OPERA AND THE CULTURE OF FASCISM

OPERA AND THE CULTURE OF FASCISM

JEREMY TAMBLING

CLARENDON PRESS · OXFORD
1996

Oxford University Press, Walton Street, Oxford OX2 6DP
Oxford New York
Athens Auckland Bangkok Bombay
Calcutta Cape Town Dar es Salaam Delhi
Florence Hong Kong Istanbul Karachi
Kuala Lumpur Madras Madrid Melbourne
Mexico City Nairobi Paris Singapore
Taipei Tokyo Toronto
and associated companies in
Berlin Ibadan

Oxford is a trade mark of Oxford University Press

Published in the United States
by Oxford University Press Inc., New York

British Library Cataloguing in Publication Data
Data available

Library of Congress Cataloging in Publication Data
Tambling, Jeremy.
Opera and the Culture of fascism / Jeremy Tambling.
p.   cm.
Includes bibliographical references (p.) and index.
1. Opera—Europe—19th century. 2. Opera—Europe—20th century.
3. Music and society—Italy. 4. Music and society—Germany.
5. Fascism and culture—Italy. 6. Fascism and culture—Germany.
I. Title.   ML1720.T36   1996   782.1′094—dc20   96–13317
ISBN 0–19–816566–8

1 3 5 7 9 10 8 6 4 2

Typeset by Pure Tech India Limited, Pondicherry
Printed in Great Britain
on acid-free paper by
Biddles Ltd.,
Guildford & Kings Lynn

This book is for
Kirsten
and
Felix

Preface

Many friends and colleagues have read all or part of this book in manuscript, and to name them reminds me of how much I have been helped: Ackbar Abbas, Hugh Chiverton, David Clarke, Peter Franklin, Jonathan Hall, Barry Millington, Nicholas Routley, Antony Tatlow, Jonathan White. None of these is necessarily implicated in anything I say. I am grateful to the many different students who during the 1980s and 1990s have listened to and discussed so much material that worked its way through to here: on *Doctor Faustus* and other texts of Mann, on *Otello*, and on Nietzsche, for instance. A conference on music and gender held in 1991 at King's College London was an important, if indirect, help. Lau Wai Wah helped materially in preparation of the manuscript. During two of the years of writing, Nicholas Routley persuaded me to take up opera direction, and our two productions in Hong Kong with him conducting, *Orfeo ed Euridice* and *Norma*, taught me much about opera. The publishers' readers who went through the book, and who remain anonymous, have also been more than helpful in their comments. I would like to thank Bruce Phillips, Helen Foster, and Janet Moth of Oxford University Press, who have made the move from script to print possible and painless.

This book was produced in London and Hong Kong. It was researched and written partly in the work conditions of Hong Kong, which provided excellent back-up facilities, and partly in London, where Pauline made research and writing a possibility and a pleasure by her own wonderful interest and commitment to opera and its social and political contexts.

I have quoted everything in English, apart from opera libretti, for which I have given translations. Citations of texts appear first in the footnotes, then are carried as tactfully as possible in the body of the text. A bibliography appears at the end.

Contents

Introduction

Opera and the Culture of Fascism

The philosopher must be the evil conscience of his age—but to this end he
must be possessed of its best knowledge. And what better guide, or more
thoroughly efficient revealer of the soul, could be found for the labyrinth of
the modern spirit than Wagner? Through Wagner modernity speaks its most
intimate language: it conceals neither its good nor its evil; it has thrown off
all shame. And conversely, one has almost calculated the whole of the value
of modernity once one is clear concerning what is good and evil in Wagner.
I can perfectly well understand a musician of today who says, 'I hate Wagner
but I can endure no other music.' But I should also understand a philosopher
who said: 'Wagner is modernity in concentrated form.' There is no help for
it, we must first be Wagnerites.

Nietzsche, *The Case of Wagner*[1]

'Il faut être absolument moderne,' Rimbaud says in *Saisons aux Enfers*: but to be
modern, we must first be Wagnerites—though, to be safe, Nietzschean ones. For
the most shameless language of modernity has turned out to be constitutive of
fascism: it has been, in fact, the 'culture of fascism', and in this Introduction I shall
illustrate what I mean by the phrase. Fascism I shall usually spell with the
lower-case, because fascism was much more than just the official politics of Italy
or Germany: it was intellectually and culturally attractive to intellectuals, writers,
philosophers, and composers, even cutting across political orthodoxies. Every
beginning is a fiction, and a starting-point for the history of fascism entails reading
much of the nineteenth century as the primeval landscape of fascism, or proto-
fascism. The phrase 'culture of fascism' includes in it this pre-fascist discourse,
which works through such markers as 1870 and 1871 (when Italy and Germany
became full nation-states) to the First World War and beyond. The prehistory
runs parallel to the work of Verdi and Wagner, the two composers who epitomize

---

[1] Friedrich Nietzsche, Preface to *The Case of Wagner: A Musician's Problem*, trans. Anthony M. Ludovici
(Edinburgh: T. N. Foulis, 1911). I cite this translation rather than Walter Kaufmann's (*Basic Writings of
Nietzsche* (New York: The Modern Library, 1968), p. 612) which on the whole I prefer, simply because here
I think it reads better.

so much of the history of the nineteenth century. And I begin with Wagner, here and in Part I, going on later, in Part II, to Italian opera. Because the writing of *The Ring* began in 1848, and because it is many years ago now (1964) that we had the first hundred years of Wagner's *Tristan*,[2] and because *Lohengrin* was first heard in Italy in 1871, while Wagner's prose writings had already been in circulation in Italy for some years previously, I take it that we can think of late nineteenth-century opera, Italian as well as German, as having some contact with Wagnerism—if only in denial of it.[3]

My references to Wagner may incline readers to the assumption that he is the book's topic, especially when they see the word 'fascism' in the title; but this should not lead to foreclosure on the argument. I have not tried to reinvent the wheel: that is, I am not interested in rediscovering that Wagner influenced the Nazi party and provided comfort to Fascism; nor are Strauss's relations with the Nazis intended to shock the reader. Unlike the Fat Boy in *Pickwick Papers*, I have no wish to make the flesh creep with revelations about which tenors or which conductors were complicit with Fascist Italy or Nazi Germany or Austria and did well afterwards. I have rather assumed a knowledge of these things.[4] In any case, the more I think about it, the less certain I become (my doubts reinforced by contemporary developments in, for instance, Italy, with its post-Fascism) about what is unique to a Fascist state. That is not the same as identifying with the 'revisionist' historians of the 1980s, German *Historikerstreit* who have denied that there was anything special about Nazi Germany, for instance, or about the death camps. The phrase 'the culture of fascism' has its pay-off in not isolating 1922–45 or 1933–45 as separate periods in Italian or German history. Traditionally, exhibitions of twentieth-century German art left out—perhaps they still do—the years 1933–45, sometimes with the argument that they might have the effect on German

---

[2] An allusion to Elliott Zuckerman's study of the influence of *Tristan* on literature: *The First Hundred Years of Wagner's Tristan* (New York: Columbia University Press, 1964).

[3] On Wagner in Italian opera, see, e.g., Julian Budden, 'Wagnerian Tendencies in Italian Opera', in Nigel Fortune (ed.), *Music and Theatre: Essays in Honour of Winton Dean* (Cambridge: Cambridge University Press, 1987); Marion S. Miller, 'Wagnerism, Wagnerians and Italian Identity', in David C. Large and William Weber (eds.), *Wagnerism in European Culture and Politics*, (Ithaca: Cornell University Press, 1984).

[4] For examples of works on musicians and fascism, see Harvey Sachs, *Music in Fascist Italy* (London: Weidenfeld and Nicolson, 1987); see also his *Toscanini* (London: Weidenfeld and Nicolson, 1978); for an anti-Strauss text, see George Marek, *Richard Strauss: The Life of a Non-hero* (London: Victor Gollancz, 1967). A broad treatment of operas in relation to politics and public affairs appears in Anthony Arblaster, *Viva La Libertà: Politics in Opera* (London: Verso, 1992), a comprehensive and useful study, which deals, however, with politics at the most overt level, so that, for instance, he sees nothing political in *Otello* or *Falstaff*, which he disposes of in two pages, whereas I give these operas a chapter each.

people of making them wish for the Nazi regime again.[5] The myth had to be preserved that this was a special, unrepeatable period. In the same way, the philosopher Benedetto Croce could think of Fascism simply as a 'parenthesis' in Italian history.[6] Even Bertolucci's film *Novecento*, which traces Italy's history through the first forty-five years of the twentieth century, is curiously end-stopped, because it seems committed to an argument that fascism ended in 1945.

Though Nietzsche liked the music of the south—that of *Carmen* and the Italians—it was Wagner he insisted on for an anatomy of modernity. The composers considered here—the later Verdi, Puccini, the writers of *verismo*, Strauss, Schreker, Zemlinsky, Weill, for example—all worked in some kind of relation to Wagnerism, whether for or against, believing it could or should be replaced or that it had reached the limits of opera. Wagnerian or not, they belong to modernity. The period of the modern includes within it *modernism*, with its emphasis on the autonomous nature of art in society, and the *avant-garde*, which contests that autonomy, and *postmodernism*, which among other things dissolves the uniqueness of 'art' and its claims to some special rooting and epistemic value. Within the period of modernity, the price to be paid is intense speculation about the self, since everything—the most intimate language of the self—is opened up. 'It is to the honour of an artist if he is unable to be a critic—otherwise he is half and half—he is "modern".'[7] One characterization of fascism might be that it attempts to close the gap that being modern opens up—to revert, out of fear of that critical self-consciousness, to pure, spontaneous action.

'The culture of fascism' also implies that culture may produce fascism, or be fascist itself, and also that fascism may produce culture: a culture which cannot simply be wished away because it contains fascist elements. We cannot free ourselves from fascism that easily. But how does opera—that non-populist, élitist art-form whose audience in the twentieth century is the opposite of the petit bourgeois one that Fascism had for its mass support—reticulate with fascism? And

[5] See Steven Kasher, 'The Art of Hitler', *October*, 59 (1992): 49–85. On the *Historikerstreit*, the arguments over the 'revisionism' of Nolte, Hillgruber, and Joachim Fest, see Richard J. Evans, *In Hitler's Shadow* (New York: Pantheon Books, 1989).

[6] Renzo de Felice, *Interpretations of Fascism*, trans. Brenda Huff Everett (Cambridge, Mass.: Harvard University Press, 1977), pp. 14, 26. The first part of de Felice's book contains an important summary of existing views of fascism. (The stress is on Italian fascism.) Alexander J. le Grand, *Italian Fascism: Its Origins and Development* (Lincoln, Nebr.: University of Nebraska Press, 1982) gives a bibliography of work on Italian fascism.

[7] Friedrich Nietzsche, *The Will to Power*, trans. Walter Kaufmann and R. J. Hollingdale (New York: Vintage Books, 1967), p. 429.

what political influence could opera be deemed to have? Apart from Wagner, of course; but we must not prejudge that issue.[8] Opera and fascism have been linked for rhetorical purposes—for example, by Spengler, the philosopher of what the historian Fritz Stern calls 'cultural despair'. In 1932, Spengler called Hitler not a hero but a 'heroic tenor' (Hitler took lessons in acting from an opera-singer, Paul Devrient), and reflected, in *The Hour of Decision* (1933) on Mussolini as 'the *lord* of his country . . . first and foremost a statesman, ice-cold and sceptical, realist, diplomat . . . Mussolini is a master-man with the Southern cunning of the race in him, like the condottieri of the Renaissance, and is therefore able to stage his movement in entire consonance with the character of Italy—home of opera— without ever being intoxicated by it himself.'[9]

One anecdote among many will serve to summarize Hitler's relation to Wagner, one given by his foreign affairs press officer, Ernst Hanfstaengel, recalling Hitler in the 1920s, on one particular occasion when he was in political despair. Hanf-staengel began to play the piano to him:

I began with a Bach fugue on the badly out of tune piano which Hitler listened to without much interest, seated in an armchair, his head in his hands, until I felt my fingers had warmed up enough to launch myself into the Prelude to the *Mastersingers*. And with this, as I had hoped, I touched Hitler's musical nerve at just the right point. He was on his feet immediately and began walking up and down the room waving his arms in the gestures of a conductor and whistling every note in a strangely penetrating vibrato which was absolutely in tune. He knew the whole Prelude by heart from A to Z, and since he also had an excellent ear for the spirit of a piece of music, I also gradually derived pleasure from our duet.

When I had finished the Finale with gusto, a radiant and completely changed Hitler stood before me, praising my playing effusively and even going so far as to say, 'You're a complete orchestra, Hanfstaengel.'

---

[8] Wagner is usually attacked on two counts: for the use the Nazis made of Bayreuth and Wagnerian ideology and for his anti-Semitism. On the latter, see Jacob Katz, *The Darker Side of Genius: Richard Wagner's Anti-Semitism* (Hanover, NH: University Press of New England, 1986), and Paul Lawrence Rose, *Wagner: Revolution and Race* (London: Faber, 1992); Barry Millington, 'Nuremberg Trial: Is there Anti-Semitism in *Die Meistersinger?*', *Cambridge Opera Journal*, 3 (1992): 247–60. Barry Millington makes use of the work of Hartmunt Zelinsky on Wagner's attitudes to Jews in his *Richard Wagner* (London: Dent, 1984); see also his 'Parsifal: A Wound Re-opened', *Wagner*, 8 (1987): 114–20; see also Dieter Borchmeyer, 'Richard Wagner and Anti-Semitism', *Wagner*, 6 (1985): 1–18; see also 'The Jewish Question', in Leroy R. Shaw, Nancy R. Cirillo, and Marion S. Miller (eds.), *Wagner in Retrospect* (Amsterdam: Rodopi, 1987); George Bridges, 'The Almost Irresistible Appeal of Fascism, or, Is it Okay to Like Richard Wagner?', *Germanic Review*, 64 (1989): 42–8.

[9] Quoted in H. Stuart Hughes, *Oswald Spengler: A Critical Estimate* (New York: Charles Scribner, 1962), pp. 127, 129.

Wagner's music had simply become second nature to him. I would even maintain that there were marked parallels between the structure of the *Mastersingers* Prelude and his speeches. In both cases the same interweaving of leitmotifs, wealth of embellishment, counterpoint and finally the powerful outburst like the sound of trombones at Wagner's act endings and Liszt's rhapsodic finales.[10]

Opera becomes a matter for critical attention in the light of this nostalgia for power it can give its listeners (especially this most famous listener), a nostalgia that works even now as a high-class aestheticist cult and longing for and pursuit of a pure experience.[11] Opera compels attention for several reasons, the first, for me being the fascination it holds: in the historical period I cover, I have managed to get in many of the operatic texts I like the most—those of Verdi, Puccini, Wagner, Strauss, for four. There is no point in saying I do not like them, however negative I get about them. The composers mentioned are not the only ones I admire, but they are enough, and powerful enough to demand an account of what in them compels interest and admiration, even when they embody some awful sympathies in politics (including gender politics). Secondly, opera is a phenomenon whose time has come, even if—especially if—the form is practically speaking dead in terms of new writing and performance of the new. I refer to the increasing popularity that opera enjoys, the fetishizing of its stars, the number of extravaganzas it produces in terms of spectacular arena-type productions, and the money spent on it. It provides a commentary and confirmation of Theodor Adorno's essay of 1938 entitled 'On the Fetish Character in Music and the Regression of Listening'.[12] Its very popularity should encourage an examination of its texts, while the high-tech forms in which it is presented fit very significantly with arguments about the 'postmodern'. These suggest relationships between art rendered totally technological—or technology rendering art wholly aesthetic—and fascist

[10] Ernst Hanfstaengel, *Zwischen Weissen und Braunem Haus. Memoiren eines politischen Aussenseiters* (Munich: Piper, 1970), pp. 55 f. I am grateful to Antony Tatlow for the translation.

[11] See Michel Poizat, *The Angel's Cry: Beyond the Pleasure Principle in Opera*, trans. Arthur Denner (Ithaca, NY: Cornell University Press, 1992), for a recent, good example of opera presented as nostalgia for a lost plenitude, where it is 'in the nostalgia for a paradisiacal unity of preseparation that the opera lover's ecstasy resides' (p. x).

[12] Adorno's essay is reprinted in Andrew Arato and Eike Gebhardt (eds.), *The Essential Frankfurt School Reader* (Oxford: Blackwell, 1978). On kitsch, see Geoffrey Nowell-Smith, 'On Kiri Te Kanawa, Judy Garland and the Culture Industry', in James Naremore and Patrick Brantlinger (eds.), *Modernity and Mass Culture* (Bloomington, Ind.: University of Indiana Press, 1991), pp. 70–9. 'Movies, radio and now television, do indeed pretend to be art, and this is often the most deceptive thing they do, bombarding audiences with products which fetishize the signifiers of artisticness. The word for this fetishism is Kitsch' (p. 76).

fantasies of total control achieved by making politics a matter of aesthetics—
through film, through architecture, through total organization (the crowd turned
into a chorus, as it were).

German fascism was violent with respect to art: its book burnings, its expul-
sions, and its promotion of kitsch are all well known. The Nazis were some of the
earliest anti-modernists in their hatred of modernist architecture, for example,
and modernist music and modernist art, all of which they identified with internationalism. In their encouragement of a national aestheticism to substitute for a
political awareness, they encouraged painting and music in general; but it is worth
noting, as a positive point about opera, something suggesting its power of
resistance to straightforward propaganda, that in the Nazi period, while 164 new
operas were premiered, 'not one Nazi opera, i.e. with a Nazi style or explicit text
and characters, was performed in National Socialist Germany'.[13] Perhaps there was
no need or room for it, but it was not for lack of encouragement; and it is a detail
worth putting against the statistic that 'in the past one hundred years Nietzsche
has inspired compositions by at least two hundred and nineteen musicians'.[14] Not
quite *mille e tre* perhaps; but it does suggest something of the importance of the
non-authoritarian, non-fascist Nietzsche for this study.

The moment of fascism and a crisis for art coincide, expressed in those 1930s
debates that emerged from Adorno and the writers of the Frankfurt school, for
whom the 'culture industry' meant the impossibility of independent, non-market-
oriented art. The 'culture industry' is a triumph of advanced capitalism, using the
full resources of technology to generate entertainment which is enjoyed passively,
having been prepackaged in response to the demands of the market-place, demands generated through the power of advertising and hype. This industry was
put in place through the whole of the period I am discussing. It was to make for
the hegemony of American popular culture (e.g. in popular music) throughout
Europe, as well as in the States, in the years immediately prior to the First World
War, and even more so afterwards. A second Marxist view, less pessimistic than
Adorno's, comes from Walter Benjamin, in 'The Work of Art in the Age of its
Technological Reproducibility' (*Das Kunstwerk in Zeitalter seiner technischen
Reproduzierbarkeit*, 1936). In this argument, technology is bringing to an end the
era of art, existing in a discreet, aura-filled existence away from the viewer who
must absorb it in a state of contemplation. Yet this holds out the possibility of a

---

[13] Michael Meyer, *The Politics of Music in the Third Reich* (New York: Peter Lang, 1991), p. 254. See also
Erik Levi, *Music in the Third Reich* (London: Macmillan, 1994).

[14] Alan White, *Within Nietzsche's Labyrinth* (London: Routledge, 1990), p. 3.

new importance for cultural production, albeit not in terms of traditional bourgeois art which relies on its uniqueness or its special cult nature.

Technology was also a concern of political conservatives, and a prompting towards reaction and fascism. For Martin Heidegger, the philosopher who joined the Nazi party in 1933 and stayed a member till 1945, the 'question concerning technology' was the dominant one in the modern world, and technology in its turn he saw as questioning the very humanist basis of art, the assumption of personal subjectivity and autonomy. Technology belongs to modernity in that it forces things out, shamelessly, into the open, into pure transparency: it fits a culture of demonstration by its power to enframe everything, a power which negates difference, such as political viewpoints. Thus technology, for Heidegger, created capitalism and communism alike: Germany was the nation in the middle, squeezed between Russia and America, which he described as being, however divergent politically, 'metaphysically the same; the same technological frenzy, the same unrestricted organization of the average man'.[15] His reaction to this was to embrace fascism as both the product of the drive of technology—and complicity with it—and as the existence which might also confront it.

Opera, which relies on its aura of uniqueness and cultic status, has been highly susceptible to technological development. Caruso's gramophone records were cut in 1902, and opera-composers such as Leoncavallo and Puccini were soon composing specially for records. The first opera to have been filmed seems to have been Max Ophuls's version of *The Bartered Bride*, in 1932, though in 1926, Strauss wrote extra music for a film version of *Der Rosenkavalier*. Just as technology currently refetishizes opera, so it worked in the aestheticizing of politics that Benjamin accused fascism of bringing about. It permits the elision of politics and art as technology, and political control being secured through the dominance of the spectacular. Opera elides with spectacle and national self-representation. For opera-houses, like national theatres and arts festivals, were—and still are—co-opted into late nineteenth-century presentations of the spectacular, the larger-than-life, as demonstrations of the power of the nation-state.

In a sense, the whole of this book looks at Benjamin's thesis of the disappearance of art: that it no longer exists, operatic art included; that this is a post-culture, in the age of its technological reproducibility, where singers cannot perform so well in the opera-house as they can on CD, where performance-art—actual people,

---

[15] Martin Heidegger, *An Introduction to Metaphysics* (1935), trans. Ralph Manheim (New Haven: Yale University Press, 1959), p. 37.

reduced to one thing only, their voice—must imitate the repro-art of laser technology. I think it almost obvious to say that opera ended somewhere around the third decade of the twentieth century as a meaningful European art-form whose existence made some difference to social discourse. Of course, there are exceptions; but the existence of some fine post-1945 composers does not take away from the minority status of contemporary opera. The miserable number of commissions of television opera come to mind. Television opera is most likely to be a video of a popular work, probably from one of the big four composers I discuss in this book. If contemporary opera is in crisis, this is inseparable from issues that were argued throughout the 1930s about the increase of kitsch (Clement Greenberg), about the power of technology to change the character of art (Benjamin, Heidegger), about the commodification of all forms of culture (Adorno, Georg Lukács), the sense that modernist autonomous art had to be impossibly difficult (Schoenberg, Adorno, Mann). For Adorno, writing in the 1930s and 1940s, 'music is inextricably bound up with what Clement Greenberg called the division of all art into kitsch and the avant-garde, and this kitsch—with its dictate of profit over culture—has long since conquered the social sphere.'[16] If contemporary opera production is kitsch, as much of it, think, I demonstrably is, then this fulfils and returns to an issue which is central to this book: Wagner writes kitsch (Adorno's most negative assessment of him); kitsch is the art of fascism; some forms of fascism (e.g. Heidegger's) proclaim themselves anti-kitsch; the critique of kitsch that Adorno offers allows for no other route than the impossible one of writing only like Schoenberg (the strategy of Adrian Leverkühn in *Doctor Faustus*).

If opera's crisis moment became apparent in the 1930s, this suggests that its history in the nineteenth century may be read with that in mind, and that it is time to take opera out of the isolation in which it often exists when discussed—isolation from the rest of culture, from politics, from society—and see it as one 'discourse' among many, inflected by culture and ideology, and inflecting those in its turn. This study, in which I try to do that, inevitably says more about the librettos than the music. This reflects my own limits of competence. But this is not a book 'about' libretti; discussion of what I have written would only be diverted by questions of whether the music distorts or mirrors the intentions of the libretto. Opera is a weave of voices, a dialogue between text, music, and

---

[16] Theodor W. Adorno, *The Philosophy of Modern Music*, trans. Anne G. Mitchell and Wesley V. Blomster (London: Sheed and Ward, 1973), p. 10.

performance, and a mixed genre, which I comment on in discussing *Falstaff*; but it also has its political unconscious[17] because of both the dominant and the marginal discourses that emerge through each opera, which do not reduce to the pairing of music and libretto. Taking the word 'text' as plural, and believing that the question as to where the text ends, where its limits may be placed, is not fixed, that the inside/outside of a text can be delimited only by a process of determining to read one way, I believe that reading an opera requires widening the scope to include other discourses informing it, sometimes unconsciously. Here, libretto and music are two voices, not the only ones.

This is not new, for opera criticism is currently losing its insulated status,[18] while opera productions have gone further in accentuating the text in terms of the contemporary, which seems important, however much it may mean that producers and the standard audiences they can expect to find are for ever at loggerheads. But the overall formalism of much opera criticism is none the less still there (though that is better than the anecdotal form of criticism). But in wishing to go beyond treating everything extraneous to the opera as mere 'background', this book will tax the patience of those who 'only' like opera. Musicians who prefer the formalist approach to opera analysis may reflect on the consequent marginalization of music and opera from the writing of cultural history. This is not because there is no subject there, as I hope this study will show.

WAGNER AND MODERNITY

A year ago I was at a hydrotherapy centre, with the intention of becoming a completely healthy person in body and senses. My secret wish was that the

---

[17] See Fredric Jameson, *The Political Unconscious: Narrative as a Socially Symbolic Act* (London: Methuen, 1981). On this, and on narrative theory, see my *Narrative and Ideology* (Milton Keynes: Open University Press, 1991), pp. 104–8.

[18] Typical signs of this change are found in the *Cambridge Opera Journal*; Catherine Clément's *Opera or the Undoing of Women*, trans. Betsy Wing (Minneapolis: University of Minnesota Press, 1988); Susan McClary's *Carmen* (Cambridge: Cambridge University Press, 1992); even my own *Opera, Ideology and Film* (Manchester: Manchester University Press, 1987); and new attention to libretti, as in Arthur Groos and Roger Parker (eds.), *Reading Opera* (Princeton: Princeton University Press, 1988). For a good review of the state of opera criticism, see Ellen Rosan, 'Criticism and the Undoing of Opera', *Nineteenth-Century Music*, 14 (1990): 75–83. On Carl Dahlhaus, see Arnold Whittall, 'Carl Dahlhaus, the Nineteenth-century and Opera', *Cambridge Opera Journal*, 3 (1991): 79–88. Also relevant to this study, John Tyrell, *Czech Opera* (Cambridge: Cambridge University Press, 1988), emphasizes the national character of Czech opera in the nineteenth century. For French opera, see Jane F. Fulcher, *The Nation's Image: French Grand Opera as Politics and Politicised Art* (Cambridge: Cambridge University Press, 1987).

attainment of physical health would enable me to rid myself entirely of art, the bane and torment of my life. It was a last desperate bid for happiness, for true, pure, enjoyment of life, such as only the consciously healthy man can know.

Wagner, quoted by Mann, 'The Sorrows and Grandeur of Richard Wagner'[19]

I have finally abandoned my obstinate attempts to complete my Nibelungs. I have led my young Siegfried into the beautiful forest solitude; there I have left him beneath a linden tree and have said farewell to him with tears of heartfelt sorrow:—he is better off there than anywhere else.

Selected Letters of Richard Wagner

For the remainder of this Introduction, I want to give a name to some of the characteristics of the 'culture of fascism' I shall be working with, and to hint at their importance as they surface in nineteenth- and twentieth-century opera. Here I shall be a Wagnerite: my examples will illuminate his work, as he also becomes an example of modernity in its most concentrated form. I want to start with Wagner the composer at a hydrotherapy centre and Siegfried the hero under the linden tree: two images with which to begin unpacking those elements of pre-fascism and modernity that are also 'Wagnerian'. These elements include a problematic form of melancholy, which links to a death-drive, an ambiguous attitude to the hero (which implies a whole gender politics) and a dual relationship to bourgeois culture.

We can begin to tap into Wagnerism by intercepting the letter to Liszt of 28 June 1857 about abandoning Siegfried. Behind Wagner's unarticulated reasons for the intermittence, there is an unconscious and a history which I shall describe and account for in this section. Wagner's tears, Adorno said,[20] are for himself, since he insists on a mythic identity with his own creatures—for Adorno, part of Wagner's desire for direct involvement with his audience and for their validation of him. They are kitsch tears, and fit Adorno's case against Wagner. 'Kitsch' itself, middle-class commodity art, is German, the word appearing first in the 1860s. The linden tree and the nature it evokes may be kitsch images as well: they fit with

---

[19] In *Thomas Mann Pro and Contra Wagner*, trans. Allan Blunden (London: Faber, 1985), p. 113. (Why does this translation render *Grösse* (greatness) by 'grandeur', with this word's overtones of pomposity?) Further references in the text. Second quotation: *Selected Letters of Richard Wagner*, trans. and ed. Stewart Spenser and Barry Millington (New York: W.W. Norton, 1987), p. 370. Further references in the text.

[20] Theodor W. Adorno, *In Search of Wagner*, trans. Rodney Livingstone (London: New Left Books, 1981), pp. 60–1.

Wagner's claims in *Mein Leben* concerning his somnambulistic state, of 5 September 1853, when he

suddenly had the feeling of being immersed in rapidly flowing water. Its rushing soon resolved itself for me into the musical sound of the chord of E flat major, resounding in persistent broken chords; these in turn transformed themselves into melodic figurations of increasing motion, yet the E flat major triad never changed, and seemed by its continuance to impart infinite significance to the element into which I was sinking. I awoke in sudden terror from this trance, feeling as though the waves were crashing high above my head. I recognized at once that the orchestral prelude to *Das Rheingold*, long dormant within me but up to that moment inchoate, had at last been revealed; and I also saw immediately precisely how it was with me: the vital flood would come from within me, and not from without.

Whatever scepticism this account affords,[21] its language of a male giving birth to *The Ring* in a kind of male parturition is crucial. Otherwise, it compares with what Freud calls 'the oceanic feeling', a desire for an earlier state of existence, one 'which might seek something like the restoration of limitless narcissism, [the desire for] "oneness with the universe" which . . . sounds like a first attempt at a religious consolation, as though it were another way of disclaiming the danger which the ego recognizes as threatening it from the external world'.[22] The Wagnerian account of the waking wet dream, looking for the birth of the author out of the waters through the birth of the music which he himself has produced, records a desire for a total mastery which is, as suggested by its/his retreat to the waters which are its/his medium, regressive, but also assertive of supreme phallic power. Nor are the waters, which recall Wagner at the hydrotherapy centre, separate from the Rhine: baptismal purity—theme of *Meistersinger* and *Parsifal* alike—occurs in a nationalistic setting. Wagner's imagined state is exactly that of Siegfried in Act 2 of that opera. In its forest murmurs he longs for the regressive state, which has to do with the mother; later, the memory of the mother is overlaid exactly by the intuition given him of Brünnhilde; so that regression and the belief in male dominance unite in him.

The linden tree is a nineteenth-century image, used from Goethe to Mann (Adrian Leverkühn is born and dies under the linden) and from Schubert to

---

[21] Wagner, *My Life*, trans. Andrew Gray (Cambridge: Cambridge University Press, 1983), p. 499. See the doubts cast on this narrative by John Deathridge, in *The New Grove Wagner* (London: Macmillan, 1984), p. 39, and Barry Millington, in *Selected Letters of Richard Wagner*, pp. 162–3.

[22] *Civilization and its Discontents*, in *Pelican Freud Library*, vol. 12 (Harmondsworth: Penguin, 1985), p. 260.

Wagner (the linden tree music, like that of Schubert's song of that name, is in E major: Wagner's music recalls Schubert's, and Humperdinck's *Königskinder* (1910), also ending with death under a linden tree and in the same key, recalls both).[23] To this feminine image[24] may be added the crowd, since the forest where the tree is suggests that, and the crowd is a classic topic for fascism, one that I say more about in Chapter 5. Elias Canetti, in *Crowds and Power*, discusses the forest as emblematic of a crowd. He picks up on its elements of shelter, compelling people to look upward so that it becomes 'a first image of awe' and then, moving from this, to become an image of an army, 'it can be felled, but not shifted'. From there, he considers the dominant crowd symbol for the Germans as the army, and the army as the forest.

The boy who escaped into the forest from the confinement of home [Canetti might be referring to Siegfried or Parsifal]—thinking to be alone there and able to dream, actually anticipated his entry into the army. In the forest he found the others waiting for him, true, faithful and upright as he himself wanted to be, each like every other, for each grows straight, and yet quite different in height and strength. The effect of this early forest romanticism on the German must never be underrated. He absorbed it from countless poems and songs, and the forest which appears in these is often called 'German'.[25]

Siegfried's entry into the forest is both a return to the mother, and a movement towards the erotic, but also, on this reading, an access to militarism, to male solidarity, and to identification of the self with the crowd: a loss of individualism in favour of a mass movement. It is also a longing for death; and, as I shall be arguing here and throughout this book, the death drive is a constitutive part of fascism.

---

[23] At the end of Humperdinck's *Königskinder*, a piece about rejection of modern life, in Act 3, the prince dies singing of his memory of the linden tree, like Tristan in Act 3, also in E major, recollecting his love. See Barry Millington, 'Humperdinck's Other Masterpiece', *Opera* (Feb. 1992): 153–8.

The linden tree gathers together associations from German mythology: *lind* means 'soft', and the soft-wood, broad-leaved species was described as feminine by Theophrastus and as tame. 'There are reports of holy limetrees hung with votive tablets against the plague; of many lime groves visited as places of pilgrimage; of lime seeds eaten by the pregnant women of upper Bavaria; of the leaves, blossom and bark of the tree applied to the body as a means to strength and beauty' (Michael Baxandall, *The Limewood Sculptors of Renaissance Germany* (New Haven: Yale University Press, 1980), p. 31).

[24] 'The first springtime stirrings of the youthful Siegfried's love life, so vividly evoked by Wagner's text and by the music he uses to underscore the meaning. What we have here, rising from the dark depths of the unconcious, is a presentient complex of mother fixation, sexual desire and *Angst*' (Mann, 'The Sorrows and Grandeur of Richard Wagner', in *Pro and Contra Wagner*, pp. 97–8).

[25] Elias Canetti, *Crowds and Power*, trans. Carol Stewart (1960) (New York: Seabury Press, 1978), pp. 84, 173–4.

Though Wagner actually finished *Siegfried*, Act 2, in the summer of 1857, and orchestrated it in 1864–5, Act 3 was not written till twelve years after this date, in 1869–71. So was it a twelve-year writer's block? In one way not, because of *Tristan und Isolde* (1857–9) and *Die Meistersinger* (1864–5), but Wagner's readiness to abandon the *Ring* cycle and to surrender a work planned over the previous ten years maps on to the history I now want to trace, and on to Wagner's own equivocalness about the crowd, the nation, and the hero. The history centres on 1848, the year of revolutions.

By November 1849, exiled in Switzerland, Wagner had completed *Das Kunstwerk der Zukunft* (The Artwork of the Future). The title connects to Marx in 1852, exiled in London and reflecting on the 1851 *coup d'état* in France. *The Eighteenth Brumaire of Louis Bonaparte* argues that the post-1848 bourgeoisie turned its back on its own political freedom, accepting its diminution in favour of a strong leader. At a moment of crisis, it preserved its economic strength and its class position in relation to the industrial proletariat by signing away democratic rights. This analysis has been used to discuss Germany in the 1930s and as an explanation for Italy's adoption of Mussolini. But Marx begins *The Eighteenth Brumaire* by describing the tendency of bourgeois revolutions to dress themselves up in the clothes of the past and to hark back to earlier models of revolution, which they argue they are repeating—but which condemn them to a logic of history-as-repetition, revolution which turns into repetition, 'the first time as tragedy, the second as farce'. The narrative of revolution becomes a matter not of progression, but of endless repeating. In contrast to this, Marx argues:

The social revolution of the nineteenth century can only create its poetry from the future, not from the past. It cannot begin its own work until it has sloughed off all its superstitious regard for the past. Earlier revolutions have needed world-historical reminiscences to deaden their awareness of their own content. In order to arrive at its own content the revolution of the nineteenth century must let the dead bury their dead. Previously the phrase transcended the content; here the content transcends the phrase.[26]

Letting the dead bury their dead entails a determined refusal of the authority of history. Marx's sense of the only way to avoid revolutions becoming merely

---

[26] Karl Marx, *The Eighteenth Brumaire of Louis Bonaparte*, in *Surveys from Exile*, trans. Ben Fowkes (Harmondsworth: Penguin, 1973), p. 149. For Marxist arguments about fascism, see August Thalheimer, 'On Fascism', *Telos*, 40 (1979): 109–22, and the introduction to this 1930 essay by Frank Adler in the same issue (pp. 95–108). See also Anson G. Rabinbach, 'Towards a Marxist theory of Fascism and National Socialism', *New German Critique*, 3 (1974): 127–53; Reinhard Kühnel, 'Problems of a Theory of German Fascism: A Critique of the Dominant Intepretations', *New German Critique*, 4 (1975): 26–50; Peter R. Sinclair, 'Fascism and Crisis in Capitalist Society', *New German Critique*, 9 (1976): 87–112.

repetitions is through a thinking which is utterly different and surprising—hence his reference to poetry, as opposed to prose, for poetry is the medium whereby the scientistic and rationalistic grounds of grammar, which pin the utterance down to what-is-already-known can be avoided. Wagner's modernism (e.g. the lack of resolution and avoidance of tonality in the music), which fits at times with this poetry of the future, shows in his wish for an 'artwork of the future'. His and Marx's reference to the poetry from the future both derive from Feuerbach's *Foundations of the Philosophy of the Future* (1843), which must:

[lead] philosophy out of the realm of departed spirits back to the realm of embodied, living spirits; out of the godly felicity of a world of thought without neediness, back to the realm of human misery. For this purpose, the philosophy of the future requires no more than a human understanding and human language. But the ability to think and speak and act in authentically human terms belongs only to the human species of the future. The present task is not yet to represent this new humanity, but to draw mankind out of the morass into which it is sunk.[27]

Working-class revolution, poetry, music, modernism, new philosophy, new humanity—these are forms of expression, modern in character, refusing nostalgia, tradition, and the past. 'The tradition of the dead generations weighs like a nightmare on the minds of the living' (Marx, *Eighteenth Brumaire*, p. 147), and Siegfried as a modern, using the logic of progress, refuses the Wanderer's authority and breaks the spear, in an assumption of personal subjectivity; the father, embodying the power of history, all that which condemns the sons to repeat the past, is refused. But the 1848 year of revolutions in France ended with the dictatorship of the Second Empire, which Marx sees as the triumph of imitation, of the simulacrum. 'They have not merely acquired a caricature of the old Napoleon, they have the old Napoleon himself, in the caricature form he had to take in the middle of the nineteenth century' (ibid. 149). In this empire, where the kitsch composer is Offenbach (or Gounod), all is imitation, and Marx's statement suggests not only that the attempt to create the Napoleonic myth is itself empty imitation, but that this imitation shows that the first Napoleon was also bourgeois imitation. Napoleon III was the triumph of spectacle and theatre and the spurious victory of Caesarism, the cult of the leader with a magical connection with the people, or so he claims, cutting out the processes of any representative institutions in his declaration that he speaks directly to and for the people.

---

[27] Quoted in Mars W. Wartofsky, *Feuerbach* (Cambridge: Cambridge University Press, 1977), p. 196.

Marx's study has been seen as a study of proto-fascism, fascism before the event, before its obvious, unmistakable manifestations in the twentieth century. None the less, Marx hopes for the end of the leader. If all is simulacral, *The Eighteenth Brumaire* concludes, then, 'when the emperor's mantle finally falls on the shoulders of Louis Bonaparte [i.e. in 1852], the bronze statue of Napoleon will come crashing down from the top of the Vendôme Column' (p. 249). When the emperor stands revealed in his imitative glory, then Napoleon will be revealed as the empty object he himself was: the bankruptcy of phallic power that builds the Vendôme column will become obvious. The Second Empire is the moment when the simulacral nature of everything marketed and made by nineteenth-century capitalism becomes obvious.

But the simulacrum has not appeared as such, and the philosopher who spoke to the 1850s was Schopenhauer, for whom there is no other representation possible than the empty phantasmagoria, the magic-lantern show; no other reality. This is Schopenhauer on old people, who

smilingly look down on the phantasmagoria of the world. They are completely disillusioned and know that, whatever may be done to adorn and deck out human life, its barren and paltry nature soon shows through such finery and tinsel. However much it may be tinted and trimmed, it is everywhere essentially the same, an existence whose true value is always to be estimated on the basis of an absence of pain, not on that of a presence of pleasures, still less of pomp and show.[28]

This is a kitsch vision of old age; but Schopenhauer, with whom I shall start in Chapter 1, had his reasons for wanting to exclude the body and its vicissitudes from consideration. It feeds Wagner's pessimism of the 1850s—that everything is delusion ('Wahn! Wahn! überall Wahn' for Hans Sachs[29]), and belongs to a retreat from politics, from Siegfried as Bakunin, to disengagement, in keeping with Flaubert's retreat at the same moment into pure Art and desire to write a book about nothing. But it is not Flaubertian in its opposition to bourgeois taste: the flight is into nostalgia and into a repro culture, which exists in the banality of

---

[28] Arthur Schopenhauer, *Parerga and Paralipomena*, 2 vols., trans. E. F. J. Payne (Oxford: Clarendon Press, 1974), i. 494.

[29] Sachs is not as simple as that: he is a manipulator of events, and his Lutheran poem sung by the chorus in the last scene suggests a nationalism; hence the reference to German art at the end. He sings of the fear of falling under foreign barbaric power—'welscher Majestät' and domination by 'welschen Dunst mit welschem Tand'. This may allude to Napoleon III's empire if French is understood by 'welscher' or French music (Meyerbeer or Offenbach) or the foreigner's foggy ideas (*Dunst* = vapours) and trifles and rubbish (*Tand*). Sachs sings about the source of kitsch being foreign, and as foggy, lacking (masculine) precision and univocality.

Hans Sachs's verse: 'Wie friedsam treuer Sitten / getrost in Tat und Werk / liegt nicht in Deutschlands Mitten / mein liebes Nürnberg' (How peacefully, adhering to its faithful customs, content in all its deeds, lies my beloved Nuremberg in the heart of Germany). That is shamelessly trite: but Wagner conceals neither his good nor his evil, and the kitsch consorts with something else that opposes the art of bourgeois culture. But the lapse back, the investment in delusion, is part of a crisis of narrative, of the inability to write a narrative of a forward, progressive movement, since bourgeois society itself is not moving forwards. The crisis of narrative is discussed by Georg Lukács, who takes the death of Balzac in 1850 to be symbolic for the end of a forward-driving narrative; but it is also in Marx's arguments in *The Eighteenth Brumaire* about France's movement from monarchy to republic to dictatorship, history is spiralling backwards. Marx saw the events of 1848 onwards as critical for narrative: here were 'heroes without deeds of heroism' and 'history without events' (p. 170); this was 'a period so poor in events and heroes' (p. 182).

Schopenhauer's philosophy fits the composer caught by the discourse of his time, which suggested that it was all over for progressive, heroic narrative. But Wagner was already Schopenhauerian and reactionary—in contradiction to the modernity I have already referred to—in the 1840s, in *Rienzi* (1842), *Der fliegende Holländer* (1843), and *Tannhäuser* (1845). A sense of nostalgia, of things that might be, but which are not possible, informs these texts. Lohengrin in the opera of 1848 departs for Montsalvat with the redemption of the historical society of Brabant incomplete. The hero has come and gone. Yet that sense of failure occurs just at the moment when meetings were being arranged at Frankfurt to create a constitution and an elected assembly for Germany.[30] Wagner's personal political idealism was not translated into the narrative of the opera. Adorno refers to the critic A. B. Marx, commenting sceptically in 1855 on the romanticism / supernaturalism of *Lohengrin*:

This drama the drama of the future? The Middle Ages a picture of our future, the out-lived, the quite finished the child of our hopes? Impossible! These sagas and fables of the wicked enchantress Venus and the Holy Grail, with all their clash of weapons, their worthy heroes, their ordeals and combat, come to us now only as the echo of the long-dead times that are quite foreign to our spirit. (*In Search of Wagner*, p. 114)

Tannhäuser also finishes equivocally. An opera which fits with the genre of the historical novel, it evokes an ideal German society—Hermann I of Thuringia, the

---

[30] For details of Wagner's activities in 1848–9, see Martin Gregor-Dellin, *Wagner* (London: Collins, 1983), pp. 148–51.

song contest held in 1206–7, and Elizabeth (1207–31). The historical novel was a prime means by which nineteenth-century nationalisms in Britain, France, Germany, Italy, Poland, and North America expressed themselves. (The word 'nationalism' seems to have been first used in Britain in 1844.) *Tannhäuser* relates to German nationalism: Wartburg is the setting because of its associations with Luther, and hence with an earlier moment of German self-assertion. The chorus 'Freudig begrüssen wir die edle Halle', Elisabeth's aria 'Dich, teure Halle', and the Landgrave's address 'Gar viel und schön ward hier in dieser Halle' are suggestive here. Ludwig Bechstein, whose history of Thuringia (1835) was Wagner's source, identified the Venusberg as the Horselberg near Wartburg, and these reconstructions of the past belong to the enthusiasm for the German nation-state which began in the 1820s—for instance, with the tricentennial celebrations in Nuremberg of Dürer's death there in 1828. This nationalism had many artistic features, such as the focus on the Rhine river, precipitated by the Rhineland crisis with the French in 1840: witness Max Schneckenburger's song 'The Watch on the Rhine' composed in 1840 and Nicholas Becker's poem 'The German Rhine' (1840), given numerous musical settings. The Rhine produces the figure of Germania (Lorenz Clasen's picture, *Germania on the Watch on the Rhine*) and, of course, *Das Rheingold*. There was Hoffmann von Fallersleben's 'Deutschland, Deutschland über alles' (1841), and as part of the palpable building of Germany, the demand in 1842 to complete Cologne Cathedral as part of a series of projects initiated by the National Monument Movement. In sport, there was the gymnastic movement, inspired by the nationalist Ludwig Jahn (1778–1852), the 'Turnvater', the patriarch doing press-ups. These clubs promoted will-power, a communal spirit, and character, as did the new singing societies: a German choral festival was held in Würzburg in the same year as *Tannhäuser*. The Crown Prince, Ludwig of Bavaria (Ludwig I of Bavaria, 1825–48), wanted a national pantheon in Bavaria, and held a competition for the design of a Valhalla, built by Leo von Klenze (architect of nineteenth-century Munich) above the Danube, near Regensburg—unconscious source material for *Das Rheingold*. Klenze and Friedrich von Gärtner were also involved with a classical Liberation Hall at Kelheim, also on the Danube, to record victory over the French in the Napoleonic wars.[31] All around Wagner were visible signs of the nation, which were worked into the operas, most of which had their genesis in the 1840s. The *Nibelungenlied* became a nineteenth-century text

[31] For details of these, see Hagen Schulze, *The Cause of German Nationalism* (1985), trans. Sarah Hanbury-Tenison (Cambridge: Cambridge University Press, 1991). See also Harold James, *A German Identity: 1770–1990* (New York: Routledge, 1989), ch. 2. On the prehistory of German fascism, see Fritz

in its own right (first printed in 1757, translated into modern German in 1827; the *Eddas* following in 1837).

But *Tannhäuser* does not belong to an affirmative nationalism. To evoke a hero who is not free seems to have been Wagner's project throughout his work, even though the stated aim of Wotan, in *Die Walküre*, is to create a hero freer than himself, the god. Wotan cannot do it, nor Wagner. The shameless modern in Wagner saw no sin in incest, and introduced it in *Die Walküre*, as earlier, almost, in *Rienzi*, thereby indicating that the only freedom or fulfilment he would settle for is an extreme, transgressive one. And he expects this transgressiveness to be foiled, so that the stress can fall on frustration. Incest in literary and critical theory suggests a foiling of narrative progression. If narrative follows, and assumes, a model of patrilinear succession, father to son, brother/sister incest deliberately intercepts this sequentiality: incest seems analogous to modernist narrative. Thus *Die Walküre* is itself a narrative of narrative frustration. But narrative is also disabled when any heroism, like Lohengrin's, is surrounded by conditions that seem simple, but are incapable of fulfilment; or when the hero, as in *Der fliegende Holländer*, is already beyond the grave, by definition unable to do anything.

Rienzi too shows defeat; in Bulwer's novel of 1835 (Wagner's source), defeat of a hero brings about the death also of the age, which is already decadent. *Rienzi* is subtitled 'the last of the Roman tribunes', quoting Byron's 'Rienzi, last of Romans', in *Childe Harold*, iv. 114. Bulwer, who followed Cooper's *The Last of the Mohicans* (1826), regularly produced such titles: the novel before *Rienzi* was *The Last Days of Pompeii*, and in 1843 came *The Last of the Barons* and in 1848, *Harold, the Last of the Saxon Kings*. My point is the affinity between Bulwer and Wagner, since writing which thinks in terms of 'the last' is already questioning the possibility of a narrative that can move forward—unless it is to be assumed that a new order is to appear. Each of these 'lasts' implies the end of an era or a race or both, and introduction of the concept of race, obviously essential for fascist or proto-fascist thought, evokes Disraeli's *Tancred* (1847), in which Sidonia, explaining the progressiveness of the Saxon race in England, as opposed to other races,

Stern, *The Politics of Cultural Despair* (Berkeley and Los Angeles: University of California Press, 1961); George L. Mosse, *The Crisis of German Ideology: Intellectual Origins of the Third Reich* (London: Weidenfeld and Nicolson, 1964); *idem, Nazi Culture* (London: W. H. Allen, 1966); *idem, The Nationalization of the Masses* (Ithaca, NY: Cornell University Press, 1975); Pierre Aycoberry, *The Nazi Question: An Essay on the Interpretation of National Socialism 1922–1975* (1979), trans. Richard Hurley (London: Routledge and Kegan Paul, 1981). On German proto-fascism, see Robert Chickering, *We Men Who Feel Most German: A Cultural Study of the Pan German League, 1886–1914* (Boston: Allen and Unwin, 1984); Ian Kershaw, *The Hitler Myth: Image and Reality in the Third Reich* (Oxford: Clarendon Press, 1987); George Eley, *From Unification to Nazism* (Boston: Allen and Unwin, 1986).

says: 'All is race, there is no other truth' (bk. 2, ch. 14). The authorial voice here is that of 'Young England', by contrast with the 'lasts' mentioned above, and the equivalent in nationalist terms of 'Young Germany' (compare the early title *Der junge Siegfried*). It is assumed that nationalism is definable in terms of its youth-fulness, its constant growing towards maturity, as well as involving a turning back to the imaginary 'youth' of a nation—its feudal condition, in other words. But is there a future for youth in Wagner?

Rienzi and *Lohengrin* both show the hero thwarted: the two operas in the middle, *Holländer* and *Tannhäuser*, both focus on the woman who must come over to the side of the damned hero at the price of self-renunciation and death. *Die Sarazenin* (The Saracen Maid), planned in 1842, uses German history (Man-fred, the illegitimate son of the Hohenstaufen emperor Frederic II, and his love for his Arabic half-sister Fatima) in order to focus on the virtual necessity of incest, the woman thereby coming over to the side of the man. It suggests the virtual abolition of existing races in the name of a new order; but this is, at the same time, the promotion of the German race, since the 'other', the Oriental woman, turns out to be linked by consanguinity to Manfred. Sidonia in *Tancred* effectively glosses the message of *Die Sarazenin* by his last comments in the chapter quoted from already: 'The decay of a race is an inevitable necessity, unless it lives in deserts and never mixes its blood.' The incest requirement means that the quest for the perfect hero and the perfect race is, paradigmatically, frustrated.[32]

The desire for a hero was a topic of the 1830s: *Rienzi* is Carlylean, in that Carlyle wrote about the importance of 'hero-worship' in *Sartor Resartus* (1833–4) before going on to write *On Heroes and Hero-Worship, and the Heroic in History* (1841) and the *History of Frederick the Great*. Carlyle wrote in the 1830s: 'All Europe is in a state of disturbance, of Revolution . . . the whole framework of Society is rotten and must go for fuel-wood.'[33] The fear in Carlyle, who loathed democracy, is of anarchy. He wishes for the great man who is not subjected to the constraints of representative democracy; his hero (e.g. Cromwell) stands for powerfully imposed order. The hero cannot be of the people, who in both Bulwer and Wagner destroy

---

[32] On the prevalence of the sister–brother motif, see Robert Gutman, *Richard Wagner* (1968; Harmonds-worth: Penguin, 1977), pp. 131–2. Further on incest, see Alan Richardson, 'The Dangers of Sympathy: Sibling Incest in English Romantic Poetry'. *Studies in English Literature*, 23 (1985): 737–54; Glenda A. Hudson, *Sibling Love and Incest in Jane Austen's Fiction* (London: Macmillan, 1992), ch. 2.

[33] Quoted in Chris R. Vanden Bossche, *Carlyle and the Search for Authority* (Columbus, Oh.: Ohio State University Press, 1991), p. 41. For associations between Carlyle and fascism, see John D. Rosenberg, *Carlyle and the Burden of History* (Oxford: Clarendon Press, 1985), pp. 94, 115–17, where we gather that his *History of Friedrich II of Prussia* (1858–65) was Goebbel's (or Hitler's) favourite reading.

him and Irene. Bulwer's Rienzi is a dreamy scholar who enters politics for revenge after his brother's death at the hands of the patricians, and is finally compromised. For Rienzi, 'amidst a discontented nobility and a fickle populace, urged on by the danger of repose to the danger of enterprise . . . he threw himself headlong into the gulf of the rushing Time, and surrendered his lofty spirit to no other guidance than a conviction of its natural buoyancy and its heaven-directed aim'.[34] Rienzi is a Romantic alien, for whom the world and the *Zeitgeist*, which is, none the less, believed in, is sullying. His friend Petrarch, by shunning the world, can 'address the world, but from without the world'.[35] But Bulwer refers to Rienzi's 'fanaticism', which 'belongs to the same part of us as Hope' (bk. 10, ch. 8) and the sense of something demonic in him gives him a death-wish ('I long for night'; bk. 9, ch. 5): 'There is a wish which a profound experience of power and pomp brings at last to us—a want gnawing as that of hunger, wearing as that of sleep . . . it is the want to die' (bk. 10, ch. 7).

Wagner emphasized 'the sinister, demonic foundation of Rienzi's character', which is tied to the death-wish, just as Tannhäuser, in leaving Venus, sings 'O Göttin, woll' es fassen, micht drängt es hin zum Tod' (Goddess, try to understand that it is towards death I am driven). Tannhäuser is spurred on by a demonic force, like the Dutchman: in the singing contest, which Wagner derived from Hoffmann, his singing is inspired by demons. *Rienzi* possibly played some part in Hitler's formation: according to his schoolfriend August Kubizek, it made a powerful impression on him when they saw a performance in Linz around 1906.[36] But, unlike Hitler, Rienzi is no populist: he does not handle the crowd. In *Die Meistersinger*, Wagner flirts with another 'fantasy', as Mann says, with 'the popular appeal of Hans Sachs, against whom "the whole guild" cannot prevail because the people are ready to do anything for him' (*Pro and Contra Wagner*, p. 138). But that heroism and affirmativeness, which makes *Meistersinger* a comedy, is rare in Wagner, and even here is produced from Hans Sachs's renunciation.

Sachs and Walther both seem anti-bourgeois heroes in *Die Meistersinger*. Wagner's post-1848 bourgeois class is ironized via Beckmesser; the knightly class is represented by Walther Stolzing, who, as Adorno puts it, 'wishes to re-establish

[34] Quoted from the account of the novel by Elliot Engel and Margaret F. King, *The Victorian Novel Before Victoria* (London: Macmillan, 1984), p. 53.

[35] Engel and King, p. 53. Bulwer's romanticism reacts consciously to Scott's comparative realism of treatment of the historical hero: see Andrew Brown, 'Metaphysics and Melodrama: Bulwer's *Rienzi*', *Nineteenth-Century Fiction* 36 (1981), 261–76.

[36] See John Deathridge, *Wagner's* Rienzi: *A Reappraisal Based on a Study of the Sketches and Drafts* (Oxford: Clarendon Press, 1977), pp. 11–12.

the old feudal immediacy, as opposed to the bourgeois division of labour en-shrined in the guilds' (*In Search of Wagner*, p. 94). In Act 2 Walther tries to get Eva to run away with him in a romantic gesture (like in Act 1 of *Die Walküre*), which is capped and foiled by the sound of the night-watchman's horn. He is terrified, clapping his hand to his sword and staring wildly before him, but the bourgeois Eva points out what the sound means, and tells him to hide under the lime-tree (*under der Linde*) until the watchman goes. We have returned to where Siegfried was left, and Siegfried and Walther parallel each other as conceptions.

Adorno points out the relationship of this gesture of Walther's to *Don Quixote* (Bloch agrees in his account of Wagner[37]). The quixotic moment is comic for those who do not recognize the solidity of bourgeois reality, now firmly in place. Yet Walther as Quixote idealizes Cervantes' hero (in terms of the Romantic, idealized—even kitsch-ridden—readings of Quixote himself common in the nineteenth century), and though the hero is undercut by comedy in this second act, he succeeds in moving both the bourgeoisie, and beyond them the *Volk* in the third act. This fantasy of control goes beyond Hans Sachs's powers, in fact, though it is secured because of him, and because he yields, playing the part of the Wanderer to Walther's Siegfried. The opera confirms Walther in terms of his inspiration reached through dreams. The bourgeois world, represented by Pog-ner, when it wishes to prove that it is not avaricious and petty-minded, can do so only by returning to the older form of social existence—the song contest. The frustrations that bourgeois existence brings about are comic here, but they are frustrating none the less, and that emphasis seems to increase after 1848, impelling more and more the rhetoric of renunciation in Wagner, and also driving him on to imagine a more and more impossible hero.

I would summarize by seeing a doubleness in Wagner's discourse from *Rienzi* onwards: the presence of an idealism, which is taken away immediately in a death-wish, and a modernity which is also conservative, just as Wotan is dreamed up in the same instant as Siegfried, and takes over his narrative. 'I no longer believe in any other revolution save that which begins with the burning down of Paris,' Wagner writes (letter of 22 Oct. 1850, in *Selected Letters*, p. 219). The language recalls Carlyle. The anarchistic impulse is inseparable from the nihilistic gesture, as quixotic as overstated. It is like Wotan desiring the end. The hero's renuncia-tion is a melancholy awareness of the impossibility of holding on to power, and

---

[37] Ernst Bloch, *Essays on the Philosophy of Music*, trans. Peter Palmer, ed. David Drew (Cambridge: Cambridge University Press, 1985), p. 156.

the fascist reaction is the one that wishes everything gone, if individual power must go. Modernity, despite or because of its progressiveness, wishes its death.

Let us return, finally in this section, *under den Linden*. In Mann's *The Magic Mountain*, the hero, Hans Castorp, is last seen at the end, in 1914, running into battle, singing Schubert's 'Der Lindenbaum'. But this music, which, with its nostalgic attachments to home and to rootedness, gives Hans Castorp the urge to fight, is the fulfilment of an earlier section in the same chapter, entitled 'Fullness of Harmony'. There, 'Der Lindenbaum' formed the last of a group of Hans Castorp's 'favourite records'. The first record contains the last section of *Aida* (the duet between Radames and Amneris, and Radames dying with Aida). The next is the climax of Act 2 of *Carmen*, the fight between Don José and Carmen, ending with his desertion to join the smugglers. The third is Valentine's 'Après de quitter ces lieux' from Gounod's *Faust*. How these three map on to Schubert is not made clear at this stage, but the reappearance of 'Der Lindenbaum' in the final section makes the connection: all these are texts of militarism, which is already liable to tend towards the state of nostalgia. In each, the soldier's commitment is productive of his death, which, in terms of the symbolism and subject-matter of the Schubert song, may be what the traveller there secretly yearns for. In all these pieces, a rhetoric of freedom and escape from bourgeois routine is productive of death, while the emotional drive that lures on each of these heroes is love, love and death being equated, as they are in the commentary on the favourite records with which the section ends. To love this music is to be attracted to dissolution, to death even on the battlefield, even though the text does not give—it does not need to—Hans Castorp's death there.

Nostalgia—the word first appears in the 1680s, to describe the homesickness of Swiss mercenaries fighting away from home in European countries—was, throughout the nineteenth century, a military medical disorder, and kept this sense up to 1914–18. It may be associated as regressiveness with militarism itself and the death-wish in battle, and with sexuality as inseparable from death.[38] I believe these things constructed sentiments traceable throughout nineteenth-century opera. A check-list of the associations of nineteenth- and early twentieth-century opera's construction of the military or those on conscripted service or those generally uprooted with nostalgia might include, in addition to the examples from Gounod, Bizet, and *Aida*, 'Va' pensiero' from *Nabucco*, 'O Signore dal tetto natio'

[38] See David Lowenthal, *The Past is a Foreign Country* (Cambridge: Cambridge University Press, 1985), pp. 10–11.

from *I Lombardi*, the Pilgrims' chorus from *Tannhäuser* (nostalgic and quasi-military), the estrangement of Lohengrin from the people of Brabant, evoked in the swan music itself, the chorus 'Patria oppressa' from *Macbeth*, the sailor's evocation of 'Heimat' in *Tristan* (though, of course, that is a very overdetermined example), Hylas's aria in *Les Troyens*, much of the mood of *La Fanciulla del West*, especially the opening and Jake Wallace's entry with 'Che faranno i vecchi miei' which returns in the ending, José's 'Ma mère, je la vois . . . oui je revois mon village' in *Carmen*, the scattered knights of the Grail in *Parsifal*, even Ping, Pang, and Pong's trio in Act 2 of *Turandot*. Wotan as the Wanderer is not too far from the spirit of 'Der Lindenbaum'. The story that Italian troops during the 1914–18 war used to sing 'Ch'ella mi creda libero e lontano' (from Act 3 of *Fanciulla*) fits here as an instance of how that nostalgic aria constructs the emotions of the real-life conscript, pushed into a war by the nationalistic fervour of Italian politics of the Right. In such ways nationalism and affectivity are connected, and militarism joined to a longing for rootedness, for nature identified with the nation.

FASCISM AND MODERNITY

> Nearly all foreign intellectuals believe that Fascism is a reactionary, conservative phenomenon. These foreigners ask: 'What do you mean, revolutionary? Does not Fascism have at the centre of its programme the restoration of the principle of authority? Does it not base its actions on the words God, King, Country, Family? Has it not declared itself many times to be a reaction to the principles affirmed by the French Revolution? Is not this perhaps the characteristic profile of a reactionary, retrograde, conservative movement?
>
> Corra, *Gli intellettuali creatori e la mentalità fascista*

Fascism rejects the Enlightenment and liberal bourgeois 'rational' values, in favour of an appeal to a national unity which is under threat, like the hero's personal power in Wagner. Bourgeois values are proclaimed to be decadent, enervating, and supportive of an internationalist *civilization* which refuses the virtues of a national *culture*.[39] But Corra, the futurist, makes fascism out to be

---

[39] On fascism in Italy, Germany, Austria, Hungary, Rumania, Poland, Finland, Norway, Britain, France, Spain, and Portugal, see S. J. Woolf (ed.), *European Fascism* (London: Weidenfeld and Nicolson, 1968). On fascism in general, see Ernst Nolte, *Three Faces of Fascism*, trans. Leila Vennewitz (1963) (London: Weidenfeld and Nicolson, 1965); Hans Rogger and Eugene Weber, *The European Right: An Historical Profile* (London: Weidenfeld and Nicolson, 1965); Walter Laqueur, *Fascism: A Reader's Guide* (1976) (Harmondsworth: Penguin, 1979); Robert Wohl, *The Generation of 1914* (Cambridge, Mass.: Harvard

modern, not reactionary, saying it is 'powerfully revolutionary with everything that extends beyond toward the dark zones in which spiritual values take place'.[40] The ambiguity of fascism, reactionary and revolutionary at once, modern and anti-modern together, is the point. And so, if we listen to Nietzsche, modernity, the culture of fascism, is itself ambiguous, in containing both extremes of being in its shamelessness—which may also be its decadence. 'Shame' almost certainly implies the sexual; and if fascism devotes itself to the family, that shows its anxious desire to recontain sexuality. A strongly contradictory set of attitudes towards decadence and sexuality run through, for instance, D'Annunzio, Wilde, and Nietzsche—all voices heard in this book—who prompt questions of gender politics and sexuality in the culture of fascism.

Gabriele D'Annunzio (1863–1938), whose novels fasten on modern Italian life as decadent and celebrate the artist as hero, began in Rome as a journalist writing in the *Cronaca Bizantina*, the title of which suggests that the decadence of the newly unified *patria*, Italy, makes it like the Roman Empire at Byzantium, not the Empire centred on Rome. He blamed decadence on the consensual liberal politics of post-1870 Italy. In the early 1890s, D'Annunzio was reading Nietzsche and listening to Wagner, and two novels, *Il trionfo della morte* (1894), discussed in Chapter 1, and *Il fuoco* (1900) use motifs from these two, while anxiously asserting the power of a threatened male sexuality. *Il fuoco* records a death in Venice— Wagner's—and the hero, a manifestation of D'Annunzio himself, helps bear the body of Wagner from the Palazzo Vendramin, where he died, to the gondola, and thence to the train back to Bayreuth for burial. D'Annunzio may even have done this, as he claimed; but it is apparent that D'Annunzio must now bear up Wagner's corpus as before he bore up Wagner's corpse. Wagner, then, is taken as being anti-decadent. That fits Cosima's hegemonic reading of Wagner at Bayreuth.

The year of *Il fuoco*, D'Annunzio, who had sat in the Italian Parliament on the Right since 1897, moved to join the socialists. The socialist party had been created in 1892; its revolutionary character had changed to a more reformist one after a shoot-out in Milan in May 1898, following riots and a general strike called in

University Press, 1979); George L. Mosse, *International Fascism: New Thoughts and New Approaches* (London: Sage, 1979). On Austrian fascism, see F. L. Carsten, *Fascist Movements in Austria: From Schönerer to Hitler* (London: Sage, 1977). On French fascism, see Eugene Weber, *Action Française: Royalism and Reaction in Twentieth-century France* (Stanford, Calif.: Stanford University Press, 1962).

[40] Bruno Corra, *Gli intellettuali creatori e la mentalità fascista* (1923), quoted in Richard A. Etlin, *Modernism in Italian Architecture, 1890–1940* (Cambridge, Mass.: MIT Press, 1991), p. 379.

commemoration of the fiftieth anniversary of 1848. The political instability was typical of the 1890s, and it shows in *Andrea Chénier*. D'Annunzio shifted position in response to the Milan riots, while making it clear, in Nietzschean manner, that 'I am beyond right and left as I am beyond good and evil', and saying of the socialists: 'I agree not with their idea . . . but with their destructive force. And I incite the ruling classes to a national renewal and to the doctrine of force for force—a doctrine of the continual struggle and the continual conquest of the world.'[41] Nationalism batters at parliamentary consensualism, and D'Annunzio represents it as poet, novelist, and opera librettist, as advocate for Italy's intervention in the war in 1915, and as the man who spearheaded the capture of Fiume in 1919. Fiume, across the Adriatic, had been pronounced non-Italian territory by the Treaty of Versailles. D'Annunzio held Fiume for fifteen months, with a use of ritual and oratory and control of the crowd that Mussolini could only learn from.[42]

Behind all this, or helping construct it, is a gender politics. It can be seen in the romantic, anti-*verismo* libretti D'Annunzio wrote for some eight or so operas or plays. There was, for example, Zandonai's *Francesca da Rimini* (1914), full of quotations from *Tristan*,[43] *Fedra* (Pizzetti, 1915), and *Parisina* (Mascagni, 1913, though D'Annunzio wanted first Puccini, then Franchetti, composer of his *La Figlia di Iorio* (1906) to set it). *La Figlia* dealt with Mila di Codra, the violent, transgressive woman of the Abruzzi region, and all these libretti were part of his self-construction as artist, nationalist, and creator of nationalist narratives of the past, preacher of Italian unity and imperialism (though his importance went beyond Italy: both Busoni and Strauss considered him for a libretto). There was also *La nave*, a verse-play with music by Pizzetti, later set as an opera by the Wagnerian Montemezzi, 'a prophetic announcement of Italy's destiny in the Adriatic'[44] as 'a tale of luxurious passion revolving around an *Übermensch* in skirts, Basiliola, who finishes by dominating the whole situation and who dies by

[41] Richard Drake, *Byzantium for Rome: The Politics of Nostalgia in Umbertian Italy 1878–1900* (Chapel Hill, NC: University of North Carolina Press, 1980), p. 214.

[42] See Michael A. Ledeen, *The First Duce: D'Annunzio at Fiume* (Baltimore: Johns Hopkins University Press, 1977).

[43] See on this Andrew Porter, 'Wagnerismo', in *A Musical Season* (London: Victor Gollancz, 1974), and on Zandonai in general, including his fascism, Rein A. Zondergeld, 'Riccardo Zandonai: The Master of the Fake Emotion', *Opera*, 35 (1984): 1191–6. On D'Annunzio's texts in general, see Jürgen Maehder, 'The Origins of Italian *Literaturoper*', in Groos and Parker (eds.), *Reading Opera*, pp. 92–108.

[44] Quoted about the first night of *La nave* by Franco Mancini, 'La scena è bella: Objectivity and Transfiguration in Gabriele D'Annunzio's Set Designs', in Pontus Hulten and Germano Celant (eds.), *Italian Art 1900–1945* (New York: Rizzoli, 1989), p. 158.

throwing herself on the pyre of the two heroes who fight for her'.[45] Basiliola in the opera shares features of Salome and Elektra. She is like D'Annunzio's Fedra, who murders and remains defiant to the end, even after taking poison. D'Annunzio's texts specialize in sexual violence, and both had political resonances in the early 1900s. *La Nave* glorified maritime Italy in the early Christian centuries; like *Il fuoco*, its action centres on Venice and the sea, and concentrates on political factions. Pizzetti, who became a Fascist in Mussolini's Italy, wrote 'primitive' liturgical music for *La nave* (his collaboration with D'Annunzio lasted from about 1905 to 1915). *La nave*'s production at the Argentina theatre in Rome in 1908, before the king and queen, was a political event: its militarism and nationalism anticipated Italy's aggression towards Turkey in 1911. As an opera, it appeared in Milan on 3 November 1918, on the evening of the armistice with Austria. Italy had driven the Austro-Hungarian army out of Italian territory with the loss, in the last offensive, of 39,000, to the Austrians' 30,000. *La nave* was D'Annunzio's triumphalism, but there was not much triumph in terms of the peace treaties or overall Italian losses (600,000 dead, half a million permanently disabled), losses that aided the drive towards fascism, as a recuperation of male power.

D'Annunzio, with his constructed masculinity and stress on women who are violently destructive to men (mirroring a set of threats to Italy), contrasts with Oscar Wilde, who provided source material for two operas discussed in this book: *Salome* and *The Birthday of the Infanta*. Belonging to the same moment as D'Annunzio and, like him, influenced by J.-K. Huysman's novel *A Rebours* (1884), a founding text of 'decadence', Wilde was radically different from D'Annunzio in being defeated by the bourgeois culture he mocked for its sexual repression (and assertion of masculine values). The impossibility of a D'Annunzio in British culture, as also the near-impossibility of opera, deserves consideration. One difference between the two is that D'Annunzio's radicalism was also populist. He did not, for instance, let Nietzsche's criticisms of Wagner, that he surrendered to bourgeois tastes, get in the way: 'It is not possible to resist the pressures of the public spirit. The general state of manners always determines the nature of the work of art.'[46] But, in addition, his cult of masculinity, while also stylized, is of the very essence of the culture of fascism. Wilde was more oppositional to his society than that, and his importance is that through his transgression of bourgeois

---

[45] Quotation from Guido Gatti, 'Gabriele D'Annunzio and the Italian Opera-Composers', *Musical Quarterly*, 10 (1924): 275–6.

[46] Quoted in Adrian Lyttelton, 'Society and Culture in the Italy of Giolitti', in Emily Braun (ed.), *Italian Art in the Twentieth Century* (Munich: Prestel-Verlag, 1989), p. 26.

gender roles, he raised questions of what decadence and nihilism mean. If D'Annunzio accused Italian bourgeois society of decadence, he was also complicit with whatever it was that he diagnosed.

'Decadent' becomes an accusation that can be levelled at anyone: at D'Annunzio or Wilde. It is clear that the term cannot be used in a single sense. As used within bourgeois culture, it implies degeneration and the abandonment of morality. As used within Marxist criticism, it applies to bourgeois culture itself. As used by Nietzsche, it implies a character and mind-set that no longer believes in life, one that has taken on itself the death-wish. For Nietzsche, it is probed by nihilism, which might be defined as that force which tests existing values to discover whether they have any survival value. Marx is a nihilist in *The Eighteenth Brumaire* when he probes the simulacrum of power at work in French society. But nihilism is not unitary. One form, complete nihilism, challenges others that do not recognize themselves as empty or protect themselves from such awareness by holding on to certain illusions or values, whereas fascism, while being actually nihilistic in the traditional sense, is also an attempt to protect the self, or a society, against nihilism. The history of Nietzschean nihilism, its increasing importance and subversion, entails the discovery that these values turn out not to last, that they devalue themselves.[47]

D'Annunzio's hyped-up virility is not simple, since it tacitly contains its own admission of the defeat of masculinity. Wilde's homosexuality and Nietzsche's placing the woman and the possibility of writing as a woman at the centre of his work[48] point up ways in which gender issues were opened by a form of

---

[47] Discussion of Heidegger and Nietzsche emphasizes the attraction of fascism for intellectuals. See e.g. Robert Soucy, 'Drieu la Rochelle and Modernist Anti-Modernism in French Fascism', *Modern Language Notes*, 95 (1980): 922–37; Fredric Jameson, *Fables of Aggression: Wyndham Lewis, the Modernist as Fascist* (Berkeley and Los Angeles: University of California Press, 1979); Alice Yaeger Kaplan, *Reproductions of Banality: Fascism, Literature and French Intellectual Life* (Minneapolis: University of Minnesota Press, 1986); for the case of Paul de Man, the bibliography defies a footnote, but see Dik Pels, 'Treason of the Intellectuals: Paul de Man and Hendrik de Man', *Theory, Culture and Society*, 8 (1991): 21–56.

[48] I do not read Nietzsche as anti-Semitic, or anti-feminist, or as consciously neither of these. R. Hinton Thomas, *Nietzsche in German Politics and Society* (Manchester: Manchester University Press, 1983) argues that Nietzsche was not an important philosopher for right-wing Wilhelmine Germany, but was more of an influence on anarchism, bourgeois feminism, and anti-nationalist trends in that society. He is thus unlike Schopenhauer, called by the socialist Franz Mehring 'the philosopher of a moneyed and philistine bourgeoisie that wanted nothing more than peace and quiet' (quoted ibid. 18). See also Geoff Waite, 'The Politics of Reading Formations: The Case of Nietzsche in Imperial Germany (1870–1919)'. *New German Critique*, 29 (1983): 185–209. But it is not my intention to smooth out a reading of Nietzsche; Hinton Thomas makes questionable, but does not cancel out Derrida's statement that 'there is absolutely nothing contingent about the fact that the only political regime to have *effectively* brandished his name as a major and official banner was Nazi', (Derrida, *The Ear of the Other: Autobiography, Transference, Translation*, trans. Christie McDonald (Lincoln, Nebr.: University of Nebraska Press, 1985)), p. 31.

Nietzschean nihilism at the end of the nineteenth century, and closed down through a violent imposition of sexual and gender codification (as in Wilde's case). Modernity is associated with throwing down barriers, opening up and making available new sexual and psychic energies. These appear in the new visibility of the proletariat, the crowd; in feminism and in the pluralizing of forms of sexual behaviour: all new evidence of the loss of earlier codifications, of 'deterritorialization' (to use Deleuze's and Guattari's term). The last three decades of the nineteenth century involved an economic slide, which threatened the politics of middle-class liberal consensualism. This was not recovered from, and it led to paranoia about those energies which had escaped, and a concern to recontain them forcibly in the declared interests of the nation as a whole. The construction, in patriarchal discourse, of the hysterical woman, of the woman as sexually dangerous or as frigid, like Turandot, the construction of the homosexual as a character-type to be legislated against, and the anti-Semitism of the period—all these are part of a neurotic fear of the other that characterizes fascism.[49] Virtually all the operatic texts of this period are marked by an anxiety about women as the 'other' of the dominant discourse, and the operatic form itself, with the place it accords to women as suffering heroines, but not suffering in silence, given a voice, or made a voice, enables this anxiety to be heard the more loudly.

Discussion of gender implies that fascism has a structure to be read psychoanalytically. Erich Fromm, Wilhelm Reich, Georges Bataille, Adorno's work on the authoritarian personality, or Alexander Mitscherlich's *Society without the Father* all offer psychoanalytic explanations. So do Klaus Theweleit's studies of the male fantasies of the *Freikorps* of the 1920s, which showed their hatred of women and Communists alike and identification of them with mud and water and everything disgusting. And there has been Julia Kristeva's work on abjection in her *Powers of Horror*.[50] The last two studies may be put together, both relating strongly to questions of shame and ambiguity of response. Kristeva makes 'abjection' the

---

[49] On the production of sexuality in the nineteenth century, see Michel Foucault, *The History of Sexuality* (Harmondsworth: Penguin, 1981); see also George L. Mosse, *Nationalism and Sexuality: Respectability and Abnormal Sexuality in Modern Europe* (New York: Howard Fertig, 1985).

[50] Julia Kristeva, *Powers of Horror: An Essay on Abjection*, trans. Léon Roudiez (New York: Columbia University Press, 1982). I discuss Theweleit in Ch. 1. On the psychohistory of fascism, see John Milfull (ed.), *The Attractions of Fascism* (New York: Berg, 1990). One of the earliest attempts to psychoanalyse fascism was by Georges Bataille, 'The Psychological Structure of Fascism' (1933); this sees society in terms of a homogeneity requiring a cultic heterogeneous figure to provide it. See his *Visions of Excess: Selected Writings 1927–1939*, ed. Allan Stoekl (Manchester: Manchester University Press, 1985). If fascism responds to male anxieties, I would like briefly to refer to two recent studies of opera which see it as not a masculinist discourse: Wayne Koestenbaum's *The Queen's Throat: Opera, Homosexuality and the Mystery of Desire* (New York: Poseidon

violent repudiation of that which threatens to take away from the defined borders of the ego and the effort to be separate from the heterogeneous—indeed, to define something as outside the self, as heterogeneous. That which is excluded is identified with the mother, with the feminine, hence Kristeva's fascists are melancholics, abjects, who spend their time separating themselves from heterogeneity, which is identified with excess and with bodily waste, in an effort to establish a pure self.

The melancholy feeds into something else, when Adorno comments on a characteristic 'envy' in Wagner (*In Search of Wagner*, p. 17): this envy, or 'rancour' (p. 50), translates Nietzsche's *ressentiment*: it is the characteristic of the nineteenth-century *petit bourgeois* who are reduced to impotence by their political and economic placement, and who cannot act, but only react, because there is no opportunity to take a political initiative.[51] Adorno sees much of Wagner's political idealism of the 1840s as envy, and he investigates it as it runs through the operatic texts' mockery of such people as Alberich, Mime, Beckmesser, and Klingsor and through Wagner's own anti-Semitism. This hatred, Adorno says, 'is of the type that Benjamin had in mind when he defined disgust as the fear of being thought to be the same as that which is found disgusting' (ibid. p. 24).[52] Disgust is motivated by fear, which means it is also a fascination with the disgusting, and an anxiety that the self may also be marginal and disgusting. This fear of the other I map on to Kristeva's abjection. It suggests that Wagner makes non-bourgeois identifications in spite of himself with the marginal and the other (I explore this in Chapter 1), while at the same time retreating into kitsch, which may be conveniently, if too neatly, formulated in Milan Kundera's terms as 'the absolute denial of shit'.[53] For this suggestion of a repudiation of the body and its otherness

Press, 1993), which, interestingly, reads opera in terms of displacement of subject-matter and doubleness of reference; and Jean-Jacques Nattiez, *Wagner Androgyne: A Study in Interpretation* (Princeton: Princeton University Press, 1993). Nattiez, however, uses androgyny as a belief in an overall unity of meaning, and there is no revaluation of gender in his text.

[51] I have suggested the importance of *The Genealogy* in the Introduction to my *Confession: Sexuality, Sin, the Subject* (Manchester: Manchester University Press, 1990). On *ressentiment*, see Tracy B. Strong, *Friedrich Nietzsche and the Politics of Transfiguration* (Berkeley and Los Angeles: University of California Press, 1988), pp. 245–50. This, I think, is one of the best books on Nietzsche; another is Gilles Deleuze's *Nietzsche and Philosophy* (New York: Columbia University Press, 1983), which also discusses *ressentiment*.

[52] Compare the Jewish Fitelberg in Mann's *Doctor Faustus* (1947), trans. H. T. Lowe-Porter (Harmondsworth: Penguin, 1968), on the German fear of being identical to the Jews: 'People talk about the age of nationalism. But actually, there are only two nationalisms, the German and the Jewish, and all the rest is child's play. . . . A German writer could not well call himself Germany, such a name one gives to a battleship. He has to content himself with German [*Deutsch*]—and that is a Jewish name, oh la, la' (p. 392).

[53] Milan Kundera, *The Unbearable Lightness of Being* (New York: Harper and Row, 1984), p. 248. For commentary on Kundera in the light of Nietzsche, see White, *Within Nietzsche's Labyrinth*, ch. 9. Several fine

(which accounts for the hydrotherapy centres) and the wish to have everything the body produces under control, compare Nietzsche on Wagner and the body: 'And now here is a fact which leaves us speechless: Parsifal is Lohengrin's father! However did he do it? Ought one at this juncture to remember that "chastity works miracles"?' (*The Case of Wagner*, p. 9). Modernity that conceals neither its good nor its evil yields a deeply contradictory Wagner: abject, disgusted, both haunted by the other and rejecting it in the name of kitsch culture. In this I believe there is something of the structure of fascism, and though it is Wagner who demonstrates it most fully, it helps to account for other operas that I discuss in this book, after *Parsifal* and *Tristan*: the late operas of Verdi and the works of Puccini, the subjects of Part II, and those of Strauss and Schreker and, in reaction to these, Brecht's and Weill's *Rise and Fall of the City of Mahagonny* in Part III.

A psychic structure which tends towards the authoritarian, to the imposition of rigid boundaries round the self, and a delineation of the subject, at a moment of gender, economic, and political crisis, ultimately takes on specifically Fascist forms. But attraction to what is called decadence and to the abject and to the other is the other side of that structure. My argument, in brief, is this: if we want to understand modernity, then, as Nietzsche said, we must understand Wagnerism, and to see that one strong aspect of modernity is itself fascist is something we can now understand better than Nietzsche could.

examples of fascist art and architecture as kitsch are given in Gillo Dorfles, *Kitsch: The World of Bad Taste* (New York: Bell Publishing Co., 1969).

PART I

Opera Beyond Good and Evil

1

The Sorrows of Richard Wagner

Steeped in sorrows and grandeur, like the nineteenth-century that he so
perfectly epitomises, thus does the intellectual figure of Richard Wagner
appear to me.

Mann, *Pro and Contra Wagner*

Relationship is everything. And if you want to give it a more precise name, it
is ambiguity.

Mann, *Doctor Faustus*

In *Doctor Faustus* (1947), the party of visitors who go to Linderhof, Ludwig II's
pastiche palace in Bavaria, call the nineteenth century 'dull and melancholy'.
Linderhof Mann describes in his Wagner lectures as exemplifying the Romantic
'primacy of the night' over the day, this being 'expressed in the very proportion of
the rooms' (*Pro and Contra Wagner*, p. 125). In ironic contrast to this world,
evocative of the mood of *Tristan und Isolde*, the company expresses the hope that,
in contrast, 'the young twentieth century' (the date is 1925) 'might develop a more
elevated and intellectually a more cheerful temper' (ch. 40, p. 416). The melancholy of the nineteenth century drove Ludwig crazy and suicidal, made Wagner
neurasthenic, and confined Nietzsche to silence and to the madhouse. And the
twentieth century was no different.

Mann divided Wagner up in terms of sorrows (*Leiden*) and greatness (*Grösse*).
The sorrows, which fit with both melancholy and abjection, will be the theme of
this chapter, but are they to be gendered as feminine, and is the greatness
masculine? Was it a certain public, bourgeois articulation of masculinity and
grandeur that held Wagner back from madness, unlike, for instance, Nietzsche?
Or perhaps it is the other way round: that the feminine is foregrounded in
Wagner, and the masculine is that which suffers, either narcissistically or sympath-
etically. Who suffers, who is wounded, and who can be 'great' here? I will argue
in this part of the book, in which I will raise gender issues for the whole study,
that Wagner collapses questions of gender so completely as to make a fascist
discourse of control essential to put things back the way they were. Gender—
where modernity conceals neither its good nor its evil, however much it may try

to repress them—challenges and constructs his melancholy, his disgust, and his fascist impulses. I also want to suggest that questions of sexual difference may enable his texts to be read differently.

This chapter and this part of the book divides into four. In the first, I will go back to Schopenhauer's impact on Wagner, and try to read again some of the symptomatic aspects of Schopenhauer's world denial and retreatism, which I described in the Introduction. These elements I link with Schopenhauer's own foregrounding of sexuality, those strains in his work that make the Will so powerful an unconscious force for his thought and fears, as well as a reading of the subject as constructed by an unconscious. In the second section, I turn the Schopenhauerian-drawn relationship between women, the will, and music into an explication of Nietzsche on Wagner. The account here is bound to be negative about Wagner, and leads into the third section, which looks at *Parsifal* and, to a lesser extent, *Tristan und Isolde* for an approach to Wagner on masculinity and on the male being fatally wounded by sexual contact; the fourth tries to reread the language in which Wagner is critiqued by Nietzsche (and also by Heidegger), in order to see how far that is a whole truth and whether the reading that Nietzsche offers of Wagner may not be turned the other way, so as to side the music with the feminine in spite of itself. The ambiguity or undecidability[1] of (Wagnerian) music is the point: it is inseparable from a sexuality and a set of gender positions that cannot be described or experienced singly, and for which a dialectic, though it may be attempted, is far too rationalist a way of proceeding.

WAGNER READS SCHOPENHAUER

Heidegger called Schopenhauer the philosopher who 'has most persistently determined the whole tone of all of nineteenth and twentieth century thought, even where this is not immediately obvious, and even where Schopenhauer's statement is opposed'.[2] In the Introduction I placed Schopenhauer within the 'the culture of fascism'; now, assuming that ground, I want to start with him, and unpick his

---

[1] On 'uncertainty' and 'indeterminacy' in Wagner, see Pierre Boulez, *Orientations*, ed. Jean-Jacques Nattiez, trans. Martin Cooper (Cambridge, Mass.: Harvard University Press, 1986), pp. 254, 266, 277. Nattiez quotes Boulez in his chapter on Boulez and Chéreau in *Wagner in Performance* (New Haven: Yale University Press, 1992), p. 88, and see his commentary.

[2] Martin Heidegger, *What is Called Thinking?*, trans. J. Glenn Gray (New York: Harper and Row, 1968), p. 39.

philosophy in terms of *ressentiment* and then of gender, and by that route to arrive at Wagner.

In 1853, when composition of *Das Rheingold* began, the year before Wagner read Schopenhauer, the journalist Ludwig August von Rochau published *Grundsätze der Realpolitik*, which begins: 'The discussion of the question who should rule . . . belongs to the realm of philosophical speculation; the practical question only has to do with the simple fact that it is power alone which can rule.'[3] *Realpolitik* thus entered the German language, and shaped a new capitalist thinking. The character of Rhine gold changed with the massive industrialization of the Ruhr valley and with coal mining (from 1.7 million tons in 1850 to 11.6 million tons in 1870). Alberich's Nibelungs are a recognition of this massive increase, with the concomitant production of metallurgy echoed in the anvil music of *Das Rheingold*. *Realpolitik* would be an encouragement to leave Siegfried under the linden tree. The mythology of the hero who conquers the woman by the force of his sword and his lack of fear is far removed from the pressures for modernization. In 1862, Bismarck became Prime Minister of Prussia, stating that 'it is not by speeches and majority decisions that the great questions of the age will be settled—that was the big mistake of 1848 and 1849—but by blood and iron'. Plenty of masculinity there. The year before Bismarck's success, 1861, 'militarism' came into play as a word. It was invented by Proudhon, in the context of France and Prussia—possibly reinvented, if it is true that it had been used in 1816 to describe Napoleonism. ('Paramilitarism', according to the OED, belongs to 1933.)[4] In contrast to this capitalist expansion and this rhetoric, in the course of the 1850s, nearly a million Germans emigrated, mostly to the United States. Wagner, too, thought seriously about emigration: in 1877 he was thinking about giving America the first performance of *Parsifal* (*Selected Letters*, p. 802).

But the philosopher who would encourage world withdrawal under the linden was also the one who would license action: and Siegfried is also a technologist, a manufacturer. By the 1850s, Schopenhauer was not perceived to be against Hegelian progress (with its Prussian inflection of the expansion and legitimization of the state). Rather, his philosophy guaranteed that the modernization and technologization of the 1850s had nothing to do with the individual, who could

---

[3] Quoted in James J. Sheehan, *German History 1770–1866* (Oxford: Clarendon Press, 1989), p. 156.

[4] See Volker R. Berghahn, *Militarism: The History of an International Debate 1861–1979* (Leamington Spa: Berg, 1981).

let the state go on with the process of supporting private property, and could turn attention to life as a matter of the personal. The philosophy depoliticizes, while de-romanticizing the 'will to live'. Schopenhauer is the ideologist of modernity, since he allows for it; but while he talks about the Will as the driving force in history, and opposes it, it is thematized ahistorically, with its particular political and economic contours never being recognized for what they are.

Resistance to the Will is thematic for one aspect of modernity. In *Buddenbrooks* (1902) Thomas Mann gives a chilling picture of the middle-aged businessman Thomas Buddenbrooks sitting down in 1874 to read chapter 41 of the second book of *The World as Will and Representation*, 'On Death and its Relation to the Indestructibility of our Inner Nature'. This reading prepares the way for the Senator's movement towards death, which happens six months later. His enjoyment of the idea of death, sitting as he does with the book before him in his comfortable summer-house, is presented as aesthetic, as 'a profound intoxication, a strange sweet, vague allurement which somehow resembled the feelings of early love and longing'.[5] This seduction by a feminine-seeming book works also for Freud, who near the end of *Beyond the Pleasure Principle* (1920), articulating the death-wish, finds that 'we have unwittingly steered our course into the harbour of Schopenhauer's philosophy. For him death is "the true result and to that extent the purpose of life," while the sexual instinct is the embodiment of the will to live.'[6]

The chapter which Thomas Buddenbrooks reads is Schopenhauer's commentary on his earlier section 54 of the first book of *The World as Will and Representation*, a chapter dealing with the process of preparation for death. One fulfilment of Schopenhauer's attitudes is in Hans Pfitzner (1869–1949), whose opera *Palestrina* (1917) drew him into a dialogue with Mann. While not a Nazi, Pfitzner had strong fascist sympathies. *Palestrina* is composed as though it were a triptych: with the artist-composer on the two outer panels, in the first and last acts, and the second act, in which the composer does not appear, given over to a display of the politics of the Council of Trent. In Schopenhauerian spirit the composer rejects the political world, not even confronting it as the opposite of him, as the opera also rejects it, parodying in the second act the world of parliamentary

---

[5] Thomas Mann, *Buddenbrooks*, trans. H. T. Lowe-Porter (Harmondsworth: Penguin, 1957), p. 509. In *Reflections of a Nonpolitical Man*, trans. Walter D. Morris (New York: Frederick Ungar Pub. Co., 1983), p. 49, Mann indicates the autobiographical nature of his reading.

[6] Sigmund Freud, *On Metapsychology, The Penguin Freud*, vol. 11 (Harmondsworth: Penguin, 1984), p. 322.

democracy. The artist is separate from that world and beyond it. *Palestrina* used an epigraph from Schopenhauer:

[Like an ethereal addition], this purely intellectual life hovers, as a sweet-scented air that is developed from the ferment over the stir and movement of the world, that real life of nations which is dominated by the *will*. Along with the history of the world, that of philosophy, the sciences and the arts pursues its innocent and bloodless path.[7]

I shall return to Pfitzner in Chapter 9, but Schopenhauer licenses in him a belief in world withdrawal, and his opposition to the will which is active in world history produces kitsch images of purity and sweetness and innocence. There is no 'gay science' (*die fröhliche Wissenschaft*) here; nor is that kind of lightness of thought allowed for in the image of the intellectual life hovering. This intellectual life is determined to keep out everything that is not of the intellect—of the life of the mind. Here is Pfitzner, quoted by Thomas Mann, discussing the differences between his work and *Die Meistersinger*.

The difference is expressed most clearly in the concluding scenic pictures. At the end of the *Meistersinger* there is a stage full of light, rejoicing of the people, engagement, brilliance and glory; in my work there is, to be sure, Palestrina, who is also celebrated, but in the half-darkness of his room under the picture of the deceased one, dreaming at his organ. The *Meistersinger* is the apotheosis of the new, a praise of the future and of life; in *Palestrina* everything tends towards the past, it is dominated by *sympathy with death*. (*Reflections of a Nonpolitical Man*, p. 311)

Mann, who writes warmly of *Palestrina* in the *Reflections*, identifies Pfitzner as, before the war, a 'romantic artist, that is: national but nonpolitical [where that term means, to Mann "conservative"]' but now 'an antidemocratic nationalist' (*Reflections*, pp. 312–13). He calls *Palestrina* 'something ultimate, consciously ultimate, from the sphere of Schopenhauer and Wagner' (ibid. 297). Relations between Mann and Pfitzner deteriorated when Mann assessed him negatively, and Pfitzner was one of those who signed a letter of protest against Mann's lecture 'The Sorrows and Grandeur of Richard Wagner'.[8]

---

[7] Schopenhauer, *Parerga and Paralipomena*, ii. 75.
[8] See John Newson, 'Hans Pfitzner, Thomas Mann and *The Magic Mountain*', *Music and Letters*, 55 (1974): 136–50. There is much of interest between the two also in Mann, *Pro and Contra Wagner*. On *Palestrina*, see Peter Franklin, *The Idea of Music* (London: Macmillan, 1986), ch. 7. On Pfitzner, see John Williamson, *The Music of Pfitzner* (Oxford: Clarendon Press, 1992). Peter Franklin's review of this in *Music and Letters*, 74 (1993): 611–13, should be consulted. Also on Pfitzner, see Marc A. Weiner, *Undertones of Insurrection: Music, Politics and the Social Sphere in the Modern German Narrative* (Lincoln, Nebr.: University of Nebraska Press, 1993).

'Sympathy with death': Mann uses the phrase quotationally in *The Magic Mountain* in relation to Hans Castorp's fascination with Schubert's 'Der Linden-baum': 'behind this so lovely and pleasant artistic production stood—death. It had with death certain relations, which one might love . . . perhaps in its original form it was not sympathy with death; perhaps it was something very much of the people and racy of life, but spiritual sympathy with it was none the less sympathy with death.'[9] Schubert has become Schopenhauerianized. In *Culture and Socialism* (1928) Mann declares that 'sympathy with death' constitutes 'a legitimate part of [his] being', along with 'a cordial acceptance of life'. The context makes it clear that the Schopenhauerian / Pfitzner identification here is to be resisted in the conditions of the Weimar Republic, as it has the capacity to draw the self away from people and towards the anti-democratic and the nostalgic cult of the aristocratic leader, an identification itself morbid. So we should gather from the strange, still élitist rhetoric that 'a conscious overemphasis of the democratic idea of life over the aristocratic principle of death has become a vital necessity'.[10] This and the episode from *The Magic Mountain* describing an erotic, death-tinged state of mind just before 1914 isolates one tendency to be drawn from Schopenhauer. But it is also a modernist drive, an identification with destructiveness, 'while the surge of warfare was at its height [Pfitzner] demonstratively dedicated a work of chamber music to Fleet Admiral von Tirpitz' (*Reflections*, p. 313). 'Klage' was dedicated to Tirpitz in 1916, Tirpitz having recently resigned in protest against attacks made on him for his advocacy of unrestricted submarine warfare. World withdrawal and technological modernization have come together. This Schopen-hauerian philosophy belongs to the culture of fascism, for though it seems to encourage passivity, it actually goes elsewhere: it allows for unlimited, cynical progress, for the power of *Realpolitik*, and for the advance of technology. It has sympathy with the submarines as much as with the abstract idea of death.

Acceptance of Schopenhauer by Wagner is not neutral; there is an investment in wishing it to be true, as much as he also wishes to be transgressive. He would like to see everything as Hans Sachs does, with detachment, not with a King Mark-like, or Wotan-like, sense of *ressentiment* and fear of the sexual as inter-ference, a breaking of boundaries and border. (King Mark's lament to Tristan about his treachery resurfaces when Hans Sachs does not want to be King Mark to Walther and Eva, who are Tristan and Isolde: which intertextuality suggests

---

[9] Mann, *The Magic Mountain*, trans. H. T. Lowe-Porter, (Harmondsworth: Penguin, 1960), p. 652.
[10] Quoted in Keith Bullivant (ed.), *Culture and Society in the Weimar Republic* (Manchester: Manchester University Press, 1977), p. 28.

that Walther's and Eva's love may also be viewed pessimistically.) But Nietzsche's criticism of Schopenhauer is that all actions which the Schopenhauerian spirit encourages actually come out of revenge and *ressentiment*. 'Man would sooner have the void for his purpose than be void of purpose,' concludes *The Genealogy of Morals*. With the example of the submarines in mind, and remembering Wotan's will in *Die Walküre*, this implies that the will takes the form of a drive towards destructiveness. As Wagner wished to fire Paris, so Wotan puts the logs around Valhalla, and wishes for the end in a destructive gesture he enforces because he cannot accept the compromising nature of life and interprets any lack of freedom as total. (I shall return to this point in Ch. 8.) The spirit which identifies life as illusion cannot, in other words, be neutral; it implies a prior *hostility* to any form of action and spontaneity, and the rhetoric with which Schopenhauer writes can be seen as a defensive gesture coming from someone wounded by life. In 'Redemption' in *Thus Spake Zarathustra*, the nineteenth century needs to be redeemed from hostility to time and its 'It was'. *Ressentiment* and the revenge instinct stem from anger at the fact that time is not in the gift of the subject, and hence neither a narrative of events nor any human destiny can be controlled. Life is a process of becoming and going, and consciousness can only watch things going away, unable to control them or make them stay. As Nietzsche puts it elsewhere: 'As Heraclitus sees time, so does Schopenhauer. He repeatedly said of it that every moment in it exists only insofar as it has just consumed the preceding one, its father, and then is immediately consumed likewise.'[11]

In Nietzschean fashion, Heidegger discusses the 'revulsion arising in the will', which, he says, is 'the will against everything that passes—everything, that is, which comes to be out of a coming to be, and endures. Hence the will is the sphere of representational ideas which basically pursues and sets upon everything that comes and goes and exists, in order to depose, reduce it in its stature and ultimately decompose it' (*What is Called Thinking?*, pp. 93–4). The activity of the personal will is, for Heidegger, to reduce the phenomenal world, to assert a mastery over it. This will to reduce, which is also the will to destroy, characterizes fascism, and a first thought will be one of surprise that Heidegger, Nazi party member no. 3125894 Gau Baden, should be so hospitable to an identification of the problem. The sense of the body as other, as not controllable by the will, just as nothing else is so controlled, becomes, then, also a source of *ressentiment*, and a further aspect of Wagner.

[11] Nietzsche, *Philosophy in the Tragic Age of the Greeks* (Chicago: University of Chicago Press, 1962), pp. 52–3.

Heidegger goes further by quoting from 'Redemption' in *Thus Spake Zarathus-tra*, refusing to speculate as to 'whether these words of Nietzsche on revenge and punishment, revenge and suffering, revenge and deliverance from revenge, repre-sent a direct confrontation with Schopenhauer, and indirectly one with all world-denying attitudes'. The suggestion is that the motivating force of Schopen-hauer's work is revenge. Heidegger, in this text from 1951, reflecting on habitual thinking as being that which works within the Schopenhauerian pattern, keeps returning to the formulation that 'we are still not thinking'—which implies the impossibility of a different form of thinking outside the conceptual modes which effectually dominate the phenomenal world, bringing it down nihilistically out of the need to control what happens. Wagner's response to this lack of control is imagined and stated by Zarathustra: 'No deed can be annihilated: how could it be undone by punishment, this is the eternal in the punishment called existence—that existence also again must be deed and guilt. "It happens then that the will at last redeems itself and will becomes non-will"—but, my brothers, you know this fable of madness.'[12] The Wagnerian inflection of revenge against time and against its 'It was' incites him to seek impossible solutions, such as I touched on in the Introduction. Existence has to be resisted, and as in the *Ring*, which describes a ring, an eternal return of deed and guilt, desire must be denied.

But withdrawal and resentment, two aspects of the same thing, both suggest male reactions to the body. Discarding the body in death is said to be the same, in a higher way, as excretion, which is taken as an example of the body in process, and 'it appears just as foolish to embalm corpses as it would be carefully to preserve our excreta'.[13] Turning this image around, it seems that Schopenhauer seriously equates the body with the body's discarded matter. This, which would be Kundera's 'kitsch' if it were not so up front, is hatred of the body, and looking forward to death as though that will free the self from the body.

But why is the body so hated? Schopenhauer, who is both fascinated and appalled by plants which reveal their will to live by shamelessly carrying their genitals exposed to view on their upper surface (*World as Will*, i. 156), I read as affronted by the sexuality of the Will. 'The sexual impulse is . . . the decided and strongest affirmation of life' (i. 329); 'Nature . . . the inner being of which is the

---

[12] Trans. by Walter Kaufmann; see Strong, *Friedrich Nietzsche and the Politics of Transfiguration*, p. 228, which makes the identification of the fable of madness with Wagner's work. (I had supposed it to be Schopenhauer's.) The whole of Strong's discussion (pp. 228–31) is relevant.

[13] Schopenhauer, *The World as Will and Representation*, trans. E. J. Payne, 2 vols. (New York: Dover, 1966), i. 277.

will-to-live itself, with all her force impels both man and the animal to propagate' (i. 330); this being possible since 'far more than any other external member of the body the genitals are subject merely to the will, and not at all to knowledge' (i. 330). These genitals, which are characteristically the 'objectified sexual impulse' (i. 108) are male; so Nature is encoded as female, as is music, which is complicit with Nature and the Will: it 'flatters only the will to live, since it depicts the true nature of the will, gives it a glowing account of its success, and at the end expresses its satisfaction and content' (ii. 457). To affirm the will is equivalent to Christianity's belief in original sin (i. 405). Music has contradictory associations; while it is the art-form that shows things as they are, it is on the side of the deceptive, the flattering, the non-controllable. It fosters no illusions. It points back to the uncontrollable body, while also urging on the self the desire to lapse away from the body.[14]

Ressentiment is thus attached to the sexual, to the body, which 'is nothing but the will objectified' (i. 100), to the affiliations that the sexual brings about, and is, in Schopenhauer's terms, bound to be misogynistic. It is this complex of issues that I now want to connect with Wagner. In this context, it is noteworthy that Schopenhauer quotes Clement of Alexandria on castration (i. 329), as if recommending that his male readers become like Klingsor. But that suggests another set of references in *Parsifal*, to Klingsor's agent and the source of all that mocks him: Kundry.

'MUSIC IS A WOMAN': NIETZSCHE AND WAGNER

> Perhaps, said Kretschmar, it was music's deepest wish not to be heard at all, nor even seen, nor yet felt: but only—if that were possible—in some Beyond . . . But bound as she was to the world of sense, music must ever strive after the strongest, yes the most seductive sensuous realisation: she is a Kundry who wills not what she does, and flings soft arms of lust round the neck of the fool.
>
> Mann, *Doctor Faustus*

If music can be interpreted from the male viewpoint as a Kundry, that would mean the end of desire for the sensuous and for bodily experience. Kretschmar

---

[14] For Schopenhauer on women, see *Paralipomena and Prolegomena*, ch. 27. Further to discussions of Schopenhauer on women and nature, see *World as Will*, i. 281. For his antagonism to sexuality, see Rüdiger Safranski, *Schopenhauer and the Wild Years of Philosophy*, trans. Ewald Osers (London: Weidenfeld and Nicolson, 1989), p. 227.

speaking to the boy Adrian Leverkühn sounds like Schopenhauer, via Nietzsche and Adorno. A first question, seeing that music has now become a Wagnerian character, would be to ask if Mann responds to the ambiguity involved in Wagner's creation of Kundry?

The figure of Kundry, the 'rose of hell,' is nothing less than an exercise in mythical pathology; in her agonizingly schizoid condition, as instrument of the Devil and penitent hungering after redemption, she is portrayed with an unsparing clinical accuracy, an audacious naturalism in the exploration and representation of a hideously diseased emotional existence, that has always seemed to me a supreme triumph of insight and artistry. Nor is she the only character in *Parsifal* whom Wagner has pushed to the psychological limit. (Mann, *Pro and Contra Wagner*, p. 99)

The schizoid state is declared to be Kundry's, not Wagner's. By contrast, I believe the drive in Wagner to be double: between the bourgeois, dignified pose and repression of the sexual in Eva and *Die Meistersinger* generally and the intense production of the sexual woman in Kundry. This duality in Wagner's discourse makes the woman destabilizing throughout: in *Lohengrin* because she will not live with the repression enjoined on her, not to ask the hero his name, and in *Parsifal* because she knows the name and sings it out with the intention to seduce. Mann writes as though Wagner were in control of these contradictions, as though Kundry did not embody Wagner's own male fantasies. It weakens Mann's assessment of Wagner's psychological strengths, and makes references to his psychological strengths conventional. It misses Wagner's shamelessness.[15]

How do Schopenhauer's views on music carry over into Wagner? First, and orthodoxly, here is Nietzsche, summarizing the impact of Schopenhauer on Wagner and suggesting the importance of the question of gender in music to Wagner, but with the wit of this, it is important to note that there is no record here of a revulsion from the woman in Wagner as there is in Schopenhauer:

[Wagner's] later aesthetic views completely contradict his earlier ones. As an example of the earlier view, we may take the treatise *Opera and Drama*, of the latter, his articles from 1870 onwards. What most impresses one is the radical change in his notion of the position of music itself. What did it matter to him that he had once conceived of music as a means, 'a woman,' which required an end, a 'man,' drama, for its completion? It suddenly dawned

---

[15] I find Mann's account of Wagner merely conventional in his discussions of Wagner as psychologist (as with Klingsor, *Pro and Contra Wagner*, p. 99) and in relation to his treatment of myth (ibid. 128). There are interesting comments on Kundry in Catherine Clément and Hélène Cixous, *The Newly Born Woman* (Minneapolis: University of Minnesota Press, 1986).

on him that Schopenhauer's theory was much more favourable to the sovereignty of music: music seen as apart from all the other arts, the triumphant culmination of all art, not concerned like the others with images of the phenomenal world, but, rather, speaking the language of the will directly from the deep source of being, its most elementary manifestation. There corresponded to this extraordinary rise in the value of music an equally amazing increase in the prestige of the musician . . . he now became a telephone line of Transcendence.[16]

This is a reminder of how Wagner shifts to such absolutism that he can call his dramas 'deeds of music become visible' (*The Destiny of Opera*) and say that 'the music sounds and what it sounds you see on the stage before you' (*On the Term 'Music-Drama'*) while his belief in transcendence takes the ultimate form of the famous desire for the invisible theatre following on from the invisible orchestra.[17] He began, in *Opera and Drama*, by taking music as female, as instrumental for the male—the drama. Music-drama reverses that argument, so that music generates its own drama. The earlier formulation in *Opera and Drama* of music as a woman, drama as a man, is inherently sexist, but when music later becomes the voice of the will, it becomes more dominant, though perhaps still female in its elementality. Wagner makes claims for music's ambiguity and power out of this, which imply a male domination of it. Something of this use of music-as-metaphysics lies behind Nietzsche's provocations in *The Case of Wagner: A Musician's Problem* where the problem is stated thus: 'Was Wagner a musician at all?' (sect. 8). In the abandonment of rules, Wagner is seen as writing 'bad music', just as, in the next section, 'Wagner is no dramatist'. In section 10, Wagner is seen to have to face the problem that people might actually understand his music, so 'he did nothing but repeat one proposition: that his music did not mean music alone!' Nietzsche's comment is that '*no* musician would speak in this way'. Put alongside Bizet, whose *Carmen* is set against Wagner in this essay, or Verdi, the case seems made. That is not to say that there is no metaphysics of music behind these other composers; only that in Wagner, music is openly ideological.

Nietzsche presses this further in *Nietzsche Contra Wagner: The Brief of a Psychologist* and in the section 'A Music without a Future'. The title plays on a Wagner title of 1861, *Music of the Future* and its Feuerbachian assumptions; also, Nietzsche's *Beyond Good and Evil* is called 'A Philosophy of the Future'. He

---

[16] Nietzsche, *The Birth of Tragedy and The Genealogy of Morals*, trans. Francis Golffing (New York: Doubleday Anchor, 1956), p. 237.

[17] For these quotations, see Jack Stein, *Richard Wagner and the Synthesis of the Arts* (Detroit: Wayne State University Press, 1960), pp. 171 ff.

comments on how late music is as a growth within the history of European culture, so that in its belatedness, 'all real and original music is a swan song'. But this comment is related to the imminent submergence—the going under—of the culture it relates to. He finishes 'A Music without a Future' by saying that 'the Germans themselves have no future', his verdict on Bismarck's Reich established in 1871 and on its nationalistic and militaristic ideology. Germany is undergoing a twilight of its idols: how does Wagner's music stand in relation to that? His subject-matter, evoking that nationalism, 'would also give unmistakable express-ion to the *spirit of his music* provided that this music, like any other, did not know how to speak about itself save ambiguously: for *music is a woman*'. Something about music resists the way Wagner tries to appropriate it for German ideology, death-driven as that is.

Music is a woman: this takes over Schopenhauer's unconscious gendering of it, and would not flatter it in his eyes, since through it (or them) and the will, the male is caught by the woman who exists only for the continuance of the species, as an agent of nature. However much Schopenhauer speaks against individuality and looks forward to seeing it taken away by death, it seems that it *must* be what he is committed to, the alternative being the life of women and sexuality, which he disparages in chapter 44 of *The World as Will and Representation*, entitled 'The Metaphysics of Sexual Love'. But in Nietzsche's case, the statement, which is *contra* Schopenhauer in its affirmation, raises the question of whether it is appropriate to think of music in gender terms. We also confront a different sense from Wagner's of what it means that music is a woman. In his Epilogue, Nietzsche returns to the issue with a comment also found in substance in the Preface to *The Gay Science* (1886), which enlarges on it a little, and from which, therefore, I quote. The context is the search for another kind of art, an art not dedicated to the desire to know:

No, this bad taste, this will to truth, to 'truth at any price,' this youthful madness in the love of truth, have lost their charm for us: . . . we no longer believe that truth remains truth when the veils are withdrawn; we have lived too much to believe this. Today we consider it a matter of decency not to wish to see everything naked, or to be present at everything, or to understand and 'know' everything.

'Is it true that God is present everywhere?' a little girl asked her mother. 'I think that's indecent'—a hint for philosophers. One should have more respect for the bashfulness with which nature has hidden behind riddles and iridescent uncertainties. Perhaps truth is a woman who has reasons for not letting us see her reasons? perhaps her name is—to speak Greek—*Baubo*?

Oh those Greeks! They knew how to live. What is required for that is to stop courageously at the surface . . . those Greeks were superficial—*out of profundity.*[18]

The French critics of the 'new Nietzsche' say that Nietzsche's writing places woman at its centre.[19] Music is a woman: truth is a woman. Nietzsche's aphorisms suggest that Wagner respects neither of these things. If music is a woman for him, it implies the possibility of domination. If truth is a woman, that suggests that truth is to be possessed. None of Nietzsche's positions are unambiguous, his writings about women especially (e.g. the old woman's advice to Zarathustra, 'Thou goest to women? Forget not thy whip!' *Zarathustra,* i. 18), and I shall finish this chapter with some aspects of his writings about Wagner that also have to do with the fear of women. But for the moment it may be worth advancing on the path that twentieth-century poststructuralist/feminist psychoanalytic readings have opened on some of Nietzsche's texts.

Feminist psychoanalytic criticism, drawing on Lacan and Derrida, has suggested that to identify truth as a woman may not necessarily imply the male conquest of truth, but rather that 'truth' may be reconceptualized not in terms of single, unitary, 'phallogocentric' statements, but in terms of otherness, or difference, which embodies elusiveness and doubleness. In masculinist ideology, which Freud identifies but does not necessarily endorse, woman is regarded as a castrated man and therefore defined by loss. To assert that truth or music is a woman is, in alternative vein, to argue that this masculinism names a way of patriarchal thinking that wishes to exclude otherness, and dubs that which is other as female, so putting it out on the margins. And that implies that truth, like music, is always other, never castrated—never, that is, brought under subjection or dominated, or brought under the power of a dominant, defining interpretation even when it seems to be. As different, and not inscribed by masculinist anxieties about the self

---

[18] Nietzsche, *The Gay Science,* trans. Walter Kaufmann (New York: Random House, 1974), p. 38.

[19] The classic reading is Jacques Derrida, *Spurs: Nietzsche's Styles,* trans. Barbara Harlow (Chicago: University of Chicago Press, 1978). See also David Farrell Krell, *Postponements: Woman, Sensuality and Death in Nietzsche* (Bloomington, Ind.: Indiana University Press, 1986), who argues for the bisexuality of Dionysos, which would be significant for an argument about music. Sarah Kofman, *The Enigma of Woman: Woman in Freud's Writings* trans. Catherine Porter (Ithaca, NY: Cornell University Press, 1985) discusses Nietzsche and women. See also her chapter on 'Baubo' in Michael Allen Gillespie and Tracy B. Strong (eds.), *Nietzsche's New Seas* (Chicago: University of Chicago Press, 1988). For oppositional views in what has become a huge debate, see Rosalyn Diprose, 'Nietzsche, Ethics and Sexual Difference', *Radical Philosophy,* 5 (Summer 1989): 27–33, and the bibliography there. I linked the affirming woman of Nietzsche to Carmen in my *Confession,* pp. 191–2. See Luce Irigaray, *Marine Lover of Friedrich Nietzsche,* trans. Gillian C. Gill (New York: Columbia University Press, 1991), for a feminist reading of Nietzsche which responds to the point that Nietzsche's contrary gods—Dionysos, Apollo, the Crucified—are all male.

whose potency must be protected—which is what prompts the impulse to dominate—it escapes single definition, remaining thus 'ambiguous' as Nietzsche says music is, not saying quite what its composer would like it to say, and never able to be pinned down as 'truth' in the 'will to truth'. If males wish to play that game of thinking in terms of the castration complex, diminishing the woman, who is not male, and creating anxiety in the male to *be* male, then there will be a return of female power in the form of 'Baubo', the name for the pudendum (Latin: *pudor*—shame), which, for Freud, is the source of deep anxiety (the wound, for the male) and of fetish-forming protectionism. To try to dominate, to control, brings its own distorting consequences.

Nietzsche's critique of Wagner accuses him of using music as a drive towards a will-to-truth, which is also a will-to-power. And the use of music as a woman in Wagner's sense in *Opera and Drama* is an attempt to think about music from a masculinist position, whereas Nietzsche's sense reverses this, and suggests that the music may actually resist that ideology—which may reverse the old joke that Wagner's music is often better than it sounds, and may suggest that part of Wagner's investment in Schopenhauer comes from his anxiety that music should become metaphysical, should be dominated by a set of concepts. If pushed to find Wagner 'fascist', the fascism might be located here.

THE LAUGHTER OF KUNDRY

> Few aspects of Wagner's music have been as seductive as the enjoyment of pain.
>
> Adorno, *In Search of Wagner*

The argument which accords a gender role to music suggests deep anxieties about gender in Wagner. Nietzsche fastens on these when he speculates on Wagner's conversion to the ascetic ideal and the rejection of women ('Wagner as the Apostle of Chastity', in *Nietzsche Contra Wagner*). Here, I concentrate on Wagner's reactiveness, finding in his operas a *ressentiment* about sexuality that constructs the quasi-fascist male, in uncertain relationship with homosexuality and the homoerotic, and certainly bonded with other males 'homosocially', a situation that is itself anxiety-forming. For example, Siegfried is fearful that he might be of the same origin as Mime, the male to whom he is bonded, and even though he knows he is not, can resolve the situation only by killing Mime. The argument may be contextualized by considering the ambiguous status of homosexuality within late nineteenth- and early twentieth-century culture. Recognition of ambiguity here does not compel agreement with Robert Gutman in his biography of Wagner that 'what seemed [in Wagner] a propensity towards homosexuality evidently remained sublimated' (p. 331), though it accords with Mann's dislike, according to George W. Reinhardt, of 'the proto-Hitlerian bad taste of the furnishings and art works of Triebschen', one of Wagner's Swiss refuges, which Mann characterized in terms of 'elements of monstrosity and *Hitlertum*' entailing 'bombastic *Kitsch*' and 'German pederasty'.[20] But Gutman makes relevant points when writing of Lohengrin's monkishness, or Tannhäuser's dissatisfaction with both Venus and Elizabeth and his attempt to conquer sex through fierce self-humiliations (p. 609), or when he notes that Ludwig II's nickname was Parsifal, the chaste hero being really the homosexual mad king. Gutman parallels the male relationships of Tristan-Melot-Mark with the court at Munich (p. 352), just as Adorno discusses the blood-brotherhood of *Parsifal* as 'the prototype of the secret societies and *Führer*-orders of later years, which had so much in common with the Wahnfried circle—that clique held together by a sinister eroticism and its fear of the tyrant, with a hypersensitivity that bordered on terrorism towards everyone who did not belong' (*In Search of Wagner*, p. 140). I compare this with Adorno's 'Totalitarianism and homosexuality belong together',[21] a statement itself fairly totalitarian. How does Wagner represent masculinity, and what investment does he make in the narcissistic male, wounded psychically or physically, spoiled by women? Is it all fed by Schopenhauerian *ressentiment* of the feminine and the body which cannot be controlled?

The wound is the mark of a break in the male subject. Siegfried feels wounded at the sight of Brünnhilde. Wagner connected Tristan's wound in his own thoughts with that of Amfortas in *Parsifal*, and in a letter of 30 May 1859 said that Amfortas was the centre and principal subject of *Parsifal*. In Act 3 of *Tristan* the hero lies under a linden tree, the third time for this setting in Wagner, and he tears the bandage away from his wound, a suicidal gesture performed at the moment when Isolde comes to bring him recovery. It is not possible to assert that Tristan's wound is genital, but the wound of Amfortas surely *is* (at least in Wolfram,

---

[20] Quoted in George W. Reinhardt, 'Thomas Mann's *Doctor Faustus*: a Wagnerian Novel', in W. John Rempel and Ursula M. Rempel (eds.), *Music and Literature* (Winnipeg: University of Manitoba, 1985), p. 110. On the subject of male bonding, which she calls 'homosociality', see Eve Kosofsky Sedgwick, *Between Men: English Literature and Male Homosocial Desire* (New York: Columbia University Press, 1985); for a critique of Sedgwick, see David Van Leer, 'The Beast of the Closet: Homosociality and the Pathology of Manhood', *Critical Inquiry*, 15, (1989): 587–605.

[21] Adorno, *Minima Moralia*, trans. E. F. J. Jephcott (London: New Left Books, 1974), p. 52.

Wagner's source), and it echoes the castration Klingsor has inflicted on himself in his attempt to atone for some sin he has committed—Gurnemanz professes not to know what. Klingsor's castration seems to follow his perception of being wounded by sin; it is an act of revenge on himself—the ascetic ideal and the desire for mastery over temptation. Klingsor is like Melot who wounds Tristan, though Tristan invites Melot's wound, accusing him of lust towards Isolde. The wound expresses the gap that has opened in male friendship, the splitting of that narcissistic unity of males, like the spear thrust that ultimately fells Siegfried. The wound in *Tristan* and *Parsifal* is the exposure of a masculinity which has lost its potency, which no longer exists in phallic supremacy and is the cause of melancholy (Freud calls melancholia an 'open wound')[22]. The agency of the wound in *Parsifal* is Kundry, the castrating female, and I have quoted Mann to connect her with music, destabilizing the dominance of the male.

The wound is also a motif in Mann's *Death in Venice*, where the protagonist, the writer Aschenbach, has written a novel about Frederick the Great (probably, and significantly, homosexual), which seems to describe his own stated attitudes which are those of the obedient writer of the second Reich—supporter of a melancholy, armoured uptightness which makes for total repression while actually enjoying the masochism which that implies. 'The new type of hero favoured by Aschenbach . . . had early been analysed by a shrewd critic: "The conception of an intellectual and virginal manliness, which clenches its teeth and stands in modest defiance of the swords and spears which pierce its side." '[23] The hero sounds like Parsifal, as though Mann were adopting Nietzsche's parody of Wagner: to translate him into modern idiom ('Parsifal as a candidate in divinity, with a public-school education': *The Case of Wagner*, p. 9). Aschenbach's hero remains 'modest', and he is obviously in retreat from one aspect of modernity, since he wants not to be shameless, but is fated to be so. The same paragraph of *Death in Venice* invokes Saint Sebastian, the hero penetrated and feminized, as the most evocative symbol of 'beauty constant under torture'. It is not just Parsifal, but Christ who is included in this circulation of images: for Parsifal, threatened by the penetration of Kundry's kiss, undergoes a profound change, clasping his hands to his heart (associating the blood which might become corrupted with the wound and with compassionate suffering) and falls into a trance, thinking of where the wound really originated:

[22] Freud, 'Mourning and Melancholia', in *On Metapsychology*, p. 262.
[23] Mann, *Death in Venice*, trans. H. T. Lowe-Porter (Harmondsworth: Penguin, 1955), p. 15.

Des Heilands Klage da vernehm ich
die Klage, ach! die Klage
um das entweihte Heiligtum:
'Erlöse, rette mich
aus schuldbefleckten Händen!'

(The Saviour's cry I hear [in my heart], the lament, the lamentation from his profaned sanctuary: 'Redeem me, rescue me from hands defiled by sin!')

Klingsor's wounding of Amfortas and Christ's wound are barely distinguished in what follows, while Kundry, who laughed at the penetrated Christ, eternally repeats her actions, first in relation to Christ, then to Amfortas, and now to Parsifal. Christ and Amfortas are both, it seems, wounded in the side, and both these wounds may be genital displacements. Kundry laughed when she saw Christ going to his crucifixion, and this returns upon her as a curse: 'ein Sünder sinkt in die Arme! / Da lach' ich—lache' (A sinner sinks into my arms! Then I laugh—laugh). But her laughter is the laugh of the Medusa,[24] and Syberberg in his film of *Parsifal* makes the hero carry a shield with the Medusa on it in the third act. It is a nihilistic laughter, which I shall develop further with the laughter of Jago in Chapter 2, and in a later discussion of nihilism (Ch. 8): its effect is to probe male illusions, and to show them up for their artificiality. This testing of illusion at the level of sexuality, male self-representations of their sexuality, makes for her modernity, exploiting what is in men, and forcing their shame into the open. Negatively, she wounds men because she knows that she has been wounded:

Die Welt erlöse, ist dies dein Amt:—
schuf dich zum Gott die Stunde,
für sie lass mich ewig dann verdammt,
nie heile mir die Wunde!

(Redeem the world, if this is your destiny, make yourself a god for an hour, and for that let me be damned forever, my wound never be healed!)

But the woman's wound, which is her 'castration', as masculinist ideology constructs that thought and as Kundry accepts it, is nothing to the offence felt by the male, and endorsed as such in *Parsifal*, Act 2. The defiled 'sanctuary' is the pure male body and the Grail temple, both already spoiled by the otherness of the

---

[24] Medusa for Freud suggests the woman as the castrating threat. See 'On Sexuality', in *The Penguin Freud*, vol. 7 ed. Angela Richards (Harmondsworth: Penguin, 1977), p. 311. 'The Laugh of the Medusa' is the title of an essay by Hélène Cixous; see Elaine Marks and Isabelle de Courtivron, *New French Feminisms* (Brighton: Harvester, 1981), pp. 245–64.

woman (other as woman, as Jewish, and Islamic and Oriental: the stage direction specifies that Kundry as the temptress wears 'a light fantastic veil-like robe of Arabian style', like the Saracen woman of the never-written opera). A society bonded on the basis of male power rejects the woman as the source of tainted blood: in *Parsifal* there are no sexual relations that do not corrupt, so Parsifal sings 'O!—Qual der Liebe!—Wie alles schauert, bebt und zuckt / in sündigem Verlangen' (Oh torment of love! How everything trembles, quakes and quivers in sinful desire). Reich, discussing the race and blood sections of *Mein Kampf,* says that 'the irrational fear of syphilis constitutes one of the major sources of National Socialism's political views and its anti-Semitism'.[25] As Adorno puts it, discussing an unconscious in Wagner, 'sex and sexual disease become identical' (*In Search of Wagner,* p. 94). (Adorno adds that Wagner feared 'the curing of diseases that had been contracted through "vice" ' (p. 94).) In the midst of all this fear, enough to send anyone to a hydrotherapy centre, there is an investment both in a pure Christ and pure Aryanism, which exists best in a context of pure homosociality. The most lyrical section of *Parsifal* (the 'Karfreitagszauber' music, which enacts that magic by casting its own spell) is written for two men over the orchestra, with Kundry referred to, but silent). That bonding of males is not negated, essentially, by the ending of *Parsifal,* with its final mixed chorus (not male only, as hitherto) proclaiming redemption to the redeemer ('Erlösung dem Erlöser!') and its obviously anti-Semitic fantasy of a Christ who is 'entirely sexless, neither man nor woman'.[26] The male attachments are not in contest with a Christianity which is fantasized as androgynous, sexless, outside questions of sexual difference, and the stage direction says it all, in that Kundry at the same time sinks lifeless and excluded to the ground.

In *Death in Venice*, Mann's paragraph describing Aschenbach's writings finishes by specifying the fit between Aschenbach's passively suffering hero and the ideology of post-1871 Germany. This is the type of hero Parsifal must become: no more pursuing 'wilde Knabentaten' (wild childish deeds, Act 2) for him. Aschenbach speaks up unironically for a *fin de siècle,* masochistic Christianity, the religion interpreted by Nietzsche as appropriate for those who believe that life is to be denied or for those driven by *ressentiment.* Mann's writing, by its ironic distance and free, indirect mode of discourse, holds itself away from these things, and

[25] Wilhelm Reich, *The Mass Psychology of Fascism,* trans. Vincent R. Carfagno (1946), 3rd edn. (New York: Simon and Schuster, 1970), p. 82.

[26] Cosima Wagner, quoted in Jean-Jacques Nattiez, *Wagner Androgyne,* trans. Stewart Spencer (Princeton: Princeton University Press, 1993), p. 171.

mocks the tones of the bourgeoisie in their world-weariness and affectation of piety and *Weltschmerz*.

Gustave Aschenbach was the poet-spokesman of all those who labour at the edge of exhaustion; of the overburdened, of those who are already worn out but still hold themselves upright; of all our modern moralizers of accomplishment, with stunted growth and scanty resources, who yet contrive by skilful husbanding and prodigious spasms of will to produce, at least for a while, the effect of greatness. There are many such: they are the heroes of the age. And in Aschenbach's pages they saw themselves; he justified, he exalted them, he sang their praise—and they, they were grateful, they heralded his fame. (p. 16)

One name that fits the 'many such' Mann describes is Amfortas, though he wishes for death, he feels so sinful. His music is virtually the first passion that is given way to in the score, as he sings of the melancholia and suffering that he must endure in ministering to the people:

> Wehvolles Erbe, dem ich verfallen
> ich, einz'ger Sünder unter allen,
> des höchsten Heiligtums zu pflegen
> auf Reine herabzuflehen seinen Segen!

(Woeful inheritance to which I am called, that I, the only sinner of my people, must tend what is supremely sacred, invoking its blessing on the righteous.)

Amfortas, with his need for cleansing, is more complex than the comparison with Aschenbach suggests: he is the son who has betrayed the patriarchy, and his passive state (even feminine, in the scale of his protestations, which are virtually given a separate 'aria' here, as though *Parsifal* were momentarily becoming traditional opera) shows the annihilation of his being that this has brought about: but impressionistically, the music also works because of the new force it introduces to the score as the record of frustrated anger.[27] The force of his avowals of guilt also evoke his own repression, which is desire for that which has destroyed him.

---

[27] Michael P. Steinberg, *The Meaning of the Salzburg Festival* (Ithaca, NY: Cornell University Press, 1990), p. 30, compares Amfortas in his bath with Marat. (Cf. Wagner as a 'sentimental Marat': Adorno, *In Search of Wagner*, p. 15.) The link between the revolutionary wounded hero and Wagner as Amfortas is suggestive. For the importance of the bath, see Matthias Theodor Vogt, 'Taking the Waters at Bayreuth', in Barry Millington and Stewart Spencer (eds.), *Wagner in Performance* (New Haven: Yale University Press, 1992), on the imagery of cleansing in Wagner's letters, which applies equally to society, the body, and the theatre: all are to be cleansed by the festival, 'the festival hill as a magic mountain' (p. 149). This is a valuable article, limited only by its endorsement of the view of Wagner and Bayreuth as curative, like a bath or a hydrotherapy centre, and accepting the ideology of the return to nature.

The mutual admiration alluded to in this passage from *Death in Venice* makes Aschenbach the perfect bourgeois, and aligns him with the repressive elements of the Reich, allowing him to write of militarism and be contemptuous of the other and of non-bourgeois emotions, so that in his novel *The Abject* he 'rejects the rejected, casts out the outcast . . . renounces sympathy with the abyss'. The fictional hero in *The Abject* is denounced for his weakness and pusillanimity. But if no abjection is experienced by the author, he does not escape being the melancholic, death-driven figure with a writer's block, unable to allow for any dissemination of himself in writing. Everything is undone, but nothing is improved when he meets his Kundry—that is, when he sees Tadzio—and is wounded in earnest and throws off all shame: 'There he sat, the master: this was he who had found a way to reconcile art and honours; who had written *The Abject* and in a style of classic purity renounced bohemianism and all its works, all sympathy with the abyss and the troubled depths of the outcast human soul' (p. 80). He is like Amfortas, save that for Wagner there is no 'classic purity' in composition, and in *Parsifal* the hatred of bohemianism is expressed in an art altogether riddled by its influence.

Tadzio—Kundry—a death in Venice endured by Wagner and by Aschenbach: these are elements in a complex of issues which Nietzsche makes more provocative when he writes in words that Mann, if not Visconti or Britten, must have acted on, 'And when I seek another word for music, I never find any other word than Venice'.[28] In another context, these words might suggest Monteverdi or even, remembering La Fenice, Verdi, but in that of *Death in Venice*, they suggest the ambiguity of desire which music represents as feminine, which cannot be recognized, because to do so would destroy the male self's autonomy, its self-possession.

It is Schopenhauerian, recalling that Schopenhauer opposed sexual love as part of the will-to-live, but included an appendix discussing homosexuality in the third edition (1859) of *The World as Will and Representation* relating to the chapter 'The Metaphysics of Sexual Love'. In this appendix he argues that Nature allows homosexuality in the young or the old, where the impulse to propagate exists, but where the effect of propagation would be to weaken the species. Heterosexual sex, then, must be frustrating to the individual who gets only the suffering and brief pleasure necessary for nature to carry out its teleological work of continuing the species: the frustration a source, therefore, of the 'revenge against life' philosophy which Nietzsche identifies in him. No form of heterosexuality can be justified:

---

[28] Nietzsche, *Ecce Homo*, trans. R. J. Hollingdale (Harmondsworth: Penguin, 1979), p. 62.

those lovers who meet 'secretly, nervously and furtively' are 'the traitors who secretly strive to perpetuate the whole trouble and toil which would otherwise come rapidly to an end. Such an end they try to frustrate as others like them have frustrated it previously' (p. 560). Lovers should cease to allow the will-to-live to operate in them. (This implies Klingsor.) They should refrain from sexual acts, and bring to an end the continual cycle of illusion. But there is an equivocation in Schopenhauer about homosexuality which nature allows for (so it is natural), but which is none the less perverted, and this ambivalence appears in the ending: 'I wanted to grant to the professors of philosophy a small favour, for they are very disconcerted by the ever-increasing publicization of my philosophy which they so carefully concealed. I have done so by giving them the opportunity of slandering me by saying that I defend and commend pederasty.'[29]

Bryan Magee reads this appendix as a confession on Schopenhauer's part.[30] Homoeroticism, both desired and repressed, becomes a further source of *ressentiment*, sexuality thoroughly dysfunctional to the subject save only in areas where it is interdicted. The important point, however, is that Schopenhauer mentions it, on at least one level justifying it as he does not heterosexual relations: it belongs to the context which refuses women. It may be compared with Klaus Theweleit's *Male Fantasies* (1977–8), which pays attention to the language and imagery employed by the Freikorps, the volunteer bands of soldiers set up after 1918 to deal with the Communist threat to Germany and cope with the fear of the masses. This psychoanalytic reading of fascism and the social character of those who became fascists discusses the Freikorps' hatred of women and the prevalence in their discourse of images of 'anxiety-producing substances' which can be

called upon to describe processes occurring in or upon the human body, especially its orifices. 'Floods,' 'morasses,' 'mire,' 'slime,' and 'pulp'—this whole battery of terms can describe bodily secretions if you start out with a negative attitude towards them. This points to a reversal of the affects originally associated with the elimination of such substances from the body: pleasurable sensations. The pleasurable sensations have been replaced by a panic defence against the possibility of their occurrence.[31]

These substances are associable with women, and Theweleit discusses the fascist interest in armouring the body, insisting on rigid boundaries, and hating the

---

[29] Schopenhauer, *World as Will*, ii. 567. The passage is cut from the earlier translation (as *The World as Will and Idea*) by R. B. Haldane and John Kemp (1883).

[30] Bryan Magee, *The Philosophy of Schopenhauer* (Oxford: Oxford University Press, 1983), pp. 322–5.

[31] Klaus Theweleit, *Male Fantasies*, vol. 1: *Women: Floods: Bodies: History* (Cambridge: Polity, 1987), p. 409.

possibility of flow from body to body, which is also a hatred of women. He discusses the putative relationships between fascism and homosexuality, though, unlike Adorno, he does not see any necessary connection between these things, and takes homosexuality in this period (a little patronizingly) as part of the construction of a maleness whose intention is to keep the woman out, in which case it might well fit with fascist ideology, or—positively, and *contra* Adorno—as a means whereby the male refuses the gender role which places him in a dominant position relative to the woman, refuses gender codification, the decodifying of sexual codes (ii. 265). The homosexuality in the Freikorps, he argues, following the ego psychologist Margaret Mahler (1897–1985), is what she calls, in another context, a 'maintenance process', an act of defence against threats of devouring dissolution. Maintenance mechanisms define the aggression of psychotic children who have not been able to form an ego, who have never 'attained the security of body boundaries libidinally invested from within' (Theweleit, *Male Fantasies*, ii. 211). Theweleit argues that in the nineteenth-century bourgeois family, where the woman's role was split between being trainer cum mother and love-object to the father, the male child was exposed to hatred (expressed in rigid toilet training) and sentimentality alternately, so he never experienced his body or being as a whole entity, with a 'pleasure-filled periphery'. Left vulnerable, the male child grows up with an inadequate sense of ego, and identifies women with the threat to that ego's stability. Theweleit characterizes those who require such armouring of their ego as 'not-yet-fully-born' (ii. 212), adding that 'only a handful of men in Wilhelmine Germany had the good fortune to be in some sense fully born—and not many more in the rest of Europe' (ii. 213). Such people lacking a sense of their own egos are not even ready for the oedipal struggle, by which the father-authority figure is thrown off. They cannot relate to another (the 'object' in psychoanalytic terms); they have problems with maintaining narcissism. He concludes: 'The Great War touched the masculinity of several German male soldiers in its most sensitive area; in the conviction that German men were born to be warriors and fighters. It deprived them of the victory they considered their "birthright" and subjected them, as Germans, to a narcissistic *wound* of the first order' (ii. 357, my emphasis).

Adorno notes that Freud turned his attention to narcissism at the moment of the First World War, as though that crisis, quite apart from showing the wounded psyches of the soldiers as they suffered under gunfire, also acted as an example of *Nachträglichkeit*, the term which conveys the idea that traumas have an afterlife, a deferred action. These wounded psyches suffered in the war, not just from that trauma (wound), but from an earlier one, whose effect was to be felt later. The war showed up the condition of German ideology and German culture as it had been before the war.[32]

The response to possessing such an inadequately constructed ego, is, in a time of crisis, to armour the self. The woman becomes a threat, a dissolution of the male ego, associated with floods and with a flow which takes the self away with it. The homosexuality of the fascist, then, Theweleit sees 'as a means of restoring the acting subject to "totality" ' (ii. 318). He argues that the particular attraction of homosexuality to the fascist male

is . . . its capacity to be associated with power and transgression. . . . [it is] one of the few remaining gaps through which he can escape the compulsory coding of feared heterosexuality; it is an escape from normality, from a whole domain of more or less permissible pleasures—all encoded with 'femininity.' As a homosexual the fascist can prove . . . that he is 'nonbourgeois' and boldly defiant of normality. His 'homosexuality' is strictly encoded; and for this very reason it never becomes sexual. Like the opposite from which it flees, it is rigidly codified . . . it is far more likely to be definable in terms of the fascist system than in terms of such things as love relationships between men. . . . escape into homosexuality ultimately functions as a reterritorialization: as an act prescribed by the social order . . . it simply reinforces dams. (ii. 323–5)[33]

The homosexuality described here, negative and repressed and involving no rethinking of gender roles, is born out of fear and desire to recontain that fear—fear of the energies and desires released by capitalist modernization, fear of

[32] On this in Freud, see his 'Project for a Scientific Psychology', in *Standard Edition of the Works of Sigmund Freud*, ed. James Strachey (London: Hogarth, 1953), i. 356–8; and *SE* xvii. 37–8 for the Wolf Man. For Adorno, see his essay 'Freudian Theory and the Pattern of Socialist Propaganda', in Arato and Gebhardt (eds.), *Essential Frankfurt School Reader*, p. 120. On the use of Theweleit and Margaret Mahler to discuss the fascist's desire to armour his ego, see Hal Foster, 'Armor Fou', *October*, 56 (Spring 1991): 65–97. There has been much controversy over Theweleit: for a favourable review, see Lutz Niethammer, *History Workshop*, 7 (1979): 176–86; for a negative, Lynne Segal, *Slow Motion: Changing Masculinities, Changing Men* (London: Virago, 1990), pp. 116–21. On the extent of homosexuality in Wilhelmine Germany—the Eulenberg scandal of 1907 was simply its most obvious example—see the essays by Isabel V. Hull and by Nicolaus Sombart in John C. G. Röhl and Nicolaus Sombart (eds.), *Kaiser Wilhelm II: New Interpretations* (Cambridge: Cambridge University Press, 1982). They suggest that homosexuality was the repressed norm. Of relevance too is James D. Steakley, *The Homosexual Emancipation Movement in Germany* (New York: Arno Press, 1975). He discusses the relationship between radical homosexuality and the women's movement in 1890s Berlin, which is a reminder of how homosexuality itself can be doubly accentuated, the source of psychic repression, as in the Eulenberg affair, or of political movement.

[33] 'Reterritorialization'—a term Theweleit derived from Gilles Deleuze and Felix Guattari's *Anti-Oedipus*. Deterritorialization refers to the centrifugal effect of energies in modernity: everything ceases to be held in by a powerful social coding. In reterritorialization, the 'new productive possibilities' of modernity, which come about from the massive circulation of energy in industrialization, are kept 'from becoming new human freedoms'. This takes place through 'the mobilization of dominant forces', the whole power of state ideology (Theweleit, *Male Fantasies*, i. 264).

woman, who is linked in ideology and imagery to the Communist threat in Germany in 1919, and the product of a desire to arm the ego.

Theweleit is suggestive for the context of Wagner's blood-brotherhoods and knights of the Grail. We may add the suggestion of narcissism, as a psychic need, which structures Parsifal in the third act of that opera. Read via Theweleit, the primordial wound would give the sense of a deficiency in wholeness, an elementary, pre-oedipal sense, with these rituals as a way of trying to complete the circle that is irrevocably open. Such a circle, in *Die Götterdämmerung* is the more vulnerable because of the existence of the 'other', Hagen, who cannot enter it but threatens it from outside. Here it must be added that Wagner's sympathies are ambivalent: he wishes to be inside the circle and to close it too (just as Siegfried rejoices that he is not Mime's son, and kills him with no sign of remorse), but he is also outside, and whatever Siegfried does, the act cannot be so easily repressed.[34]

Wagner's dream, quoted in the Introduction, of the waters of the Rhine implies his yearning for a restoration of limitless narcissism. The psychoanalyst Richard D. Chessick refers to the fascination that *Tristan und Isolde* holds as coming from 'the empathy it produces for the pain and suffering and rage of two wounded narcissistic people who must relieve this discomfort even if it means death'.[35]

But are these people narcissistic because that is their fault, or because they cannot establish their ego? Theweleit speaks as an ego psychologist, assuming that the ego can normally be established. But the ego might be compared more to Schopenhauer's 'representation', as a fictional construct, and as armour against 'the world as will'. Jacques Lacan, who speaks in opposition to ego psychology, speaks of the formation of the individual taking place in 'a drama ... which manufactures for the subject ... the succession of fantasies that extends from a

---

[34] Derrida suggests that 'what the word *disgusting* denominates is what one cannot resign oneself to mourn'. 'The disgusting can only be vomited', because what is mourned is incorporated into the subject (Jacques Derrida, 'Economimesis', *Diacritics*, 11 (1981): 23). Mime is disgusting to Siegfried, but he is not mourned, and the hero suffers no melancholia from his loss (where melancholia would suggest the inability to absorb loss, to incorporate it into the subject's being). Derrida on the disgusting should be compared to Kristeva on the abject; I read *Siegfried* as a repressed text, in that it works to let go of Mime so easily; its anxiety is to protect the narcissistic self-completeness of Siegfried.

[35] Richard D. Chessick, 'On Falling in Love: The Mystery of Tristan and Isolde', in *Psychoanalytic Explorations in Music*, ed. Stuart Feder, Richard L. Karmel and George H. Pollock (Madison: Connecticut: International University Press, 1988), p. 482. See also Chessick's '*The Ring*: Richard Wagner's Dream of Pre-Oedipal Destruction', *American Journal of Psychoanalysis*, 43 (1983): 361–74. On the relationship between Wagner and psychoanalysis, see Carl Dahlhaus, *Richard Wagner's Music Dramas*, trans. Mary Whittall (Cambridge: Cambridge University Press, 1979), pp. 147–8: 'it is not inconceivable that the second act of *Parsifal* and the third act of *Siegfried* exercised an unacknowledged influence on the development of psychoanalytic theory.' Dahlhaus accepts, it would seem, Mann's sense of Wagner as a psychologist.

fragmented body-image to a form of its totality that I shall call orthopaedic—and, lastly, to the assumption of the armour of an alienating identity, which will mark with its rigid structure the subject's entire mental development'.[36] Lacan sees an alternation in the subject of a series of violent fantasies of the body in pieces, never formed into a whole, and the no less violent assumption of an ego which is defined *as* armour—which itself has fascist connotations. In Lacan, belief in a pure ego is a dangerous fiction. It is not so much a question of armouring the ego, as I earlier put it in discussing Theweleit, but more a matter of seeing that the ego *is* armour. Parsifal in armour in Act 3 is a fantasy of the pure ego, the ego being, for Lacan, a neurotic structure. The very assumption of ego identity is alienating. On this basis, the wound fits with fantasies of the self as fragmented. Parsifal knows nothing in the first act. He is not constituted as a single subject: he is as though schizoid in not knowing the significance of his actions, which implies that there is nothing to draw the fragments together. Gurnemanz calls him a fool, and the opera invests in overcoming the power of the fool; but the fool can only triumph—this is the textual impossibility that defeats Wagner—by also having the armour of the pure ego. Can the male cease to be so masculinist? Though Parsifal is presented as the holy fool, this takes place from a masculinist construction that invests in him as always the male ego, and that makes any narrative of his development spurious.

Parsifal as an ego comes into fullest being in the *Karfreitagszauber* music, which musically seems to describe and complete a circle, and also silences the woman and her laughter, which is alluded to. It takes place over a dialogue between Parsifal ('Wie dünkt mich doch die Aue heut so schön!') and Gurnemanz, whose single-line comment explains the meaning of the music just heard. A key change makes for Parsifal's negation of the joy: all that blooms should weep. Gurnemanz provides the negation of the negation: 'Du siehst, das ist nicht so', commenting on how Nature now does *not* see Christ on the cross (it does not see the suffering of the male, but this is recalled in the urgency of the music), so man will now walk on the green grass with a gentle tread, and redeemed nature now lives its day of innocence. Parsifal completes the section (beginning and ending with 'die Aue') by qualifying this rapture:

> Ich sah sie welken, die einst mir lachten,
> ob heut sie nach Erlösung schmachten?

---

[36] Jacques Lacan, *Écrits: A Selection*, trans. Alan Sheridan (London: Tavistock, 1977), p. 4.

Auch deine Träne ward zum Segenstaue:
du weinest!—sieh! es lacht die Aue.

(I saw them fade that once laughed at me: and are they dissolving in longing today for salvation? Also thy tear is like the blessed dew; thou weepest! but see! the meadows are laughing.)

What once laughed at him were the flower maidens, who are linked with Kundry; now Kundry weeps, and the fields—the flower maidens sublimated, as it were, into an inoffensive, sweet nature—laugh, and on them 'der Mensch' (man) walks. 'Man' I read as the male, who walks on the flowers, and music, like flowers, blooms in the rising and repeated tune that climbs higher and more sensuously to the high strings heard just before Gurnemanz's 'Das dankt dann alle Kreatur'. Once the flowers climbed darkly and threateningly round Parsifal: now it is the music which does so. The melody is orchestral, rather than carried by the voices, and it seems to equate the orchestral sound with the woman (the world as will tamed), heard below the male voice, while also suggesting that the proper function of music is to be weeping, as Parsifal thinks that all things should weep on Good Friday (though Gurnemanz turns this round) and that the beauty of the flowers, their laughter, which is de-sexualized, takes place because Kundry alone, no longer schizoid and fragmented, but constrained into a single identity and silenced, weeps (and 'weinest' reaches the highest note sung within the section). The music can be as attractive as it is, and as much a set piece, in the logic and coherence of the passage, because it has recodified the woman's status.

The ego which is established is male: *Parsifal* as a title contrasts with *Die Walküre* or *Tristan und Isolde*. Chessick's account of this last text is incomplete in not seeing the difference between Tristan's and Isolde's wounds. Tristan's wound, another name for which is his desire, which proclaims him as incomplete, is systemic, part of his being, and he covers it in Act 1 by the company of sailors, whose mocking chorus sets up a male bonding to exclude the woman. Tristan in Act 3 sings a narrative ('Muss ich dich so versteh'n') of the wound inflicted on him by Sir Morold that he came to Ireland to be healed of by Isolde. Now wounded again, two wounds are linked: that associated with Isolde and that dealt by the betraying friend, Melot. But the wound is more psychic than that suggests. His narrative associates music as a 'Klage Klang' with the death of both his parents (like Siegfried, like Parsifal) and with drifting in the boat to Ireland, where music seems to drive the boat towards Isolde as the emblem of death. What he has in mind is the situation which Isolde described in her Act 1 narrative. His words are:

Die Wunde, die
sie heilend schloss,
riss mit dem Schwert
sie wieder los!

(The wound she had healed and closed she ripped open again with the sword.) But Isolde in her narrative does not describe wounding Tristan: she says she let the sword fall while she bent over him. The fantasy is his own: the male's, of the dominant woman with the sword (the castrating woman), and of himself like a Prometheus caught in an endless cycle of being wounded, opened up to desire (*Sehnsucht*) by the woman who may in his mind have features of Melot, and who turns from cutting him with the sword to poisoning him, where poison has the same valency as giving him the torments of love. Tristan fantasizes an Isolde like Kundry: the woman who allows the man to lose his possession of his own ego.

It is easy to read this as though Tristan's view was authoritative. In D'Annunzio's novel *Il trionfo della morte* (1894), commenting on nineteenth-century music's evocations of death in Schumann, Chopin, and Grieg, D'Annunzio focuses on *Tristan*, giving an account of a performance as remembered by the hero who saw the opera at Bayreuth. As though following through these male fantasies, which are part of the culture of fascism, he reads its subject-matter as the destructiveness of Isolde: 'Passion aroused in her a murderous desire, awoke out of the depths of her being an instinctive antagonism to life, a longing to destroy, to annihilate.'[37] The love relationship is itself destructive, reactive, an act of hatred against 'time and its "It was"'. According to this argument (in the context of D'Annunzio's novel, where the aristocratic hero, Giorgio, insists on murdering his lower-class lover, Ippolita, while committing suicide himself), the love 'was rancour against that time when love did not exist, against the empty useless past' (p. 283). D'Annunzio takes the opera as showing the woman pulling the man into the darkness after her. He also suggests that the body itself might be what the wound symbolizes. The wound suggests a gap, a split, which prevents the attainment of desire, as well as being itself the condition of desire. He writes of Act 2:

Their sighs of passion changed to anguished sobs, an insurmountable obstacle interposed between them, parted them, estranged them, and left them solitary. And that obstacle was their own bodily substance, their actual personality. A secret hate was engendered in both their souls—a longing to remove that obstacle, to annihilate it; a longing to destroy and be destroyed. (p. 284)

[37] Gabriele D'Annunzio, *The Triumph of Death*, trans. Georgina Harding (London: Dedalus, 1990), p. 280.

The love is born of *ressentiment* directed against the body, even though, of course, it uses the body in love-making; but the love must work to annihilate the body. This is suggestive for Tristan's fantasies of Isolde standing over him with the sword, and for his own complicity with that imagined violence when he rips the bandages off at the moment when her presence and his own healing are assured. Where D'Annunzio helps is in the identification of the hatred of the body with the fear of the woman, the sense that these two are in some way the same.

That Tristan fantasizes that Isolde has wounded him means that he is 'always already' wounded, and there is no recognizable point in his past which can be narrativized in terms of a wounding. In his psychic memory, in the *Nachträglichkeit* from which he suffers in Act 3, it seems always to be in place; he has always been a fragmented being. Loving a woman may give the impression of wholeness, but tearing off the bandages says that nothing 'orthopaedic' (so Lacan) works: the wound is already there. Isolde, whom he says also gives the wound, takes on features of Kundry, just as Tristan's music in its chromaticism has associations with that of Amfortas, wounded through Kundry. From the standpoint of the ego which is armour, the male constructs his sexuality as a wound in the psyche, a gap in the armour; but if Wagnerian heroes, like Christ, must be like Aschenbach's imaginary heroes in terms of 'the conception of an intellectual and virginal manliness, which clenches its teeth and stands in modest defiance of the swords and spears that pierce its side' (*Death in Venice*, p. 15)—and is it the side?—then it is not surprising that Kundry laughs. It is what Wagner's texts most fear, but it is also what they seek: to be shamed by the woman, and to experience fragmentation. Or, to experience the self as a wound, and not to be able to use any of the orthopaedics—bandage or armour, or the anonymity of namelessness, or associations with other males—to be unable to form any ego.

OPERA, OR THE UNDOING OF MEN

> If one is to be fair to this writing, one has to suffer from the destiny of music as from an open wound.
>
> Nietzsche, *Ecce Homo*

In *Tristan und Isolde*, there is a recognition of difference: Isolde, too, has been wounded: she is incomplete. Isolde prompts the wish to turn the argument around, from Wagner's male narcissism to a tendential feminism in the text. Her first words are: 'Wer wagt mich zu höhnen' (Who dares mock me?)—she is no

Kundry—as if in response to the voice of the sailor singing to the 'irisch Kind', whose sighs, whose breath, whose singing even, seem to increase the gap, the distance, between the two—the sailor and the Irish girl. The off-stage sailor seems to dramatize her own loss. The words 'Wehe, wehe, du Wind!' (Sigh, sigh (or blow, blow) you wind) and 'Weh', ach wehe mein Kind!' (Ache, ah, ache, my child) pun with suggestions of sighing, woe, pain, and drifting, and seem to anticipate Isolde's death, even as they also imply that the woman's breath may destroy the male. The pains include labour pains: no wonder Isolde feels mocked.

Isolde's wound is her humiliation in being taken by Tristan to King Mark. The first act focuses on Isolde, in the downstage, dominated position, and shows her rage, shut in on herself by the curtains of her tent, feeling her loss of power as the sorceress, which seems to be emphasized for her as a lack by the singing of the sailor. The gap in her subjectivity, what *The Birth of Tragedy*, chapter 18, calls 'the eternal wound of being', she needs to fill through Tristan. The fantasy she sings of in her narrative in Act 1 ('Den hab ich wohl vernommen') is about wholeness: of being able to heal the wound of the knight; of being able to match together the pieces of the sword; of being able to see that Tristan and Tantris are the same; of being able to relate the disparate narratives of different men she has loved; and finally, in her alternation of third-person and first-person narrative, of trying to get out of a schizoid state to which she none the less gives way. In pursuit of that fantasy of wholeness, and as the destabilizing sorceress, like Ortrud in *Lohengrin*, she plans Tristan's death along with her own.

Isolde is clearly inscribed by loss throughout: that is evident in the 'Liebestod'. But what seems rare in Wagner is the recognition of it; and the closing of the opera with that extraordinary expression of desire, celebrates the woman, and gives voice to her lamentation and her *jouissance*. By comparison, Brünnhilde's tragedy at the end of *Die Walküre*, though moving, is presented as though it were Wotan's, the music at the last giving him the higher affectivity.

None the less, with this Wagner on the side of the woman, I want to return, finally, to Nietzsche's criticism of Wagner. I have suggested a dual valency of music considered as a woman: the impulse to dominate that this implies, but also, in the 'Liebestod', the ability of the music to affirm the woman's part. Wagner has not fared well in this chapter: he has evoked a male circle anxious to preserve its completeness, fearful of the wound, and terrified of anything that could damage an ego in fear of being exposed and unable to establish itself. But the traffic is not all one way. Nietzsche on sexuality is also problematic, and his writings do not allow simply for the opposition of Nietzsche *contra* Wagner. It is also Nietzsche *contra* Nietzsche and Wagner *contra* Wagner. The ambiguity is important: however much Nietzsche attacks Wagner, he will not distance himself from him, even in his last text, *Ecce Homo*, in the section on 'The Birth of Tragedy':

> A psychologist might add that what I in my youthful years heard in Wagnerian music had nothing at all to do with Wagner; that when I described dionysian music I described *that* which *I* had heard—that I had instinctively to translate and transfigure into the latest idiom all I bore within me. The proof of this, *as strong a proof as can be*, is my essay 'Wagner in Bayreuth': in all the psychologically decisive passages I am the only person referred to—one may ruthlessly insert my name or the name 'Zarathustra' whenever the text gives the word Wagner. (p. 82)[38]

Wagner is being read by Nietzsche as though his actual texts are allegories of what could be; as though Wagner need not be taken literally, but as the secret allegorist of another scene. This is like Adorno saying that 'there is not one decadent element in Wagner's work from which a productive mind could not extract the forces of the future' (*In Search of Wagner*, p. 153). Adorno closes his study by saying that there are moments when the music 'breaks the spell it casts over the characters' (p. 156), instead of casting a spell over the characters and over the listener. When the music splits from the characters like this, it becomes allegorical, suggesting another way of reading: a double reading, which is allegorical, since allegory says something is other than what it is. But, Nietzsche adds, 'Wagner did not recognise himself in this essay.'[39] Wagner read literally, not allegorically: in opting to be the public 'Wagner' of Bayreuth, he failed to be another 'Wagner' who might be more like Nietzsche.

The interchangeability of Nietzsche and Wagner as two ways of accentuating one problem—modernity—is important: 'Nietzsche' and 'Wagner' are allegories of each other.[40] And that illuminates their contradictory positions on gender. But it may be best to approach this problem through another text, via Heidegger

---

[38] The last part of this section (from my quotation on) is really on 'Richard Wagner in Bayreuth', and alludes specifically to sects. 4, 9, and 6 in that order, though it should be said that Hollingdale's translation, by simply referring to page numbers is, if not misleading, unhelpful on this point.

[39] So Walter Kaufman translates it in *Basic Writings of Nietzsche* (New York: Random House, 1968), p. 730—better than Hollingdale's 'He failed to recognise himself in this essay'.

[40] Allegory here may be understood in the terms of Walter Benjamin, *The Origin of German Tragic Drama*, trans. John Osborne (London: New Left Books, 1977). Benjamin understands allegory as the breakdown of definite stated meaning: 'any person, any object, any relationship, can mean absolutely anything else' (p. 175), and one situation can swing round into its opposite: Wagner into Nietzsche. Thus Adorno, using Benjamin, says that 'there is not one decadent element in Wagner's work from which a productive mind could not extract the forces of the future' (*In Search of Wagner*, p. 153). Adorno reads Wagner allegorically: the operas as the negative, his readings the photograph.

reading Nietzsche. Heidegger's studies of Nietzsche help in a reading of the implications of Nietzsche's critique of Wagner, and illustrate the problems that twentieth-century fascist philosophy has with what Wagner represents.

Heidegger wrote extensively on Nietzsche in the years 1936–44. He says that Nietzsche is the philosopher of the 'will to power'. Heidegger assumes that phrase in Nietzsche to be definitional for Nietzsche's reading of humanity: the mark of the human is that it has within it the will to power. Further, he takes Nietzsche's thought of eternal return to be the basic motif of his philosophy: it is the motif which makes Nietzsche a metaphysician, just as the belief in the will to power makes him a philosopher who assumes the unchanging character of human nature. These are aspects of Nietzsche's thought that Heidegger resists, since the philosophy he stands for assumes no humanist definition of the human, and he attacks all forms of metaphysics as being ways whereby the human represents things so as to give himself a privileged status.

The phrase 'will to power' is often thought to link with blackshirts and men in uniform, and so be right wing. In Nietzsche, however, it has to do with the power to interpret existence, and to give a representation of it. Although the phrase has been taken to coincide with those aspects of his thought which suggest the legitimacy of domination, Heidegger—such is the contradiction in his own thought as the philosopher who had identified himself with Nazism—resists it. In his meditations on *The Will to Power*,[41] he examines Nietzsche's statements on art as an example of the will-to-power. But for Heidegger, the destiny of art is to be enframed by technology: in the modern world, art exists only to be used, not as autonomous, not as an alternative or a critique of it. Indeed, Heidegger argues that aesthetics comes on to the agenda for discussion, at the end of the eighteenth century, only when it is clear that art's time is going. He sees Wagner's attempt to evoke the *Gesamtkunstwerk* as a proof of the disappearance of autonomous art: as the concept of art becomes impossible, so Wagner tries to shore it up by making the term cover more and more phenomena.

But it is clear that Heidegger dislikes this, and he quotes Nietzsche on it: *The Will to Power*, section 839, from notes written at the same time as *The Case of Wagner* (1888). Here Nietzsche pronounces Wagner a hypnotist, and refers to his

---

[41] *The Will to Power* was put together after Nietzsche's death by his sister, Elizabeth Forster-Nietzsche, and Peter Gast, from notes and fragments. It does not comprise a book in its own right; hence it is difficult to read it for a consistent teaching, which is what Heidegger tries to do. On Nietzsche's sister, who made him out to be an anti-Semite and who doctored his writings to increase his right-wing appeal, see H. F. Peters, *Zarathustra's Sister* (New York: Crown Publishers, 1977), part 5 of which deals with Nietzsche's posthumous career.

'repellent avoidance of logic and squareness in his rhythm; the lingering, soothing, mysterious, hysterical quality of his "endless melody" ', taking the *Lohengrin* prelude as an instance of a 'somnambulistic trance' and quoting an Italian woman, a 'Wagnerienne', as saying 'Come si *dorme* con questa musica' (How one sleeps to this music). Heidegger approves of this Nietzschean statement, and on the basis of it refers to Wagner's 'dissolution of everything solid into a fluid, flexible, malleable state, into a swimming and floundering; the unmeasure, without laws or borders, clarity or definiteness; the boundless night of sheer submergence'. He takes it as the mark of Wagner's dependence on Schopenhauer, who, by this token, is also to be seen negatively. For Heidegger, the positive aspect of Nietzsche, by contrast with Wagner, was that Nietzsche became Dionysiac not by submerging himself, but by his approach to art 'leash[ing] its force and giv[ing] it form'. He continues:

Wagner did not belong to that group of men for whom their own followers are the greatest source of revulsion. Wagner required Wagnerians and Wagneriennes. . . . [Nietzsche's] opposition to Wagner involved two things. First, Wagner's neglect of inner feeling and proper style. Nietzsche expressed it once this way: with Wagner it is all 'floating and swimming' instead of 'striding and dancing,' which is to say it is a floundering devoid of measure and pace.[42]

Heidegger alludes here to several passages in Nietzsche. But it is worth checking Heidegger's references. One, from *Human, All Too Human*, written in 1879, and marking the break with Wagner, is called 'How modern music is supposed to make the soul move'. It discusses 'endless melody' in terms of

imagining one is going into the sea, gradually relinquishing a firm tread on the bottom and finally surrendering unconditionally to the watery element: one is supposed to *swim*. Earlier music constrained one—with a delicate or solemn or fiery movement back and forth, faster and slower, to *dance*: in pursuit of which the needful preservation of orderly measure compelled the soul of the listener to a continual *self-possession*. . . Richard Wagner desired a different kind of *movement of the soul*: one related, as aforesaid, to swimming and floating.

Nietzsche links this to arguments about the 'brutalization and decay of rhythm itself' and to the 'loss of limit and proportion' which he sees as 'the *all too feminine*

---

[42] Martin Heidegger, *Nietzsche*, vol. 1: *The Will to Power as Art*, trans. David Farrell Krell (1961): (New York: Harper and Row, 1979), p. 88. Quotations from *The Will to Power* trans. Walter Kaufmann and R. J. Hollingdale (New York: Vintage Books, 1967), p. 442. Other quotations from *Will to Power* appear in the text, under the number of the section.

nature of music'.[43] Now it would seem possible to find here an anti-feminism in Nietzsche. Who is the sexist, Nietzsche or Wagner?

But it might be possible to reread this, recalling Nietzsche's sense of the 'shamelessness' of modernity, that it does not allow for repression, but produces subjects who must say just what they think, and do as they will. The utterance could be taken as that of a dramatic voice, a masculinist one thoroughly frightened by the feminine nature of music. The speaker might be an over-inquisitive, phallogocentric male who has tried to get at 'the truth' of things and been revolted by music's lack of shame, its Kundry or 'Baubo' character, its ability to shock. The excess, the 'shame' even, of Wagnerian modernism, compels the masculinist ego in horror to armour itself—which toughness is the very condition of fascism.

So the Nietzsche passage allows for a double reading. But Heidegger also alludes to a passage in Nietzsche's *The Gay Science*, section 368, which was revised for *Nietzsche Contra Wagner* and called 'Wherein I Raise Objections'. As before, I quote from *The Gay Science*, where the comments are prefaced by the warning 'The cynic speaks', reinforcing the point that utterances in Nietzsche are voices from personae, not to be taken as the voice of a single identity, that of 'Nietzsche'. It should, indeed, be said that in these two versions we do not have the 'same' thing being said; they are different critiques, coming from different directions. However, it is on *The Gay Science* version that I wish to fasten: 'My objections to the music of Wagner are physiological . . . [The] "fact" is that I no longer breathe easily once this music begins to affect me; that my foot soon resents it and rebels; my foot feels the need for rhythm, dance, march; it demands of music firstly of all those delights which are found in *good* walking, striding, leaping and dancing' (sect. 368). The cynic, who asks for 'perfection' and for 'good golden and tender harmonies' is 'antitheatrical', declaring that 'in the theatre one is honest only in the mass; as an individual one lies, one lies to oneself'. In the theatre, 'there one is common people, audience, herd, female, pharisee, voting cattle, democrat, neighbour, fellow man; there even the most personal conscience is vanquished by the levelling magic of the great number; there stupidity has the effect of lasciviousness and contagion; the neighbour reigns, one becomes a mere neighbour' (ibid.). This speech is placed in the context of talking to an 'upright Wagnerian', and the passage ends: 'I forgot to mention how my enlightened Wagnerian replied to these physiological objections: "Then you really are merely not healthy enough for our music?" '

---

[43] 'Assorted Opinions and Maxims, 134', in *Human, All Too Human*, trans. R. J. Hollingdale (Cambridge: Cambridge University Press, 1986), p. 244.

The Gay Science is effectively dialogic, a weave of voices, so we may hesitate over the ascription to Nietzsche of any one point of view. I think the section may be illuminated by section 370 (revised in *Nietzsche Contra Wagner* as 'We Antipodes') and called 'What is romanticism?' Here, Wagnerian-Schopenhauerian romanticism is in view:

Every art, every philosophy may be viewed as a remedy and an aid in the service of growing and struggling life; they always presuppose suffering and sufferers. But there are two kinds of sufferers: first, those who suffer from the *overfullness of life*—they want a Dionysian art and likewise a tragic view of life, a tragic insight—and then those who suffer from the *impoverishment of life* and seek rest, stillness, calm seas, redemption from themselves through art and knowledge, or intoxication, convulsions, anaesthesia and madness.

Reading back to the cynic's voice from this, and taking as a clue the comment by the Wagnerian that the cynic is not healthy enough, suggests that his problem and his reason for not liking Wagner might be impoverishment of life. That, in section 370, is said to produce art which deals in 'mildness, peacefulness and goodness in thought as well as deed', the opposite in timbre of that nervous music which includes within it 'decomposition and negation'. In section 368 the upright Wagnerian would respond by saying that health is the prerequisite for listening to Wagner. Though it is easy to imagine this Wagnerian as thoroughly 'masculine' in his uprightness, there are other things to be said as well. The objections to Wagner's music, which are normally taken to be 'standard' Nietzschean objections to Wagner—the clichés of Wagnerian/Nietzschean commentary—are voiced, but by the cynic, someone who sounds like Wagner as rendered by Nietzsche: accused of suffering from impoverishment of life. This is not just Nietzsche *contra* Wagner, but Wagner *contra* Wagner in the mouth of Nietzsche.

We can go further. The previous section (367) distinguishes between 'monological art' (exclusive, restricted, single-voiced: I shall return to the term in Ch. 3 in relation to Bakhtin) and 'art before witnesses'—public art, art which may also, therefore, lead to the shamelessness of display. In section 368, the cynic turns his back on public, theatrical art, and seems to want monological art, which is drug-like in being associated with forgetting, and is defined as something cultic, religious, and auratic. The interesting point, however, is that this desire for monological art, outside the theatre—or, rather in such a *Festspielhaus* as Bayreuth—is refuted by the close of section 368.

And the cynic's demand for a music which is upright, masculine, in control, is akin to the demand for a monological, single-voiced text. The desire for something crisp, like the marches of *Tannhäuser* or *Die Meistersinger*, or for the Grail knights in *Parsifal*, is a masculinist wish (put negatively) or a Dionysiac wish (put positively). The cynic, who in Nietzsche is usually the person speaking from a reactive position, like Schopenhauer, implicitly declares that he is outside that.[44] For him, the music is too feminine, or non-Dionysiac. Perhaps this is Wagner talking to himself (the masculinist as the cynic), regretting that he writes the music he does and not another kind. But if that is true, it must be emphasized that Wagner would then be reacting against his own music in a way *not* endorsed by the enlightened Wagnerian, who indeed seems grateful that he writes the feminine music he does. More teasing is the thought that if he wrote the other type, tuneful, bright, full of rhythm, dance, and march (more Italian), he would be monological; and to write that would be a false solution. Further, the cynic speaks too loosely: march and dance are different from each other; the Dionysiac can use the dance but not the march, which has its own militaristic implications.

The argument has become fairly vertiginous here, and demands some conclusions to be drawn.[45] I shall return to the cynic in Chapter 9, and discuss him as a decadent; but in the meantime I want to stress that his criticism both is and is not a Nietzschean sentiment. It is that in so far as someone signing with the name 'Nietzsche' wrote it, but it is not just that; it is part of a cross-over between Nietzsche and Wagner where Nietzsche *contra* Wagner is also Nietzsche *contra* Nietzsche and Wagner *contra* Wagner (and Nietzsche's Wagner *contra* Wagner's Nietzsche). And the end of section 370 looks to an end of 'romantic pessimism',

[44] For the link between the cynic and Schopenhauer, see Nietzsche, *Genealogy of Morals*, essay 3, ch. 7. Nietzsche aligns the cynic and the Epicurean in *Human, All Too Human*, sect. 275 (p. 129) and associates the Epicurean with the Christian and the romantic in *The Gay Science*, sect. 370, in opposition to Dionysian pessimism. The cynic is committed to joylessness: 'it is as though he walks abroad naked in the teeth of the wind and hardens himself to the point of feeling nothing' (*Human*, sect. 285, p. 130).

[45] Another sense of what is entailed in the cynic being one aspect of Wagner: at the end of Nietzsche's autobiography, *Ecce Homo*, the text reads, in a piece of Nietzschean self-definition, 'Have I been understood? *Dionysos against the Crucified.*' On the basis of *Ecce Homo*, 'Nietzsche' as a name and a person is a duality of two gods who suffer, Dionysos and Christ, but in different ways. Perhaps the cynic speaks against 'the Crucified' in section 368, in which case the crucified might be feminine and a Parsifal-type hero—one who sympathizes with suffering, with the crucified, rather than laughing at him, like Kundry. But then is not Parsifal identified more properly with the male than with femininity? Is the cynic *complaining* that Wagner's music is on the side of sympathy? In which case, the enlightened Wagnerian seems to be saying you have to be really healthy to even think about the crucified. At each stage in the argument we see two positions offered, each of which divides into two further subject positions (e.g. the crucified as the sufferer who must be sympathized with; the crucified as the person who demands sympathy in a coercive way, forcing a point of view on another). What appears here is the lability of identity, including gender identity, the recognition of difference within identity. Kaufmann glosses the passage from *Ecce Homo* from *Will to Power*, sect. 1052 (the whole section).

which it also sees as the characteristic discourse of the nineteenth century. None the less, it is interesting that Heidegger should have picked up on the strand in Nietzsche's critique of Wagner that relates to sexual politics and to questions of gender in music, and has taken it as the sole voice of Nietzsche. Wagner requires Wagneriennes; in the theatre, males become female, as the cynic complains; the music submerges the listener who cannot impose upon it signs of a domination which take the form of noting its rhythm or detecting its proper style. Worst of all, in the first quoted passage (p. 64), from *The Case of Wagner*, the revealing word is 'hysterical', which immediately, if unconsciously, invokes women negatively. If music is a woman, so much the worse for it in public esteem. But I have argued that this, at least, cannot simply be taken as Nietzsche *contra* Wagner; it is also one aspect of Wagner's text in dialogue with another aspect, and an encouragement to look for dialogism, not for monological art, in Wagner's music.

To sum up: on one reading, Nietzsche exposes an anti-feminism in Wagner. On another, it is Nietzsche who is anti-feminist. On a third, he shows that Wagner constructs himself in masculinist terms as the 'cynic'. But this is in opposition to the 'enlightened Wagnerian' in himself—who might see the unconscious speaking in the cynic's text as the language of Siegfried and the late nineteenth-century cult of nature and the body. The cynic's refusal of the theatre originates from refusal of the 'mass'. But refusal of the 'mass' (in favour of the exclusivity of Bayreuth) might suggest an underlying proto-fascism in the stress on individualism and the lonely self. (Besides, remembering that Wagner wanted to purify the theatre and wondering about the implications of that, which is more the mass: a Bayreuth audience or the audience in the 'ordinary' theatre, flea-pit though it might be?) A music with rhythm, to which you can dance or march or walk, might take on male characteristics—unless Dionysos is bisexual. And the language of floundering, of being submerged, recalls Theweleit on the language of the Freikorps and their anxieties about women, crowds, and Communists—all that would prevent the imposition of order. Certainly in the drama between the fragmented body and the ego as armour, it is easy to see that the critique of Wagner having no form slips back into the fear of having no ego: that Wagner's music does not form an ego, because an ego would be alienating, neurotic, the assumption of a single (male) identity.

Heidegger, speaking almost in Theweleit's terms—and in the 1930s—writes approvingly of Nietzsche: 'In opposition to the "complete dissolution of style" in Wagner, rules and standards, and above all the grounding of such, are here [in *The Will to Power*, sect. 838] demanded clearly and unequivocally; they are identified as what comes first and is essential, beyond all sheer technique and mere invention and enhancement of "means of expression" ' (*Nietzsche*, i. 130). Heidegger reads an anti-feminism in Nietzsche which he then repeats and endorses.

If this is the case, we are left with a Wagner who is not only contradictory for Nietzsche, but dysfunctional for 1930s fascist discourse, in that his 'romantic pessimism' (ibid. i. 133) gives rise to a music that awakens deep psychic fears in the authoritarian personality. We have passed from a masculine Wagner who uses music as female to a feminine Wagner whose music is disturbing to Nietzsche because of its lack of distinction, form, and order. So Nietzsche seeing music as a woman outside the control of the male *logos* becomes ambiguous, while Heidegger in this case wants to read in a phallogocentric way. For him, Wagner's music was an attempt to rescue life in all its modern inchoateness; but he damns Wagner with faint praise: 'Rising on swells of feeling would have to substitute for a solidly grounded and articulated position in the midst of beings, the kind of thing that only great poetry and thought can create' (ibid. i. 88). But he is not simply damning Wagner, since his point is that technology has exposed the lack of a basis for any humanism or humanist goals: only Nazism could confront the course of planetary technology.[46] By contrast with this technology, Wagner's music looks nostalgic in its reactiveness.

Nietzsche is dual about Wagner, because the latter represented everything that he saw as dual in modernity. Wagner's music is an open wound: there is no suture to it; it is split, double, unresolved, and it suggests fragmentation and the lack of a centred subject. A completed modernity, such as Heidegger's, has no use for it. It seems appropriate to finish these questions concerning Wagner by noting that on one reading at least, Nietzsche's, he provides a femininity capable of questioning the fascist basis on which the modern subject is set up. Femininity proves to be a critique. It is an insight with which to approach late nineteenth-century Italian opera, in its masculine (Verdi) and feminine (Puccini) forms.

---

[46] I refer to Heidegger's statement in 1935, with a parenthesis added in 1953, that 'the works that are being peddled about nowadays as "the philosophy of National Socialism" . . . have nothing whatever to do with the inner truth and greatness of this movement (namely the encounter between global technology and modern man) [but] have all been written by men fishing in the troubled waters of "values" and "totalities" ': *Introduction to Metaphysics*, p. 199. On the subject of Heidegger and fascism, see Victor Farias, *Heidegger and Nazism* ed. Joseph Margolis and Tom Rockmore (1987) (Philadelphia: Temple University Press, 1989); Pierre Bourdieu, *The Political Ontology of Martin Heidegger* (1988), trans. Peter Collier (Stanford, Calif.: Stanford University Press, 1991); Richard Wolin, *The Politics of Being: The Political Thought of Martin Heidegger* (New York: Columbia University Press, 1990); and *Critical Inquiry*, 15 (1989). But this only touches the secondary literature; see Joseph G. Kronick, 'Review Essay: Dr. Heidegger's Experiment', *boundary* 2, 17, 3 (1990): 116–53; Michael E. Zimmerman, *Heidegger's Confrontation with Modernity* (Bloomington, Ind.: Indiana University Press, 1990).

PART II

The Modernization of Italian Opera

2
Verdi and Imperialism: *Otello*

Those are composers! And what operas! What finales! To the sound of guns!
Verdi on Garibaldi's army, May 1860

The Risorgimento, an opera in itself, reached its triumphal conclusion when, on 20 September 1870, Italian troops entered Rome by Porta Pia, and the imperial city joined with the emergent nation-state. The Italian parliament first met in Rome on 27 November the following year. It was headed by a constitutional monarchy: Vittorio Emanuele II until 1878, Umberto till 1900, and Vittorio Emanuele III until 1946. It was a kingdom and monarchy which satisfied few, and successive governments seemed to contain in themselves the seeds that would produce Mussolini's march on Rome at the end of October 1922. And the founding of Mussolini's organization the Fasci Italiani di Combattimento (on 23 March 1919), which became a party in November 1921, seems to belong to a narrative set in place by 1871. Its constitutive elements and discursive structure were never so self-consciously articulated as by Nietzsche in the German case, but I want to examine these elements, which add up to a culture of fascism, through late Verdi and Puccini.

Verdi, the liberal and former republican, whose name had been an acronym in 1859 for Vittorio Emanuele Re D'Italia, and who had worked for the 1861 settlement which had given the Piedmontese monarchy to Italy in general, and briefly sat in Parliament in 1861, bears little relationship to any proto-fascism. But the relationship of Verdi's thinking to the political discourse of post-1871 cannot be defined simply in terms of his conscious opinions, because it goes beyond his stated views or thoughts or those of his more Bohemian collaborator of that period, Boito. It opens up questions of what is not consciously registered in discourse, what could not be recognized till much later. Though it is easy to find many contributors to Italian culture who were proto-fascist and aware of it, and Verdi was not one of them, the limits of thinking that are permitted within any ideological formation impose discursive structures not consciously registered as choices. Conceptualizing the unconscious of a period means seeing what controls its range of options in thinking. Criticism of *Otello* (1887) or *Falstaff* (1893) requires going beyond the intentions of the writer and of his work. A short example of what I mean may be given from *Simon Boccanegra* (1857, revised with Boito in 1881). Both versions have plots almost impossible to follow: the contemporary critic Abramo Basevi said of the 1857 one that he had to read it through *six times* (his emphasis) to make sense of it.[1] Only six times? *Simon Boccanegra* may not be the worst opera plot, but the difficulty in following it stems from the difficulty of seeing what is at stake, which invites speculation that the subject-matter may be such that no one has any interest in clarifying it. Its difficulty is symptomatic of a problem, a form of unconscious repression. By the end of this opera, which has much in common with *Rienzi* in setting, accent of the hero, and transgressive incest (father/daughter here, not brother/sister), there is much less democracy around than there was at the beginning. The plebeians elect Boccanegra as Doge, rigged though the election may be. Two-thirds of the way through, a middle-class (Guelph) revolt takes place which is foiled by Gabriele Adorno, the Genoese aristocrat, who is declared by Boccanegra to be the next leader. The fear of working-class rebellion in Act 1, scene 2 (Verdi in 1881 specifically compared this with the Paris Commune[2]) and of middle-class rebellion in Act 2 leads to the new leader who is not the product of the people's choice. In all this, with Amelia the embodiment of the nation, there is a strong political unconscious which worked its way through Italian politics between the end of the Risorgimento and the beginning of fascism.

This chapter concentrates on *Otello* in the light of the discourses of imperialism and the struggle for a hegemony based on an imagined national unity headed by a monarch and promoting the interests of the middle classes, as these things prevailed in Umberto's Italy. *Otello* and *Falstaff* (next chapter) are usually treated as autonomous works of art, products of a genius that had had a lifetime to mature and had the seductive power of Boito to stir to further achievement. They are tightly organized, and do not let much slip past conscious control (*Falstaff* throws off all shame to the least degree of all the operas I discuss, though there is fear of adultery, and perhaps some shame in being in a laundry basket). These operas, even *Falstaff*, are still derivative from the opera form that uses a separate number structure, which is obviously their difference from Wagnerian opera and from a Schopenhauerian inspiration which is inseparable from a belief in actions and the

---

[1] Quoted in Julian Budden, *The Operas of Verdi*, vol. 2 (London: Cassell, 1978), p. 250. Basevi, incidentally, found in the opening of the 1857 version the presence of Wagner, 'the well-known subverter of the present state of music' (p. 254).

[2] See Budden, *Operas of Verdi*, ii. 260, quoting Verdi on the female chorus in Act 1, sc. 2: 'Besides, it's well known that women play an important part in popular uprising: think of the Paris Commune.'

intellect being controlled unconsciously. In so far as Verdian operas, unlike Wagner, hardly recognize an unconscious and therefore the existence of
repression, they may be themselves more repressed, less modern. But despite
the restraints they show, I believe it is possible to focus on those elements of
the texts that do not suggest a unified work of art, but point to underlying
contradictions, evoking competing discourses at work in Italian society. These
discourses thus suggest the need to historicize the operas. We cannot just ask
questions such as what Verdi did to Shakespeare, as though we had a sure sense of
the meaning of Shakespeare's text that would entitle us to comment on Verdi's
understanding of it, as if we were dealing with an ahistorical Verdi and an
ahistorical Shakespeare. How Shakespeare exists means many different things:
how the texts worked at the time of their writing, including their mediation of
previous texts; how they worked in the context of nineteenth-century Italy, and
how, at the end of another century, they look to us, when our reading articulates
with that text aspects of the discourses and ideologies we live in and by. These
differences make all thought of a common approach to Shakespeare (Verdi's and
ours together) impossible: there are several Shakespeare texts involved, belonging
to different centuries—the sixteenth, the nineteenth, and the twentieth. And
Verdi is not isolated either; in his *Otello* other discourses can be found, which
perhaps unconsciously possess his text, like the anti-democratic move in *Simon
Boccanegra.*

  This approach is familiar in literary studies, in particular to those who have been
working in the critical theory developed since the 1970s and to those who have
used Foucault or have worked in the spirit of 'new historicism'. I do not assume
its newness to those working in music history, though I think its impact has yet
to be felt fully in the study of opera. Since I am addressing the question of the
political within a cultural discourse, this means considering how nationalism and
imperialism could turn silently into proto-fascism. So let me start with a classic
new historicist move, one which preludes discussion of a text by reference to a
historical anecdote, usually one not found in orthodox histories, which is then
used in improvisational style to illuminate the text, as if it were the missing key to
interpretation, in fact.

  My example is not improvisatory, for it is historically famous and of obvious
importance, but it rarely features in discussion of the music. At the heart of the
opera is the representation of the 'other' of the European: the black. Verdi referred
to the opera as his 'chocolate project', and initially, in 1881, thought of Othello as
'an Ethiopian without the usual turban', declining, therefore, to see him as

Oriental, like a Turk.[3] *Otello* opened in Milan on 5 February 1887. On 26 January, between 400 and 500 Italians under Lieutenant-Colonel De Cristoferis were slaughtered at Dogali in Ethiopia, by the soldiers of the local Tigre chieftain, Ras Alula, in a humiliating reversal of Italy's imperialist designs on East Africa. The disgrace, which was felt internationally, was widely seen as contributing to the death that summer of the Prime Minister, Depretis, who was born the same year as Verdi (1813). It was perceived as a scandal of apparent failure analogous to Gladstone's failure to support General Gordon in the Sudan in 1885. When the Italian could be put to shame by the black, while in *Otello* the black is put to shame by the Italian Jago, then the black, the African, appears in two moments of close proximity, and in two—or are they two?—manifestations. The opera, though it was never said so, must somehow have fitted into the crisis of this defeat, must somehow be taken as negotiating this problem of national defeat. In part it did so simply by being opera and being by Verdi. In fact, the connection *was* stated: Hanslick said of the opera's première that it was 'a matter of national consequence, and the governmental crisis was forgotten, along with the military disasters in Abyssinia'.[4] It sounds as though the 'forgetting' of the military defeat was a matter of negotiation, in relation to the necessary success of the opera.

Italy's African adventure had begun earlier, in the decade leading to the unification centred on Rome, and this history can be mapped on to Verdi's work. In 1869, with the Italian government's connivance, the Rubattino shipping company occupied the port of Assab on the Red Sea coast. Ethiopia had been touched, its sovereignty impaired, even though Assab was under nominal Turkish and actual Egyptian rule. It is no coincidence in terms of the discourse of the moment that *Aida*, the idea of which was proposed to Verdi in the autumn of 1869 and was first produced in Cairo in December 1871, features Egypt taking Ethiopia into captivity. Aida is the black Ethiopian slave/princess deriving from Meyerbeer's *L'Africaine* of 1865 (who prompts, among further representations of the 'other',

---

[3] Quoted in James Hepokoski, *Otello* (Cambridge: Cambridge University Press, 1987), p. 171. The chapter is important for its dealing with the way *Othello* was received in nineteenth-century Italy, and arguing that Schlegel's view of Othello was a confusion in Shakespeare's mind of 'a Moor of North Africa, a baptized Saracen', with 'a real Ethiopian' (p. 165), and suggesting that for Boito, it was decisive that Othello was 'a negro' (p. 170). Verdi refers to Otello as 'the African' in letters. See Frank Walker, *The Man Verdi* (London: Dent, 1962), p. 476. Hepokoski's chapter on the *Otello* libretto in Groos and Parker (eds.), *Reading Opera*, pp. 34–59, should also be consulted.

[4] Eduard Hanslick, *Music Criticisms 1846–99*, trans. Henry Pleasants (Harmondsworth: Penguin, 1963), p. 276.

Madama Butterfly). In thematic terms, the woman in love with a member of the dominating colonial or imperialistic power suggests the willingness of the colonized to be just that: under domination. The sexual and the imperial themes go together. And such a willingness existed in Khedive Ismail, who wanted *Aida* and an opera-house and a Cairo that would reflect nineteenth-century Paris. 'My country is no longer in Africa. I have made it part of Europe.'[5] *Aida* was to be a national opera, opera being one of the means by which a country took on aspects of its colonial masters. (In fact, the Cairo opera-house was to be unsuccessful, and was baled out by Italy, bringing it more under the sphere of Europe.) Signs of a colonial mentality towards Egypt appear in Verdi's lack of interest in the project (while others thought about Cairo, he thought of Milan for the première) and even in Mariette's source material: though he was (or because he was) an Egyptologist, he actually neglected to be accurate about Egypt (this shows when Egypt acquires a temple of Vulcan).

Aida closes the decade of Verdi as a public, international composer. *La Forza del destino* (1862) had been produced for St Petersburg, and revised in 1869 for Italy; its source material, *Don Alvaro, o La Fuerza del Sino*, of 1835, is interesting in that the eponymous hero is Peruvian, thus recalling the independence wars of Peru against Spain in the 1820s. Verdi works with a hero himself the 'other', who is pursued with implacable hatred by the European, Don Carlo, who finally rouses him to act when he suggests that his code of honour is deficient by the hegemonic European standard. The theme anticipates much of *Otello*. There was also *Don Carlos* (1865) for Paris, which also saw a revised *Macbeth*. Each opera received a home-coming in Italy; but they belong to Italy's desire to make a grand opera statement about itself abroad in the years of unification from 1861 to 1871. Thereafter, it seems, in the new decade of grand opera (*opera ballo*), Verdi virtually wished to retire.

Aida does not, of course, belittle Ethiopia. Its third act plays positively on the nostalgia of the homeland ('O patria mia'), and Amonasro's words to Aida echo old Risorgimento values: 'Pensa che un popolo, / vinto, straziato, / per te soltanto risorger può': think that a vanquished, tormented people through you alone can rise again. The clash within ideology is apparent: the triumphalism of Act 2 may transfer to Italy—Dynley Hussey calls the opera 'a musical celebration of the final realization of Italian unity which was achieved at the expense of the Vatican

[5] Hans Busch, *Verdi's* Aida: *The History of An Opera in Letters and Documents* (Minneapolis: University of Minnesota Press, 1978), p. 6.

[doubtless portrayed in the Egyptian priests] during the year of its composition'.[6] But Ethiopia is Italy as it was, before the Risorgimento, and the contradiction— that Italy was now much more like the less sympathetic Egypt as it appears in the opera—may be what lay behind Verdi's willingness to retire, like Rossini in 1830. The bourgeois liberal would read Italy's existence in Egypt's. In 1878, after the Congress of Berlin, from which Italy had come away seeming to possess nothing in colonial terms, Crispi, Italy's version of Bismarck, urged the colonizing of Tunisia and Libya, but the country was forced to recognize France's possession of Tunisia in 1881, which act pushed Italy towards the Triple Alliance with Germany and Austria-Hungary (1882). An excuse to persevere with Ethiopian expansion came in 1884, when African tribesmen in Assab (bought by the Italian government from the Rubattino shipping company in 1882), killed Gustavo Bianchi, an Italian scientist and explorer, in a raid. Assab had been declared the first colony, with Britain's agreement; part of the history of Italy's foreign policy in the last thirty years of the nineteenth century was trying to keep Britain's support, against France and so as to dilute the Triple Alliance. A punitive expedition sent out from Italy in 1884–5 produced expansion along the coast to Massawa and the conse- quent need to ensure that Ethiopian trade went through Massawa as a trading- post. But it was the troops moving inland from Massawa who were cut off and killed at Dogali.

It is worth completing now this narrative of the imperial adventure, beyond the opening night of *Otello*. In March 1888, the Abyssinian emperor, John IV, agreed to give compensation for Dogali and to permit Massawa to be used as a trading- post, but in March of the following year he was killed by the Madhist force at Metemma, and his head carried off to Khartoum. His successor was Menelik, who signed the Treaty of Uccialli with Italy in May 1889. The Prime Minister, Crispi, joined up these Red Sea possessions now apparently guaranteed to Italy to form the colony of Eritrea, and then proceeded to the conquest of Somalia, which became a colony in 1905. Such adventurism was not carried out without consid- erable opposition at home, but it was felt that there was no way Italy could pull out of Africa without, as it was put, 'serious damage to the monarchy'—the king being Umberto, himself no symbol of national unity.[7] The hegemony of bour- geois Italy, united not on republican but on constitutional monarchic lines, was

    [6] Dynley Hussey, *Verdi* (London: Dent, 1940), p. 193.
    [7] The statement is quoted by Martin Clark, *Modern Italy 1871–1982* (London: Longman, 1982), p. 100. On the African adventure generally, see John Gooch, *Army, State and Society in Italy, 1870–1915* (London: Macmillan, 1989), ch. 5.

in question. Menelik then rejected the terms of the Treaty of Uccialli, and this provided an excuse for Italian expansion to continue. Troops moved inland from Massawa to take Agordat, and then, under General Baratieri, took Kassala in the Sudan. In January 1895 reinforcements were sent to occupy the Abyssinian region of Tigre, with its capital at Adowa, resulting in 150,000 square kilometres of Abyssinia being declared to be under Italian sovereignty. Kassala and Adowa were held to be the key symbolic positions, which were not to be moved away from.

Such adventurism invited a response from Menelik, and the fight-back began in November 1895, climaxing in the total humiliation of Italian troops at Adowa, 1 March 1896. Some 4,600 Italian troops were left dead, and many men were wounded and captured. More died at Adowa than had been lost in the whole Risorgimento. Thus ended for the moment Italy's experience with the 'other' it had tried to colonize, and its status as a European power was only diminished further. The fall-out from Adowa brought down the Prime Minister, Crispi; it turned the future leader of the nationalists, Enrico Corradini, into a patriot; it awakened demands for redress: in 1911, on the fifteenth anniversary of Adowa, Corradini began his nationalist weekly *L'idea nazionale*, venerating the memory of Crispi, lamenting bourgeois Italy's decadence, and urging the importance of war. That year (29 September) Italy began war on Turkey by invading Tripoli.

Italy's Abyssinian adventurism resumed in October 1935 when Italy was a fascist state; on 2 May 1936 the emperor, Haile Selassie, abandoned Addis Ababa; on 9 May Mussolini proclaimed the new Roman Empire. Alfredo Casella's one-act opera *Il Deserto tentato* opened in Florence on 19 May of the following year, with a dedication to Mussolini and in praise of his campaign. The militarism of the subject of the opera, which draws on 'orientalist' discourse, is avoided by a literal mystification of the issues, by a use of the rhetoric of 'Second Futurism' and its interest in *Aeropittura*. This language allowed for avoidance of reality, promoting 'cosmic idealism' instead, and images of weightlessness and formlessness.[8] In the spirit of this, Casella referred to the opera, itself inspired by an account of a flight over Ogaden, as

a mystery . . . of profoundly religious and martial character, evoking the abstract voices of a virgin nature anxious to be fertilised by human civilization; there would be the arrival of

---

[8] Compare Enrico Prampolini, the futurist writer and pro-fascist, describing the idea of *Aeropittura*: 'I maintain that to reach the highest realm of a new extraterrestrial spirituality we need to transcend the transcription of visible reality, even in its formal properties, and launch ourselves towards the total equilibrium of the infinite, thereby giving life to images latent in a world of cosmic reality' (quoted by Enrico Crispolti, 'Second Futurism', in Emily Braun (ed.), *Italian Art in the Twentieth Century* (Munich: Prestel-Verlag, 1989), p. 168).

a group of aviators, who descend from the sky into the horrible desert, like modern Argonauts; their struggle against the *dark* forces of barbarism and the snares of nature; and finally peace, after the transformation of the colossal surroundings by gigantic human edifices.[9]

This opera was intended, like the campaign itself, to make up for Adowa, that 'sad and mediocre epoch', as Casella called it in his autobiography (p. 32). Opera itself was to be renewed, like the deserts of Ethiopia, by being returned to 'its point of origin, the miracle plays [compare Pizzetti's *La sacra rappresentazione di Abram e d'Isaac* (1926–8), derived from a fifteenth-century mystery play] and the old mysteries', while also (an anti-Puccini statement) 'animating it with the breath of current reality' (p. 214). Giving both opera and imperialism a quasi-religious sanction—it is, for example, noticeable how much of Pizzetti's operatic material is religious in nature—makes each appear an alibi for the other, and both belong to the triumph of the nation-state, itself conceived as a kind of spectacular opera:

On the afternoon of October 2 [1935] sirens called the nation to hear the voice of the Duce, as he committed Italy to its great African adventure. In the ancient square of Siena, so rich in art and history, the gathering of people seemed a gigantic evocation of the 'Commune' and it was particularly impressive that the voice seemed to come from the top of the Municipal Palace. Night descended during the address, making that historic hour incomparably solemn. (p. 211)

Celebration of Mussolini's Roman Empire appeared also in Carmine Gallone's film *Scipione l'Africano*, made in 1937 at the new Cinecittà studios.[10] Pizzetti, himself an opera composer and, like Casella, a member of the 1880s generation of musicians, wrote the music for the film, and conducted the 'Hymn to Rome' from the film for the Duce when he came to open the studios. In this historical epic, which drew on Rome's war with Carthage, we may see grand opera reaching its apotheosis in cinema, the medium of twentieth-century Italian popular culture, a fulfilment of Italian opera.

The events of the 1930s had their roots in 1880s colonialism: fascism was not just a parenthesis in Italian history. Going back to Verdi, how might we argue that *Otello* mediates any of these issues? Unlike the later Pizzetti and Casella, Verdi kept his independence in composing, and the opera is not a response to or a

---

[9] Alfredo Casella, *Music in My Time* (1941), trans. Spencer Norton (Norman, Okla.: University of Oklahoma Press, 1955), p. 214; my emphasis.

[10] On *Scipione*, see James Hay, *Popular Film Culture in Fascist Italy* (Bloomington, Ind.: Indiana University Press, 1987), pp. 155–61.

commentary on the events at Dogali. The view of art as reflecting issues in society is exactly the opposite of what I want to argue for throughout this study; the opera neither reflects nor criticizes state ideology, but exists as another voice within the discourses at work in this colonial adventure. On a personal level, Verdi himself represented a liberal opposition to such wild enterprises, as his conversational comments on the British in India, in September 1896, suggest:

Here is a great and ancient people now fallen prey to the English. But the English will regret it! Peoples allow themselves to be oppressed, vexed and maltreated,—and the English are sons of bitches. Then comes the moment when national sentiment, which none can resist, awakes. That is what we did with the Austrians. But now, unfortunately, we are in Africa, playing the part of tyrants; we are in the wrong and we will pay for it. They say we are going there to bring civilization to these people. A fine civilization, ours, with all the miseries it carries with it. Those people don't know what to do with it, and moreover in many ways they are more civilized than we.[11]

It is dangerous to read too much into a report of a conversation, but it is interesting none the less, revealing several splits within Verdi's attitudes. Feelings of Romantic revolution are there, and an abiding appeal to nationalism, and the unwilling sense that there may be a continuity between both these and imperialism. Perhaps guilt over imperialism is shifted on to the British, who are, however, secretly envied. Their anticipated defeat gives a pleasure which is that of both envy and a recognition of the historical futility of imperial adventures. In its sense of there being a single standard of civilization, which emanates from Europe, but which the Ethiopians seem unexpectedly to possess, it is an expression of orientalism, as Edward Said famously defines it. Orientalism names the way in which a dominant discourse overcomes its fear of the other by purporting to describe it from the reference point of its own position, which is taken as normative. The phenomenon appears in Verdi's sense that the colonized people do not know what to do with 'civilization': that proclaims the dominance of the European position. It is both a weak defence of, and a weak attack on, imperialism. Verdi's appeal to nationalism as that which prompts resistance is significant, for this nationalism was, of course, strongly productive of twentieth-century fascism. But to investigate the ways in which *Otello* partakes of the discourses of orientalism, nationalism, and imperialism, while moving within a nineteenth-century liberalism, means considering how 'the other' is rendered within the text.

[11] Quoted by George Martin, *Aspects of Verdi* (London, Robson Books, 1988).

Stephen Greenblatt, in *Renaissance Self-Fashioning: From More to Shakespeare*, a key text within 'new historicism', reads Shakespeare's *Othello* as a text whose experiences articulate the colonialism at work in sixteenth-century European discourse with regard to the Americas. Greenblatt's work is indebted to Said and Foucault, whose work on the power of discourses to dominate was influential for the thesis of *Orientalism.* To summarize Greenblatt's arguments briefly, Iago's polytropic improvisatory skills succeed in compassing the downfall of Othello, the black, the non-European, by a process of prestidigitation. Renaissance skills in diplomacy are shown to be what they are: two-tonguedness, with an ability to think not only in the dominant discourse of the European, but also to represent the colonized subject to himself in a language he must take over and internalize: the dominated thinks of himself or herself in the language of the dominant. Anthropology, that classic nineteenth-century liberal discipline, is the one which renders the other as the same by its use of a 'scientific', 'objective' language in which to speak the practices of the colonized other. But of course the language is not objective: it is the positivist, rational discourse of the European. Greenblatt's argument turns on the sense that the improvisatory and uncommitted language which Iago uses has to be accepted in its literal and truthful sense by Othello: that the colonized cannot perceive the will to power that lies within the speech of the colonizer.

Here is a reading, not without problems of its own,[12] which moves away from the famous A. C. Bradley/F. R. Leavis encounters with the play which question whether its centre is Iago's diabolism or Othello's self-regarding pride.[13] Neither of those readings gave any weight to Othello's colour, which means that they both assume, in weighing up the merits of Iago and Othello, that they may be judged by the same humanistic—actually European—standards, that there is no difference that needs to be drawn attention to. It is another case of 'orientalism'. Greenblatt's reading at least places the play in the area of imperialism, as in its later nineteenth-century stages I would suggest that no European text—certainly not *Aida* or *Otello*—can be free of it. But *Aida* shows Verdi's liberal

---

[12] See my *Confession: Sexuality, Sin, the Subject*, for further discussion of Greenblatt's reading; for Greenblatt, see his *Renaissance Self-Fashioning: From More to Shakespeare* (Chicago: University of Chicago Press, 1980); for Edward Said, see his *Orientalism* (1978; Harmondsworth: Penguin, 1985). Said's account of *Aida* in his *Culture and Imperialism* (London: Chatto and Windus, 1993) is also relevant. On Said, see Paul Robinson, 'Is *Aida* an Orientalist Opera?' *Cambridge Music Journal*, 5/2 (1993): 133–40.

[13] A. C. Bradley, *Shakespearian Tragedy* (London: Macmillan, 1904); F. R. Leavis, 'Diabolic Intellect and the Noble Hero: The Sentimentalist's *Othello*', in *The Common Pursuit* (London: Chatto and Windus, 1951).

sympathies, which do not suggest conscious racism—certainly not that of Crispi, for example, urging revenge after Dogali—for 'our national flag must be respected even by savages'.[14]

None the less, references to colour in Boito's libretto for *Otello* do appear, more marked than in Shakespeare: in the Act 1 duet—Desdemona's 'le tue tempie oscure' (your dusky temples)—and the Act 2 quartet—'forse perché ho sul viso quest' atro tenebror' (perhaps because I have on the face this dark gloominess)— and in the ensemble finale to Act 3, where the references are more suggestive and inspired by Boito. Desdemona's images of mud and sun are suggestive, working in relation with what the other characters sing, Cassio referring to the lightning, Roderigo singing of clouds covering his destiny and then of the 'lugubre luce d'atro balen' (the mournful light flashing darkly), as he intuits what Iago wishes him to do, and Lodovico singing of Otello's 'man funerea' (dark, funereal hand). The opposition between lightning and sun, mud and heaven, woman as angel versus black primitive man, continues with the chorus singing of Desdemona's 'viso santo, pallido' (pale, saintly face) and of Otello as 'quell'uomo nero è sepolcrale, e cieca / un' ombra è in lui di morte e di terror' (that black man is deadly, and blind; a shadow of death and terror is in him).

> Strazia coll'ugna l'orrido petto!
> Gli sguardi figge immoti al suol.
> Poi sfida il ciel coll'atre pugna,
> l'ispido aspetto ergendo
> ai dardi alti del Sol.

(He tears with nails his hairy breast. His eyes are fixed unmoving on the ground. Then he challenges heaven with dark fists, raising his bristly face towards the high rays of the sun.)

But this alignment of death, blackness, the atavistic, the heavily physical, and the sense of damnation is only one set of discourses within the text, which in any case is constructed by contradictions. Though it may deal with Otello as racially the 'other', it still wishes to claim him for Italian nationalism. Boito regarded Giraldi Cinthio's source narrative of the unnamed 'Moor' in the *Hecatommithi* (1566) as based on fact, since it referred to Cyprus becoming the property of Venice, and he thus placed the events of the story as occurring in 1525 (so that costumes for *Otello* matched this dating, making it historical drama). Further, the

---

[14] Quoted by Dennis Mack Smith, *Italy and Its Monarchy* (New Haven: Yale University Press, 1989), p. 86.

collaborators argue, the model for the Moor might have been Cristoforo Moro, a Venetian lieutenant of 1508. Perhaps this figure, according to Boito, might be fused with Francesco da Sessa, a southern Italian called 'il capitano moro'. 'Moro is not an uncommon name among white Venetians, while also black Africans, referred to as Ethiopians, were officers in the service of the republic.' Working from this possibility that Othello might have been Italian, Verdi in 1881 thinks that Shakespeare meant 'the Venetian Giacomo Moro', having confused Cristoforo Moro with the procurator Giacomo Moro who died in 1377. It was a 'bad mistake' of Shakespeare to make him a Moor.[15]

Thus Boito and Verdi are as dependent on Cinthio as on Shakespeare for their material. Shakespeare is not perceived as the original, but as working over traditional Italian literature. And a massive recuperation is at work to exclude the other altogether, by making Cinthio's Moor an Italian, thus saving his nobility and heroism and making it unnecessary for the Verdian text to say much about colour. In the research on Cinthio's narrative there is the beginnings of a desire for a national epic, and for the reclamation of Italian literature as well as Italian music, then commonly seen as afflicted by Wagnerism. Verdi calls it a 'decadence' when in 1881, on the eve of the signing of the Triple Alliance, he comments: 'Yes, we no longer have any literature or art or sciences of our own. Everything is foreign and already we are two-thirds not Italian any more, not even politically' (quoted by Busch, *Verdi's* Otello, i.125). He was opposed to German influences; hence he sided with France against Germany in 1870, for instance. Similarly, he was hesitant about Wagner. His nationalism makes Otello a virtual Italian, and thereby softens any racism. Thus the question of the representation of the black is solved by *not* representing him—Otello as an Ethiopian is virtually invisible in the text written for 1887. Thus are questions of national defeat by the other resolved.

The very public, nationalist overtones of the text may account for the opera's avoidance of the sexual issues that mark Shakespeare's play. In Cinthio, the Moor and Desdemona have been married for some time. In some ways it seems that Verdi goes along with that. But in Shakespeare's play, Cyprus, Aphrodite's island, is to be the place of the consummation of Othello and Desdemona's marriage. The duel between Cassio and Montano, a parody of the carnivalesque celebrations that accompany newly-weds to bed in Mediterranean countries, have the effect of

---

[15] See Hans Busch, *Verdi's* Otello *and* Simon Boccanegra *in Letters and Documents*, 2 vols. (Oxford: Clarendon Press, 1988), i. 215; ii. 756.

getting Othello out of bed. The language of Iago explaining to Othello what happened to cause such a riot is suggestive in implying that the marriage has not in fact been consummated:

> I do not know, friends all but now, even now
> In quarter, and in terms, like bride and groom.
> Devesting them to bed, and then but now,
> As if some planet had unwitted men,
> Swords out, and tilting at other's breast
> In opposition bloody.[16]

Certainly the play suggests the way in which men may be 'unwitted' by others, and the word may include a sense of being made impotent. The wedding sheets that Desdemona has laid on her bed and in which she dies are also suggestive of unsullied virginity. In Verdi, she has placed on the bed her white bridal robe, which does not carry the same symbolic charge. It is pointless, of course, to be novelistic about this and to try to settle the question of Othello and Desdemona's relationship one way or the other—whether Desdemona dies a virgin or not—but the play certainly sets up a structure where Cassio is the common object of desire of both Othello and Iago, whose envy of him is patent, and also of Desdemona. It will be recalled that Cassio acts for Othello as a substitute wooer of Desdemona. Cassio's desires, in addition to this structure, are further directed away from that circle towards Bianca, a figure brought in by Shakespeare and omitted by Verdi, though referred to in the opera. Desire is displaced, directed past the immediately available person or object towards something indefinable beyond, just as the attachment which Othello shows to the handkerchief is not to that simply, but to something for which it substitutes and which is not definable—as desire, that Freudian/Lacanian term, can never be. That something which is the end of desire seems to be the 'it' of the statement 'It is the cause, it is the cause, my soul' (*Othello*, Act 5, sc. 2), lines introducing a monologue that the opera omits. But what the 'it' is, is unsayable; it is part of the structure of desire that, for Lacan, belongs to the symbolic order of language into which humans are inserted.[17]

---

[16] Shakespeare, *Othello*, 2. 3. 170–5. ed. M. R. Ridley (London: Methuen, 1958).

[17] On the structure of desire in *Othello*, see Peter L. Rudnytsky, 'The Purloined Handkerchief in *Othello*', in Joseph Reppen and Maurice Charney (eds.), *The Psychoanalytic Study of Literature* (Hillsdale, NJ., 1983). For Lacan, the moment 'when desire becomes human is also that in which the child is born into language' (*Ecrits: A Selection*, trans. Alan Sheridan (London: Tavistock Publications, 1977), p. 103). The whole essay, 'Function and Field of Speech and Language in Psychoanalysis', discusses the symbolic order and insertion into it.

As for Cassio's part within this structure, it seems significant that he unwittingly 'unwits' Othello by stopping his marriage celebrations by his duel, and that the climactic moment of Act 3 (and Act 2 of the opera) is the imaginary account by Iago of Cassio's wet dreams about Desdemona (compare Boito's words for Cassio: 'L'estasi del ciel tutto m'innonda' (The ecstasy of heaven drowns me)). Shakespeare's account of Cassio is framed in a homoerotic context, omitted by Boito, where Iago makes the imaginary Cassio make love to him in sleep as though he were Desdemona, while lying beside him (3. 3. 425–32): a substitution, which, like the handkerchief, suggests how interchangeable objects of desire are, how labile, thus demonstrative of how desire is not itself finally attached to any object—and certainly not to one only. This fantasizing of Cassio, which comes from Iago as much as it is meant to appeal to Othello's scopic drive (the Freudian term for the urge to see, to witness sexual intercourse, to become 'the supervisor' (3. 3. 401)), makes an imaginary Cassio the elusive object of desire for both men, and strongly colours the way that jealousy is constructed within the text: as something like the fear that someone else possesses what the self in fact can never possess, possession not being possible (a point borne out by the interrupted wedding night). Desire as flow, as not codifiable, as circulating endlessly, as shameless: these issues link strongly to those Theweleit discusses in *Male Fantasies*: their power is felt in the deterritorializations implied in modernity, and fascism in particular is anxious to recontain them, to shut the borders again, to control desire.

And desire *is* contained in *Otello*. Very little of this interest survives in the opera, where it is not obvious that Otello and Desdemona are newly-wed; and the duet between the two that closes the first act and appears to resolve the storm and conflict present among the males in the first part has indeed the opposite effect, in suggesting that Otello is in possession of his object of desire. None of the anxieties about male and female sexuality that make the Shakespeare play so disturbing—and modern—are allowed into the opera. The jealousy which becomes essential in Act 2, even giving rise to a later motif to begin the third act, is not focused on anything within the individual psychology of the character, as Leavis argued, seeing it as reaching towards problems in Othello's own psyche. Nor does it have to do with the structure of desire to which he is subjected as a colonial servant working for the patriarchy of Venice and forced to speak a language of European sophistication that is not his. Rather, it remains a fixed element associated with nineteenth-century Italian opera in all the clichés spoken about it. Similarly, Iago is taken out of the realm of the sexual altogether, and is given the 'Credo' which transforms him into a Mephistopheles figure. The change does much more than transfer Germanic influences, Goethean and Weberian, or even Wagnerian, into Italian opera. It allegorizes the text so that Desdemona in her saintliness and Jago in his diabolism become alternative influences upon Otello, who has the potentiality of each. It also takes the textual events out of the realm of commentary almost altogether. If Jago's sources of inspiration are so flatly malign, they are beyond the scope of discussion, and questions of ethical judgement hardly arise.

But these negative comments do not point to a textual failure in what is obviously one of the most famous, striking, self-assured operas of the nineteenth century. Rather, they point up an ideological crisis of representation: what can be allowed on the stage in 1887? Or again, why do Verdi and Boito invest so much in self-assurance, confirming, for instance, the highly *Italian* nature of their project? The removal of the anxieties I have spoken of may suggest that the need has been felt to repress them. Signs of this appear in the text's equivocations or contradictions, which may now be spelled out.

Thus Otello is both African and Italian; he is and is not newly-wed; the opera both is and is not named after him, for its working title was *Jago*, which points to a lack of assurance about what should be its centre, Italy or Ethiopia. Another equivocation hangs over Desdemona as a real or an ideal figure, marked out by melody, especially in the Act 2 quartet, and like the Virgin Mary, as suggested by the way she is spoken of in the Act 2 and 3 ensembles. Her music in Act 4 guards her as a special object: for instance, the 'Salce' music is presented in a closed form, with no interruptions from Emilia (a contrast to the Shakespeare presentation: see *Othello*, Act 4, sc. 3), which would give another voice, another set of attitudes, and another timbre. Similarly, the music invests much in her voice being heard without any instrumental backing, making her into a pure presence. The closure of form referred to almost replicates this closing off of the woman: she is knowable, a firm personality, and an ideal one. Verdi referred to Desdemona, as a woman, as 'a stupid little thing', but added: 'She's the type of goodness, of resignation, of sacrifice . . . beings that exist in part and that Shakespeare has poeticized and deified' (letter of 22 April 1887).[18] But it is not Shakespeare who idealizes her or makes her sing the Ave Maria, but Verdi, and that suggests an anxiety about women's sexuality and the degree to which women can be seen as

---

[18] Quoted in William Weaver and Martin Chusid (eds.), *The Verdi Companion* (New York: W. W. Norton and Co., 1979), p. 161.

real or as types, and what seeing them as real would entail. These problems are displaced on to a reading of Shakespeare.

A third equivocation appears in the very character of the opera: whether it should be regarded as pure Italian or as German-inspired. The Goethean inspirations for the character of Jago are relevant. Wagnerian music became the other of Italian music, to the anxiety of those, Verdi included, who wished to maintain national boundaries in music, and felt that Italian opera with its insistence on melody was being threatened by a newer interest in the symphonic and the orchestral. Such invasions into a national music are represented as of a piece with Italy's need to preserve a national and international status not dependent upon Central European powers. *Otello* opened in the year that the Triple Alliance was renewed, affirming Italy's links with Germany.

To these problematic discourses of nationalism, imperialism, and the sexual, I want to add another, equally relevant for Wagnerism: decadence. The word can receive varying emphases: what it refers to depends on who uses it, since it has been a term of abuse adopted by both left and right. The word embodies a struggle for control of a hegemonic discourse, for a dominant way to describe someone else, and thereby marginalize both that person and their actions. Nor is discussion of decadence separable from the subject of 'degeneration', which in the second half of the nineteenth century became a powerful term with which to conceptualize people's mental and physical states. Its influence was first felt in the writings of B. A. Morel (1809–73), in his treatise *Dégénérescence* (1857), which set the agenda for an ideology and right-wing politics suggesting that nineteenth-century progress was threatened by degenerate behaviour, madness, alcoholism, cretinism, and criminality. It affects naturalism in literature and verismo opera, and also exists in *Otello*. Boito's imagery of mud, the 'livido fango' into which Desdemona has been pushed in Act 3, receives added force from Jago's words in the Credo. He says he is born 'dall a viltà d'un germe o d'un atomo' (from the vileness of a germ or an atom), repeats 'vile son nato' (that he is born base), and feels 'il fango originario' (the primeval slime) in himself. Further, man is determined 'dal germe della culla' (from the germ of the cradle). This is the discourse of disease belonging to a Zolaesque nineteenth-century naturalism: behind Boito's self-consciously poetic language is the suggestion of syphilis or of congenital, hereditary degeneracy. Syphilis would be a marker of degeneracy; though a disease of the bourgeois, it was linked with every group marginal to the bourgeois—with women, foreigners, criminals, and deviants of all forms. Cesare Lombroso (1836–1909), the Italian theorist of degeneracy, in his *L'uomo delin-*

quente (1875), discussed the putative physical features of those thereby constructed as 'criminal types', and something of this and of racial assumptions about the African seem to be in Verdi's wish, expressed in a letter of 24 September 1881, to have Jago played as 'a long and thin figure, thin lips, small eyes set close to the nose like a monkey's, broad, receding brow, and the head developed behind'. Jago begins, with this simian image, to approach a characterization of the black, as though his and Otello's colours were being reversed, and as if the work was affirming Italian virtues in Otello while damning degenerate, other qualities in Jago. But then the ironic mode of Jago is referred to in this same letter, that mode which displays itself so much in the trills that play in his music and his laughter at the end of the Credo, obligatory for every Iago. The laughter is a nihilism which probes any humanism (such as the love of Otello and Desdemona), and may be compared with the laughter of Kundry. In keeping with this nihilism, Verdi describes Jago as having

an absent, *nonchalant* manner, indifferent to everything, witty, speaking good and evil almost lightheartedly, and having the air of not even thinking of what he says; so that if someone were to reproach him: 'What you say is vile!' he could answer: 'Really? I don't think so . . . we'll say no more about it.'[19]

Verdi describes a fictional construct with no internal consistency, which is not surprising, since it is overdetermined, a production of the condensation of contradictory discourses. (We could add to this overdetermination the fact that Boito and Verdi also thought of Jago as analogous to the Jesuit—model, in anticlerical liberal thought, of casuistry, of use of the truth rather than commitment to it.) But to consider Jago in the light of Lombroso's work might be suggestive. Lombroso's version of degeneracy differed from the French model of Morel, in that he believed that behaviour could regress atavistically. Daniel Pick suggests that the anxieties which lie behind his work came from 'the chimera of [Italian] national unity'.[20] Italy, though unified officially, was radically divided between north and south: the south was widely regarded in the north as a segment of Africa, as not Italian at all. In *L'uomo bianco e l'uomo di colore* (1871), Lombroso characterized the white as the creator of national unity; but, as Pick points out, 'inside the triumphant whiteness, there remained a certain blackness' (p. 126). That is, perhaps part of Italy was not Italian but really African. Or perhaps part of Italy

---

[19] Hepokoski, *Otello*, p. 100.

[20] Daniel Pick, *Faces of Degeneration: A European Disorder, c.1848–1918* (Cambridge: Cambridge University Press, 1989), p. 119. The subject of the construction of certain types of people as marginal is the topic of Michel Foucault's *The History of Sexuality* (Harmondsworth: Penguin, 1981).

had regressed to criminal or mad levels, which meant that not all Italians were true Italians. Lombroso's taxonomy of criminal types attempts to assist in the creation of a specious unity by making people read the signs of degeneration in their midst. Perhaps, then, the very indecisiveness of the opera about Jago and Otello—who really stands in for the black?—represents an uncertainty about what can be expected of a true Italian.

Verdi's portrait in his letter of how he imagines Jago is suggestive of a critique of the nihilist as conceived by the bourgeois. Turgenev is usually assumed to have been the first to use the word 'nihilist', in *Fathers and Sons* (1864), and the anarchist/nihilist, rejecting bourgeois society, could be equated by that society with the 'decadent' and degenerate. Verdi's letter dates from five years before Nietzsche's *Beyond Good and Evil*, but it gives a superficial critique of just that kind of anti-bourgeois text, as also of Nietzsche's refusal of the binary oppositions of 'good' and 'evil'. Similarly, it is ten years before *The Picture of Dorian Gray*, but is highly suspicious of the dismissal of sincerity and commitment to truth that Oscar Wilde displays—as in the preface to the *Picture*: 'There is no such thing as a moral or an immoral book. Books are well written or badly written. That is all.' Nietzsche and Wilde stand here as two nihilists who in some ways are Jago-like.

Moreover, the ambiguity about Jago's nihilism, despite Verdi's letter, extends to the conditions of his creation as a character. In 1881, Boito and Verdi intended to give his name to the opera, like Mefistofele, rather than Faust, in Boito's 1868 opera of that name, and the character was therefore not to be regarded as simply negative, but heroic in its own way. (Very few nineteenth-century operas are named for their villains.) The brindisi, for instance, seems to go beyond its dramatic context of inciting Cassio to drink, invoking, indeed, the heroic, or rather Dionysiac, spirit of *The Birth of Tragedy*:

> Chi all'esca ha morso
> del ditirambo
> spavaldo e strambo
> beva con me
> . . . .
> Il mondo palpita quand'io son brillo!
> Sfido l'ironico Nume e il destin!

(He who has tasted the bait of the dithyramb [the spirit of the Dionysiac dance in Greek tragedy], defiant and wild, drink with me . . . The world vibrates when I am lit! I dare the ironic Gods and destiny!)

The energies here recall Boito's antecedents in the anti-bourgeois, bohemian *scapigliatura* movement of the 1860s, as well as the Nietzschean commentaries on the spirit of music as Nietzsche glimpsed this in Wagner. In making Jago a gambler who defies destiny, they create him an ironist, and thus affirm his kinship with such figures as Nietzsche and Wilde. They go way outside the tightly held moral/religious assumptions involved with Otello and Desdemona. Jago is the decadent whose influence on such innocents as Cassio, to say nothing of an 'Italian' soldier such as Otello, is corrupting and destabilizing for bourgeois values. That is one reason why he is almost totally excluded from Act 4 of the opera. The opera does not consciously wish for anything Dionysiac to be in it, anything of the spirit of *The Birth of Tragedy*, which would subvert tidily held ideologies. But the music of the brindisi is infectious: it draws everyone into it, collapsing social structures, mirrored in the breakdown of its strophic form towards the end, and annihilating the distinctiveness of individual voices. In the brindisi, Cassio becomes shamelessly drunk, so providing an image for the circulation of desire that cannot be contained, but which spreads out to others, and on which Nietzsche on the Dionysiac as the loss of the centred self and Theweleit on the fascist fears engendered by the concept of flow are the best commentaries.

Yet the decadence is dual in its implications: Jago is presented contradictorily. His questioning of the pieties of conventional thought makes him both modern and decadent, like D'Annunzio in relation to his society. He is an ironist who also *refuses* irony, as in 'sfido l'ironico Nume', and irony, in Kierkegaard or in earlier German Romantic philosophy, is one of the essential qualities of any 'modern'. Nietzsche, indeed, discusses it in *The Birth of Tragedy* as the legacy of Socrates, who, for Nietzsche, effectively destroyed the Dionysiac, and commenced the course of European nihilism. For Jago (or for Verdi), not to allow the ironic mode would mean to pretend that the path of nihilism need not be trodden. In one sense, Jago is a nihilist; in another, he denies nihilism. The refusal of modernity is also apparent in the refusal of irony—rejection of irony as destiny's mode of existence—and it pairs with something else—his will to power exerted over Roderigo, Cassio, and Otello. These things link him with aspects of fascist thought. The refusal of irony which is implicit in trying to wield power suggests decadence in a sense mentioned in the Introduction, but waiting closer definition (I will come back to it when discussing Schreker). This decadence is reactive and unable to accept present reality in all its difference from the self and non-accountability to it. What can be said here is that the pairing of anti-bourgeois feeling which questions bourgeois piety with regressive authoritarianism is basic to fascism. So Jago's desire for total control is relevant, though in the brindisi he *does* recognize that this cannot be total, since the power over irony cannot be his, and that ironic elements, which belong to whatever is 'other', will always destabilize his schemes. The brindisi is begun by a proto-fascist, who has not quite thrown off all shame, whose interest is in using chaos and anarchy in order to bring about order again, as a totalitarian force, when Otello stops everything. Jago in the brindisi suggests the devil's advice to Adrian Leverkühn in *Doctor Faustus*, prompting him towards a musical excess which runs parallel to fascism: 'creative, genius-giving disease . . . that rides on high horse over all hindrances and springs with drunken daring from peak to peak is a thousand times dearer to life than plodding healthiness.' The devil's advice is: 'you will lead the way, you will strike up the march of the future, the lads will swear by your name—' (p. 236). Jago, like Adrian Leverkühn, 'dares to be barbaric'. But the barbarism in Jago is that energy which is ultimately directed against flow and desire: it is a parody of that Nietzschean drive which the devil evokes. If I were staging the brindisi, I would make the scene's energies evocative of the controlled chaos of the Nazis in the *Kristallnacht.*

Thus Jago is and is not ironic, is and is not nihilist. Otello is not ironic, and not, therefore, a modern, but may, like Wotan, be nihilistic because of his death-wish, of which more in the next chapter. But Jago is decadent in every sense in which I have used the term so far. Jago as the secret (Italian/African) outside, as he is constructed by the text, fits with a racist ideology, one fearful of the stranger in the midst, fearful of the break-out of degeneracy. As the inside outsider, it is significant that he kills no one—not Emilia, not even Roderigo in the opera (a contrast with the play). It is the Venetians, both the real and the honorary ones, who turn out to be killers—Cassio of Roderigo and Otello of Desdemona. Nor should Cassio's wounding of Montano be forgotten. The outsider makes the Italians come to grief. Or perhaps the point should be that not all Italians are true Italians. They become degenerate in their turn. The ability to show this up, which Jago possesses, is his power of irony. It is an ability that Verdi does not show: hence the constantly ennobling music given to Cassio and Otello, and to the most certainly unironic Desdemona.

Within the smoothness of Boito's adaptation of Shakespeare's play lie many anxieties. Jago is a figure of fascination: in the first act a controller of the crowd, whom he stirs up to fight, Italian against Italian, as he then stirs up Otello, even manipulating him within the crowd scene that closes Act 3. One parallel to Jago might be provided from an example given by Daniel Pick. From 1875, and for ten years onwards, various European cities, including Italian ones, saw performances of a hypnotist called 'Donato', who appeared on stage and magnetized audiences (Pick, *Faces of Degeneration*, pp. 149, 169–70). Donato was the stage name of a Belgian ex-naval officer, D'Hont, who seems to have been a fake, and was eventually unmasked on stage. His theatrical performances may be suggestive for a reading of Mann's novella about fascist control, *Mario and the Magician*, which I will discuss in Chapter 4; but this kind of mass deception is close to what Jago stands for, controlling people, making them do things apparently outside their range of expectations, taking away their autonomy. But perhaps that autonomy was only their self-control.[21]

As opera, *Otello* should have been minatory for Italy. For Jago's doubleness with regard to his nihilism and ironizing and his two forms of decadence points to all that was weak in the fragile Umbertian consensus of liberal-humanist values. It suggests that this humanist façade, symbolized in the marriage of Otello and Desdemona, could not hold; that with pressure applied to it, it would collapse, and that while violence might destroy it, it also ultimately required to be maintained through violence. A further anatomy of that society appears in *Falstaff*, to which I will now turn.

---

[21] The readiness to be deceived, which is a theme of *Otello* and which points to Verdi's own dominant rationalism (his 'positivism'), is brought out by Lombroso becoming a spiritualist in the 1890s, falling under the spell of the Neapolitan medium Eusapia Paladino. It sounds like an episode from Italian opera itself. (See Braun (ed.), *Italian Art*, p. 27.)

3
The Laughter of Falstaff: Comedy and Italian Politics

Verdi's music, or, rather, the libretti and plots of the plays set to music by Verdi, are responsible for a whole range of 'artificial' poses in the life of people, for ways of thinking, for a 'style'. 'Artificial' is perhaps not the right word, because among the popular classes this artificiality assumes naïve and moving forms. To many common people, the baroque and the operatic appear as an extraordinarily fascinating way of feeling and acting, a means of escaping what they consider low, mean, and contemptible in their lives and education, in order to enter a more select sphere of great feelings and noble passions. Serial novels and below-stairs reading (all that literature which is mawkish, mellifluous, and whimpery) provide the heroes and heroines. But opera is the most pestiferous, because words set to music are more easily recalled, and they become matrices in which thought takes shape out of flux. Look at the writing style of many common people: it is modelled on a repertory of clichés.

However, sarcasm is too corrosive. Remember that we are not dealing with superficial snobs, but with something deeply felt and experienced.

Antonio Gramsci[1]

Otello was a national opera, displacing anxieties about the nation-state (fears that these two things might not be the same, that the hyphen might mark a disjuncture) on to the figure of Jago, a terrorist-like, dispossessed figure who subverts the state. But the final Boito–Verdi collaboration seems to displace politics altogether. *Falstaff* (1893) is usually, and rightly, regarded as a little gem of music and text fully integrated, of ensemble rather than of solo writing, finishing Verdi's career in a way that could not have been predicted—comic, not tragic, signing off over fifty years of composing with the fugue where 'tutto nel mondo è burla', so that, we learn, nothing is to be taken too seriously. In this fugue, it seems that Verdi provides a commentary on his own operatic progress. So, in any case, it has been

---

[1] *Selections from Cultural Writings*, ed. David Forgacs and Geoffrey Nowell-Smith (London: Lawrence and Wishart, 1985), pp. 377–8. The whole section, pp. 377–80, which links oratory (cf. fascist oratory) to opera, is relevant.

narrativized, excessively in my view, by Verdian commentators, who are thus allowed, as though on the author's own say-so, to treat his art as self-enclosed, autonomous, unrelated to history or to the 1890s in Italy. If, however, *Otello* circulates appropriately amidst discourses at work in Umbertian Italy, then *Falstaff*, six years later, should not be omitted from consideration of its relation to those discourses too. I think, in fact, that the greater smoothness of *Falstaff* is linked to the greater intensity of the political issues involved in that last decade of the century, the sense that more is at stake. Having argued that, I want to finish off my comments on Verdi by returning briefly to *Otello*.

The idea that in *Falstaff* Verdi wishes not to connect the text to anything else, that it exists as a delightful comic exercise in isolation from the world he had retired from, is itself suggestive of a politics. 'Tutti gabbàti' (all are deceived) provides a formal closure to the text, thus implying that nothing that comes before should be taken too seriously. The wonderful ending of the first scene of the second act, with Falstaff and Ford exchanging politeness before going out of the door to the swanky march that laughs at them both, is a perfect example of what this opera does so well: ironize nearly all attitudes—though, significantly, not those of the lovers. The debt in this ending to the Susanna/Marcellina exchanges in *The Marriage of Figaro* is noticeable, but the wish to ironize seems basic to late Verdi, which might make him a 'modern'. But *I Pagliacci*, first staged nine months earlier, had also played on the idea of life as no more than art: 'La commedia è finita' concludes that text by suggesting that the role of the clown is the one played at all times by everyone. Such an assumption of role playing which necessitates self-ironizing may well belong to bourgeois Italy's 1890s sense of lacking a place and a role: could the serio-comic opera of Italy in Ethiopia be taken at face value internationally?

Italy was governed by the flamboyantly operatic Crispi (1887–91), by di Rudini (1891–2), and by Giolitti (1892–3), who was followed again by Crispi in December 1893 until the news from Adowa came through in 1896. While the country pursued its African adventure, it was also caught by elements at home that would destroy the ability of that conservative–liberal society to hold any consensus. Both Crispi and Giolitti were compromised, and Giolitti brought down, by the Banca Romana scandals, which broke in 1892 and continued in 1893. (They had been implicit as scandals since 1889.) Further bank crashes, the Credito Mobiliare (November 1893) and the Banco Generale (January 1894), added to the sense of Italy having no credit-worthiness. Then there was socialism—the Italian Workers'

Party had begun in 1882 in Milan, and its growth was rapid—and there were the fasci, groups of workers concentrated in Sicily whose strength was first manifested in Palermo in 1892. The first Fascio dei Lavoratori, a peasant organization suffering from loss of profits on sales of wine, fruit, and sulphur, was founded in Catania by Giuseppe de Felice Giuffrida, a local politician of the left. Other groups followed in Palermo and other Sicilian towns: there were 162 groups by October 1893. Importantly, the Fasci dei Lavoratori and Fasci Siciliani marked the beginning of a new political meaning for the Latin word *fasces*, rods or branches carried round an axe, and carried by lictors (executioners) as a mark of power. To cede the *fasces* was to acknowledge the authority of another. And *fasces* could also mean a crowd. The obedience of the crowd, and the popular nature of fascism, its reliance on a popular party, are both implicit within this etymology. Nor was this the first time that the fasci had appeared in Italy: a popular nationalist, Garibaldi-inspired party existed in Bologna in 1872, and a League of Democracy in 1879, founded under Garibaldi, who died in 1882. This was revived in 1883 as the Fascio della Democrazia, on a ticket opposing Depretis and Italian foreign policy and parliamentarianism and 'trasformismo' (that is, Italian consensual politics).[2] The fasci of southern Italy, unrepresented in such a popular northern opera as *Cavalleria Rusticana*, were not industrialized, unlike the socialists of Milan or the north, who consequently resented them for their peasant status, their anarchism, and their contradictory allegiance to the monarchy and to the Church.

From May 1893 onwards, under Giolitti, the leaders of the fasci were liable to be arrested, with the military being sent into Sicily. Crispi himself was Sicilian, and, with working-class support, had been Sicily's most popular politician, but the new fascist leaders in Sicily supplanted his popularity, so that, as the new Prime Minister, with something of a personal resentment against them, he declared martial law in Sicily in January 1894, and suppressed the movement. De Felice was imprisoned for eighteen years; the socialist party was dissolved; and the Catholic Church was evoked to help fight disorder. The result was a series of anarchist bombings from that year onwards, including the assassination of Umberto in July 1900. Fear of revolution is present in Giordano's *Andrea Chénier* (1896).[3] Giordano (1867–1948), himself a southern composer, had in *Mala Vita*

---

[2] See on this Christopher Seton-Watson, *Italy from Liberalism to Fascism, 1870–1925* (London: Methuen, 1967), pp. 68, 96, 157–63.
[3] I have quoted Bruno Corra in *Gli intellettuali creatori e la mentalità fascista* (1923) on fascism's opposition to the French Revolution (see Introduction). The number of operas with a French Revolution or Napoleonic setting all written by Illica might be considered in this light: *Andrea Chénier*, *Tosca*, his

(1892) dealt with such verismo themes as tuberculosis and prostitution and the Naples working class. (Such an opera could not have expected a good reception in a country fearful of its ability to sustain national unity between the north and the poor south—and it was not popular.) Giordano may be seen to become more conservative-reactionary in the operas that follow, as also in his life under fascism. That is illustrated in *Fedora* (1898), his opera about anarchism. The action is set in Russia, immediately after the nihilists' assassination of Alexander II in 1881. Sardou's play, which formed the basis for Giordano's opera, was first staged in 1882 as a vehicle for Sarah Bernhardt (along with her Tosca and Cleopatra and Théodora—and what might have been her Salome, on similar lines, for Oscar Wilde, if the production had taken place). These parts present the noble, if not regal, woman, who has flights of grand passion, which drag her lovers down with them. In *Fedora*, the situation provided an opportunity for the representation of anarchism at La Scala; here anarchism, represented by Count Loris Ipanov, is romantic and upper class, so not at all connected with class struggle, and it succumbs to the force of love. Further, the dangerous figure is the woman (the point holds also with Tosca), not the man, and the opera shows her taking poison at the end and dying, as in all the vehicles for Bernhardt. The impassioned woman's death scene allows for melodramatic excess, but also recontains the passion.

Looking at the 1890s and Verdi's part in that decade, the conception of Falstaff can be seen to be an indirect result of the various contradictions represented by such a politician as Crispi, a Sicilian adventurer and a Garibaldian six years younger than Verdi, who died the same year as him. His energies are the faded remnants of the corsair spirit of Simon Boccanegra, himself possibly owing something to Garibaldi. In 1895, two years after the opening of *Falstaff*, Crispi was formally attacked by his former ally, Felice Cavallotti, with a list of all the crimes he had perpetrated in office and before. Crispi, whom Italian fascism took as one of its precursors, and who turned to further and further authoritarian and bloody measures against the socialists and the fasci, could be accused of virtually every sin. He had been charged in 1878 with bigamy, which had kept him out of politics for some years; he was accused of having been a pro-Bourbon lawyer before 1860; he had been a physical coward during Garibaldi's Sicilian adventure; he had been

planned *Maria Antonietta* for Puccini, and Franchetti's *Germania* (1902). It is an interesting footnote to *Andrea Chénier* that the French fascist Robert Brasillach, while in prison awaiting execution, identified with this poet (linking the Revolution to the French Resistance and the Liberation, and himself to the aristocrat)—see David Carroll, 'Literary Fascism or the Aestheticizing of Politics: The Case of Robert Brasillach', *New Literary History*, 23 (1992): 697.

involved in the Banca Romana scandals; he had been implicated in corruption with a view to personal gain by getting Umberto to give Italy's highest decoration to Cornelius Herz, the partner of Baron de Rheinach, the villain of the seedy company that had been building the Panama Canal until it was bankrupted in 1889, with its leaders sentenced in France—at the same moment (February 1893) as the opening of *Falstaff*.[4] The parallels with Falstaff's sins, smaller scale no doubt, need little underlining, and all these points about Crispi were well known in the Italy of the 1890s, long before Crispi was faced with them—and faced them down. His 'artistic life', as Cavallotti called it (Thayer, *Italy and the Great War*, p. 69), survived, but even it could not live down the defeat at Adowa.

In Crispi's (Falstaffian) career we see something of that 'controlled chaos' that J. P. Stern sees as characteristic of fascist Germany, and which I began to illustrate as a concept by reference to the brindisi in *Otello*. The authoritarianism does not go with control and order: the state tolerates illegalities, and goes above the rule of law; state institutions are conflictual, each with each, in an incoherence which seems systemic and structural. As Stern puts it, ' "there was always something going on" is the phrase on the lips of people who, in Germany today, try to convey the atmosphere of the Third Reich to those who did not experience it.'[5] Fascism was helped to survive in power by constant political activity that was never quite out in the open, with the overall incoherence that results. And *Falstaff* similarly works by something 'always going on' in it: in its rush and bustle of plot and counter-plot, each scheme planned and carried out without the full knowledge of other parties who might normally be expected to be a part of it. If Stern's formulation is suggestive for the fascist state, it works too for the Italy of which Crispi was Prime Minister, which is why the analogy with *Falstaff* seems relevant. If this chaos suggests a nihilism—the rule of law is not observed because there is actually no commitment to rationality—this maps on to one dominant image in *Falstaff*, that of bankruptcy. Falstaff's empty purse and Dr Caius's pocket picked while asleep come to mind; and personal 'honour' is declared no more than an empty word, 'aria che vola'. Bankruptcy and nihilism take many forms, some literal. The sense of loss of credit from the collapse of capitalist enterprises in the 1890s fits with this opera, just as *Die Fledermaus* (1874) with its theme of one last waltz before the bourgeois goes to prison fits with the collapse of the Vienna

---

[4] See John Thayer, *Italy and the Great War* (Madison: University of Wisconsin Press, 1964), ch. 3, pp. 74–5 for the Cavallotti/Crispi confrontation.

[5] J. P. Stern, *Hitler: The Führer and the People* (London: Fontana, 1975), pp. 114, 117.

stock-market, when a hundred firms were declared insolvent on one day, 8 May 1873. But the lack of credit also had to do with the very claims to legitimacy of the post-Risorgimento liberal Italy, where right and left—Crispi had been identified with the republican left—spoke the same language of protection of middle-class interests, and were identified with compromise. As far as both nationalists and socialists were concerned, conviction politics seemed squeezed out.

As an operatic text, *Falstaff* comes down on the side of the middle-class inhabitants of Windsor, and its resolution allows the Crispi-like hero both his afflatus, his ability to live above the rule of law, and his incorporation into the middle-class world. If *Falstaff* is uncommonly silent on political matters, as is virtually no other Verdi opera save *Otello*,[6] it may be worth thinking of the politics of Crispi's and Umberto's Italy being displaced in the text: not referred to openly, but everywhere present in the bankrupt Falstaff making another bid for credit and credibility by courting the middle-class world. Yet this displacement, although it is a necessary aspect of all discourse (since there is always a gap between what can be represented—in terms of what counts as representable, or realistic—and the actual conditions of history), also exhibits a retreat from political seriousness. It can work only by choosing to be superficial, by not looking at anything but the middle-class world, and by a text that confirms pleonastically at the end what has been known from the beginning. There are no surprises in this opera; nothing is discovered; there is no comic recognition. This retreat is evident when *Falstaff* is compared with, say, the strongly politically conscious *Marriage of Figaro*, whose musical influence we have noted, as it appears in the night music of the last scene or in the bustle of Act 2, scene 2. The separation between art and life that *Falstaff* promotes—which is aestheticism—is found again in the comic operas of Strauss. Indeed, Wagnerian, Verdian, and Straussian comedies all exhibit a deepening textual repression by comparison with Mozart, a repression of politics, deepening in accordance with their historical moment of writing.

Such repression of the political is intrinsic to some other Italian operas of the 1890s. Mascagni's peasants may be intended to represent ordinary life, but they have nothing to say that we might expect from Sicilians in the 1890s at the very moment when agrarian failure was pushing peasants off the land and into the fasci organizations, or into emigration. Verismo involves a textual repression: the peasants are less interesting than, for instance, those presented in the prelude to

---

[6] See on this Paul Robinson, *Opera and Ideas: From Mozart to Strauss* (Ithaca, NY: Cornell University Press, 1985), ch. 4.

Don Carlos (the episode dropped before the first night in Paris). It looks like kitsch; the futurists regarded it as vulgar. D'Annunzio tried to make it more intense, less picturesque, in the *La Figlia di Iorio* (1906). But political issues and opera are kept apart: it is not surprising that *La Bohème*, three years after *Falstaff*, should have excised a reference, however mocking, to the radical thought of the bohemians in Paris or any attempt to link them seriously to the Commune and the events of 1871, attempts which would have put radical politics back on the agenda of a group who, as they were constituted in France (and as the *scapigliatura* in Italy), were indeed political.[7]

In such circumstances, where bourgeois art cannot comment, perhaps because it cannot afford to on its own conditions of discourse, the interest turns to the historical, and the sets for the first Milan production of *Falstaff* show a detailed recreation of an imaginary English Elizabethan Windsor, something which later English and New York productions have followed through. The designer Adolph Hohenstein travelled to London, Windsor, and Paris in order to research authentic period details for the production. The whole belongs to that 'invention of tradition'[8] referred to in the Introduction in relation to Germany, everywhere discoverable in European nation-states of the last part of the nineteenth century, and evidence of the hold that history had for that century, imposing a sense of a past which could be retreated into and demanding its recreation in the present. In Britain, similar elements of nostalgia for the past are to be found in *The Yeomen of the Guard* (1888), *Ivanhoe* (1891), and *Merrie England* (1902). The past as recreated for *Falstaff* is, firstly, that of England, a country which Italy was flattering and seeking approval from throughout the Umbertian period, particularly in regard to its foreign policy in Africa and because Italy needed Britain for its industrialization, since 90 per cent of Italy's coal was imported from Britain. Comparisons of the English Parliament with the Italian, favourable to the first, were also frequently made by Crispi. (Thayer makes the point that Crispi stressed such comparisons to diminish the authority of the Italian Parliament, and so to

---

[7] See Arthur Groos and Roger Parker, *La Bohème* (Cambridge: Cambridge University Press, 1986), pp. 57, 142–7. For bohemianism in Paris, see T. J. Clark, *The Absolute Bourgeois*, (London: Thames and Hudson, 1973). On the negative reception of verismo opera, seen as a function of mass culture, see Adriana Guarnieri Corazzol, 'Opera and Verismo: Regressive Points of View and the Artifice of Alienation', *Cambridge Opera Journal*, 5/1 (1993): 39–53.

[8] Eric Hobsbawm and Terence Ranger (eds.), *The Invention of Tradition* (Cambridge: Cambridge University Press, 1983).

undermine the fragile democracy Italy possessed: this supports Thayer's general argument that these were the years of the forging of fascist doctrine.)

But the past evoked in *Falstaff* is also that of Italy. Andrew Porter quotes Boito's sense that Shakespeare's *The Merry Wives of Windsor* has a 'clear Tuscan source', since *Il Pecorone*, published in 1558, and from which Shakespeare took his material, was attributed to 'Ser Giovanni' (that is, Boccaccio). The *Decamerone* (2. 7) gives the source for the lovers' lines 'Bocca baciata non perde ventura / Anzi rinnova come fa la luna'. Accordingly, the libretto contains suggestions of a choice of words derived from the Italian Renaissance.[9] As with *Otello*, the aim is to produce an official art, fitting the positive presentation of Italian history. Significantly, the lovers' words turn out to be traditional—as though the wish were to suggest that this bourgeois world of smug wives and jealous and respectable husbands could also be productive of Petrarchan love, instead of what seems more likely, a materialistic culture. Fenton, the aristocrat, is idealized in a way that Shakespeare's play refuses. The attempt to bring together love and bourgeois values suggests that the past is being elevated into an imaginary wholeness, like the apparent seamlessness of the music, while the present, with its politics, drops out.

SHAKESPEARE TO VERDI: NATIONAL THEATRE, NATIONAL OPERA

The 'seamlessness' occurs as the music rushes on with no pause for introspection. Here it is necessary to say something about *The Merry Wives of Windsor*, but, as with *Otello*, not to comment on how Verdi might have understood his source material, but to offer a reading which may raise questions about the text and so promote an active reading of *Falstaff*—by which I mean one that does not begin by assuming as a matter of course the success of the opera, as though criticism were called upon only to comment on its excellences. Thus I assume some points about Shakespeare's play which, though not beyond argument, seem fairly likely. *The Merry Wives* was written for performance on 23 April 1597 at the St George's celebrations in Whitehall at which the names of the knights to be elected to the Order of the Garter were revealed, the celebration taking place two months later at Windsor. Hence the final masque, at the climax of which Falstaff is pinched,

---

[9] Andrew Porter, 'Translating Falstaff', in John Nicholas (ed.), *Falstaff* (London: John Calder, 1982), pp. 47 ff.; see also James Hepokoski, *Falstaff* (Cambridge: Cambridge University Press, 1983), pp. 29–30. On Verdi generally, any commentator must be much in debt to Julian Budden's three volumes, *The Operas of Verdi* (London: Cassell, 1973–81).

contains lines celebratory of the Order of the Garter (5. 5. 38–80). It may be that this writing of the play also included the commission, from Queen Elizabeth, to write a play with Sir John Falstaff in love in it, and it seems likely that the character of Falstaff had already appeared in *1 Henry IV* (1596) and that *2 Henry IV* was interrupted to write *The Merry Wives*, *Henry V*, which records the death of Falstaff, being written in 1599.[10]

Now this suggests that the play itself is in the service of a nationalism and contributes to an ideology of 'Merrie England'. Perhaps all *fin de siècle* texts are liable to such things: just like the opera commissioned by Genoa in 1892, Franchetti's *Cristoforo Colómbo* (1892), a grand opera in Meyerbeer–Wagnerian style dealing with the colonial encounter of 1492, which Verdi advised on for the choice of composer. In the case of *The Merry Wives*, the Garter celebrations in 1597 belong to that same determination to preserve the imaginary unity of the nation-state. (The Order had been set up in 1350, Edward III wanting to re-create a past chivalry, that of King Arthur's court.) In the play, Welsh and French speakers (Sir Hugh Evans, omitted in Verdi, and Dr Caius), appear in order to permit laughter at the idea of foreigners attempting to speak what was already, by 1597, called 'the king's English' (1. 4. 5). Similarly, the characters in the play are identifiable types, as though offering a picture of bourgeois England in a state of unity. There is even the suggestion that tradition is being created, as with the legend of Herne the Hunter (4. 4. 28–38) and his oak-tree, which was certainly productive of further and later legends after 1597. Or take the line that ends the penultimate speech of the play—'let everyone go home / and laugh this sport over by a country fire'. A 'country fire' in Windsor in the 1590s might well have been possible, but it comes across as a boosting of Englishness and of old customs. Nowadays, Windsor is filled with imitation Elizabethan mansions and electric fires especially designed to look like old country logs, and the place is a microcosm of the way in Britain the present tries to pretend that it is still the past: a tendency endemic to English ideology. And the site, Windsor, is itself not reassuring—the contrast with the Eastcheap of the Henry plays is telling indeed. The wives are not feminists who belong with those other Shakespearian figures of resistance to patriarchal rule, such as Viola or the women of *Measure for Measure*, but are blue-rinse matrons of the Thatcher cast, privileged suburban bourgeoisie. This element seems all too much integrated into the opera.

---

[10] On these details of dating, see Jeanne Addison Roberts, *Shakespeare's English Comedy* (Lincoln, Nebr.: University of Nebraska Press, 1979). Quotations from *The Merry Wives of Windsor* are from the Arden edition, ed. H. J. Oliver (London: Methuen, 1971).

Of course, this negative reading over-simplifies. But I am not implying a negative judgement of the play; rather, I am trying to suggest how it mediates contradictions within the discourses it is part of. Falstaff is rejected twice in the plays he appears in: once here and once in *2 Henry IV*. In the context of the history play, his rejection is highly political. But the importance of Falstaff is precisely his relationship to the political, which is why his appearance in a comedy is less interesting than his destabilizing influence proves to be in plays so aware of the nation-state as the two *Henries*.

The point could be put in the terms of the Russian literary critic Mikhail Bakhtin (1895–1965), in his work on the 'polyphonic' or dialogic novel. Falstaff provides the dialogic—that is, non-single, non-unitary—set of discourses that split apart the monological, single-minded, (certainly single in intention) discourses which make up the political realm and which Hal tendentially but finally accedes to in *2 Henry IV*. When Falstaff says 'I am not only witty myself, but the cause that wit is in other men' (*2 Henry IV*, 1. 2. 8–9), the words provide an apt illustration of Bakhtin's dialogism. Wit, which implies the awareness of doubleness and the perception of differences within utterance, manifests itself in Falstaff, and thus splits in two all those other tight-lipped utterances of the politicians who, like Hal himself, are actually converted momentarily to a recognition that their utterance is attended by an opposite otherness, the language of the other. Bakhtin stresses that the language of the other haunts any discourse, which means that language in use, as addressed to another, is never singly-voiced, but double, polyphonic. The 'other' voice that speaks in it is, however, repressed in monologistic discourse, the voice of the colonized being one instance, though denial of otherness is a feature of the fascist drive itself. Bakhtin takes the novel, rather than the epic, drama, or poetry, as the art-form most responsive to polyphony; for the novel, whose history he traces back to the classical period, has a low, subversive role, often being disparaged by high-minded guardians of 'literature'. As Bakhtin puts it,

the novel parodies other genres (precisely in their role as genres); it exposes the conventionality of their forms and their language; it squeezes out some genres and incorporates others into its own peculiar structure, reformulating and reaccentuating them.[11]

<hr/>

[11] M. M. Bakhtin, *The Dialogic Imagination*, trans. Caryl Emerson and Michael Holquist (Austin, Tex.: University of Texas Press, 1981), p. 5. Bakhtin discusses Pushkin's *Eugene Onegin* as a typical dialogical novel: on Tchaikovsky's opera (1879) he argues that this 'reaccentuation . . . has had a powerful influence in the philistine perception of this novel's images, greatly weakening the quality of parody in them' (p. 421). The

The novel is always in some degree subversive of 'higher', more intentionally monologistic utterances, beginning by questioning the conditions of utterance that it—and other genres—live by, and it is open to other problematic, unconscious forces that are the conditions of utterance. It could be asked whether this kind of self-reflexivity is possible in nineteenth-century opera.[12]

These comments of Bakhtin fit the case of Falstaff well, since he is the very demonstration of the otherness of speech. Even his famous commentary on honour (*1 Henry IV*, 5. 1. 127–41), which is incorporated into the opening scene of *Falstaff*, is not to be taken as a simple rejection of a code of honour: for it is presented as a catechism, parodying the language of the Church addressing a catechumen, so it exists in a language quite different from Falstaff's—the language of that which is other to him. It is not possible simply to attribute such a parodying speech, containing its own dialogism, to one character, Falstaff. To do so closes a gap that the text's dialogism leaves open. The character Falstaff exists as the interweave of different voices which speak in him; these are deployed in him as wit. But wit itself is described as characteristically produced not from the subject's autonomy, but from outside as though through the effects of drink—this is the topic of the speech made on 'a good sherris-sack', which takes over the person (*2 Henry IV*, 4. 3. 84–124).

The wit of Falstaff in the *Henries*, then, is the name for those strongly other elements in the character that are so destabilizing to the foundation of the nation-state, and which in the late nineteenth century would wreak the possibility of fascism. The destabilizing power means that Shakespeare shows the society he bears such an uncertain relation to rejecting him twice—in the guise of both tragedy and farce. For Hazlitt, the rejection begins in *The Merry Wives*, with the dramatist taking away his wit and eloquence from him. 'Instead of making a butt of others, he is made a butt of by them. Neither is there a single particle of love in him to excuse his follies: he is merely a designing, barefaced knave, and an unsuccessful one' (quoted by Roberts, *Shakespeare's English Comedy*, p. 91). This may overstate the case, but it is suggestive of something emergent in *The Merry*

---

opera he sees as working back towards the monologic, taking away from Pushkin's text its playing with romantic and realist genres.

[12] Verdi seems ambivalent here. In the context of *Aida*, he draws attention to the doubleness of music: 'beneath these lawyer's words [those of Amneris] there is the heart of a desperate woman burning with love. Music is splendidly able to succeed in depicting this state of mind, and, in a certain way, in saying two things at once' (letter, 26 Oct. 1870). Yet this music must be in the service of something consistently dignified, monologic; therefore 'this duet must be lofty and noble, as much in the verse as in the music . . . In other words, nothing common' (quoted by Busch, *Verdi's* Aida, pp. 86, 87).

Wives which does not just come from the generic move from a history play to a comedy. The character of Falstaff generates profound anxieties because of his destabilizing dialogism, but his rejection also produces anxieties, for the whole issue of wit is mapped on to questions of sexuality. The wives' humour affirms a respectability—'wives may be merry and yet honest too' (4. 2. 96). Merriment is thus kept within bounds, in order to preserve a kind of dignity which in Mrs Page, the speaker here, is quite consonant with her highly unscrupulous desire to marry Anne off to Dr Caius for her own respectable reasons, in the same way that her husband schemes to marry Anne off to Slender. These faults, which point up the discreet charm of the bourgeoisie, receive but little punishment in the play, by contrast with the scapegoating of Falstaff.

The wives' opposition to Falstaff takes the form of the wish to 'dishorn the spirit' (4. 4. 63), one meaning of which is certainly to render impotent; Fall-staff as a name suggests the loss of phallic power, and the symbolic, or not so symbolic, pinching of Falstaff at the end implies a dismembering as though Actaeon were being torn apart by his hounds.[13] It evokes the fantasy of the body in pieces that I referred to in Chapter 1. The refusal of carnival and energy and the male fear of castration are linked. Indeed, Roberts (*Shakespeare's English Comedy*, pp. 45–6) goes so far as to suggest that the name of the character was modified in the writing of the *Henries* and the *Merry Wives* from Oldcastle to Falstolfe to Falstaff in symmetry with the moves towards a complete rejection of Falstaff as a figure of impotence;[14] this would make a bourgeois puritanism overcode the political censorship that might also have dictated the change. It fits that the second trick played on Falstaff involves his dressing up as the old woman: it is a cross-dressing (man into woman) unprecedented in Shakespeare, though it recurs in the last scene with the duplicated tricks played on Slender and Dr Caius, one of which is used in *Falstaff*. But Falstaff's feminization is not included in *Falstaff*: noticeably, no such anxieties exist in Verdi's opera. (If we wished to maintain the contrast of this opera with *Figaro*, we might note how much cross-dressing is an important element of that text and part of its characteristic subversion of roles, both sexual and social.)

Even more than in Shakespeare, the wives are impeccably middle class in their humour; after the scherzo that Alice sings, 'Gaie comari di Windsor! è l'ora / L'ora

[13] For the Actaeon illustration, see John M. Steadman, 'Falstaff as Actaeon: A Dramatic Emblem', *Shakespeare Quarterly*, 14 (1963): 231–44.

[14] The topic of the mutations of Sir John Oldcastle to Sir John Falstaff through three or four plays is controversial; see Gary Taylor, 'The Fortunes of Oldcastle', *Shakespeare Survey*, 38 (1985): 85–100.

d'alzar la risata sonora!' (Merry wives of Windsor, it's time, time for raising the loud laugh), comes her declaration of bourgeois limits:

> E mostreremo all'uom che l'allegria
> D'oneste donne ogni onestà comporta
> Fra le femine quella à la più ria
> Che fa la gattamorta.

(We'll show the men that the joy of honest women carries all honesty; amongst women the worst is the one who plays the hypocrite.)

The laughter will not be subversive, as Bakhtin suggests its power to be: it imposes no threat to patriarchy, but protects it. These wives have little to do with, say, Nora, in Ibsen's *The Doll's House* (produced in Milan in 1891). 'La risata sonora' is as far as it could be from the laughter of Kundry or of Iago. To invoke *The Marriage of Figaro* again for comparison, the tricks that Susanna and the Countess plan to play on the Count, inevitably involving Figaro as well, imply strong threats to male hegemony, which Figaro's fourth act aria, 'Aprite un po' quegli occhi', registers with its minatory horns in the orchestra, as does virtually all the Count's music. The laughter of Susanna is feared by both the Count (Act 3) and Figaro (Act 4). In the speed and lightness of *Falstaff*, where issues and music flash by breathlessly, as though avoiding inspection, there is no place for the women to assert any sexually independent position in regard to the male. The issue is left as silent as it was with Desdemona in *Otello*.

There is very little rejection of Falstaff in the opera, because at no point do his schemes come near to penetrating the carapace of middle-class culture. Adultery, as a transgression of bourgeois sensibility, and therefore so much at the centre of bourgeois plots in nineteenth-century texts, appears in Umbertian opera in working-class or peasant and marginal groups, in those treated of in *Cavalleria rusticana* and *I Pagliacci*. There is no chance of anything transgressive happening 'dalle due alle tre' in *Falstaff*, despite the musical paralleling this verbal motif. Ford may think that adultery is on the go between two and three, and Falstaff in the last scene may think of trying it with two at once, so making three . . ., and the 'jealous' aria may give the possibility of adultery a little credibility, but as regards this aria, I think it is relevant that Julian Budden sees this aria as a throwback to a convention that Verdi had mastered very much earlier. To take the aria 'É sogno? o realtà' as a piece of convention, its placing justified because of the Shakespearian insistences on Ford as jealous, seems to me to emphasize that anxieties about the sexual have been kept out: bourgeois stability is preserved, and Ford soon forgiven.

In *Falstaff*, both wit and sexuality are diminished. Let us go back to those two speeches of Falstaff I alluded to in discussing the Shakespearian character: about 'honour' and 'sherris', to pick upon the wit. The 'honour' speech is used by Boito in the first scene, though the 'honour' discussed in the play is part of a knightly order, and is not the same as the personal, middle-class honour which Pistol and Bardolph lay claim to in Boito's text and which Falstaff, like any venture capitalist, has none of, and is happy to dissociate himself from. In this context, the sentiments of the speech are indeed to be taken as Falstaff's, and the effect is a narrowing of the character—in fact, the loss of those elements of dialogism which set off the Shakespearian creation. The 'sherris-sack' speech appears in the opening to Act 3, for there drink rises to the brain

> e quivi risveglia il picciol fabbro
> Dei trilli; un negro grillo che vibra entro l'uom brillo.
> Trilla ogni fibra in cor, l'allegro etere al trillo
> Guizza e il giocondo globo squilibra una demenza
> Trillante! E il trillo invade il mondo!

(and there wakens the little maker of trills; a black cricket [or trick] that vibrates in the man lit up. Every fibre in the heart trills, the joyful air quivers to the trill and a trilling madness upsets the joyful world. And the trill invades the world.)

Trills were heard at the climax of the passage on honour, as part of the whole ironic structure of that solo, as they appear here, gradually taking over the whole orchestra. They are a basic motif of the opera, allied to those orchestral moments which celebrate laughter, such as in the march that celebrates Falstaff's sense of his own phallic power before 'Va' vecchio John'. In *Otello* the trill belonged to Jago's music, and Frits Noske comments on its function there: it 'often leaves the impression of a jeer, but also pictures gentle persuasion. In the drinking song and in the third-act terzetto it may have the ambiguous meaning of both playfulness and devilry.'[15] There may be the intention to connect elements of Falstaff with Jago's irony and nihilism (as in the 'honour' solo). Jago's music moves towards Falstaff's in his brindisi. Falstaff's words echo the brindisi specifically in the common word 'brillo' (Falstaff the Dionysian), while the 'negro grillo' even

---

[15] Frits Noske, *The Signifier and the Signified: Studies in the Operas of Mozart and Verdi*, 2nd edn. (Oxford: Clarendon Press, 1990), p. 149.

suggests the black as the subversive and necessary, as though rewriting or revising the tragically intense nationalism of *Otello*. Yet these moments of a Nietzschean gay science are momentary. Laughter, which breaks up strict operatic form, connects in Jago with his nihilistic subversion of bourgeois marriage. But there is a diminishing here to a humour where the trill corresponds to the concept of wit that does not shake the certainties of the bourgeois.

As for sexuality in Verdi's opera, to add to wit, we must return to the play for a moment. In *The Merry Wives*, Falstaff begins the last scene by appearing 'with a buck's head', which may imply that, like Bottom in *A Midsummer Night's Dream*, his metamorphosis goes further than just wearing horns; he has become something other than what he was, the personified animal who, in contrast to what happens to Bottom in the *Dream*, is attacked, not seduced, by the Fairy Queen. The elements of fantasy and masque and bourgeois reality are overlaid on each other, and while Falstaff's second disguise in the play (this one being a further descent from the old woman of Brainford) belongs to his rejection, it also suggests how he cannot be considered in single, monological terms: he is what his disguises imply.

Disguise, like wit, breaks up the unitary, centred self. Verdi's last scene, set under the oak where, in legend, the Black Huntsman hanged himself, seems to quote from Act 2 of *Un Ballo in maschera*, where Riccardo and Amelia meet at the foot of the gallows at midnight: the conjunction of death and fertility, derived from the semen of the hanged man ('Where it falls, mandrakes grow': *Waiting for Godot*), is suggestive. But the issues of adultery, with which that earlier opera deals at so many levels, ending the act with the fine comic irony that the conspirators celebrate in the wonderful laughter of 'E che baccano sul caso strano', mocking the idea of married love, are here softened, and the language of wooing of Falstaff to the wives is made considerably more genteel in Boito than in Shakespeare.[16] The sexual is swallowed up in the romantic in the relationship of Fenton to Nanetta. And the scapegoating of Falstaff is also softened and made harmless. His own words about wit, which I quoted earlier, appear when he sings these words having recovered from his discomfiture: 'Son io che vi fa scaltri. L'arguzia mia crea l'arguzia degli altri' (It's me who makes you smart. My wit creates the wit of others). 'Son io' is sung three times, ascending the scale for each repetition, and the delaying, climactic utterance releases itself in laughter in the orchestra as he

---

[16] Gabriele Baldini refers to Boito's 'preciosity' in relation to his libretto for *Otello*, in *The Story of Giuseppe Verdi*, trans. Roger Parker (Cambridge: Cambridge University Press, 1981), p. 123.

descends slowly and then rapidly down the scale on the final line. In Verdi the words provide the moment whereby Falstaff is enabled to put a gloss on the whole affair, affirming his own victory. If he has been bested, he has provided the weapon of wit himself; so he remains supreme, not entering into any form of dialogism, just as it is he who expands the meaning of the trill. If he sings 'Son io' with such confidence, the text may be seen to keep him as the ultimate patriarch at the centre of those centrifugal forces that are involved in his wit, whereas the last scene of *The Merry Wives* dissolves him into the company and decentres him, suggesting that identity is itself a matter of successive and simultaneous disguises. In centring Falstaff like this, the dialogic goes: this text is careful what it lets in.

But opera starts from a basic and obvious multi-layeredness, so that any opera *could* easily be dialogic, more so than spoken drama: it is words plus music, both visual and aural, as a medium, not a single medium. And if it is plural, double, that would make it 'feminine' in gender terms, recalling the discussions of French psychoanalytic criticism in Chapter 1, where we saw Wagnerian music to be disturbingly feminine. Not only would opera be ambiguous, and therefore outside precise definition; it would also imply that the pluralities of parody and irony belong to the form. The critic and psychoanalyst Julia Kristeva, whose *Powers of Horror* I have referred to, uses Bakhtin's work particularly to associate laughter and parody and women. So opera, when it is comedy, might empower the woman: Kundry's laughter, which she takes to be her curse, is an important subversion of male fantasies. Perhaps Syberberg was right to describe *Parsifal* as a comedy.[17] If opera has the capacity to associate with laughter and parody and doubleness, then it becomes feminine, which is the possibility from which opera as an institution flees, which explains why the form is so massively recuperated as serious, single-minded, and definite in its presentation, to say nothing of its composition. In the Boito–Verdi or Hofmannsthal–Strauss collaborations, much of the thinking between librettists and composers was to bring the two disparate elements of words and music together. Wagner's interventions on the subject of words and music try to keep together its elements of utterance, diminishing the sense of the artificiality of its discourse, though the music may yet allow for a dialogism through its leitmotifs. At stake is the wish to make the discourse seem natural and free, not ideological: which is how any discourse that aspires to be hegemonic wishes to seem. A dominant discourse cannot afford to be seen as

---

[17] For Syberberg, see Eric L. Santner, *Stranded Objects: Mourning, Memory and Film in Postwar Germany* (Ithaca, NY: Cornell University Press, 1990), p. 117. On laughter as associated with women, see Pam Morris, 'Rerouting Kristeva: From Pessimism to Parody,' *Textual Practice*, 6 (1992): 42–3.

parodic, self-questioning, full of laughter at itself and at its mode of utterance, and laughing at the operations of power. Thus the music, as a narrative as well as an expressive force, underlines, rather than questions, the actions on stage.

Such a process is marked in the Verdi–Boito libretto and even some of the music of Verdi that I have discussed: it is not so apparent, perhaps, in some earlier texts, such as *Un Ballo in Blaschera* or *Don Carlos*, where the very intractability of the material forbids it. But in *Falstaff* even the polyphony of the fugal 'tutto nel mondo è burla' dissolves plurality into an overall unity and single meaning. So, like Mascagni's opera *L'Amico Fritz* (1891), it is called a 'commedia lirica'. Feeling—especially that which protects order and patriarchy—is promoted above all in Mascagni, and to a lesser extent in Verdi. And the closure in *Falstaff*, the cutting-out of other elements in favour of a single determinate meaning, also worked in *Otello*, which I want to return to now. *Otello* concludes with the 'bacio' music heard first in the love duet closing Act 1. The kiss motif is heard first in the orchestra, as something Wagnerian, before Otello asks for a kiss: it comes as though from the unconscious, as though it embodied the force of the Schopenhauerian will. Otello is held by something stronger than himself—'la gioia m'innonda sì fieramente' (joy floods over me so fiercely). Within the music of the duet, the love of Otello has been linked with death—indeed, to a death-wish far exceeding anything equivalent in Shakespeare, which has been expressed a little earlier: 'Venga la morte! e mi colga nell' estasi / di quest' amplesso / il momento supremo' (Let death come, and the supreme moment take me in the ecstasy of this embrace). It echoes *Tristan*, and inserts that Wagnerian/Schopenhauerian mood into Italian opera (though Baldini suggests that *Un Ballo in Maschera* is Verdi's *Tristan*).

Thus the return of the 'bacio' theme is heavily suggestive. At the end of the opera, something of its connection with death is more manifest. The music supplies the completion of Otello's last words, 'un altro bacio', and thus suggests union with Desdemona. But this recall is in a context wholly unironic: the whole situation is endorsed by the music. There is no criticism of Otello and of his jealousy; nor is any critique of his suicide possible. The nihilistic aspects of Jago's cruelty, which could be seen as important testings of the nature of this marriage—testings that find it lacking—are negated. In Shakespeare's text, the final self-justifying speech, 'Soft you, a word or two before you go', illustrates how Othello has been bought up by the state. His final words:

> And say besides, that in Aleppo once,
> Where a malignant and a turban'd Turk

Beat a Venetian and traduc'd the state,
I took by the throat the circumcised dog
And smote him thus.

(5.2. 353–7)

indicate that he sees himself as the Turk, and that he reads his offence in killing Desdemona as a sin against the Venetian state. The patriarchy of Venice is the winner. Othello's stabbing himself is, as it were, a circumcision, where this implies a castration, a cutting-away of the self in the final subjection to the imperial power.

The speech is removed in Verdi's opera. The state is gone: Otello is virtually alone on stage. It seems as though this is private, not state, tragedy, as though the state was not there, has receded, as the political recedes in *Falstaff.* We are left with an orchestral endorsement of his suicide, which we have seen to be not separate from his overall death-wish. The motif in the orchestra does not disallow Otello from appearing on his own absolute terms; the death-wish is fulfilled, the closure complete. Where elements of an alternative view of the suicide are denied, where the statements of the text are made so monologic, it seems to me that we are brought back to wonder what desires are held back by such a closure, what anxieties the text conceals here and in *Falstaff.* In *Otello* the final deaths are fatal, but not nihilistic. The death-wish is heroic, which is how the Schopenhauerian argument is accentuated in Italian opera: as a D'Annunzio-like triumph of death. Or, as the lovers sing at the end of *Andrea Chénier,* 'Viva la morte!' *Otello* shows the triumph of a simpler heroism in a bourgeois period of politics: the state is in one sense kept out, perhaps wisely; its contemporary reality is certainly not confronted. But then Verdi could not have foreseen the way in which the death-wish, death as triumph and the cult of the soldier-hero, would have reasserted itself in Italy's reactionary politics.

The forceful combination of orchestral motif and the voice working together as elements in that *Gesamtkunstwerk* that would unite everything in one is tendentially monologistic. That is not, of course, a total truth: Hepokoski (*Otello,* p. 159) finds elements of the love duet in Act 1 in Jago's 'Era la notte' in Act 2, where the context is anything but confirmatory of the attitudes presented in the love duet: instead, these attitudes are warped by Jago's imaginations. Hepokoski also points out that Jago was at one stage to have listened to the love duet. (In *Othello,* Iago does listen to the equivalent dialogue between husband and wife (Act 2, scene 1) and comments 'aside' on it.) While the effect of the return of the duet may work backwards from Jago's solo to imply that the love music was not so simple as all that, in its attitudes towards love and desire between the sexes, none the less, leaving Jago out of the Act 1 scene altogether tends towards a simple, grand ennobling of the marriage. It is also true that the 'bacio' music is not confined to the two appearances discussed.[18] These other appearances qualify an argument about monologism; but there is still a textual and ideological simplification here, or that is the intention, even if the music undoes it. The power of opera as a nineteenth-century discourse lies in its pleonastic forms of utterance, orchestral music backing up the narrative contained in the singing and acting.

Such pleonasm is undone by the spirit of laughter, feared and repressed, tamed in *Falstaff*. Part of the culture of fascism I take to be the need to ensure pleonasm and the homogenizing of utterance. An art-form whose dominant late nineteenth-century expression permitted little self-reflexivity or no more than local irony, smoothing things over in favour of monologism, as these late Verdi operas did, coincides with the more authoritarian nation-state that Italy was becoming under Crispi. It is as though Verdi turns his back on the side of modernity that stresses doubleness, irony, and ambiguity. The Italian state could never exhibit homogeneity and a union of national interests, as was evident in a politics which demonstrated something more like incoherence. Contrasts between outward lack of order and the presentation of total order in public art suggest the use that the state had for an art of homogeneity and of the monologistic. Verdi never provided this consciously, but he fitted the dominant discourse of the 1890s, both as it was and as it wished to be.

---

[18] It is heard harmonically in Desdemona's words to Otello about Cassio, 'D'un uom che geme', in Act 2, and also in distorted form in the orchestral introduction to Act 3, both of which are at a distance from any single meaning that could be ascribed to it. Furthermore, in its two occurrences in Act 4, the 'bacio' music is overlaid with the music associated with the handkerchief, so that what speaks of the doubt in Otello's mind is not overriden, even if its last appearance suggests a moralizing impulse: so much for doubts of Desdemona's infidelity. See Roger Parker and Matthew Brown, 'Rehearings: Late Verdi: "Ancora un bacio": Three Scenes from Verdi's *Otello*', *Nineteenth Century Music*, 9 (1985): 50–62.

4
Puccini and the Swish of Tosca's Skirts

The yearning for modernity that afflicted Italian culture after unification . . .

Bianconi, *New Grove Dictionary of Opera*

Puccini was promoted by Ricordi as the successor to Verdi. But the differences between the two reflect a shift in Italian politics and discourse. One way of describing the differences comes in Mosco Carner's view of the two composers, which is everywhere present in all his writings on Puccini. He takes Verdi's timbre as masculine, Puccini's as feminine. By the 1890s, when Freud began publishing—*Studies in Hysteria* with Josef Breuer, the same year (1895) that Wilde was convicted for homosexual practices (Whose hysteria was this?)—sexuality had been established in medical and legal discourse as something basic and individual in men and women alike, at the foundation of their individual personality, the source of a whole mode of domination whereby perversion, decadence, sickness, and racial impurity would all be mapped on to the sexuality of each individual. If we decided that there was anything 'feminine' about Puccini, it would have to be after recognizing that masculinity and femininity are matters of cultural construction. To be labelled as masculine, or to label oneself that, while it does not assume the possession of any essential quality, entails taking a normative position within the symbolic order whose values are always patriarchal. So to be labelled as feminine means to take a minor role, and to be identified with what lacks stability, the lack of the patriarchal—to be identified with lack itself, according to Jacques Lacan. Hysteria, classically regarded as feminine, was emphasized as such afresh in late nineteenth-century discussions of sexuality. The idea of opera out of control, in which the orchestra 'screams the first thing that comes into its head', as Joseph Kerman refers to the reprise of 'E lucevan le stelle' after Tosca's suicide,[1] makes for an argument that Puccini's texts may be hysterical, also that they reflect his ambivalence about women, having, according to Carner, both a need to destroy

---

[1] Joseph Kerman: *Opera as Drama* (London: Faber, 1956; rev. edn. 1988), p. 15. 'Screaming' is important in Puccini, as in Wagner. See Philip Friedheim, 'Wagner and the Aesthetics of the Scream', *Nineteenth-Century Music*, 7 (1983): 63–70, for the importance of the cry in post-Wagner opera, including *Elektra* and *Lulu*. Freidheim refers to Cavaradossi's cries in *Tosca* as verismo, but says that these 'are categorically different from those of Wagner. Wagner's screams never reflect physical pain, but [are] rather the outburst of pent-up emotions in a sudden outburst' (p. 70).

them but covertly identifying with them. Such an alliance, as it has been worked up in criticism, disadvantages Puccini, since hysteria and the feminine are paired in ideology: compare Wilfrid Mellers's casual reference to Puccini's 'febrile intensity and neurotic self-involvement'.[2] Every commentary on Puccini makes the point that he is in love with all the women he describes in music. That may point to a feminism within his work, which would be very interesting; but since the women in the operas are nearly all destroyed, it may also imply a guilt, which is Carner's point, and a wish to save the male self from the power of the dominating female.

Carner's work is not feminist; it is not hard to find him going back with approval to music which is 'strong-fibred and virile' in a setting 'markedly masculine, brutal, almost machismo' in *La Fanciulla del West*.[3] Nor does his psychoanalytic reading of Puccini as 'feminine' address the question of how femininity is constructed within a culture, existing at a wider level than that of individual psychology. It is not just Puccini who is marked by an emotionality commonly culturally ascribed to women. If he distinguished his *Manon Lescaut* from Massenet's *Manon* with the statement 'Massenet feels [the emotion of the plot] as a Frenchman, with the powder and the minuets. I shall feel it as an Italian—with desperate passion' (Carner, *Puccini*, p. 57), Leoncavallo's libretto for *I Pagliacci* ought also to come to mind: the prologue declares that the text was written 'with sighs and tears', and Canio is supposed to sing 'Vesti la giubba' while sobbing. Very different from the laughter of Jago—or Kundry. It would be possible to take the argument further by asking what subtends the use of the figures of the *commedia dell'arte* in Leoncavallo. (How popular these were to become may be gauged from their use in, for instance, Strauss, Busoni, Puccini, Schoenberg, Picasso, and Severini.) The Pierrot figure, for instance, adapted from Watteau's *Gilles* and given a new circulation by Laforgue in the 1880s, is a modernist creation, but he is anti-Wagnerian in his lack of heroism and commitment to an idea, and suggestive of androgyny. The painting of Lulu in *Erdgeist* shows her in Pierrot costume, for instance: the motif carries through to *Lulu*, which indeed makes more of Lulu as bisexual. The Pierrot desexualizes, dehumanizes, and makes ironic.[4]

In this chapter and the next I want to look at the question of a possible femininity in Puccini's texts. But to broaden the discussion, I will first look at

[2] Wilfrid Mellers, *Music in a New Found Land* (New York: Hillstone, 1975), p. 202.
[3] Quotation from his sleeve-notes to the Deutsche Gramophon recording, 1978.
[4] See Martin Green and John Swan, *The Triumph of Pierrot* (London: Macmillan, 1986).

verismo or Umbertian opera—that of the last decade or two of the nineteenth century—and then at the younger generation of Italian composers who were critical of Puccini, and were indeed fascist. With regard to the first comparison, the question is how such operas as *Otello* (1887), *Cavalleria Rusticana* (1890), *I Pagliacci* (1892), *Manon Lescaut* (1893), *Falstaff* (1893), *La Bohème* (1896), *Andrea Chénier* (1896), *Iris* (1898), *Tosca* (1900) and *Madama Butterfly* (1904) may be considered together, especially if these are regarded as decades in which fascist thought is nascent. If we keep to 'feminine' to describe Puccini, the most popular composer here apart from Verdi, are there implications for considering fascism itself in gender-related terms? In any case, what affinities are there between these works—not the only ones of the decade, of course—and proto-fascist discourse? That Mascagni allied himself with fascism, like Giordano and Puccini to a lesser degree, is interesting but not unexpected.[5] But these individual allegiances are not so much the point if the dominant discourse is itself fascist in tendency. Here fascism will be likely to be the unconscious even of a work that tries to sever its ties from that discourse.

For these were years foundational for fascism. Such historians as John Thayer, Richard Drake, and Dennis Mack Smith emphasize the disillusionment that the successive governments established in Rome after 1871 produced and the whole cult of what Drake calls generally 'the politics of nostalgia'. Middle-class liberal Italy, not successful in foreign policy (e.g. with Africa), nor in uniting the north and south with their separate economic problems, not regarded highly internationally, nor able to stave off working-class unrest, moved more and more towards a nationalism and authoritarianism which was, like Crispi, anti-parliamentary democracy. 'Trasformismo', 'an ugly word for an even uglier thing' according to the nationalist poet and Wagnerian Carducci (Thayer, *Italy and the Great War*, p. 44), was the politics of moving both right and left in Parliament closer to the centre, to that liberal, bourgeois class whose centre was the north, with its roots in Piedmont. It was identifiable as a politics based on positivist values, and positivism was the antithesis of the culture of Carducci, and of the writers influenced by him, including some of the *scapigliatura* group, which included Boito; of Illica, the

---

[5] See Harvey Sachs, *Music in Fascist Italy* (London: Weidenfeld and Nicolson, 1987). See Puccini's letter to Adami of 30 Oct. 1922, the day after the march on Rome: 'What do you think of Mussolini? I hope he will prove to be the man we need. Good luck to him if he will cleanse and give a little peace to our country!' (*Letters of Giacomo Puccini*, ed. Giuseppe Adami, trans. Eva Makin, rev. edn. by Mosco Carner (London: Harrap, 1974), p. 297).

omnipresent librettist of the 1890s and 1900s, of D'Annunzio, or Corradini, founder of the Nationalist Association, or Croce.

One feature of these operas that could align them to a proto-fascist moment is a renewal of violence in them, itself quite shameless, with whipping (*I Pagliacci*), torture (*Tosca*), sexual sadism (a feature of nearly all of them), and unbearable pressure put on the women. There is a concentration on extremity of experience: one Puccini heroine dies in the heat, another in the cold, for instance; and Tosca's death is anticipated by Iris throwing herself down a shaft in a brothel to her death in a sewer below, the same singer, Hariclea Darclée, doing both. There is also the malicious delight in deformity (in *I Pagliacci* the deformity of Tonio evokes both Rigoletto and Alberich and even the grossness of Falstaff, and extends to the husband in Zandonai's *Francesca da Rimini*). Both *Andrea Chénier* and *Tosca* are concerned with rape: Gerard demands that Madeleine gives herself to him in exchange for Andrea Chénier, which she is ready to do in the name of sacrifice; Scarpia finds Tosca less willing to offer herself. Arias conclude with demonic laughter, howls, rage, or weeping. *I Pagliacci*, which ends with a double murder, is more violent than *Cavalleria*, where death at least takes place as the result of an off-stage duel fought for honour. The sense of shock, which Walter Benjamin discusses as the characteristic mode of experience in modernity in his *Charles Baudelaire: A Lyric Poet in the Age of Capitalism*, fits with the shortness (only one act in some cases) of verismo opera. Stressful action belongs to the advent of the detective novel, itself largely a *fin de siècle* development—Jack the Ripper, Sherlock Holmes, and the word 'thriller' all belong to the years 1888–9. Joseph Kerman describes *Tosca* as 'that shabby little shocker' (*Opera as Drama*, p. 205), and quotes Shaw to the same effect on Sardou's original play (ibid., p. xiv).

In what follows I use *Tosca* as a reference point, the Sardou play which might have been set by Verdi and become Verdian, or by Franchetti and become Wagnerian, but which in the event became Puccinian. I try to raise some questions about femininity, and towards the end of the chapter I will situate this in the context of Italian politics and perceptions of Italy as feminine and feminizing. In the next chapter, I will look at the way in which masculinity is constructed in *Madama Butterfly* and *Turandot*.

Tosca was first heard on 14 January 1900 in Rome, the nation's capital, not at La Scala, and before Queen Margherita, Umberto's wife. The presentation suggests a gesturing towards the presentation of an imaginary national unity on the opera stage. *Tosca* was national opera, whose subject-matter mapped straight on to the place of performance, for the church of Sant' Andrea della Valle, the Farnese palace, and the Castel Sant' Angelo are obvious landmarks of Rome. The opera-house mounts art which spectacularly reproduces the nation's monuments, and repro art is to be admired as being as good as the real thing. Reproductions of monumental architecture on stage are likely to appear kitsch and simulacral, and this opera as public or media event aestheticizes politics: the arguments will be familiar from the Introduction. So the Teatro Costanzi in Rome was taken over by the fascist government in 1926, to reopen as the Teatro Reale dell'Opera in 1928.

The running together of art and life is obvious in the details of Puccini taking actual words and music for the church music in the first act, and in the third reproducing the authentic sound of the Matins bells rung from Saint Peter's, climbing Sant' Angelo early in the morning to get the impression of church bells ringing, and looking for traditional shepherds' songs from the Campagna for use at the beginning of Act 3.[6] There is an intentional breaking of the gap between conventional representation and actual reality in the name of further realism. Italian opera, like German music-drama, becomes ritual, ceasing to be at some conventional distance from the audience and becoming something else. *Parsifal* (1882) offers itself as more than opera, the interdiction on performances other than at Bayreuth implying the desire to tie the sacred experience to a particular place which has thereby virtually holy associations. The Ave Maria in *Otello* is similar. Desdemona singing the actual words of a prayer can hardly not appear like a singer out of a Verdi requiem, and the audience must, I think, find that any possible emotional reactions which they possess against Desdemona are removed by the exhibition she offers of traditional Italian piety. Opera becomes the religion of the nation-state as Desdemona appears as an imaginary figure of Italian national unity.

Tosca invites comparison with *Otello* as national opera, but has a different emphasis on the roles of the sexes. Desdemona's piety is subordinated to the much more passional relationships of the men. In *Tosca*, the heroine's name may well connect her to the Italy of public culture: Tosca could recall Tuscany as a name and so the world of Florence (cf. Floria) and the Arno river, quasi-symbol of literary Italian (as when Manzoni said he dipped the language of *I Promessi Sposi* in the Arno); in the figure of Tosca, Italy appears in feminine form. Noticeably,

---

[6] Mosco Carner, *Puccini: A Critical Biography* (2nd edn., London: Duckworth, 1974), p. 108.

this is the first portrayal of an Italian woman in Puccini. Further, in an interesting gender reversal, she is deliberately conceived within the limits set for Otello in Verdi's opera. Scarpia comments on how her jealousy may be aroused: 'Per ridurre un geloso allo sbaraglio / Jago ebbe un fazzoletto, ed io un ventaglio' (in order to bring a jealous man to distraction, Iago had a handkerchief, I a fan). 'Già il veleno l'ha rosa' (already the poison has consumed her), Scarpia's words near the end of Act I, equally recall Jago. Tosca's 'Vissi d'arte' may also recall Otello's farewell to his warrior existence, 'Ora e per sempre addio'. Yet, if the text evokes *Otello*, Tosca's violence, stabbing Scarpia, which represents his 'feminization' in being penetrated, evokes a different set of energies from those Verdi mobilizes. Scarpia's statement of his own decadence, sung while drinking, recalls Jago's Credo, the difference being, however, the omission of the sexual as a motive in Jago, a textual fact which is reversed in Scarpia. His espousal of rape and violence in the sexual realm and rejection of the repertory of effects in lovers' wooing, which, because of their 'mellifluousness', belong in ideological terms to the feminine, points to a determined rejection of the feminine in favour of pure phallic power.

> Ha più forte
> sapore la conquista violenta
> che il mellifluo consenso. Io di sospiri
> e di lattiginose albe lunari
> poco m' appago. Non so trarre accordi
> di chitarra, né oròscopo di fior,
> né far l'occhio di pesce,
> o tubar come tortora!
> Bramo. La cosa bramata
> perseguo, me ne sazio e via la getto,
> volto a nuova esca. Dio creò diverse
> beltà, vini diversi. Io vo' gustare
> quanto più posso dell' opra divina!

(Violent conquest has a stronger flavour than gentle consent. I am little satisfied by sighs and vows at milky lunar dawns. I do not know how to draw harmony from guitars nor horoscopes from flowers, nor to make dalliance [literally, fish-eyes] or coo like the turtle-dove. I crave. I pursue the thing craved, satiate myself of it and cast it away and turn to new allurements. God created diverse beauties and wines. I want to taste as much as I can of these divine works!)

This reading gains momentum from the sounding of the 'Scarpia' motif at 'Bramo' and continued thereafter, the return of an effect which perhaps in its volume suggests an anxiety haunting it, a desire for total maleness, more Giovanni than Don Giovanni. This desire functioning through sound would certainly be the case with Mascagni, who said of his 1921 opera *Il Piccolo Marat* that 'it had muscles of iron. Its power lies in its voice. It doesn't speak, it doesn't sing: it *shouts, shouts, shouts!* I wrote the opera with my fists clenched, like my soul' (quoted by Sachs, *Music in Fascist Italy*, p. 107). The contrast between Mascagni and Leoncavallo, as discussed at the beginning of this chapter, is worth noting; Mascagni wants to be masculine, but the force of the declaration would be dubbed hysterical if it came from a woman.

With Scarpia, compare Gerard in *Andrea Chénier*, who moves politically from left to right, like Mussolini himself. At the beginning of the opera he is the servant whose father is also a servant and whose oppression he is justly angry about; in the later scenes he has become an apparatnik of the French Revolution, in which capacity he lusts after Madeleine, the aristocrat whose mother he served. In a confessional solo derived from Jago's Credo, he sees himself as full of hatred for the idealists of the Revolution, concluding:

> Sono un voluttuoso!
> Ecco il novo padrone: il Senso!
> Bugia tutto!
> Sol vero la passione!

(I am a sensualist! See my new master: the Senses! Everything else is a lie. Only passion is true!)

This excited confession of decadence and nihilism fits with a fascist and proto-fascist exaltation of the instincts and an anti-positivism which refuses any rule of rationality. As with Puccini, the important point about Gerard is not his feeling that he is above passion, which would make him a patriarch within the revolution, but the declaration of being a sensualist, which links him, in ideology, to the feminine, like the people he opposes or loves. To decide that the excitement here is nearly hysterical would be to suggest that late nineteenth-century opera promotes that hysterical sense, a refusal of anything except the senses as they are appealed to in music and spectacle, and a passion that is stirred up through operatic plots and the violence represented on- and off-stage.

Tosca redoes aspects of *Otello*, but without the dominant masculinity—just as the male fear of adultery heard in *Falstaff* receives no comparable accentuation in Puccini, and as Sardou's sexual sadism in the character of Scarpia is actually softened by Puccini, according to Carner (*Puccini*, p. 354). The awareness of sexuality and particularly of the feminine cuts across Verdian assurances, and points to shifts in ideology. Scarpia and Tosca are opposites: in comparison to the investment each makes in the other, Cavaradossi seems unimportant, certainly less commanding than Scarpia. The Act 1 curtain comes down to Scarpia's statement that Tosca makes him forget God; Act 2 concludes with Tosca's meditation on Scarpia's past power, and Act 3 sees her jump with her last lines, insinuating that she and Scarpia will meet again (before God, of course; but I think it is more important that this implies that they are eternal opposites rather than that there will be a final meting out of justice). 'Every woman adores a Fascist' Sylvia Plath wrote in her poem 'Daddy' (*Ariel,* 1963), and the disturbing power of this opera connects with the idea that the woman and Scarpia are necessary to each other. To make a comparison, Conan Doyle in *The Memoirs of Sherlock Holmes* (1892) had Holmes and Moriarty, clutched together as necessary to each other, going over the Reichenbach Falls. Is not Moriarty another figure of both decadence and fascism (the 'Napoleon of crime'): half Nietzsche's *Übermensch,* as conceived within popular culture, and half master criminal? Tosca in the opera jumps to her death with the sense that the fight between her and the dead Scarpia—untouchable by law—is not over yet. The eroticized woman, who lives by the power of her seductive voice, and the policeman who wants to entrap her are connected by the operatic text, which thereby makes the proto-fascism necessary and recurrent, a matter of destiny, and creates a woman who can be the vulnerable yet dangerous object of male fantasies. Scarpia needs to assert his masculinity, for Cavaradossi's descriptions of him as a licentious bigot who refines his lust with religious practices ('bigotto satiro che affina / Colle devote pratiche la foia / Libertina'), while they make him potentially Dionysian in the reference to the satyr, also turn him into something like a fetishist: lust works when supplemented by something other to it. It makes Scarpia a decadent, as I earlier described his credo as being the language of decadence; so it connects fascism with one of the very things that the violence of the fascist aims to destroy. And that decadence is present elsewhere in the opera.

For example, note how *Tosca* draws attention to clothes, specifically women's clothes, throughout—as Act 2 of *Manon Lescaut* defined a meretricious form of empty love by its use of clothes and adornments ('In quelle trine morbide'). Such an interest in clothes and what they conceal and reveal is present even in the poster advertising the first performance of *Tosca.*[7] Here, Puccini sits writing the opera (or

[7] Reprinted as plate II in Martin Cooper (ed.), *The New Oxford History of Music: The Modern Age 1890–1960* (Oxford: Oxford University Press, 1974).

perhaps stands, looking over a garden wall—at any rate, he is visible only from the chest up), quill in his right hand; his left hand is drawn up to his chin in a gesture of contemplation. What he is looking at—what he is inspired by to write—is the woman whose back is turned towards us, her pelvis thrust out towards him. Who is this woman? She is Tosca; she is opera; and Rome, since she invites him with an outstretched hand which carries laurel leaves towards Rome itself: the Castel Sant' Angelo is to be seen in the far distance. An eroticized Rome invites the provincial Puccini to come to the capital, to fame and to national status. Her dress is diaphanous; her gesture that of a singer—that is, theatrical; she wears high-heeled shoes, and her legs are visible beneath her skirts. Our eyes focus on her, and move from her in her veils towards Puccini behind and to her left: our eyes, our gaze, meets his at the point of intersection which is the body of the woman. At the same time, she is somewhat ghostly, as though she evokes the power of the voice, the power of the diva: in which case, there would be a reason for putting together her partial nudity and the voice she symbolizes. Voice and body meet, as in *Doctor Faustus* the musician Adrian Leverkühn describes the voice as 'abstract . . . but . . . a kind of abstraction more like that of the naked body—it is after all, more a pudendum' (ch. 8, p. 70). The singer's pudendum is where our and Puccini's eyes meet—the Puccini created by the discourse that creates this poster.

The poster is not Puccini's work, but it suggests the power of then contemporary discourses to link opera, the erotic, the nationalistic, the cult of the archaic (this is a pastoral world), and the fetishistic, as suggested by the clothes. In the opera, Tosca appears in Act 1 saying that she has heard a woman's dress rustling, and Angelotti's sister intends that her brother, like a true freedom fighter, should make his escape in women's clothes, and has hidden in the chapel a dress, a veil, and the fan, which may well also keep the associations of the fetish, which would explain Scarpia's interest in it. If Angelotti had indeed got away in such a disguise, it would have been an example of the transvestism I drew attention to in discussing *The Merry Wives* and *Falstaff*. Above all, there is a revealing direction in the score as Tosca goes out from singing the love duet with Cavaradossi in Act 1 ('Mia gelosa'). This wonderfully seductive piece ends with her exit, with the strings playing on the bridge, meant to sound, as a note in the score says, 'like the rustle of a skirt'. It is a touch of verismo, to wish to mime the sound of the woman walking out, but it is also suggestive in a metonymic way, implying that the whole music of *Tosca*, especially its lyricism, its constant moving back to the love theme, has an equivalence to women's skirts—skirts to be adored if the woman is the mother, to be played with if they are the lover's. The stress on Tosca's clothes is not confined to this: Cavaradossi's last meditation on Tosca in 'E lucevan le stelle' is on how he 'fremente / le belle forme disciogliea dai veli!' (quivering, loosened the beautiful body from its veils). In the same way, Ping, Pang, and Pong fantasize about Turandot being undressed as a bride and taken behind 'soffici tende' (soft curtains)—'gloria al bel corpo discinto / che il mistero ignorato ora sa!' (glory to the beautiful unclad body now initiated into the mystery!). But the unveiled body of Turandot is still veiled behind the curtains; and indeed in Act 1, the three have sung very slightingly of her body without veils as just 'carne cruda'.

Attention to the body and its veils appears not only in *Tosca* and *Turandot*, but also in Mascagni and Illica's *Iris* (1898), where in the brothel scene the wealthy lover Osaka says to the virginal Iris, 'Oh come al tuo sottile corpo s'aggira / E s'informa di te la flessuosa / Notturna vesta' (How your subtle body is enfolded and suggested by your supple night-dress), and the brothel-owner, Kyoto, puts her into even more skimpy garments, 'in una vesta / Ancor più trasparente di codesta, / come se indosso avesse a veste il nulla, / vedrete qual trionfo di fanciulla' (in clothes more transparent than these, as though she was wearing nothing at all, you will see the triumph of that girl). Here the garments, which are and are not visible, match the sense of Japanese paper walls that are both there and not there. In *Turandot* and *Iris*, and markedly in *Tosca*, where the focus is on 'normal' life, attention to women is not separate from an interest in the fetish, in the clothes which supplement the body and fill out the lack by which the feminine is constituted in patriarchal culture. If the fetish, one of Freud's topics in the *Three Essays on Sexuality* (1905), suggests that male attention to the woman is displaced on to objects or things that stand in a metonymic association with her, it may be added that this need to supplement and to take away from the woman comes about from profound male anxieties about the feminine as lack, thereby suggesting that the truth about masculinity may be that it, too, is constituted by lack.

There are several elements of this fetishizing of the feminine in *Tosca*. Cavaradossi's aria 'Recondita armonia', sung about the portrait of a lady, is an instance. It exists as a lyrical moment in the first part of the act, and is accompanied by the sacristan's comments (an 'operatic' moment which is compromised by a more non-'operatic' voice, an instance, it seems to me, of Bakhtinian dialogism in the text). Cavaradossi celebrates the woman who represents the repentant Mary Magdalene, who has the features of the revolutionary Marchesa Attavanti, and who is painted with Tosca in mind, as the very embodiment of Italian opera in its power to seduce. There could hardly be a more effective setting out of the way women are perceived in late nineteenth-century ideology, of the range of positions that they are allowed to occupy, as icons of religious devotedness, as exemplars of the 'New Woman' of the 1890s, as figures of the Muse. And, significantly, all these are interchangeable in the one portrait, one portrayal of the power of the phallic brush, which claims to be able to represent women, and whose power is represented, as though in a process of synaesthesia, not by painting but by music: Tosca is right to be jealous of Cavaradossi's disclaimers. Moreover, the lyrical moment entails singing not about an actual woman, but about a portrait which thus displaces her. It is an instance of the fetishizing of the woman, and for that reason the sacristan's very limited remarks have their place too in the dialogism—they go a little way towards preventing the total idealization of the woman.

But the voice is the fetish. Tosca, like Mimi and Cio-Cio San, is heard off-stage before she appears. The effect is stronger in *Madama Butterfly*, for, before the singing voice is heard, Sharpless has already described it, giving an account of how she came to the consulate, and he didn't see her, but heard her—'Di sua voce il mistero l'anima mi colpì. / Certo quando è sincer, l'amor parla così' (the mystery of her voice touched my soul; certainly, when love is sincere, it must speak like that). Any voice has much to do to cope with that build-up, that investment in it. In psychoanalytic terms, since this appeals to the priority of ear over eye, it may evoke the omnipresence of the mother's voice, heard before seen and recognized, and suggestive of a power that physical presence does not necessarily have, since the voice is not dependent on it. Similarly, in Act 2 of *Andrea Chénier*, the hero sings of how a woman's voice speaks to his heart, telling him to believe in love, telling him that he is beloved. He also tells of how he has been receiving letters from a woman: later in the act Madeleine appears, and confirms the dream he has had. Puccini and Giordano shared a librettist in Illica, but the similarity is suggestive beyond just this incidental detail: it indicates how the woman, in male representations of her, is built up from parts, from associative aspects which have the function of idealization—of the fetish, in fact. And to note this fetishizing, which is reversed in *Turandot*, where the princess appears first without singing, is to comment on the ambiguity that hangs over everything in Puccini: this is an art which both responds positively to femininity and which also furthers its fetishizing. Negatively, Turandot stands silent, withholding her voice like the mother who withholds the breast in Melanie Klein's psychoanalytic terms—the bad mother who drives the male child towards the father by this gesture. The silence of the mother, in turn, produces the need to fetishize the woman as unknowable.

This ambiguity persists in other related areas of Puccini. For example, does he have a politics as regards Italy? Or a religious position? I will return to the ending of *Tosca* Act 1, marked, exceptionally for Puccini, as 'Finale primo' as if to give it great definition. According to Mosco Carner,[8] Puccini fails to contrast Scarpia's music with the religious tones of the chorus singing the Te Deum: his voice follows the religious drift of the music. This is true, but the related point should be made that the use of the Te Deum is ironic, state ideology being used cynically to support a reactionary monarchy which thinks it is safe from Napoleon. In that sense, religion itself is not at a distance from Scarpia. Taken at face value, which is one way it is intended to be, the Te Deum offers a standard so absolute by which to evaluate Scarpia that any sense of his wickedness must be virtually completely conventional—not, that is, created in any individualistic way through Puccini's art. And, on that face value, the audience are, as it were, being persuaded into a religious experience themselves, where the gap between the actual church of Sant' Andrea and the faithfully reproduced setting of the church on the stage is as nearly closed as possible. Yet matters are not so simple, because of the political motivations underlying state religion. The opera promotes the sense of something like a national experience of unity, and since the text shows that the Te Deum's function is manipulative and ideological, it illustrates how art and religion are both used as part of the ideological state apparatus. Whereas *Otello* suggests that Desdemona's religiosity wins, Tosca's trust in the Church is seen to be deluded and the source of her tragedy, since she cannot be confided in by the revolutionaries: and the Church's power is revealed as cynical and nihilistic.

The anticlerical arguments here, with art being placed against religion in the opening exchanges between Cavaradossi and the sacristan, mediate contemporary debates in Italy at the time and in Catholic Europe about the status of the papacy. The declaration of papal infallibility announced by Pius IX in 1870 came after a decade of antagonism between the forces of the nascent Italian kingdom and the papacy, so that the papacy was to be represented, as by the Ultramontanists, as in a state of siege, against the values of the modern world. In 1864, a papal encyclical had numbered eighty errors associated with secularism and the new Italian state. Both *Don Carlos* and *Aida*, with their different kinds of priest, may constitute a comment on this papal intransigency. After Rome was possessed in 1870, Pius IX excommunicated the founders of the Italian state, and Catholics were forbidden

---

[8] Mosco Carner, *Tosca* (Cambridge: Cambridge University Press, 1985), p. 108.

to vote in parliamentary elections (an edict he had affirmed in 1868, and again in 1874). His successor, Leo XIII (1878–1903), continued a policy of opposition to the state, and was more opposed to socialism; but a change of direction was visible in the 1890s, and the reign of Pius X (1903–14), which condemned Modernism (1907), saw fundamental changes of approach, ending in a pact with the state in 1913. Verdi, Boito, and Puccini were all agnostic; yet it is *Otello* that invests in the power of a specifically Catholic consolation. Puccini's music, more mocking in general, as Ashbrook points out[9]—whether Voltaire-like, alongside Cavaradossi and Angelotti, or Kundry-like—plays on the imagined resolution of Church and State in the first act of *Tosca*. It locates Scarpia's decadence in his uses of religion, and settles for no other consolation than the erotic—as in 'E lucevan le stelle' in the last act; no hymn to art and life, as in the version of Illica's libretto which Franchetti nearly set; nothing that would exalt the political realm. In a sense the mocking tone that Ashbrook notes goes with a form of nihilism.

PUCCINI AND BOURGEOIS SOCIETY

I once thought Puccini reactionary, along with much other Umbertian opera, partly on the basis of Joseph Kerman's arguments, partly for the way he treats his heroines, and also because I could not believe that such popular music could be other than purely establishment-oriented, and therefore unchallenging; but now I am not so sure, and my ambivalence stretches over this chapter and the next. To come to some assessment of Puccini and his politics is important, but it could be better done now by working outside the value-judgements implicit in Joseph Kerman's famous, if negative, reading, which presuppose the possibility of a single coherent way of taking the text, one that does justice to all its features. It might be better to stress the contradictions that mark Puccini's work. Thus there is the determined degradation of the woman in *Tosca*, and the pleasure in showing and describing physical torture, and the death by firing squad of Cavaradossi. These things are not apologized for; the dramatist in Puccini is drawn to them for their theatricality. Does the sadism perhaps make *Tosca* a proto-fascist text? But then what of the 'real' proto-fascist, Scarpia? (And if we find verismo opera inherently reactionary, is there nothing to be said for Mascagni using contemporary peasant life as opposed to romantic historical figures, such as those in *Otello* or *Falstaff*?)

[9] William Ashbrook, *The Operas of Puccini* (Oxford: Oxford University Press, 1985), p. 26.

The beginning of a response might come by returning to the comparison with the 'masculine' Verdi. There, ultimate power is in the hands of the patriarchy; but in Puccini, through the melodramatic plots sanctioning violence against young innocents, patriarchy is thoroughly undone, as with Scarpia. *Tosca* is anticlerical, anti-police, and revolutionary, 'Volterrian' like Cavaradossi. To the tragedies of Tosca and Cavaradossi and Angelotti must be added Napoleon's success at Marengo and the power of the off-stage figure of the Marchesa Attavanti, whose impact is marked, since Cavaradossi is painting her, and who disturbs both Tosca and the patriarchal world of reactionaries by the force of her beauty. Verdi's operas are historical dramas in which the heroes are aristocratic soldiers or princes. Bourgeois opera of the nineteenth century receives from Verdi heroic figures whose relationship to economic production is gracefully avoided: the move to Shakespearian drama at the close consolidates the tendency to bracket off these matters from consideration (it is hardly necessary to worry how Falstaff will survive financially). Puccini's texts, like those of other Umbertian operas, seem much more aware of economic determinants, and Rodolfo, Andrea Chénier, Cavaradossi, and Tosca, for instance, are presented as artists, a 'feminine' kind of occupation, which puts them on the margins of their society. *La Traviata* antici- pates *La Bohème* in some ways, but does not seem an exception to this charac- terization of Verdi, where the life of the *demi-monde* is made respectable by the values of the bourgeoisie. Alfredo redeems Violetta temporarily to a bourgeois existence, in which she in turn quells his (no doubt sexual) ardent spirits ('spiriti bollenti'); but the text allows her to return to the *demi-monde*, meaning that she has not been redeemed really: that is her place, high though the price of her suffering is. She does not belong in bourgeois society. By contrast—with the influence of *Carmen* strong here—there is no moving out of the bohemianism of *La Bohème*. Indeed, it is implied that there is nowhere to go. The point made about patriarchy in Verdi may be extended by saying that while *La Traviata* endorses sacrifice to the predominant bourgeois shapes of life represented by Germont, Alfredo's father, these shapes being the pattern of societal order which is always ultimately endorsed, there is, by comparison, no normative societal order in Puccini; there are only exploiters or representatives of the young and innocent and feminine. Thus the solitary scene for Manon Lescaut and the student des Grieux which closes the opera of that name, while it witnesses their defeat, also testifies to the absence of the social. Mosco Carner's point (*Puccini*, p. 322) that the music for des Grieux and Manon Lescaut is interchangeable only stresses the linking of the feminine with the bohemian in society in Puccini's thinking.

Rodolfo and Andrea Chénier alike sing of love as the highest value—in Giordano's opera as being revolutionary—rather than bourgeois values.

In *Falstaff*, there is a normative, controlling bourgeois society, whose existence mediates problems in late nineteenth-century Italian government. But its absence in Puccini marks out his work in several ways, and is suggestive of an attitude towards Italy which makes him more decisively modern. It is no coincidence that Puccini, like Franchetti (whose fascist attitudes appear in his 1922 opera *Glauco*), was well known for his love of cars and speed. As an embryonic futurist, his interest in machines marks him out as modern. Scarpia's disdain for moonlight and serenades also marks him out as interested in speed. And Puccini's modernity was self-conscious: a letter of 18 March 1920 refers to creating 'a *Turandot* by way of the modern mind', and fits with his attitude to America. In 1906, Puccini wrote that 'to look to the future of opera one has to look to America'.[10] *La Fanciulla del West* was one of the first major European operas to have been premièred at the New York Metropolitan (10 December 1910). The date is of more than casual interest: Virginia Woolf, thinking of Britain specifically, wrote that 'on or about December 1910 human nature changed . . . All human relations shifted—those between masters and servants, husbands and wives, parents and children. And when human relations change there is at the same time a change in religion, conduct, politics and literature.'[11] (But it is also important that Italy held its first nationalist congress, with Corradini, in December 1910: with a different kind of modernism being preached, of readiness for war, along with nostalgia for 'Italy'.) *La Fanciulla* was the eventual work 'modern in construction' with which 'to go on, but *on*, not back' to succeed *Butterfly* (23 Feb. 1905, *Letters*, p. 167). Consideration of the modernity of *La Fanciulla* begins with its reaccentuation of Italian opera in the displaced setting of the West, a liminal space, which is temporary in character because of the shifting fortunes of people there, as though it were being seen under the influence of speed. But *Il Trittico* also opened at the Metropolitan, and *Turandot* at one time was thought of for the same opera-house. An American, David Belasco, provided the plays for both *Madama Butterfly* and *La Fanciulla*, and another was proposed at the time of the gestation of *Turandot*. Study of Puccini's fascination with America, of which more in the next chapter, could begin by considering the last act of *Manon Lescaut* in comparison to Massenet's

---

[10] See Maria F. Rich, 'Opera USA Perspective: Puccini in America', *Opera Quarterly*, 2 (1984): 31. The whole issue is devoted to Puccini.
[11] Quoted in James McFarlane and Malcolm Bradbury (eds.), *Modernism* (Harmondsworth: Penguin, 1976), p. 33.

setting, which does not leave France. In Puccini's opera we see negative fascination. But the equivocal attitude persists and shifts, going along with the massive
scale of Italian emigration to the United States in these very years. Economically,
Italy was demonstrably inferior to the United States, including the rates it could
afford to pay singers such as Caruso, who sang in New York (as also in Buenos
Aires) for far higher fees than La Scala could manage. And the question this
prompted—important also for Italian nationalists—was, *Where was Italy's centre?*
Or even, *Where was Italy?* Could it be identified in any complete sense with the
peninsula which had been unified in 1870? (Wagner's readiness to move to
America will also be recalled.) Could it make sense to be a successor to Verdi, the
musician of the nation, when, clearly, that nation which his music had encouraged into being was in process of being proved to be elsewhere, displaced,
decentred?

One aspect of modernity may be the recognition of a loss of centre, in which
case Puccini's texts contrast strongly with Verdian moral standards. *La Fanciulla
del West* may be thought of as a decentred text, presenting a society based on
primitive lynch law; the violence there looks forward to *Turandot,* which shows
an absolutist, primitive, non-bourgeois society; but *Turandot,* as a work of the
1920s, certainly shows the wish for a centre. *Fanciulla* repeats some material from
Tosca—the wounded hero in Act 2; Rance as a figure of violence and attempted
rape, repeating elements of Scarpia; Minnie caught between the two figures; in
addition, Mr Johnson and Rance both raise psychoanalytic issues which are
modern—Johnson/Ramerrez as a split self, Rance as a psychotic whose nihilism
recalls Jago's Credo, but whose sadism is new and post-Freudian. And the whole
non-Italian, non-nationalist setting seems to make a difference. The film critic
James Hay points to the changing depictions of women in Italian films coming
from American myths. Referring to Puccini's source, Belasco's play with its
heroine, Girl, he says that while this 'Western melodrama was certainly not the
first American work to break from the conventional model of heroine as either
victim or hag, it clearly reformulated a role that for over a century had become
relatively standardised in popular European forms', while 'the period of silent film
had . . . frequently encouraged roles and images that seemed to transcend questions of a woman's place in the work force and her competition with men in an
urban environment'.[12] Minnie, the heroine whom Puccini is *not* in love with—

---

[12] James Hay, *Popular Film in Fascist Italy* (Bloomington, Ind.: Indiana University Press, 1987), p. 118.
There are interesting essays on *Fanciulla* in John L. DiGaetani and Josef P. Sirefman, *Opera and the Golden
West: The Past, Present and Future of Opera in the USA* (Cranbury, NJ: Associated Universities Press, 1994).

there is no identification, hence no masochistic impulse towards the suffering female in the music—represents a feminism which finds its completion in the non-violent, soft ending, a musical farewell that is piquant and affirmative. There is no society for Minnie and Johnson to relate to; there must be an appeal to the myth of the wanderer—the American as the hero always on the move. I conclude that Puccini seems not to believe in anything holding bourgeois society together. There is no unity—just as in *Andrea Chénier* there is nothing in the revolutionized state of France (reading Italy for France here) worth preserving. Hero and heroine remain outside it at the end, waiting for execution. The absence indicates that the myth of the nation-state could not hold, and nor could accompanying bourgeois liberal values.

This distinctive modernism separates Puccini from Pizzetti and others of the 'generazione dell' ottanta' (so called by the anti-fascist critic Massimo Mila), many of whom supported the fascists. Both Pizzetti, writing in 1910 and then in 1914 (Musicisti contemporanei: Saggi critici), and Fausto Torrefranca (1883–1955), attacking Puccini in *Giacomo Puccini e l'opera internazionale* (1912), disliked the internationalism of modernism. As Carducci, who died in 1907 had put it, 'today we are too French, too English, too German, too American: we are individualists, socialists, authoritarians—everything except Italians.'[13] The reference to America fits Puccini: it is important that Mussolini disliked the United States, whose popular culture he felt was invading Italy and preventing fascism's total hold. In 1929, in a year of propaganda against the United States, America was pronounced that 'grease-stain which is spreading through the whole of European life'.[14] Puccini was accused by Torrefranca of being too French in musical taste (it is worth considering the comparative absence of Italian settings for his operas),[15] as well as of being too bourgeois (Ashbrook, *Operas of Puccini*, p. 196). Torrefranca felt that Puccini's music did nothing for nationalist Italy.

Pizzetti hated speed, modern life, and modernism in music, and regarded bourgeois existence as decadent; Casella and Malipiero became more hostile to modernism after the war, and there was a resistance common to all three of these composers to Italian lyricism and the stress on the voice (it is tempting to read this as a resistance to the voice as the other, the feminine) and a corresponding

---

[13] Quoted by Richard Drake, *Byzantium for Rome: The Politics of Nostalgia in Umbertian Italy 1878–1900* (Chapel Hill, NC: University of North Carolina Press, 1980), p. 21.

[14] Quoted by Dennis Mack Smith, *Mussolini's Roman Empire* (London: Longman, 1976), p. 28.

[15] See Jay Nicolaisen, *Italian Opera in Transition: 1871–1893* (Ann Arbor: UMI Research Press, 1980), p. 280.

nationalistic desire to turn back to older forms of Italian music, to instrumental music and polyphony. Pizzetti's sense of decadence was unlike D'Annunzio's; the common dislike of the Italian Parliament they shared did not, with him, fit with a romanticism or rhetoric. He collaborated with D'Annunzio from 1905 to 1915, turning to opera composition around 1909, with a reading of Euripides and a setting of D'Annunzio's *Fedra*. But *Fedra* in Pizzetti's hands became a text dealing with aspirations for a loftier love beyond this life, an aim to find serenity after anguish, and a reforming wish in music, to make it 'reveal continuously the mysterious depths of the soul'. The contrast with Puccini's operas of passion and incident is striking. After a disagreement with D'Annunzio's aesthetics over two further pieces, Pizzetti wrote his own libretto for *Debora e Jaele* (1922), the first of three operas with heavily religious subject-matter, *Lo Straniero* (1922–5) and *Fra Gherardo* (1926) being the others.

The biblical plot of *Debora e Jaele*, from Judges, fitted a number of national stereotypes. The Hebrews accuse Jaele of consorting with the enemy, Sisera. Debora placates them by promising victory over him. She convinces Jaele to go to the enemy camp to kill Sisera, but Jaele is unable to do this. The Hebrews begin the war; Sisera flees and seeks refuge with Debora, who kills him to save him from humiliation and torture. The mood of much of the music is declamatory. Debora is the inspired prophetess, with an overpowering, inflexible will; Jaele the loving woman, with the soul of a woman that love transforms and transfigures. Sisera is the 'heroic captain, kind and true hearted, who attempts to oppose the law of love to that pronounced by divine commandment and succumbs', and the populace, who come off worst, are passionate, 'variable and violent, now frenzied with hate and warlike fury, now depressed and complaining, a creature of manifold and shifting aspects, amorphous material to be shaped by the leaders of men and heroes'.[16] The emphasis on the chorus, which influenced *Turandot*, comes from Greek drama, but points to the need for authoritarian control, which is also felt in an operatic style that rejects emotionality and subjectivity in favour of self-sacrificing love. Women are put to entirely different purposes from Puccini by Pizzetti. Here they stand for the motherland (which D'Annunzio appealed to in his rhetoric at Fiume); Turandot, compared with Debora, is seen as dysfunctional for China and the source of destructiveness. The religious character of Pizzetti's text ministers to nationalist myths in which the woman is important emotionally as a support to masculinity.

---

[16] Quoted by Guido Gatti, 'Ildobrando Pizzetti', *Musical Quarterly*, 9 (1925): 283.

Pizzetti scorned Puccini's subject-matter as being 'drammetto di piccole medio-cri anime borghesi'. But 'mediocre bourgeois souls' are just what Puccini parodies in *Gianni Schicchi*, which may be a response to these criticisms; 'mediocre' seems to be a significant term of disparagement in the culture of fascism. Casella in his classicism, with its 'return to order' theme, shared with such Italian painters as de Chirico, Felice Casorati, Savinio, and Severini, declared himself against 'passion-ate' art, meaning verismo and the desperate passions of Puccini. Pizzetti in his negativity towards Puccini condemned him for an inability to feel passion. Puccini is made out to be insincerely passionate. Pizzetti refers to his 'absence of thematic elaboration', which 'demonstrates the incapacity of the composer's mind to receive the impressions of life in their infinite variety and hence his impotence to live fervidly a life that is profound and intense because overflowing with innumerable impressions'.[17]

The refusal of 'bourgeois' passion by Pizzetti or Casella relate to what could be heard from the futurists or D'Annunzio or the Corradini-led nationalists (who all in measure supported fascism). The futurists and nationalists went with Mussolini only for a time, but fascism had both a modern and an anti-modern rhetoric behind it, and a central contradiction constructing it—its support for technology and the machine, which was an anti-humanism, while preaching reaction,[18] melancholic nostalgia, and Italian nationalism. Yet such melancholy was also anti-humanist in its classicism, which it claimed to derive from *The Birth of Tragedy*, and in its readiness, as de Chirico put it, 'to see everything, even man, as a thing'.[19] Turandot's body is seen as a 'thing' by Ping, Pang, and Pong, which would align Puccini to that discourse, and also make him a figure between futurism and the metaphysical painters such as de Chirico. None the less, I would

---

[17] The first Pizzetti quotation is from David Kimbell, *Italian Opera* (Cambridge: Cambridge University Press, 1991), p. 586; the second from Guido M. Gatti, 'The Works of Giacomo Puccini', *Musical Quarterly*, 14 (1928): 27. For Casella, see his *Music in My Time*, p. 229. For these composers, see David Ewen (ed.), *The Book of Modern Composers* (New York: Alfred A. Knopf, 1942).

[18] The word 'reactionary' itself changes its emphasis in the 1890s, from meaning being in favour of the aristocracy and, basically, the values of the old regime, pre-Risorgimento, to meaning being against the masses, rejecting mass society. See Alexander J. le Grand, *The Italian Nationalist Association and the Rise of Fascism in Italy* (Lincoln, Nebr.: University of Nebraska Press, 1978), p. 1. Two relevant texts for understanding the Italian culture of fascism are: A. James Gregor, *Young Mussolini and the Intellectual Origins of Fascism* (Berkeley and Los Angeles: University of California Press, 1979), and David D. Roberts, *The Syndicalist Tradition and Italian Fascism* (Manchester; Manchester University Press, 1979). On the relationship between futurism and fascism and on the aestheticism of futurism, see Anne Bowler, 'Politics as Art: Italian Futurism and Fascism', *Theory and Society*, 20 (1991): 763–94.

[19] Quoted by Elizabeth Cowling and Jennifer Mundy, *On Classic Ground: Picasso, Léger, de Chirico and the New Classicism 1910–1930* (London: Tate Gallery, 1990), p. 74.

like to close this chapter by emphasizing the differences between Puccini, Pizzetti, and Casella, in whom there is perhaps an anxiety at work in the hostility to romantic passion. For Puccini's music, while it is not outside the discourse of fascism, points up a dominant hysteria instinct in that discourse: reads it in terms of instability, of reason which collapses into its other, of men who are really feminine, or who have been feminized. The ascription of hysterical femininity to the figures of *I Pagliacci*, to Giordano's Gerard and to Scarpia, is sexist, but taken another way, that ascription can also be used, and become, a source of liberation.

The feminine seems to be associated with the absence of bourgeois patriarchy; but this feminine which belongs to the art of Puccini is ambiguous, since the weakening of bourgeois power in Italy, France, Austria, and Germany was associated with the rise of fascism. To put these points together, a hint might be taken from the clichés passed around about Italians in the years after 1871, that the nation itself was feminine, lacking maturity and decisiveness, 'feminine' being a comment passed on Mussolini himself.[20] The historian Richard Bosworth cites Maurice Barrès of the fascist grouping Action Française saying that Italy was 'designed for dilettantes who were a bit weak, elegant and incapable of all effort', marked out by 'sterility, while leaving [people] the voluptuous pleasures'.[21] The English ambassador to Rome, Sir Francis Bertie, Bosworth records as saying, with reference to the country's foreign policy: 'Italy was like a woman with two lovers whose jealousy of each other she utilised for her own profit' (ibid., p. 5) Further, Italians were like children. The futurist Marinetti (1876–1944), who attacked femininity and feminism in all its forms, as though in reaction to these clichés, preached in the futurist manifesto of 1909 that 'we want to glorify war—the only cure for the world—militarism, patriotism, the destructive gesture of the anarchists, the beautiful ideas which kill and contempt for women'.[22]

Bosworth suggests how to extend this point about Italy as feminine by referring to *Death in Venice* (1912), whose opening page, referring to a 'menace' that hung over Europe's head for months, may allude to the instability caused when Giolitti took Italy into the Libyan war against Turkey, a war Bosworth calls 'the only war of aggression waged by a recognized Great Power against another traditional member of the Concert since 1870, . . . a microcosm of the greater war to come' (*Italy*, p. 99). *Death in Venice* deals with feminization. So does Mann's later short

---

[20] Dennis Mack Smith: *Mussolini* (1981; repr. London: Granada, 1983), p. 132.
[21] Richard Bosworth, *Italy and the Approach of the First World War* (London: Macmillan, 1983), p. 3.
[22] Quoted by James Joll, *Intellectuals in Power* (London: Weidenfeld and Nicolson, 1960), p. 182.

story, *Mario and the Magician* (1929), set in the fictitious Italian seaside resort of the Torre di Venere—the tower of Venus, which thus connects a sense of sexual luxury with the nationalism, xenophobia, and prudery of the Italians. The last of these qualities is manifested when the German middle-class narrator (the Italians dislike the Germans because of the First World War) allows his 8-year-old daughter to go naked on the beach. This Italian middle class is none the less conned by the conjurer Cipolla, fascinated and hypnotized by him, and the episode serves as a critique of Italian fascism, which Mann had observed at first hand in 1926.

The text is a warning to Germany, against the prestidigitation of a force 'by which today Munich and tomorrow Berlin could be made Italian' (Mann, on 17 Oct. 1930, after the Nazi party had strengthened their position in the Reichstag).[23] Cipolla, as magician, may echo aspects of German culture: Wagner, for instance, as a conjurer, or Klingsor, fake seeker after virtue, castrate and the destruction of all who come into his garden through the employment of Kundry. Later, of course, Mann was to see Hitler too as conjurer and fake artist. The text focuses also on the German narrator, whose fascination with Cipolla is part of the way that he is controlled by what he comes across in the Torre de Venere: the narrator, whose tone of superiority to the events means that he, with his family, is dangerously close to being dragged in by them, fits with the uncommitted German, like Zeitblom. Alongside these German references, there is, however, the specifically Italian criticism. Mario, the working-class waiter and not an artist at all, shoots Cipolla when he hypnotizes him into kissing him, thinking that he is his beloved; obviously the question of what people do when hypnotized could be suggestive of what their unconscious desires are, so the text comments on the Italian mentality that has allowed itself to be swayed by such a conjurer as Cipolla, the Mussolini figure.[24]

Both Mann's novellas suggest how Italy, despite its imperialism and its aggression, could be represented not as any violent threat, but as seedy and degenerate, characterized by an inward, deathward movement, symbolized by Venice attracting Aschenbach towards his own dissolution and death. Or, to supplement Thomas Mann, who is, after all, representing the 'other' power, that of Germany,

[23] Quoted by Ilsedore B. Jonas, *Thomas Mann and Italy*, trans. Betty Crouse (University, Ala.: University of Alabama Press, 1979), p. 60.

[24] See Eugene Lunn, 'Tales of Liberal Disquiet: Thomas Mann's *Mario and the Magician*: Interpretations of Fascism', *Literature and History*, 11 (1985): 77–100. This reads the text in the light of recent theories of fascism.

and being nationalistic himself, D'Annunzio's novels could come in with their urgent need to reassert patriarchy, while recognizing the impossibility of doing this. In *L'innocente* (1892), the cuckolded father kills 'his' son—his wife's child— in desperation over the loss of his patriarchal power. His negating action, of course, destroys his fictitious status as the 'patriarch', since he now has no title to being a father.

Patriarchal Italy, it seems, stood in a vulnerable relationship towards what has been called 'the feminization of culture', which took place throughout this period of proto-fascism. Barbara Spackman uses the phrase when she discusses D'Annunzio, but we have already seen it in discussions of Wagner's music. D'Annunzio's novels of the late 1880s and 1890s, before the adventurism at Fiume in 1919, and his association with the fascists who were, however, anxious to keep him at arm's length, record an increasing turning away from women and the erotic. They go from initial male conquest and enjoyment to repentance and flight from the flesh.[25] The turn away is towards a pure maleness, seen most fully in *Il fuoco*, in which the hero, Stelio, leaves at the end to renew Italian art from its core, and his mistress, based on Eleonora Duse, gives him up, realizing that she cannot stand in his way.

But the process of leaving the woman that runs through D'Annunzio's texts is attended, as Spackman argues, by a sense of sickness, of loss of phallic power, of domination by 'furies, chimeras, androgynes, hermaphrodites and Medusas.' Such tensions which disallow the power of the male basically refuse patriarchy. The split Barbara Spackman observes in *fin de siècle* Italy is between those elements of normal bourgeois society who, as it were, simply precluded women and the decadents, among whom she thinks of D'Annunzio, and, I would add, Puccini. The decadents could not exclude women; rather, they made their presence into a problem, a pressing fear and anxiety which displayed itself in the morbid, sick conditions of the men. In that, paradoxically, lay their healthiness: that they had not excluded women, or their passion. The hero of *L'innocente* knows that he has been cuckolded, and knows he can do nothing about it, except in a murderous nihilistic move.

---

[25] Barbara Spackman, *Decadent Genealogies: The Rhetoric of Sickness from Baudelaire to D'Annunzio* (Ithaca, NY: Cornell University Press, 1989), p. 215. Spackman takes the phrase from Christine Buci-Glucksmann's book *La Raison baroque: De Baudelaire à Benjamin*. Spackman's work comprises an important reassessment of D'Annunzio. The comment about the retreat from women she takes from Paolo Valesio (quoted p. 154).

Italy, even at the end of the nineteenth century, seemed to be the place important for producing a sense of the other's otherness, and of going over to the other's side. Is it not relevant that Nietzsche, read so intently by D'Annunzio for the cult of the *Übermensch*, was supposed to have collapsed in his madness in Turin on 3 January 1889, while putting his arms around a horse which was being beaten?[26] Italy becomes the place for the dissolution of patriarchal power, in Nietzsche, in D'Annunzio, in the depiction of Wagner's death in Venice at the end of *Il fuoco*, in *Death in Venice*. In these ways, the sexist ascription of 'feminine' to Italy turns into a way of 'undoing' the naming power.

Thus, if Tosca embodies features of contemporary Italy, the fittingness may not be just that countries are often represented in statuary for instance, as women; nor may it necessarily be part of a putting down of Italy's political situation. It reads the hysteria in Tosca's 'folle amor', of which she sings to Cavaradossi and which activates her jealousy, as an aspect of her enslavement to clericalism, as well as a fitting embodiment, or mythicizing, of Italy in her embattled condition. But just as Scarpia underestimates the opposition of Tosca, and sees her protestations as so much opera—'Mai Tosca alla scena / Più tragica fu!' (Tosca on stage was never so tragic)—so there is the sense that the heroine, Italy, who is both operatic *and* hysterical is more than a match for those forces which would drag her down. It was fitting to make Tosca an *opera diva*. It is the spirit of Italian opera—as it were, the spirit of *Otello*—that is everywhere celebrated in this text. If that spirit is not distant from the way that fascism is represented, it at least points, on one reading, to a doubleness in Puccini.

---

[26] The volume edited by Thomas Harrison, *Nietzsche in Italy* (Saratoga, Calif.: Anma Libri, 1988), is useful for both Nietzsche and D'Annunzio.

5

From *Madama Butterfly* to *Turandot*: The Crowd and the Gamble

Death by a man—whether they do it themselves, like Butterfly, or are stabbed, like Carmen, the provenance of the knife, or the choking hand, or the fading breath, is a man, and the result is fatal.

Clément, *Opera, or the Undoing of Women*

So Catherine Clément comments on the 'undoing of women' in those most famous operas *Otello, La Bohème, Madama Butterfly,* and *Turandot.* In the last two, women fit with those themes of Orientalism noticed in discussing *Otello. Madama Butterfly* is relevant for Puccinian politics in dealing so plainly with areas of racial and sexual exploitation which unite in the death of the woman. So it is worth beginning a chapter which will discuss *Madama Butterfly* and, in more detail, *Turandot,* by contextualizing *Madama Butterfly,* and doing so alongside Mascagni's Japanese opera *Iris* (1898). This last was set to a libretto by Illica, who had prepared it initially for Franchetti, as a successor to their collaboration *Cristoforo Colómbo* (1892).

Interest in the relationship between America as colonizing power and Japan distinguishes *Madama Butterfly* from *Iris,* which has no foreigners in it, save the foreign imaginations which write it, but *Butterfly* maps sexual politics on to imperialism and, more, pursuit of the imaginary exotic as the 'other' of Western experience. The United States forced the hand of a previously isolationist Japan in 1854, and made it open up to the West; and one result was the Western imperialist interest in Japanese commodities, first displayed in London in 1862, and later in Paris in 1876. Two posters for the original production of *Iris* indicate that this opera was regarded as an equivalent of *art nouveau,* which itself appropriated Japanese motifs.[1] Both the butterfly and the iris are key Japanese motifs in

---

[1] William Weaver has reprinted one poster, by the Polish-born artist Leopoldo Metlicowicz, in *The Golden Century of Italian Opera* (London: Thames and Hudson, 1980), p. 180. Malcolm Haslam, *In the Nouveau Style* (London: Thames and Hudson, 1989), p. 121, reprints another, by the Italian Adolfo Hohenstein, influenced by Paul Berthon. On Japanese motifs in Europe generally, see Siegfried Wichmann, *Japonisme* (London: Thames and Hudson, 1981).

art nouveau, and they suggest anti-industrial, anti-utilitarian, anti-modern tendencies within the movement and also, in the cult of beauty, a tendential feminism, present in *Iris*. Women are often flowers in *art nouveau*: the flower maidens of *Parsifal* recall Adorno's alignment of Wagner to the aestheticism of *art nouveau* (*In Search of Wagner*, pp. 101, 150). Adorno sees such aestheticism as the revelation of the character of the commodity: art is a form of commodity (ibid., p. 90), little more than advertising, and it is advertisements for *Iris* that project and frame an interest in art for art's sake. Iris is a flower-like aesthetic object, whose fate is to be bought up.

She compares herself in her first aria to a doll, but in keeping with the apoliticism of aestheticism, the text is also sadistic, which fits its verismo context. In the first act, Iris is snatched away from her blind father and from her country home by Kyoto and Osaka (the *Rigoletto* echoes are strong), and confined to a brothel in the city. She refuses attempts at seduction, but, exposed to the gaze on the balcony of the brothel, she is 'seen' by her father, who, thinking she has gone there voluntarily, throws mud at her. She kills herself by throwing herself into a sewer. In the third act, the rag-pickers working the sewers find her dying, and she is given a last vision of the emptiness of male egoism as the voices of Osaka, Kyoto, and her father come before her, before she is received by the sun and turned into a flower herself amidst a whole stage filled with flowers. This is a non-modern Japan which combines a sexual sordidness/splendour with a pre-pubescent innocence; there is no social context for Iris as there is for Cio-Cio San; no Bonze, no mother, no relations, only the egoistical father who needs Iris for eyesight (the word-play is evident), no Suzuki, and no 'impartial' male, like Sharpless, to place the action at all. Fantasy elements replace this sense of a naturalistically conceived drama. The sun, its music given to an unseen chorus who sing at the beginning and the end, and Fuji mountain, the flowers, the sense of human life being no different from that of plants or animals—these elements which all belong to the retreatism of *art nouveau* become the basis for a criticism of patriarchy and urban life.

William Weaver quotes Bastianelli, one of the 'generazione dell'ottanta' on the existence of a 'strange erotic sadness' in *L'Amico Fritz* (1891), Mascagni's second opera. Its love theme and wealthy class setting have nothing to do with the kitsch peasants of *Cavalleria Rusticana*. Mascagni, whose origins were working-class, identified with socialism until 1920, though Harvey Sachs indicates that the composer vacillated in terms of politics up to the time of his identification with fascism.[2] The sadness, which Weaver also finds in Giordano's *Andrea Chénier*, may characterize the 1890s: it fits *Iris*, where the heroine is subject to morbid fantasies throughout. Her attempts to draw flowers in the brothel produce snakes instead; in depicting the sky, the result is a black veil. The expressionistic images here, which involve an explicitly made identification of pleasure with death, suggest male sadism and fantasy which in one way are eager to confront the woman with sexuality, but the dreaminess of the rag-pickers' music, for instance, points to an equal male identification with turning away from life. It is as though the opera knows it can go nowhere, and is unable to make any larger political assessment of its Italy. And some such reason must be invoked to account for the stunning blows to Mascagni's popularity after the success of *Cavalleria Rusticana*. The inability of opera to deliver a contemporary realism, so that verismo opera was short-lived in Italy, means the escape to a fantasy Japan, where art is presented as delusion and as the source of violence to woman (permitting her rape). The affections are simultaneously brutalized and made tender in this opera, which, while it shows the destruction of the woman—and there is only one woman in the opera—effectively makes the woman the symbol of life which is better not lived.

The differences from *Madama Butterfly*, where two cultures are represented, are strong. *Butterfly* opened in Milan on 17 February 1904. On 10 February, the Russian–Japanese war had begun, the climax to Japanese expansion within the Pacific. Japan had entered Korea in 1875, and had fought China in 1894–5, during which time it had taken Formosa, and occupied the Liatung Peninsula in China itself, which it was later forced to cede as the Triple Alliance (Russia, France, and Germany) became fearful of Japanese advances. At the same time, Japan was virtually humiliated by the United States over Hawaii, which was annexed by the States in 1897, and was forced to a concession of power to the States in the Philippines, which the Americans occupied in 1898. The Pacific was the theatre for both American and Japanese imperialism in the 1890s; the historian Akira Iriye draws parallels between the American and Japanese aggression in the 1890s, and points to the ideological pressure to expand which was being exerted on the Japanese in the 1890s by their own economists and politicians. He quotes the writer Watanabe Shujiro on the need for an aggressive stance: 'Why should we alone be governed by moral scruples in international affairs?'[3] One result of Japanese expansion was the Anglo-Japanese treaty signed in February 1902,

---

[2] See Sachs, *Music in Fascist Italy*, pp. 106–20.

[3] Akira Iriye, *Pacific Estrangements: Japanese and American Expansion 1897–1911*, (Cambridge, Mass.: Harvard University Press, 1972), p. 39.

whereby two island states and empires recognized each other in a form of symmetry, a treaty welcomed by the Italian government, and one whose main aim was the halting of Russian expansion in China.[4]

This militarism and aggression, in which Japan learned late but quickly the lessons of imperialism taught by Britain, France, Germany, and the United States, and after 1895 became identifiable as the 'yellow peril', could not be gathered from *Madama Butterfly*, the narrative of which suggests a weak, feminine little country inhabited by a people content to wait for 'one fine day', sitting out the night in non-retaliatory sweetness. It could be argued that the West needed to represent Japan to itself in such a feminine, miniature, non-aggressive way, and, above all, as so economically backward, because of its fears that the reality was very different. In which case, this depiction of Japan, along with several others by Saint-Saëns, Sullivan, Messager, and Mascagni, has an ideological function: to represent Japan as a quaint, pacific, other that accepts exploitation. But of course it is true that the narrative picks up from other elements within the prior colonization of Japan, including the whole cult of 'japonaiserie' (Baudelaire's term of 1861). Pierre Viaud, who called himself Pierre Loti (1850–1923), provided source material for *Lakmé* (1883) and for Puccini through his novella *Madame Chrysanthème* (1887). This is material dealing as though autobiographically with Loti's marriage, Japanese style (as Pinkerton describes it), to a geisha, a marriage which lasts for one summer. The material was rewritten—indeed, written anew—by John Luther Long in his American short story 'Madam Butterfly', and made into a one-act play by Belasco in 1900, where, for the first time, Cio-Cio San (Loti's Ki-Hou-San) commits suicide.

But Loti seems symptomatic of a Western attention to Japan, and those symptoms need exploring. He had a naval career, which aligns him with Pinkerton; his autobiographies (of which there were two) register a nostalgia for 'the colonies':

oh what magic and mental turmoil there was during my childhood in the simple word 'the colonies' which at that time denoted in my mind every far-off tropical land with its palm trees, enormous fruits, Negroes, animals and adventure . . . oh 'the colonies'! How can I describe everything that stirred in my head at the very sound of that word! A piece of fruit from the colonies or a book or a shell from over there, immediately became virtually enchanted objects for me.[5]

---

[4] Ian H. Nish, *The Anglo-Japanese Alliance* (2nd edn., London: Athlone Press, 1985).

[5] Quoted from *Le Roman d'un Enfant* by Alec G. Hargreaves, *The Colonial Experience in French Fiction* (London: Macmillan, 1981), p. 23.

As with Casella on Ethiopia (see Chapter 2), the colonial space is assumed to be free of people: it is nature, itself presented as a collection of objects for collecting: the shell, the fruit, the Negroes. People are not there, or, when they have to be represented—as Japanese—they become 'these little people with slit eyes and no brain' (ibid., p. 35), the physical characteristic of littleness which is insisted on throughout being the index to moral and intellectual qualities which are made to match. Madame Chrysanthème herself becomes a 'plaything', a 'dog', a 'cat', a 'doll', an 'insect'; and the narrative asks (it is written in the first person, as a 'journal of a summer of my life'): 'What can take place in that little head? . . . I'll bet one hundred to one that nothing takes place there. And even if it did, I wouldn't care.'[6] Mosco Carner's references to Loti's 'exquisite poetic touches' and sense of 'delicacy and loving care with which he describes the fragility of (the geisha's) world' (Carner, *Puccini*, p. 380) are inappropriate: the tone is cynical and no better than exploitative.

In this 'journal', ennui and loneliness become the reason for marrying Madame Chrysanthème, and it is not assumed that the woman suffers—Irene Szylionicz writes that 'Loti's final image of the mousmé are of her playing with the piastres he gave her, and of her prostrating herself on the threshold of their abode as he departs' (*Pierre Loti*, p. 80). But there is more to be said about Loti, for his homosexuality, which Clive Wake makes the centre of his study of the writer,[7] means that there is the constant motif in the texts of the handsome sailor who accompanies Loti: here Yves, based on a figure Loti knew. The sailor displaces attention from the Japanese woman; indeed, it may be said that the whole episode with the woman exists as a displacement for something else. Here, above all, we may ask the question that Frantz Fanon uses in thinking about the white man's desire for black Africa: What does the man want? Perhaps the woman is inwardly despised because she is female, not male, perhaps the whole cavalier attitude towards her represents a desire for assertion of maleness. Wake notes that Loti was bored by Japan, which contrasts sharply with the nostalgia we have seen to mark out his attitudes to the notion of the colony; but his attitude to both the colony and the geisha go together in what seems a highly repressed text. Neither are wanted, though both provide temporary ways of thinking about otherness; but the violence at work betrays the fact that one way of representing reality (broadly,

---

[6] Quoted by Irene L. Szylionicz, *Pierre Loti and the Oriental Woman* (London: Macmillan, 1988), pp. 75, 56, 76.

[7] Clive Wake, *The Novels of Pierre Loti* (The Hague: Mouton, 1974).

the homosexual) has been enforcedly replaced by another, and this is not what the man wants.

By comparison, it is time to look at Puccini's rendering of what the man wants, as given through the libretto of Illica and Giacosa:

PINKERTON.   Dovunque al mondo
              lo Yankee vagabondo
              si gode e traffica
              sprezzando i rischi.
              Affonda l'ancora
              alla ventura—
              (*he breaks off to offer Sharpless a drink*)
              Milk-punch o wisky?
              Affonda l'ancora
              alla ventura
              finchè una raffica scompigli
              nave e ormeggi, alberatura . . .
              La vita ei non appaga
              se non fa suo tesor
              i fiori d'ogni plaga . . .
SHARPLESS.   è un facile vangelo . . .
PINKERTON.   . . . d'ogni bella gli amor!
SHARPLESS.   è un facile vangelo
              che fa la vita vaga
              ma che intristisce il cor.
PINKERTON.   Vinto si tuffa,
              la sorte racciuffa.
              Il suo talento
              fa in ogni dove.
              Così mi sposo all'uso giapponese
              per novecento
              novantanove anni
              Salvo a prosciogliermi ogni mese . . .
SHARPLESS.   è un facile vangelo . . .
PINKERTON.   America for ever!

(Pinkerton: Throughout the world the Yankee wanders enjoying himself and trading, ignoring all risks. Milk-punch or whisky? He casts his anchor at random until a squall upsets ship and moorings and riggings . . . and life isn't satisfying to him unless he makes his treasure the flower of every shore, the love of every beauty. If he's beaten, he tries his luck again. He does whatever he pleases wherever he goes. So I'm marrying in Japanese fashion for nine hundred and ninety-nine years, save that I can free myself every month Sharpless: It's an easy-going creed, which makes life fun, but which saddens the heart.)

This number, which is effectively a denial to Pinkerton of a complete aria, since it is interrupted both by himself and by Sharpless, deserves study on many counts. Pinkerton keeps trying to sing a quatrain, starting with 'Dovunque', 'Affonda', and 'Vinto si tuffa'. But the first time he begins the quatrain 'Affonda', which speaks of the Yankee's free-and-easy ways (with a word-play no doubt intended on his anchor which he casts wherever he wants to), he breaks it to offer Sharpless milk-punch or whisky, and the second time he begins the same verse, it develops chromatically into a vision of shipwreck which also spoils the form of the verse, lengthens it, and thereby renders its neat unity again non-existent. A similar chromaticism is heard in the next quatrain ('La vita ei non appaga'), as Pinkerton sings of the dominance of the sexual—life isn't worth living if he can't get the best woman in every country—and this verse too is interrupted, this time by Sharpless, singing 'È un facile vangelo', which he repeats after the verse is finished, but with the rhyme-words of the verse, 'È un facile vangelo / Che fa la vita vaga / Ma intristisce il cor', save that the two 'È un facile vangelo' statements have to rhyme with each other, which underlines, perhaps, their and the creed's triteness. Pinkerton continues with the next quatrain, which is immediately followed by the non sequitur of 'Così mi sposi', which seems like an attempt at another four-line verse, and is responded to again by Sharpless, 'È un facile vangelo'. Earlier, Pinkerton has referred to the ability to cancel a 999 years' lease any month; now it becomes clear that this is because he intends marrying in Japanese fashion. The whole solo is intended to explain—this is the force of 'Così'—that the roving Yankee's aim throughout life is wholly sexual. But Pinkerton has finished non-consequentially, and can only complete the number by his toast, 'America for ever', which again seems to begin the quatrain, and which needs—indeed, has asked for—a conclusion from Sharpless, who repeats the toast. The tenor seems to acknowledge that of himself he cannot end, but also that he must prevent the dialogue (dialogic, like that between Cavaradossi and the sacristan) from splitting into open argument (i.e., through hearing Sharpless's disapproval of him) by the appeal to national patriotism, to the flag (the 'Star-Spangled Banner' has been alluded to throughout the quatrains, and in a context which suggests Bakhtinian parody).

Many interesting points emerge from this. Pinkerton begins by singing about the Yankee in the third person, but in the non-consequential 'Così mi sposi' moves to the first person, thus making apparent a prior wish to shift guilt on to the archetypal commercial fly-by-night, roving, modern American, the 'Yankee'. His inability to finish both in the second verse, which he has two shots at, and also at the end, reveals, despite the swagger and smoothness, an evasiveness which goes along with an uncertainty about what happens: it would seem as though the second verse envisages his death by shipwreck, though this is deflected almost immediately by the statement that life isn't worth living if he can't secure the best 'fiori d'ogni plaga'. This deflection could suggest the power of the death drive within him: the shipwreck is permitted to destroy him simply because it isn't possible to have every woman from every country, and that is recognized (and affirmed by the opera's ending), or the stakes are set so high—he must have 'ogni bella' in a dash for speed and experience (I recall Puccini's interest in speed)—simply because of the likeliness of death. But death is likely only because he places himself in a position where it is only to be expected.

Two conclusions follow: the Yankee (is this a term of self-hatred on Pinkerton's part?) is a gambler—note 'rischi', 'ventura', 'vinto si tuffa / la sorte racciuffa'—and he has a death drive which is a motive force behind his imperialism (an imperialism we have noted in historical terms already), especially his sexual imperialism. He is willing to go on until the squall finally upsets the ship. If beaten, he throws himself in again into the pursuit of happiness; but that pursuit is already detectable as being of death. Such pursuit, as Sharpless notes, makes him a melancholic, both in the sense that he has a nostalgia for what is past and gone, hence the death wish, and also in a sentimentality about home, which is registered in the use of the kitsch material of the 'Star-Spangled Banner'. The musical text performs a critique of imperialism as kitsch-inspired, exoticism as an empty dream. In this attitude, the individual Yankee is of no importance; but Sharpless and Pinkerton clink glasses at 'America for ever'. The nation is important; and because it is important, the nation spreads itself round the globe. Hence we have the remarkable intrusion into Italian opera of American words and phrases and American music. Further, Pinkerton's commitment to marry a real American wife later on ('una vera sposa americana') and his and Sharpless's plan at the end, in which Madama Butterfly co-operates, effectively, for the child to become an American, will be handed over to the American patriarchy, which must be preserved. These are moves which belong to nationalism and imperialism alike.

Much of what is described here fits an anatomy of fascism, I believe, and I want to focus on three of its aspects which seem not accidental in Puccini: the gambling, the death-wish, and the melancholy, the latter point relating also to

Mascagni. Discussion of them may move forward through consideration of *Turandot.* But we may conclude this section on the earlier opera by noting the quality of the critique Puccini offers of Franklin Benjamin Pinkerton, lieutenant on the gunboat *Lincoln* (Loti's ship is called *La Triomphante*). It seems much stronger than the way Arthur Groos depicts the whole 'tragedy' which he sees as resulting from 'a contradiction between the principals' fantasies about each other and about reality'.[8] Pinkerton's perceptions are fantasies which he holds about himself and America: Groos's formulation is not adequate to convey the sense of inner violence within Pinkerton, which makes him a morbid figure, self-destructive, and hence destructive of others (it is perhaps not coincidental that even Kate can say little in his presence). Most of the fantasies that Cio-Cio San entertains are largely of Pinkerton's making, in any case.

GHOSTS OF WAGNERIAN OPERA: TURANDOT

In the title of their book on the opera, William Ashbrook and Harold Powers call *Turandot* 'the end of the Great Tradition'. William Weaver finishes his *The Golden Century of Italian Opera: From Rossini to Puccini* with this work, premièred on 25 April 1926; while David Kimbell says that 'it is difficult to feel that anything that could properly be described as an Italian operatic tradition survived much beyond the First World War'.[9] The ending of opera and the event of the war are not unrelated. David Forgacs, in his *Italian Culture in the Industrial Era, 1880–1980*, apparently sees no need to give space to Italian opera as an aspect of Italian popular culture; and John Rosselli (like Kimbell) argues that the common passion for opera was gone by 1869, that 'Italian opera had been closely bound up with the world of the old sovereigns. It was shaken when the 1848 revolutions shook their rule; when in 1859–60, they departed for good, Italian opera began to die.'[10] Rosselli refers to the Italian Parliament in 1868 as no longer subsidizing the opera-houses which the united Italy had taken over from the old states, and imposing a 10 per cent tax on all theatre takings, thus squeezing opera-houses considerably. He also points to economic pressures in the 1870s, notably an

---

[8] Arthur Groos, 'Lieutenant B. F. Pinkerton: Problems in the Genesis of an Operatic Hero', *Italica*, 64 (1987): 666. See also, for a musical reading of the text which makes this kind of point, Allan W. Atlas, 'Crossed Stars and Crossed Tonal Areas in Puccini's *Madame Butterfly*', *Nineteenth-Century Music*, 14/2 (1990): 186–90.

[9] David Kimbell, *Italian Opera* (Cambridge: Cambridge University Press, 1991), p. xiv.

[10] John Rosselli, *Music and Musicians in Nineteenth-Century Italy* (London: B. T. Batsford, 1991), p. 71.

agrarian depression, which affected landowners' incomes; like Kimbell, he stresses that the copyright laws of 1882 made successful operas into big business, and so cut down on new writing, a point also emphasized in the shift from the impresario as determining the repertoire to the publisher, such as Ricordi. Such points only increase the sense that Italian opera was destined to become more marginal: the operas I have discussed were designed for great state occasions, belonging to an Italy that needed the public work of art, as an image of the state. *Turandot*, as Ashbrook and Powers note, was given a spectacular staging in the Verona Arena in July 1928, as also in 1938. In Puccinian opera the anxiety of the composer is to achieve that earlier popularity which opera had enjoyed through melody, through melodrama, through the projection of an immediate relationship between composer and audience (the thirty curtain-calls for *Manon Lescaut*, for example). The 'generazione dell'ottanta' had no such aspirations to be of the people, and much less survives of the operas of Respighi, or Pizzetti, Casella, or Malipiero.

One of the most interesting aspects of *Turandot* is how it seems to be composed with an awareness of the approaching end of a form which fascism was powerless to save, and was actually, in the character of the musicians of the 'generazione dell'ottanta', virtually all associated with fascism, instrumental in destroying; fascism being here a death drive, as this is described in Freud's *Beyond the Pleasure Principle* and recognized as a feature of modernity through Schopenhauer's work, while it is also interpreted as a self-appointed gamble to save a civilization. Such a gambling spirit is a recognizable part of the discourse of the 1920s and 1930s. J. P. Stern quotes from Spengler's *Decline of the West* (1918) to focus on its pertinence in his series of meditations on Hitler and Germany:

Hitler had no need to read Spengler's *Decline of the West* to understand its message for the times: 'The history of this age is no longer a witty game, conducted in polite, social forms and concerned with a nicely calculated less or more, a game from which one may withdraw at any time. To stand fast or to go under—there is no third way.' At all times, and increasingly as Hitler's career proceeds to its end, the *No* is envisaged as a real possibility, the *Götterdämmerung* pathology which Nietzsche had attacked in Wagner is translated from a private obsession to the praxis of national and international politics.[11]

Stern argues that Hitler's *Yes*, which he demanded from Germany (as he also quotes D'Annunzio at Fiume in 1919 soliciting a 'Yes' from Italians), contains a death drive. It is a theme I will return to later in the chapter.

---

[11] Stern, *Hitler*, p. 41.

In *Turandot*, the gambling motif referred to in relationship to Pinkerton continues, just as it was also present in Act 2 of *La Fanciulla del West*, where Minnie and the sherrif gamble for Mr Johnston, and Minnie wins by cheating. In *Turandot*, despite being told by Ping, Pang, and Pong in the first act, 'La vita non giocar' (don't gamble with life), Calaf gambles three times: once on being able to answer three riddles (a gamble which recalls the two gamblers in the first act of *Siegfried*, Wotan as the Wanderer and Mime); once that no one will be able to discover his name (this is the gamble which does not pay off, as it leads to Liù's death); third, when he tells Turandot his name, and thus invites his own death. But he is a gambler as someone who has already lost once: re-meeting his father at the beginning of the opera, among the crowds in Peking, he sings that the usurper of his father's crown is searching for them both to kill them: 'Non c'è asilo per noi, padre, nel mondo!' No place is safe for them. He gambles for a kingdom as much as for Turandot, out of the position of displacement and exile. The topic of displacement, of the lack of a centre, we have noticed as marking out Puccini, as it marked out the 600,000 Italians per year who were emigrating, many to the United States in the decade prior to 1914. It is tempting to link such an attitude to risk to Puccini's own melancholy, which was not his only; comparison could be made with de Chirico, whose paintings thematize melancholy—for example, the picture of that name of 1912 and *Mystery and Melancholy of a Street* (1914). This mood of cultural despair I also associate with William Ashbrook's comment, referred to in the last chapter, on the amount of 'mocking music' in Puccini,[12] and with Ping in *Turandot* saying when he sees the dead Liù that 'per la prima volta / al vedere la morte / non sogghigno' (for the first time I look on death without sneering). If the sneering attitude fits a *fin de siècle* nihilism, it is interesting that it stops here: as though the sacrificial violence of Liù, which accords with the fascist calls to sacrifice in the name of the leader, brings back humanism and stops mockery and parodic attitudes dead in their tracks. For Martin Cooper, the melancholy is associated with despair, 'passione disperata':

If this despairing quality in Puccini's lyricism had its immediate origin in his own personal psychology, it also corresponded to a more general mood in the public, a vague emotional unrest and presentiment of future disaster that found poignant expression in the almost funereal melodies, which have often escaped notice among Puccini's innumerable expressions of erotic passion. In Act II, scene 5 of *Tosca* the Andante sostenuto, with muted violins

---

[12] William Ashbrook, *The Operas of Puccini* (Oxford: Oxford University Press, 1985), p. 26.

playing on the G string, could be the funeral march, not simply of Scarpia, but of a whole civilization, like the slow movement of Elgar's Second Symphony written ten years later.[13]

To this comment, which will recall *two* funeral marches in *Turandot*, for the Prince of Persia and for Liù, which form an interesting symmetry with each other, there is to be added both Puccini's confession of a 'Neronic instinct', and that 'I have the great weakness of being able to compose only when my puppet executioners move on the stage' (Carner, *Puccini*, p. 276). Reference to Puccini's cruelty has been common since Richard Specht's book of 1931. Pinkerton may have something of Puccini in him, just as the torture of Liù may echo the mental torture of the Puccini's servant Doria Manfredi, partly at the hands of Puccini's wife (as Turandot), which led to her suicide. But the sense of impending execution, which hangs over *Turandot* and threatens Calaf, may also imply a danger, felt as a death-wish, to the male composer himself.

Gambling, the death-wish, melancholy—to these three must be added the whole difference of this opera from earlier Puccini texts. The stage direction says it all in referring to the walls of Peking, with the massive bastions that run right across the stage and the decapitated heads hanging above. This is monumental art using the chorus in a way it was never used in *Madama Butterfly*.[14] The chorus exist as the obedient subjects of plenary power, the power of empire; and the law is established by the Mandarin who sings at the beginning. And whose is the power? Ashbrook and Powers, drawing on the opera's fire–ice symbolism (Turandot as the moon, Calaf as the source of warmth), insist that it is not Turandot but the Emperor: 'the immobile pure white C-major centre of music and drama alike [is] the hieratic figure of the Emperor . . . the Son of Heaven—the heaven in which both sun and moon reside.'[15] Imperial power, Asiatic despotism: it is no accident that these things fit with the spectacular force with which Mussolini's fascism displayed itself. (In this connection of ideas a reason may be found for the locale of Bertolucci's film *The Last Emperor*, which certainly deals with Fascism, in a mediated way, and at the historical period of Mussolini's Fascism, though in China, not Italy.) But certainly power inheres more in Calaf than in Turandot, whose anger and ice, increasing as she becomes more frustrated and unable to

---

[13] Cooper (ed.), *The New Oxford History of Music: The Modern Age 1890–1960*, p. 155, 156.

[14] On the political role of the chorus in nineteenth-century Italian opera from Rossini to late Verdi, see Philip Gossett, 'Becoming a Citizen: The Chorus in *Risorgimento* Opera', *Cambridge Opera Journal*, 2/1 (1991): 41–64.

[15] William Ashbrook and Harold Powers, *Puccini's* Turandot: *The End of the Great Tradition* (Princeton: Princeton University Press, 1991), p. 42; see also pp. 120, 122.

control the situation, only increase her attractiveness to him. Furthermore, he does not suffer from what Mosco Carner refers to as 'hysterical outbursts', referring to Cavaradossi.[16] The charge of hysteria we have seen to be familiar in discussion of Puccini, extending by implication from character to composer, aligning him with unstable feminine sympathies in so far as Cavaradossi as a character is endorsed by Puccini. Here the stress is on maleness, and feminine sympathies do not function in Puccini's view of Turandot.[17]

The opera could be seen as an exercise in how to tame the woman. To say this would align it with fascist rhetoric, which sees the crowd and the woman as images for each other. 'The Fascist leader conquers a crowd and subdues it as he would a woman or a horse.'[18] In *Turandot*, Liù serves faithfully and blindly, and commits suicide because once, in the palace, Calaf smiled at her; she is ready to die for the leader who picks out the person from the crowd. Turandot turns from ice to warmth when Calaf kisses her passionately in a violent action which certainly at least begins to repeat the act of rape performed by the invader against Princess Lou-Ling ('trascinata / da un uomo come te, come te / straniero'). The violence in *Turandot* takes many forms, some grotesque. The decapitated heads have been mentioned, but in the first act, the crowd's incitements to the executioner, declaring their readiness to torture—'noi siam pronti a ricamar le vostre pelli' (we are ready to embroider your skins)—belong to a way of thinking that runs throughout. The moon becomes a severed head; Ping, Pang, and Pong sing of Turandot's raw flesh beneath her clothes that cannot be eaten; the palace is the slaughterhouse, the place of strangling, impaling, throat-cutting, skinning, decapitation, and disembowelling; Ping sings of Calaf finding a brick wall to knock his head against, and the power of the Tao and then of the void ('il niente') is sung of, 'nel quale ti annulli'—in which you will be annihilated. This Schopenhauerian sentiment of nihilation continues the ground of Jago's Credo; indeed, it fits Puccini's melancholy; in this act, the sense of dominant illusion returns repeatedly. But it also accords with the Fascist ideology which declares the individual to

---

[16] Carner, *Turandot*, ed. Nicholas John (London: John Calder, 1984), p. 1984.

[17] She was identified as the type of the 'new woman' in the first-night review by the critic Andrea Della Corte; see Ashbrook and Powers, *Puccini's* Turandot, p. 155.

[18] Eugene Weber, *Varieties of Fascism* (New York: Van Nostrand Reinhold, 1964), p. 35. The passage is quoted by Barbara Spackman, 'The Fascist Rhetoric of Virility', in an issue of *Stanford Italian Review* called 'Fascism and Culture' (8 (1990)). Spackman quotes the work of Maria-Antonietta Macciochi, *Elements pour une analyse du fascisme* (Paris: Union générale d'Edition, 1976), on women in Fascism, quoting Hitler: 'in politics one must have the support of women; men will follow by themselves' (quoted, p. 83).

be of no importance.[19] Ping, Pang, and Pong sing of their homes in pastoral China in the second act, but they join in with the sadism expressed by the off-stage crowd. Turandot's description of a primal rape, which caused an originary cry of pain and outrage to break out, as Catherine Clément says, makes Turandot 'a woman possessed'. She quotes 'This cry took refuge in my soul', saying that 'here is the familiar hysteric'.[20] Turandot's second riddle (the answer is 'blood') appeals to a primal atavism:

> Guizza al pari di fiamma,
> e non è fiamma.
> È talvolta delirio.
> È febbre d'impeto e ardore!
> L'inerzia lo tramuta in un languore.
> Se ti perdi o trapassi, si raffredda.
> Se sogni la conquista, avvampa, avvampa!
> Ha una voce che trepido tu ascolti,
> e del tramonto il vivido baglior!

(It burns like flame but is not flame. Sometimes it is frenzy. It is fever of force and passion. If you lose, or go off, it becomes cold. If you dream of conquest, it flares it. It has a voice which you hear trembling, and the vivid glow of the setting sun.)

In relation to this, Catherine Clément's commentary is suggestive, pointing to the blood spilling from men in torture and war and to menstrual blood—that which the icy body of Turandot would seem to deny in its frigidity—and also the blood of Liù in Act 3; but then it is also phallic, the blood of an erection, which itself belongs to the realm of the gamble ('se ti perdi, o trapassi, si raffredda'), the death of the male resulting from the gamble being lost. Hope which fires the blood and Turandot, the name of the ice which incites that blood, these answers to the first and third riddles, circulate round that central image of blood, and both point to a phallicism central to this opera.

The violence of Act 3 includes Liù's torture and death and the anarchic attacks of the crowd, including Ping, Pang, and Pong, upon Calaf and his party. Those who attack have already been threatened with death unless Calaf's name is discovered before dawn (the inevitable period of the sun, the end of the moon and

---

[19] See on this Zeev Sternhell, *Neither Right nor Left: Fascist Ideology in France*, trans. David Maisel (1983: Berkeley and Los Angeles: University of California Press, 1986), pp. 33–8.

[20] Catherine Clément, *Opera, or the Undoing of Women*, trans. Betsy Wing (Minneapolis: University of Minnesota Press, 1988), p. 100.

its feminine domination). The way that Liù's death goes uncommented on in what follows, the part which focuses on Turandot as the irresistible object of desire (after she has driven one woman to her death), certainly belongs to the contradictory nature of the ending, to the failure to write a *Tristan und Isolde* love duet, a failure not separable from Puccini's death. Liù was Puccini's addition to Carlo Gozzi's plot; but it was not clear in Puccini's mind that her death would turn Turandot's heart. Puccini seemed to go no further than to say: 'I think that Liù must be sacrificed to some sorrow, but I don't see how to do this unless we make her die under torture. And why not? Her death could help to soften the heart of the Princess' (letter of 3 Nov. 1922, a week after the march on Rome, quoted by Ashbrook, *Operas of Puccini*, p. 206). Calaf hardly comments on her death: it remains an almost isolatable incident, whose sadistic impulses, in the composer choosing to place it there, are not easy to characterize. And since, at that point, as Toscanini memorably said at the first performance, the master laid down his pen, the violence and the affirmation of love remain in contradiction with each other, except that Calaf's final gamble which se-cures his victory also belongs, because it is a gamble, to the melancholy and near-despair that is inseparable from the violence at work in the text and the music.

Pinkerton and Calaf gamble, and in Chapter 2 I suggested that Jago could be seen as a gambler. In 1928, an essay of Freud's appeared called 'Dostoevsky and Parricide', which sets out links between masochistic elements in Dostoevsky and the subject-matter of *The Brothers Karamazov*, which is the killing of the father, as though by all of his sons. Those masochistic elements are further linked to Dostoevsky's 'addiction' to gambling, which Freud interprets as a self-punish-ment: playing till he had lost everything, as though punishing himself for the wish to kill the father, the father perceived as the castrating figure, who, paradoxically, must be killed, in order that the boy may enter into any sexual existence. Gambling replaces masturbation, Freud's 'primary addiction'.[21] I am not con-cerned here with the validity or otherwise of Freud's arguments, which I actually think are too much involved in his own model of psychoanalysis, not risky or speculative enough—not gambling enough. I am more interested in their sugges-tiveness for a reading of *Turandot*, where fantasies of a castrating woman replace the castrating father—Turandot appears on the balcony to signal the Prince of

---

[21] Quoted in *Art and Literature*, in *The Penguin Freud*, vol. 14, ed. Albert Dickson (Harmondsworth: Penguin, 1985), p. 459.

Persia to go to decapitation. Gambling which is motivated, in Freud's terms, by the desire to lose, fits with the death-wish, which Freud wrote about in *Beyond the Pleasure Principle* (1920). We have seen J. P. Stern's use of this motif in order to explain something about Hitler and fascism: that 'the death wish is at the heart of the will to power' (Stern, *Hitler*, p. 34). But, in contrast to this view, it should be noticed that gambling pays off for Calaf: he is put beyond 'castration' by it; he succeeds in replacing the old patriarch, the Emperor, with his own patriarchy. This involves the recodification of the woman out of her position as threat to patriarchy in that she has refused to marry and to be possessed by the male. At the end, she is brought into the traditional role, where she speaks in terms of 'love'.

The fantasy, then, in *Turandot* involves the complete victory of the male: 'Vincerò! Vincerò!' No wonder these finishing words of 'Nessun dorma' were made so much of in the British televising of the 1990 World Cup: the victory of the male is also the victory of a nation-state, for international sport and national ideology go together. Pinkerton's gamble is revealed to be futile; Calaf's, triumphant. One difference between the two is that Pinkerton, whose desire for whisky may suggest his lack of independence, his insecurity, is characterized by an unconsciousness, by an awareness that his ego is not wholly in control of the situation, as the love duet with Cio-Cio San suggests. Whereas Calaf has no such introspection, and indeed no awareness that he is gambling at all: 'the riddles are three, life is one' expresses his confidence in the face of unnerving odds. The confidence makes him a hero: this man does not gamble to lose, in contrast to Freud's argument, though Freud's point may hold its validity in relation to the whole text (where Puccini is the gambler, as it were), which itself fails in the gamble of being completed before the composer's death. The difference between Pinkerton and Calaf may owe much to Italy's shift towards a politics of violence and fantasy in the years after 1918, akin to the violence and (male) fantasy in the opera itself.

With reference to this violence, it is worth coming back to the question of the crowd in this opera: the 'popolo di Pekino', that anonymous body, 'la nera infinita umanita', the gloomy human crowd who long for hope, who call out to it and implore it as it flies above them. *Turandot* belongs to the moment of the discovery of the crowd: given their decisive study in 1895 by the French doctor and writer on all things scientific, Gustave Le Bon (1841–1931). Le Bon belongs to a prevalent discourse at work in Europe in the second half of the nineteenth century, one desperately afraid of the power of the working classes, of women, of the effects of alcohol, of the possibility of degeneration, and of the loss of national glory, particularly focused after France's defeat in the Franco–Prussian war of 1870. His very popular text on the crowd, *La Psychologie des foules* (1895), provided research findings used by Freud, for instance, in his essay 'Group Psychology and the Analysis of the Ego' (1921). The importance of Le Bon lies in his perception of the importance of the crowd as the powerful force of modern life and modern politics. Marxism may think in terms of class society: the discourse of those theorists of the crowd who belong with Le Bon shows, rather, a sense of mass society, that which needs to be led by a strong leader.[22]

Crowd psychology became topical in France in the Third Republic, in part as a fearful response to the events of the Commune in 1871 and in the face of such right-wing populism as Boulanger's (himself almost an operatic hero, who committed suicide over the grave of his mistress), which reached its climax in 1889. The General Strike of May Day 1890 was a source of Georges Sorel's thinking, as much as of the sense that the 'ERA OF THE MASSES' (Le Bon's phrase) had arrived. Zola's *Germinal* (1885) picked up on previous miners' strikes, and seemed to prelude another of January 1886 (discussed by Barrows, *Distorting Mirrors*, pp. 20–1), in which it was rumoured that Watrin, the deputy director of the mining company of Decazeville had been trampled on by a group of women and castrated by them (it happens in *Germinal*, with the figure of Maigrat). Women as castrating hordes and crowds as women: women as warriors, as vampires, as castrators, and as cannibals—this last theory was Lombroso's contribution, discussing revolts in Naples in 1799 and Palermo in 1866: these are anxious images constructed by late nineteenth-century patriarchy (Barrows, *Distorting Mirrors*, p. 57; Pick, *Faces of Degeneration*, p. 93), fitting another dominant image of the crowd as drunken, as a collection of alcoholics. For Gabriel Tarde, an early theorist of the crowd, writing in 1893, 'by its whimsy, its revolting docility, its credulity, its nervousness, its brusque psychological leaps from fury to tenderness, from exasperation to laughter, the crowd is feminine, even when it is composed, as is usually the case, of males' (quoted by Barrows, *Distorting Mirrors*, p. 149). Pick's thesis brings together the fear of revolution in France (revolutions marked out the years 1798, 1830, 1848, and 1870–1) and the coming into play of the

---

[22] See Susanna Barrows, *Distorting Mirrors: Visions of the Crowd in Late Nineteenth-Century France* (New Haven: Yale University Press, 1981), and Serge Moscovici, *The Age of the Crowd* (Cambridge: Cambridge University Press, 1985), for analysis of this topic. On Le Bon, see Robert A. Nye, *The Origins of Crowd Psychology* (London: Sage, 1975). See also Daniel Pick's *Faces of Degeneration*. For Freud, see *Civilization, Society and Religion*, in *The Penguin Freud*, vol. 12, ed. Albert Dickson, pp. 91–178.

discourse of degeneracy which I discussed with reference to the construction of Jago. To suggest that revolution is either the work of degenerates or allows degenerates to surface is powerful ideology, appealing to all those whose ideal is liberal progressivism; and to see women in the revolutionary crowds as both degenerate and revolutionary is to play on powerful fears. This model of the crowd as a woman may be compared with Le Bon:

Crowds are everywhere distinguished by feminine characteristics, but Latin crowds are the most feminine of all. Whoever trusts in them may rapidly attain a lofty destiny, but to do so is to be perpetually skirting the brink of a Tarpeian rock, with the certainty of one day being precipitated from it. (Quoted by Moscovici, *Age of the Crowd*, p. 110)

In the previous chapter, I referred to Tosca as the type of the Italian nation. As female, within this ideology of Le Bon, she is easily swayed by the proto-Fascist Scarpia, her jealousy a marker of the way the crowd moves backwards and forwards in its emotional commitments. But if at the end she goes over something like a Tarpeian rock, she has none the less dispatched the corrupt agent who would control the crowd; her stabbing of Scarpia bears out the character of the woman as depicted by the anxieties of patriarchy, and in itself looks forward to the power of Turandot. Similarly, *Andrea Chénier* presents a leader of the masses in the Gérard of Act 3, and throughout implies a contempt for the crowd, manipulated into singing 'La Carmagnole': again, that opera seems to have motivations in a contemporary awareness of the crowd as a new formation.

For Le Bon, to understand a crowd was a hypnotist's art; as though in the atmosphere of *Mario and the Magician* he says it needs to be controlled, as a herd which has reverted to a more primitive state of racial being, and that idea of control leads him to the idea of a leader. Such a leader, quoting Freud on Le Bon,

must himself be held in fascination by a strong faith (in an idea) in order to awaken the group's faith; he must possess a strong and imposing will, which the group, which has no will of its own, can accept from him . . . leaders make themselves felt by means of the ideas in which they themselves are fanatical believers. . . . he ascribes both to the ideas and to the leaders a mysterious and irresistible power, which he calls 'prestige' . . . a sort of domination exercised over us by an individual, a work or an idea . . . it would seem to arouse a feeling like that of 'fascination' in hypnosis. (Freud, 'Civilization', p. 108)

'Fascinating fascism' indeed, as Susan Sontag calls it. But the importance of seeing that the language and technology of fascism fascinate the crowd rests upon a prior sense that the leader believes his own rhetoric, too much romantic pessimism being dysfunctional for fascism.

I have noted Crispi's repressive response to socialist uprisings in the 1890s in Italy; Zeev Sternhell points to the significance of the Marquis de Morès proclaiming the doctrine of the *faisceau* in 1894 (Sternhell, *Neither Right nor Left*, p. 45) in a context of anti-Semitism, as with the Dreyfus case. 'Anti-Semitism' as a word seems first to have appeared in France in 1879. De Morès's wish was to mobilize the proletariat around it as an idea whereby to secure an imaginary French unity (the integration of the proletariat into the nation). Sternhell's thesis is that fascism, a mass movement with an anti-Semitic force, originated in France in the new Right associated with Boulangism, a new Right which differed from the old in being both anti-parliamentary (like Italian nationalist politics of the 1890s) and in favour of direct action by the people. Whereas the old Right had despised the crowd, the new Right wished to use it. Sternhell argues that the emergence of this new Right, which he contrasts to Bonapartism, 'which despite its populist and authoritarian character, belonged to a society where the participation of the people in the political process was limited,' laid the groundwork for fascism (ibid., pp. 26–7).

Le Bon and his sense of the populist leader, the new age of the crowd, and the crowd as that which must be controlled as a woman—these ideas engage not only France, but, more spectacularly, Mussolini directly, and I am arguing for their place in the structure of *Turandot*. But while Calaf may exhibit features of the hero whose skill goes beyond rationalism and human limitation (answering the riddles, like Oedipus answering the Sphinx's riddle), it still remains to say something about the violence which seems to show a regression to the primitive (the primitive Oriental). Here Georges Sorel's *Reflections on Violence* (1906) may help, where Sorel argues for the power of myth as the motor force of history. The *Reflections* looks forward to a war which will bring to power men who have a will to govern, bourgeois France having lost that along with its moral sense. His myth is of the proletariat, the crowd mobilized (the syndicalist movement), ready to fight in a struggle 'which, like the Napoleonic battle, is to annihilate completely a condemned regime'.[23] In Italy, Sorel's impact was felt in the revolutionary syndicalist movement—for instance, in the Italian general strikes of 1904 and 1908, but also in both nationalism and Italian imperialism. At the heart of Sorel is the stress

---

[23] Quoted by Jack J. Roth, *The Cult of Violence: Sorel and the Sorelians* (Berkeley and Los Angeles: University of California Press, 1980), p. 48.

on myth for the masses, on the proletariat taking direct action against bourgeois liberalism, on direct experience, struggle and action based not on rationalism, but on a sense of mastery. Sorel sees the American as the embodiment of a kind of mastery he is pleased to call Nietzschean: 'The master still exists before our eyes, and . . . it is he who brings into being at the present time the amazing greatness of the United States.' Later, Sorel speaks of 'the extraordinary parallels between the Yankee, capable of any task, and the ancient Greek mariner, sometimes pirate, sometimes colonist or merchant', and refers to

the parallel between the hero of antiquity and the man who dashes off to the conquest of the Far West. Paul de Rousiers has sketched an excellent portrait of the prototype of the master: 'To become, and remain, American, life must be regarded *as a struggle* and not as a pleasure; one must seek victorious effort, energetic and effective action, more than amusement, more than leisure embellished by the cultivation of the arts and the refinements peculiar to other societies. Everywhere . . . we have discovered what makes the American succeed, what constitutes his nature; it is moral value, personal, active and creative energy.' The same profound scorn that the Greek had for the barbarian, the Yankee has for the foreign worker who makes absolutely no effort to become truly American.[24]

A myth of Greek greatness substantiates another myth, that of the Yankee, the cowboy (and here might be mentioned the writer of westerns, Karl May (1842–1912), dealing with 'Old Shatterhand', favourite reading of Hitler). The hero, initially called Karl, belongs to the 'Wild West', and exists in an alliance with the 'Redskins' against the villainous Yankees—corrupt Americans of the north, men whom Pinkerton describes, but who are really the same as he is. The critique of American imperialism in *Madama Butterfly* might be regarded as belonging to the Sorelian myth about America. Because Pinkerton is not part of that Wild West ideology, it is significant that he is a figure of defeat, at least in moral terms. But perhaps Puccini is not all Sorelian: the admiration for the American male in *La Fanciulla* is also undone by the strength of the supporting heroine, who will not allow male destructiveness its way.[25]

In Sorel, myth operates in the sphere of pre-capitalistic, pre-modern society, in which individual action, working through violence, is mastery. Croce called

---

[24] John L. Stanley (ed.), *From Georges Sorel* (Oxford: Oxford University Press, 1976), pp. 213–14. Sorel refers to Paul de Rousiers's *La Vie américaine: Ranches, fermes et usines* (1899).

[25] On Karl May, see Christopher Frayling, *Spaghetti Westerns: Cowboys and Europeans from Karl May to Sergio Leone* (London: Routledge and Kegan Paul, 1981).

Reflections on Violence 'the breviary of Fascism' (quoted by Roth, *Cult of Violence,* p. 248). Mussolini took over areas of the stress on myth, and, accepting that violence meant that 'we accept whatever means may become necessary, the legal and the so-called illegal', said in 1922: 'We have created a Myth—a Myth that is a Fate, a passion. It does not need to be a reality, it is a stimulus and a hope, belief and courage. Our myth is the Nation, the grandeur of the Nation, which we will make a concrete reality' (quoted, ibid., pp. 210, 211).

The wish for mastery and the acceptance of violence: I think that the person who watches *Turandot,* unless he or she can make that viewing an active questioning process, has to accept and become complicit in a measure of violence that belongs to that European discourse which in Italy saw an imperialist war (1911), engagement in the First World War in spite of initial strong feelings that the country should keep out of it, and the institutionalized violence of the rise of fascism. That Italy entered the war at all, in the face of liberal neutrality and socialist disdain for fighting other capitalists' wars for them, owed much to the reactionary forces of nationalism which made the pressure for participation ultimately irresistible: the historian Adrian Lyttelton argues: 'in a real sense, Fascism itself was born in 1914–1915; and the split between interventionists and neutralists produced a violent laceration of the political fabric, a bitterness of feeling, more characteristic of a civil than of a "national" war. The divisions in the country and their consequences cannot be understood except in the light of the relationship, or lack of it, between the State and the mass of the Italian people.'[26] That Italy entered the war seems to have been a turn of the screw towards violence which did not end after 1918. A Sorelian culture obtains, the banality of which is captured in the fascist and Sorelian French novelist Pierre Drieu la Rochelle, who speaks of his orgasmic delight in violence: 'On August 23 and October 29, 1914, in the course of two bayonet charges, I experienced an ecstasy . . . I consider equal to those of Saint Theresa' (quoted by Roth, *Cult of Violence,* p. 197).

In *Turandot* something has happened whereby the restraints felt earlier in the portrayal of the Puccinian hero have been taken away. Busoni's *Turandot* (1917) gives a heroine who is 'a person of considerable intellect, driven to savage extremes in the search for her equal', while Kalaf 'is a fiery idealist with a truly Faustian urge. "I wish for the exceptional" is his call—and he achieves it.'[27] The comparison

[26] Adrian Lyttelton, *The Seizure of Power: Fascism in Italy 1919–1929* (Princeton: Princeton University Press, 1987), p. 3.

[27] Antony Beaumont, *Busoni the Composer* (London: Faber, 1985), p. 242.

with Busoni, the Italian composer who could not settle in Italy, makes the point finely: Puccini's work is comparatively anti-intellectual (indeed, bourgeois) and sheerly materialistic, representing a glib coarsening of Nietzsche's sense of the self going beyond itself.

Calaf does not represent an ideal; instead, he replaces an old, etiolated order as surely as the new rising sun. (Is the Emperor here Victor Emmanuel III, who made Mussolini Prime Minister after the march on Rome? Is he Giolitti, the old liberal politician, who represented the old parliamentary democracy that fascism overthrew?) Calaf's conquest, signalled in 'Nessun dorma', is affirmed when he induces the woman to ask 'Come vincesti?' (How did you conquer?) and to reply to her own question by saying that, as opposed to all the other princes who wanted to claim her, 'I feared you'. 'C'era negli occhi tuoi / la luce degli eroi. / C'era negli occhi tuoi / la superba certezza' (In your eyes shone the light of heroes. In your eyes [was] proud certainty). Such a fantasy of the new leader recalls not the world of *Tristan,* but that of *Parsifal,* who also triumphs as the unknown hero from outside (Lohengrin, Parsifal, and Calaf are similar here), and, more specifically, Siegfried, who does not know what fear means. Nor, of course, do any of these culture heroes know what degeneracy means: they are all noble.

Calaf as a fantasy where Mussolini was the reality: is it possible to read the text against that endorsement of the hero who bangs on the gong with the force of destiny? A small point against would be to notice that 'Nessun dorma' seems tacked on as an older-style aria almost detachable from the whole; certainly it seems to be readily packageable as a commodity, as I have already noted that this has been its fate. That might perform a critique of Calaf by showing him as two-dimensional. It also seems interesting that the opera uses the ghosts of Turandot's past suitors. The text thus breaks the boundary between fantastic reality and what might be characterized as psychodrama (Calaf listening to a Schreker-like 'ferne Klang', as it were) or sheer fantasy. But if the prevalent tone of nihilism means anything, it may suggest that there is no difference between the living and the dead. In the same way, the chorus pray to the ghost of Liù, giving her more respect when dead than when alive, and the spirit of Princess Lou-Ling still lives in Turandot. These interchanges between the dead and the living may suggest a fantasy world of primitive belief; or perhaps they make the events of the opera more phantasmagoric, recalling Adorno and Wagner, and hollow out assertions of possession and power into nothingness. If that is so, then the text may perform its own critique, its nihilism fitting the emptiness of fascist displays and rhetoric, just as the melancholy and sense of anonymity that hovers over the opera becomes the key to a lack of belief in its events.

And there are other ghosts in the text: one the music of *Tristan und Isolde*, which Puccini wished to reactivate in the last duet, but died before writing, the second the duet itself. If he had lived to write the love duet which would belong to the world of *Tristan*, a work he greatly admired, he would have been guilty of a misrecognition. His death, which meant that he did not stray into that discourse, has something uncanny about it, like the gamble itself. For *Tristan* celebrates the D'Annunzio-like hero who is marked out by his perpetual convalescence—his sense of himself as flawed, wounded as far as his patriarchal power is concerned: the message is equally portrayed in *L'innocente* and *Il trionfo della morte*. If Calaf were Tristan, he would have lost the gamble: he would have desired to lose it. Puccini's wish to evoke Wagnerian opera was nostalgic, revealing both an idealization of the Wagnerian hero and a failure to register how Italian operatic discourse had changed, had become a ghost. In the 1920s, the possibility of being a Tristan had vanished in the face of a newer discourse which demanded a Calaf. Calaf answers the riddles, but has no interiority; there is nothing to be discovered about him. He has no ghosts attending him. In Straussian terminology, he would be the hero of an opera called *Der Mann ohne Schatten*. He is simply the myth of the complete man: Otello without the jealousy and the death-wish, Jago without the decadence and the nihilism, a fantasy of Italian ideology. The situation of the love duet, which would imply loss of completeness in moving out into mutuality, might be ghosted on paper in a libretto, but not set to music. The aim of the opera is to close the gap between aspiration and achievement, to realize the full fantasy of controlling power which itself is on the side of the great and the good. But just as the regime under which the opera was written signally failed to realize its fantasies, so operatic form and Puccini's life, both pushed to their limits, collapsed and died. The irony should not be lost that this opera, which arguably drives the trends of operatic thinking to one logical conclusion, and gives it a powerful, even wonderful, send-off, not only failed to be completed, but also ended the Italian operatic tradition.

PART III
Opera, Gender, and Degeneracy

6
Daughters of Kundry:
Salome and *Elektra*

The music is the ultimate in modernism. Nobody has ever gone beyond it. Strauss's so-called 'progress' is all twaddle. Every one of them continues to feed and draw on *Parsifal*. What a terrifyingly *expressive* art! The accents of contrition and torment that he practised all his life achieve their ultimate intensity only here. Tristan's longing pales beside this Miserere. Piercing details, gripping moments, the most refined and ardent cruelties. But does it still have a future? Does it not already belong to history in terms of ambience, tendency, taste?

Mann, *Pro and Contra Wagner*

It happened that the first Austrian performance of *Salome*, conducted by the composer himself, was to take place in Graz, the capital of Styria, in May 1906. Adrian and Kretschmar had gone to Dresden to see its actual première, and he told his teacher . . . that he wanted to be present at this gala performance, and hear again that successful revolutionary work whose aesthetic sphere did not at all attract him, but which of course interested him in a musical and technical sense, particularly as the setting to music of a prose dialogue.

Mann, *Doctor Faustus*

Going to this performance of *Salome* aligns Leverkühn with Mahler, who was at Graz on 16 May, as were Berg, Schoenberg, and Zemlinsky. According to Stefan Zweig in *The World of Yesterday*, so was the young Hitler. But was *Salome* much more than a continuation of *Parsifal*'s obsessions about the woman? Or was *Elektra*, which Mann found 'uninteresting' (*Pro and Contra Wagner*, p. 41)? Klingsor calls Kundry Herodias when he evokes her in *Parsifal* Act 2, so Salome is literally a daughter of Kundry. Opposition to Kundry in *Parsifal*, which shows in Wedekind's *Erdgeist* and *Büchse der Pandora*,[1] nevertheless repeats features of Kundry, most clearly demonstrable by the time we come to *Lulu*. A fixation with gender issues as they are rendered here is also a crisis for modernist opera, and contains its own politics within it.

[1] See Ulrich Müller and Peter Wapnewski, *Wagner Handbook*, trans. and ed. John Deathridge (Cambridge, Mass.: Harvard University Press, 1992), p. 90.

In this chapter, I want to look at *Salome* and then *Elektra*. With *Salome*, it will be useful to contrast Strauss and Wilde in terms of their gender politics; with *Elektra*, the attitude towards women and emotions that works through Hofmann-sthal is influenced by the reactionary and quasi-fascist writings of Otto Weininger, which I shall discuss, before mapping the way the 'woman question' is posed on to a reading of Austrian politics on the eve of the First World War. In the next chapter, also on Strauss, I look at his reaction away from Modernism after the First World War, and his reactionariness: signing the letter of protest from Munich against Thomas Mann in response to the criticisms of Wagner expressed in 'The Sufferings and Grandeur of Richard Wagner'; volunteering the same year, 1933, to conduct *Parsifal* at Bayreuth in place of Toscanini, who had withdrawn. The modernist has become the fascist's lap-dog. So was the modernism itself meretricous? Was it really already of the past?

GODDESSES OF HYSTERIA

> [*Salome's*] atmosphere is sickening and stale . . . it is not a question of bourgeois morals, it is a question of healthiness. The same passions can be healthy or unhealthy according to the artists who experience them and the characters in whom they are incarnate. The incest of *Die Walküre* is a thousand times healthier than conjugal and lawful love in these rotten Parisian comedies, the names of which I should prefer not to mention. Wilde's *Salome* and all those who surround her, save only that brute of a Jochanaan, are unhealthy, unclean, hysterical or alcoholic, oozing with a perfumed and mundane corruption. It is in vain that you transfigure your subject by multiplying a hundredfold its energy and enveloping it in a Shakespearean atmosphere; it is in vain that you have lent emotional tones of a moving nature to your *Salome*.
>
> Romain Rolland[2]

What are we to make of this contrast between Wagner and Wilde? One trans-gresses the sexual in brother–sister incest, and Nietzsche calls him decadent; the other, who parodies Wagner in *Salome*—the wooing of Jochanaan by Salome evokes Kundry trying to seduce Parsifal—was certainly held to be decadent by his own bourgeois society. Rolland's word 'healthy' appears, with its derivatives, five

---

[2] Quoted by Norman Del Mar, *Richard Strauss*, 3 vols. (1962; London: Barrie and Jenkins, 2nd edn. 1978), i. 283.

times in this letter; operatic art should be healthy. The word maps on to several things already referred to in the course of this study: it evokes Jago, arguments about degeneracy, Wagner on sexuality, Theweleit's proto-Nazis, and fascist rhetoric about biological decline.

For Rolland, *Salome* was a *fin de siècle* text, associated with his first experiences of hearing Strauss conduct in 1898, when he felt that there was a 'Neroism in the air' as a result of 'Germany's dizzy promptings' which had been called up by Nietzsche, and which existed both in Strauss's music and attitudes and in the imperialism of the Kaiser. (We may compare with this Puccini's 'Neronic instinct'). In 1900 Rolland saw in Strauss 'the powerful reflection of that heroic pride, which is on the verge of becoming delirious, . . . that contemptuous Nietzscheanism, . . . that egotistical and practical idealism which makes a cult of power and disdains weakness'.[3] These are familiar critiques of the 1890s and of the power of Modernism. But we should not, perhaps, treat them too seriously. The Kaiser was equally bourgeois when, in 1892, he called secessionist art in Berlin 'art from the gutter'. In looking at attacks on decadence, we must see who is making the critique, and what interests are being policed.

To get at the 'decadence' of *Salome*, it will be well to look first at the figure of Salome herself in the nineteenth century. The source material for Wilde's play uses a deliberately unhealthy hero in Joris-Karl Huysmans's novel *A Rebours* (1884), 'Against the Grain' or 'Against Nature'. The title may sound like an invitation to reread history, public ideology, and bourgeois culture, to reread against the grain. But it is more mixed than that. 'Decadence' had been used earlier in the century to convey the sense of a decline of a civilization,[4] and Des Esseintes is the aesthete/aristocrat whose body is worn out through generations of inherited weakness. He possesses 'two masterpieces' of Gustave Moreau (1826–98) thematizing Salome, *Salome Dancing before Herod* and the water-colour *The Apparition* (both of 1876).

The Salome motif pervades bourgeois and anti-bourgeois culture: in, for example, Heine's poem *Atta Troll* (1841), where Herodias is the embodiment of Semitic poetry and a figure of unrequited love; Mallarmé's 'Hérodiade', begun in 1864; Flaubert's *Trois Contes* (1877); Massenet's opera *Hérodiade* (1881), which uses

---

[3] Quoted in Rollo Myers (ed.), *Richard Strauss and Romain Rolland: Correspondence* (London: Calder and Boyars, 1968), pp. 112, 122.

[4] See Ian Fletcher (ed.), *Decadence and the 1890s* (London: Edward Arnold, 1979); Jean Pierrot, *The Decadent Imagination 1880–1900*, trans. Derek Coltman (Chicago: University of Chicago Press, 1981).

Flaubert's text; Laforgue's *Moralités légendaires* (1886), which parodies the tone of the earlier narrations; Wilde's play of 1891, and Beardsley's illustrations for its English publication. Alongside these specific versions of the Salome theme are others that are more general, but also influential: Baudelaire's 'Les Femmes damnées', Flaubert's *Salammbô* (1862), Villiers de l'Îsle Adam's *Isis* (1862); the *Beheading of John the Baptist* (painting by Puvis de Chavannes, 1869); and Delacroix's earlier *Beheading of John the Baptist*. The motif of the woman holding the head of her lover looks back to the ending of Stendhal's *Le Rouge et le noir* (1830). Klimt's 'Judith I' and 'Judith II' continue the subject in 1901 and 1909.[5]

The appearance of two Salome paintings in *A Rebours* then clicks into a whole repertory of images of the primitive Oriental woman. Orientalism inspires Moreau: his paintings of *femmes fatales* include the *Thracian Woman Carrying the Head of Orpheus* (1864) and *Oedipus and the Sphinx* (1866). *Salome, Helen of Troy Standing above a Heap of Bodies, Galatea, Cleopatra, Bathsheba, Andromeda, Delilah*, all painted in the 1880s–1890s, contribute to the sense of women as idols and as castrating. The Salome of Moreau's first famous picture links her gesturally to the goddess of fertility, Diana of the Ephesians, who is above Herod's head, and Moreau's own commentary on the painting runs:

this woman represents eternal woman, a frivolous, often fatal character, passing through life holding a flower, searching for her vague ideal. Often terrible and walking, always crushing everything under foot, even geniuses and saints. This dance takes place, this mysterious promenade is performed in front of death, who watches her incessantly gaping and attentive, and in front of the executioner with the sword that strikes. She is the emblem of a terrible future, reserved for those who search for a nameless, sensual and unhealthily curious ideal.[6]

---

[5] For commentary on all these, see Pierre-Louis Matthieu, *Gustave Moreau* (London: Phaidon, 1977), pp. 121–6; Jean Paladilhe, *Gustave Moreau: His Life and Works* (London: Thames and Hudson, 1972), pp. 97–102; Elliot L. Gilbert, 'Tumult of Images: Wilde, Beardsley and *Salomé*', *Victorian Studies*, 26 (1983): 133–59; Helen Grace Zagona, *The Legend of Salome and the Principle of Art for Art's Sake* (Geneva: Droz, 1960). For links between Salome and French feminism and deconstruction, see Françoise Meltzer, *Salome and the Dance of Writing* (Chicago: University of Chicago Press, 1987), ch. 1. For application to the opera, see Sander Gilman's essay, most conveniently found in Groos and Parker (eds.), *Reading Opera*; Lawrence Kramer's articles 'Culture and Musical Hermeneutics: The Salome Complex', *Cambridge Opera Journal*, 2 (1990): 269–94, and '*Fin de Siècle* Fantasies: *Elektra*, Degeneration and Sexual Science', *Cambridge Opera Journal*, 5/2 (1993): 141–65; Nicholas John, (ed.), *Salome and Elektra* (London: John Calder, 1988); Derrick Muffett, *Salome* (Cambridge: Cambridge University Press, 1989).
[6] Quoted by Julius David Kaplan, *The Art of Gustave Moreau* (Epping: Bowker Publishing Co., 1982), p. 58.

This is similar to Des Esseintes's conclusion about the Salome that Moreau depicts dancing before Herod:

She had become, as it were, the symbolic incarnation of undying Lust, the Goddess of immortal Hysteria, the accursed Beauty exalted over all other beauties by the catalepsy that hardens her flesh and steels her muscles, the monstrous Beast, indifferent, irresponsible, insensible, poisoning, like the Helen of ancient myth, everything that approaches her, everything that sees her, everything that she touches.[7]

In *The Apparition*, where, as if in a monstrous erection, the head of John the Baptist rises off the dish, high into the air, to gaze at Salome, she is 'a true harlot, obedient to her passionate and cruel female temperament, here . . . she roused the sleeping senses of the male more powerfully, subjugated his will more surely with her charms—the charms of a great venereal flower, grown in a bed of sacrilege, reared in a hot-house of impiety' (ibid., p. 68).

This perception of the woman can be paired with Des Esseintes's nightmare which comes after he has collected plants as unnatural-looking as possible, plants which mime the corruption of flesh. This makes him reflect on the primacy of corruption:—'It all comes down to syphilis in the end' (ibid., p. 101). The virus which he perceives as causing universal decay is on the plants as well. The fantasies of the dream entail seeing 'the image of the Pox' (ibid., p. 103) in the vision of a woman and of a sexless figure on a horse; the woman loses her teeth, which has obvious associations with syphilis, and may also point to castration fears; the dream progresses to the sight of 'enormous white pierrots . . . jumping about like rabbits in the moonlight' (ibid., p. 104) and then to fantasies of a woman. 'Naked but for a pair of green silk stockings', she modulates into the flower (Salome is associated, in the Moreau painting, and in Des Esseintes's commentary on this, with the lotus), and then into the virus. The woman's corruption is evident, but the man is impelled to draw near:

He was almost touching her when black Amorphophalli sprang up on every side and stabbed at her belly, which was rising and falling like a sea. He thrust them aside and pushed them back, utterly nauseated by the sight of these hot, firm stems twisting and turning between his fingers. Then all of a sudden, the odious plants had disappeared and two arms were trying to enfold him. . . . He made a superhuman effort to free himself from her embrace, but with an irresistible movement she clutched him, and held him, and pale

[7] *A Rebours*, trans. as *Against Nature* by Robert Baldick (Harmondsworth: Penguin, 1959), p. 66.

with horror he saw the savage Nidularium blossoming between her uplifted thighs, with its swordblades gaping open to expose the bloody depths. (ibid., p. 106)

The Amorphophallus has been brought to him in a series of Orientalist and imperialistic (and kitsch) fantasies as 'a plant from Cochin-China with leaves the shape of fish-slices and long black stalks crisscrossed with scars like the limbs [*membres*] of a negro slave'. The Nidularium 'open[s] its sword-shaped petals to reveal gaping flesh-wounds' (ibid., p. 99). The woman is seen as castrated, and with a potential castrating impact on him as the seducing figure, while she is also the personification of unnatural nature, the virus.[8] She is herself phallic, as well as a mixture of plant and human life (a portrayal of degeneracy), and belongs among other figures of ambiguous sexuality. Perhaps the figure on the horse is a fantasy of the father, and the first woman is the mother. Perhaps the Pierrots (who I discussed in Chapter 4) are desexed. The fantasy of the lack of teeth, which recalls an earlier incident in the novel of a visit to the dentist (ch. 4), full of castration and rape anxieties, fits with a dream recorded by Edmond de Goncourt, in his *Journal*, belonging to Bastille Day, 14 July 1883, almost exactly the same time as the incident in *A Rebours*:

I dreamt last night that I was at a party, in white tie. At that party, I saw a woman come in, and recognised her as an actress in a boulevard theatre, but without being able to put a name to her face. She was draped in a scarf, and I noticed only that she was completely naked when she hopped onto the table where two or three girls were having tea. Then she started to dance, and while she was dancing took steps that showed her private parts armed with the most terrible jaws one could imagine, opening and closing, exposing a set of teeth. The spectacle had no erotic effect on me, except to fill me with an atrocious jealousy, and to give me a ferocious desire to possess myself of her teeth—just as I am beginning to lose all my good ones. Where the devil could such an outlandish dream come from? It's got nothing to do with the taking of the Bastille.[9]

---

[8] See Charles Bernheimer, 'Huysmans: Against (Female) Nature', in Susan Robin Suleiman (ed.), *The Female Body in Western Culture* (Cambridge, Mass.: Harvard University Press, 1985), pp. 373–86.

[9] Quoted by Pick, *Faces of Degeneration*, p. 96. Pick refers to Peter Gay, *The Bourgeois Experience: Victoria to Freud*, Vol. 1: *The Education of the Senses* (Oxford: Oxford University Press, 1984), pp. 198–9, where Gay gives an 'orthodox' psychoanalytic explanation of this. See Gay, *Education of the Senses*, pp. 197–213, for a treatment of the nineteenth-century 'castrating sisterhood'. But Pick's discussion of late nineteenth-century fear of women (*Faces of Degeneration*, pp. 87–96) seems altogether more precise and less reliant on assumptions about general truths—'man's fear of woman is as old as time' is Gay's (*Education of the Senses*, p. 169) beginning of the whole chapter. On degeneration generally, see J. Edward Chamberlain and Sander L. Gilman (eds.), *Degeneration: The Dark Side of Progress* (New York: Columbia University Press, 1985).

As a male fantasy, the castrating woman, evoking Lombroso's equations of the degenerate, the criminal, and the revolutionary, had everything to do with the storming of the Bastille. Georges Sorel in the 1890s saw a woman's depravity, her degeneration, to consist in prostitution, which he called 'the essence of female crime' (quoted by Pick, *Faces of Degeneration*, p. 105). An association of ideas extends from the hysterical crowd and the revolutionary woman as prostitute, who thereby gives character to the crowd. Pick connects this with France's late nineteenth-century 'extraordinary obsession with hysteria' (ibid., p. 95), and Salome is 'the goddess of immortal Hysteria'.

The patriarchal fear of the last three decades of the nineteenth century was not solely of women, but of political destabilization, of the bourgeois losing its position. But there is a huge violence implied against women, none the less, and a fear of their loss to the national economy. Such French theorists as Le Bon feared that feminism would take the form of a 'grève des ventres' (a womb strike); women failing to reproduce and build up France's population, which seemed, after 1871, to be woefully down in contrast to Germany's. In the attempt to keep women within the bounds of patriarchal demands, Max Nordau, author of a famous study called *Degeneration* (1893), recommended 'female castration' (*De la castration de la femme*, 1892) as a response to what he took to be the hysteria and near-insanity of women. This form of violence (recommending, presumably, clitorectomy) does not make him utterly dissimilar to the more obviously violent Jack the Ripper who killed women in London in 1888, removing their uterus and viscera. The Ripper, called 'The Whitechapel murderer', was discussed by Krafft-Ebing in the second edition of his volume of sexology *Psychopathia Sexualis* (1893). Krafft-Ebing surmised that he ate parts of the flesh of his victims.[10] The White-chapel murders were used by Wedekind, who read Krafft-Ebing, in *Büchse der Pandora*, and entered opera via *Lulu*.

The womb, part of Pandora's box, is the Greek *husteron*; the hysterical woman as Salome in *A Rebours* is unstable because of her womb and her monthly changes; hysteria was gendered as a female condition in the nineteenth century through the power of medical discourse, making woman a 'natural' hysteric, basically ready to run wild. Woman as nature is a powerful myth: Des Esseintes works with it in his fantasies, as when he thinks of the evisceration of the woman in 'the sepulchral rites of ancient Egypt, the solemn ceremonies of embalment, when practioners and priests lay out the dead woman's body on a slab of jasper, then with curved

[10] Richard von Krafft-Ebing, *Psychopathia Sexualis*, 10th German edn., trans. F. J. Rebman (London: Rebman Ltd., 1901), p. 86.

needles extract her brains through the nostrils, . . . and finally, . . . insert into her sexual parts, in order to purify them, the chaste petals of the divine flower [i.e. the lotus]' (*A Rebours*, pp. 66–7).

The castration fantasies of the nightmare do not affect only the man, but also the woman. If the insertion of the flower into the body imitates intercourse, it is also analogous to a castrating action. So the 'savage Nidularium' acts also to castrate the woman: it is Jack the Ripper again. *A Rebours* looks for an art which is outside nature; hence the aestheticizing of reality, the bejewelling of the dead body, like the tortoise covered with precious stones (ch. 4) which kill the tortoise beneath. The tortoise, too, may evoke the female sex organ.[11] Alternatively, the nightmare of Des Esseintes may suggest the loss of sexual distinction, the fear that both men and women may actually be castrated, that there is no basis for difference; in which case there may well be fear of anarchy at the level of class, sex, or race.

SALOME

Before turning to Strauss, it should be considered how these things—the basis of a whole discourse about women—work out in Wilde's *Salome*. Oscar Wilde's play, written in French in 1891 and translated in 1894, was not performed in London because of censorship, but was staged in Paris in 1896 and in Berlin in 1902, in a production by Max Reinhardt, which Strauss saw. It was the beginning of a taste for using Wilde for operas: Schreker's pantomine *Der Geburtstag der Infantin* followed in 1908, based on the short story of 1891, 'The Birthday of the Infanta', and Schreker continued this theme with *Die Gezeichneten* (1913–15). Zemlinsky's *Eine Florentinische Tragödie* (1916) followed a verse-play that Wilde wrote in 1894 and that Puccini considered for a libretto. *Der Zwerg* (The Dwarf, now better known as *The Birthday of the Infanta*) succeeded in 1921.

Perhaps something intentionally operatic informed the writing of Wilde's *Salome*. Its rhythms and repetitions, for instance, bring it near to a libretto, and certainly Bernhardt, for whom it was designed, helps to link it to *Tosca*, in Sardou's version of which she starred.[12] Wilde's reference to the text's 'refrains whose recurring motifs make it sound like a piece of music and bind it together

---

[11] See Rodolphe Gasché, 'The Falls of History: Huysmans's *A Rebours*', *Yale French Studies*, 92 (1988): 201.

[12] See Kerry Powell, *Oscar Wilde and the Theatre of the 1890s* (Cambridge: Cambridge University Press, 1990), ch. 3. On the work generally, see Richard Ellmann, *Oscar Wilde* (London: Hamish Hamilton, 1987), pp. 320–6.

as a ballad' (quoted by Del Mar, *Richard Strauss*, i. 241) suggests a use by Wagner. A difference between Wilde's play and Strauss's opera, however, picks up on the fact that Strauss pushes the text over into the obviously operatic, whereas Wilde's play remains camp, in which it also differs from *A Rebours* and most other nineteenth-century versions of Salome/Herodias. Being camp and being operatic have sometimes been taken to be the same, but they need distinguishing.

'Camp' is a term almost created by its use in Susan Sontag's 'Notes on Camp', which is dedicated to Oscar Wilde, and which defines the term with reference to assorted examples, saying that it is 'the consistently aesthetic experience of the world. It incarnates a victory of "style" over "content," "aesthetics" over "morality," of irony over tragedy.'[13] Earlier, Christopher Isherwood discussed 'High Camp' as 'the emotional basis of the Ballet . . . and of course of Baroque art . . . You're expressing what's basically serious to you in terms of fun and artifice and elegance . . . Baroque art is largely camp about religion. The Ballet is camp about love. . . . Mozart's definitely camp. Beethoven, on the other hand, isn't.'[14] Sontag's essay is more interesting in taking camp as a mode of irony. Camp cannot be tragic, because tragedy demands an investment in feeling which is endorsed definitely, whereas camp recognizes the doubleness, the inherently parodic nature, of utterance. It is this that makes a feminist reading of Wilde's *Salome*—there are several—difficult to sustain, because it demands a commitment that camp would be unwilling to give. Whereas kitsch does not work by irony, and asks for an acceptance of simplified, laundered emotions, camp does not; it plays up its bad taste: it 'asserts that good taste is not simply good taste, that there exists, indeed, a good taste of bad taste' (Sontag, *Against Interpretation*, p. 291). In a way that Sontag's essay does not emphasize, we may now, in the light of more recent gender studies, see good taste as gendered (which means that it may be directed towards a straight sensibility) and ideologically bourgeois. Bad taste, which is, of course, defined as such by that dominant ideology, is a necessary challenge to it in gender terms. An example given by Sontag of camp in opera is Bellini (the unspoken contrast to him would be Verdi, masculinist to the core); but Sontag finds *art nouveau* to be camp, and in the same spirit, says that the operas of Strauss are camp, but not those of Wagner (ibid., p. 278), since he offers his music and themes as too important to be camp.

---

[13] Susan Sontag, *Against Interpretation and Other Essays* (New York: Octagon, 1986), p. 287. For a recent approach to camp, see Andrew Travers, 'An Essay on Self and Camp', *Theory, Culture and Society*, 11 (1993): 127–43.

[14] Christopher Isherwood, *The World in the Evening* (London: Methuen, 1954), p. 125.

If Strauss's *Salome* was found to be camp, that would imply a close following of Wilde, and would mean a critique of Romain Rolland, for whom the category of camp, the idea of subversion by style, would mean little. But it has yet to be proved that Strauss is camp. Wilde gives the primary emphasis in his play to the idea of the violation of taboos, taboos of sexual, racial, and class difference, the incest one being primary. The young Syrian looks at Salome, and the page of Herodias looks at him, homosexually attracted to someone who is perhaps also his brother. Herod looks at Salome, thus suggesting one incest on top of another (relations with the daughter after relations with the wife who is actually his sister-in-law). Salome looks at Jokanaan. The young Syrian used to look at himself in the water (p. 545).[15] He is a narcissist. (The phrase 'Narcissus-like' to describe a psychological attitude, one quickly identified as a perversion, was first used in 1898 by Havelock Ellis.) The young Syrian compares Salome to 'a narcissus trembling in the wind' (p. 540), a comparison omitted in the opera. At the end, Salome says to the head of Jokanaan, brought to her on a shield as though it were a delicacy on a plate (part of the camp), 'I was a virgin and thou didst take my virginity from me' (p. 559). This again evokes a violated taboo, however much it is a fantasy that is being described (the words are cut in the opera). Taboos, however, are what everyone in this text wishes to break, and it seems undeniable that the text wishes to support that: its radical nature is its nihilistic questioning of any basis on which taboos are set up.

Kerry Powell (*Oscar Wilde*, p. 167) quotes Jane Marcus, who identifies Salome as Wilde's 'New Woman,' his Hedda Gabler. The linking to a play also written in 1891 is suggestive. Hedda's 'unnaturalness' in that play, which goes through her relations to everyone—pulling their hair, insulting the aunt's hat, refusing to take hints about pregnancy, destroying the 'child' (the manuscript of Lovborg and Mrs Elvsted), and enticing Lovborg to kill himself beautifully—is part of a nihilism like Jago's, which exposes 'nature' as so much bourgeois ideology. That, in its turn, is like Kundry's laughter, which, reading backwards from Wilde's *Salome*, can be identified as being of the same order as her undermining of late nineteenth-century bourgeois morality, whose illusory and attenuated nature is becoming obvious, and challenging it right at the source—with the character of Christ, the hero of weakness, of passivity, preaching life as self-denial. That reading is, of course, Nietzschean, and would not have pleased Wagner, though in Chapter 1

---

[15] Quotations from Wilde here and elsewhere are taken from *The Works of Oscar Wilde*, ed. G. F. Maine (London: Collins, 1948).

I quoted from *The Gay Science* to show that the antithesis Wagner/Nietzsche might not be as simple as that.

Salome effectively uncovers the perversity in virtue; Jokanaan's sadistic prophecies are really invitations to violence, as when he shouts from the prison, 'Let the people take stones and stone her . . . let the war captains pierce her with their swords, let them crush her beneath their shields' (p. 550). These words seem to have reference to Salome, but Herodias says that these words apply to her. Herod keeps their referentiality open by saying, 'He did not speak your name', but of course the killing with the shields—a visual symbol of the act of repression, covering up an offensive representation of something—is exactly what, following from these instructions, he learns to instruct his soldiers to do to Salome. Salome is right to accuse him of sexism and hatred of women in her words 'Thou didst treat me as a harlot, as a wanton, me Salome' (p. 559)—again, words cut from the opera. These may suggest that the fantasy at work in her sense of deflowerment actually corresponds to a male fantasy of Jokanaan's, a desire for penetration, enacted in the image of piercing with swords. Salome identifies herself with the moon on account of its virginity—'Yes, she is a virgin. She has never defiled herself. She has never abandoned herself to men, like the other goddesses' (p. 540). Again, the opera cuts these words, and weakens the association with the moon (and therefore makes Salome more threatening sexually, though it is also true, as Del Mar points out, that Salome's own motifs are heard as she sings about the moon, so implying that the reference is to herself). Salome tries to assimilate Jokanaan to herself by saying of him in both play and opera, 'I am sure he is chaste as the moon is' (p. 543), thus attributing to him her own softness and lack of violence; but though she is right that he is chaste, in other respects she has picked the wrong man, has got someone who is desperately anti-female. I associate this statement about his chastity with her promise to give Narraboth a little green flower when she sees him next (p. 542). It is camp, a touch of aestheticism which cuts out all traces of the fearful, castrating woman. She likes men who are not a threat to women. By contrast, Narraboth's suicide is a desperate, self-repressive, guilt-inducing violence analogous to Jokanaan's verbal violence. Romain Rolland's reading of Jokanaan oversimplifies. It may be that the virtuous are less violent than the vicious in this text (Herod, Herodias) only because they have less power to be so.

Herod's response is inherently repressive: the prison for Jokanaan is out of sight, down below; at the end, he wants the torches to be put out, and the moon and stars to be hidden, but in the play, not the opera, he also says: 'I will not look at things, I will not suffer things to look at me' (p. 559). Jokanaan is as uptight as Herod about not looking, and almost seems to rely on the soldiers to keep him from the dangerous woman: 'Who is this woman who is looking at me? I will not have her look at me. Wherefore doth she look at me with her golden eyes, under her golden eyelids? I know not who she is. I do not wish to know who she is. Bid her begone. It is not to her that I would speak' (p. 543). He goes back into the prison saying, 'I do not wish to look at thee. I will not look at thee, thou art accursed, Salome, thou art accursed' (p. 545). Again the opera lessens the impact by cutting the opening repetition.

Looking and not looking is a trope constantly at work in the play. The body of the young Syrian has to be hidden; the moon, in contrast to such repression, is a naked woman (again these words are not in the opera)—'The clouds are seeking to clothe her nakedness, but she will not let them. She shows herself naked in the sky' (p. 546). Herod is anxious not to look too deeply, and says in an epigrammatic moment worthy of *The Importance of Being Earnest*, 'You must not find symbols in everything you see. It makes life impossible' (p. 553, but not in the opera). He believes that 'it is not meet that the eyes of a virgin should look upon [Jokanaan's head]' (p. 555)—again, this precise formulation is cut from the opera—and adds: 'Neither at things, nor at people should one look. Only in mirrors should one look, for mirrors do but show us masks' (p. 556). Looking in the mirror returns us to Narcissus, and implies that the scandal of Salome, like the moon, is her desire to go beyond this, and to probe what the culture of Herod and of Jokanaan, two halves of a single entity, it appears, leaves out. Again, this statement is not in the opera libretto. Norman Del Mar argues that Jokanaan's music is not different in kind from that of the decadents of the palace, which may, therefore, indicate that the opera takes them together as part of a linked discourse, that Strauss understands that the two male worlds go together.

It is not to fault the opera to note what it has omitted from the play, but omissions none the less make for a text of considerable difference. Strauss takes the material more solemnly than Wilde, which destroys the camp and turns the material back towards kitsch: this would seem to be true of the Dance of the Seven Veils. I am thinking of Strauss's comment that 'operas hitherto based on Oriental and Jewish subjects lacked true Oriental colour and scorching sun' (quoted by Del Mar, *Richard Strauss*, i. 243). The word 'true' here is worth highlighting, for the result is more Bavarian than Oriental, the emphasis being given by the elements of the waltz (Bavarian and Viennese and, of course, nineteenth-century) heard in Salome's music, as at Salome's 'Wie süss ist hier die Luft!' in her first entry and

'Wie gut ist's, in den Mond zu sehn'. The young Syrian is taken out of the narcissistic alterity which he possesses in Wilde's text, and given the name Narraboth, which domesticates him. In Wilde, Salome calls him by this name while persuading him to bring Jokanaan out of prison, but there is no authentication of that name outside her text; Strauss simplifies. The music for Jokanaan moves towards endorsing a religious tone. Jokanaan (as in Wilde) calls Salome the daughter of Herodias after Narraboth has killed himself, as if, by associating her with the sins of her mother, putting responsibility for his death on to her, and he then sings that Salome must go and seek Christ in Galilee. The tone softens, and the intention is certainly to underwrite the sense of an alternative world (as with the words of the First Nazarene, we are within the world of *Parsifal* here). The effect is a softening of the nihilism practised by the Wilde text. A comparison of the Wilde and Strauss texts at this point, where Narraboth kills himself, shows that the cutting of other reactions to his suicide makes Salome more obsessive, and gives Jokanaan the edge by making him appear more justified, more absolute a figure than he really is. Salome may be transgressive in wanting to touch him and kiss him, but he is doing his best to deny that he has a body at all.

Ernest Newman compared the last long solo of Salome to the 'Liebestod'. The emotionality, however, is much more projected towards the past than is the case with *Tristan*, which is itself an opera whose subject is the cancelling out of the past and of mundane reality. Wilde supplied the words, but not the waltz theme, of 'Nichts in der Welt / ist so weiss wie dein Leib. Nichts in der Welt / war so schwarz wie dein Haar' (Nothing in the world is as white as your body; nothing in the world was so black as your hair), while 'hörte ich geheimnisvolle Musik' (I heard mysterious music) is strongly Marschallin-like in its nostalgia; and the voice pauses after 'Musik' to foreground the sound that Salome imagined. There is no distancing of the voice from the music in the orchestra: it endorses and, indeed, echoes and repeats the sentiments, with the use of what would become Hollywood-type high strings and echoes of the voice which leads the orchestral sound, as in the section from 'Nicht die Fluten'. The doubling and repetition make for the refusal of irony, and thus turn the music away from camp. Herod's expressionist horror follows Salome's monologue, but then the voice of Salome is heard singing out of the night in which she is veiled. The 'taste of love' that she sings about gets its full endorsement from the sweetness of the orchestral sound, and the slowness which moves towards the climactic discord after 'Ich habe ihn geküsst' establishes that whatever the strangeness of the situation—the woman estranged from all else, crooning to the relic of her 'love' like the alienated figure of *Erwartung*—the love is recognizably operatic, nineteenth-century romantic, simpler in quality than the love of *Tristan*, in that it has no obvious metaphysic behind it. Romain Rolland was right to speak of the 'emotional tones of a moving nature' in the opera; for the opera moves away from the camp modernism that plays with humanist projections of emotions into something less avant-garde, in fact, more 'Wagnerian', at any rate, more nineteenth-century: the rediscovery of the nineteenth century in the atmosphere of *Salome* is what turns it back towards kitsch. Only the anxieties about the castrating modern woman remain.

If this is avant-garde opera, it comes out of a deeply conservative mind, one characterized by Rolland in 1891 as not free from the unhealthiness it engaged with, 'a man more strong than inspired; of vital energy, nervy, morbidly overexcited, unbalanced but controlled by an effort of will-power which rescues music and the musician . . . sickness hidden beneath the strength and military tautness' (quoted by Del Mar, *Richard Strauss*, i. 284). We come back to basic contradictions in the discourses that construct Strauss: a right-wing appropriation of Nietzsche (as in the setting of *Also Sprach Zarathustra*); a fascination with decadence, which he plays both with and against; antagonism to the independent woman, while also recognizing her powerful appeal; and a desire to recontain the threats she poses in terms of nineteenth-century ideology. The opera turns Salome back towards a Kundry character whose laughter is perverted and hysterical, whereas Wilde makes her a product of style, of aesthetic control, and her nihilism is camp. In the opera Salome is a virgin who has lost her chance of romantic love, as though Strauss were finally unwilling to describe musically the woman who might be a total threat to the bourgeois.

SEX AND CHARACTER

What was typical and new in the image of Salome may be seen by a comparison with Wedekind's Lulu. Wedekind called her 'Die Urgestalt des Weibes' (the original paradigm of women) in the prologue to *Erdgeist* after seeing Gertrud Eysolt's acting (she also played Salome and Elektra in Max Reinhardt's 'quasi-operatic' productions of these plays).[16] Wedekind distinguishes between the woman as 'Frau' (her social character) and the woman as 'Weib' (her sexual character), a distinction also made by Karl Kraus (1874–1936), editor of the Viennese satirical journal *Die Fackel* (1899–1936). Kraus admired Wilde's *Salome*

---

[16] See J. L. Styan, *Max Reinhardt* (Cambridge: Cambridge University Press, 1982), p. 24.

in Berlin (1902) because, he said, it showed up 'brutal male morality', and showed 'Weiblichkeit', which was 'ethically scarcely definable', demonstrating the woman as naturally polygamous, so that the prostitute is the sensuous woman fulfilling her 'natural destiny'.[17] There seems little change here, in this characterization, from the image of Kundry. And in *Elektra*, there are still echoes of *Parsifal*, as also of *Salome*. Elektra describes Aegisthus as a woman, which links him to Herod in relation to Herodias, for Herodias says that Herod is sterile (which makes him a Klingsor). Sander Gilman points out that Herod's music makes him, musically, no more than another Jew. Anti-Semitism has been added in, and this association of woman and Jew (the two meet in Kundry) fits with the philosophy of the Jewish Otto Weininger in *Sex and Character*, a book asking whether there can be ethical relations between the sexes.

Sex and Character, which had run through eighteen editions by 1930, appeared in Vienna in 1903, the year the 23-year-old Weininger shot himself. This suicide, which had Schopenhauerian overtones of refusing the will, has been interpreted as a gesture of self-hatred. 'Self-hatred' as a term comes from Theodor Lessing, whose book *Jüdischer Selbsthass* (1930) made use of Weininger as an example of the Jew's revulsion from himself and desire not to be perceived as Jewish.[18] Weininger's family admired Wagner: his own views about Jewishness seem to have been derived from the Bayreuthian H. S. Chamberlain.

Weininger, who became a Protestant the day he graduated, regards the human as bisexual, where the male stands for rationality and the female for unstable sensuality. Woman is aligned with the Jew and the homosexual (Weininger seems also to have been homosexual). The self is constructed as dual and unable to make the two parts of the personality (male/female) speak to each other; thus relationships between the rational male and the woman/Jew/homosexual are impossible, just as sexual intercourse could never be justified anyway, since it always involved using the other person merely instrumentally. An ethical consideration maps on to a deep misogyny, which seems to express an internalized hatred of his own character, the internalizing of an anti-feminist, homophobic, anti-Semitic, proto-fascist discourse. In the psychomachia that Weininger subscribes to, the woman

---

[17] Edward Timms, *Karl Kraus, Apocalyptic Satirist* (New Haven: Yale University Press, 1986), p. 71. On Vienna generally, see Carl E. Schorske, *Fin de Siècle Vienna: Politics and Culture* (New York: Alfred A. Knopf, 1980).

[18] See Peter Gay, *Freud, Jews and Other Germans* (Oxford: Oxford University Press, 1978), pp. 194–6. Gay's view is attacked by Allen Janik in Ivar Oxaal (ed.), *Jews, Antisemitism and Culture in Vienna* (London: Routledge, 1987), pp. 75 ff.

is sexual continuously, the man only intermittently; the man possesses a penis, but the woman is possessed by her vagina. Much of this deeply influential psychology Weininger learned from Wagner, especially from his Kundry, whom he called 'probably the most perfect representation of woman in art'.[19] Thus there follows in *Sex and Character* a virtual account of Kundry as a picture of woman, mystified and dehistoricized, and perhaps displacing an account of what both the Jew and the homosexual are like.

> Woman can reach no more than a vague half-consciousness of the fact that she is a conditioned being, and so she is unable to overcome the sexuality that binds her. Hysteria is the only attempt on her part to overcome it . . . the most notable examples of the sex (I have in mind Hebbel's Judith and Wagner's Kundry) may feel that is because they wish it that servitude is a necessity for them, but this realisation does not give them power to resist it; at the last moment they will kiss the man who ravishes them, and succumb with pleasure to those whom they have been resisting violently. It is as if woman were under a curse. At times she feels the weight of it, but she never flees from it. Her shrieks and ravings are not really genuine, and she succumbs to her fate at the moment when it has seemed most repulsive to her. (p. 279)

There is more in the same vein: and what applies to Kundry is also true of the homosexual, seen as the feminized man, and the Jew, since 'Judaism is saturated with femininity' (ibid., p. 306). Weininger compared Wagner to Christ, and called him 'the greatest man since Christ's time' (ibid., p. 345) in a context which alludes to the tradition of Clement, the Church Father, that Christ did actually speak to Salome, as a Magdalene figure (or as a Kundry). Strauss's *Salome* appeared the year after *Sex and Character*, and works within Weininger's discourse; all non-patriarchal sexualities are doomed, and 'patriarchal' also means Aryan. The woman needs to be emancipated from herself; she can be released only when males have vanquished their own sexuality, which is nothing but a psychic wound to them when it breaks out in force. But Wagner has already enabled the thought that the male might narcissistically desire to be wounded. Perhaps that is the secret of the opera Wagner planned in 1849 on Jesus of Nazareth, in which the hero wills his own destruction, and only the woman—that is, Mary Magdalene—divines that he wishes to be betrayed.

Thinking of Schopenhauer, within whose influence he writes, Weininger comments on the first Act of *Götterdämmerung* and on Siegfried's journey down the Rhine that

---

[19] Otto Weininger, *Sex and Character* (6th edn. Heinemann, 1906; New York: AMS reprint, 1975), p. 319. Some interesting comments on Weininger appear in Slavoj Zizek, *The Metastases of Enjoyment: Six Essays on Woman and Causality* (London: Verso, 1994), ch. 6.

a man only comes to his fulness when he frees himself from the race [i.e. the cycle of generation], when he raises himself above it. For paternity cannot satisfy the deepest longings of a man, and the idea that he is to be lost in the race is repellent to him. The most terrible chapter in the most comfortless of all the great books that have been written, the chapter on 'Death and its Relation to the Indestructibility of our Nature' in Schopenhauer's *The World as Will and Idea* is where the permanence of the will to maintain the species is set down as the only real permanence. (ibid., p. 223)

I commented in Chapter 1 on this section of Schopenhauer, discussing Thomas Buddenbrook's feelings of despair at bourgeois existence in Mann's *Buddenbrooks.* Weininger shows that the pessimism of that novel is that bourgeois existence does not permit a Siegfried, and that the male, with whom Schopenhauer identifies, cannot be content with subordination to the power of the will, which indeed seems to be female. The gamble of Nazism—of fascism in general, as a struggle to get beyond both bourgeois existence and the woman as the power of nature, of the will—is enshrined here, and Weininger provides an apologia for it. He makes evident the masculinist cast of Wagner and his music; at one point he argues that the absence of women in music generally can be accounted for by its abstract quality; women could not be involved since women have no imagination! (pp. 118–19). This follows from Schopenhauer: 'Women can have remarkable talent, but not genius, for they always remain subjective' (*World as Will and Representation,* ii. 393). Music is thus gendered as male: this is the opposite side of Nietzsche's contention that music is a woman. Weininger would have no toleration for the seductiveness of music, seducing the male composer from his purpose, like the will making the male give his time and talent to procreation, seducing him from his Siegfried- or Parsifal-like purpose.

Imposing an impossible ethical dimension on the human, while also refusing the characters of women who are identified with everything of an unacceptable other, Weininger affected much of modernist discourse. Though Freud rejected Weininger's thesis of an original universal bisexuality, the influence is felt in Hofmannsthal, Schreker, and Zemlinsky, names that occupy much of the remainder of this book. *Elektra* (Hofmannsthal's play of 1903, first performed as an opera in 1909) is Freudian, but gathers much of its misogyny from Weininger, and, significantly, it closes with the plight of Orestes, the male now being tortured for having followed through an 'ethical' action in killing his mother and her lover. But also, Elektra was seen by Hofmannsthal as 'unfeminine', by contrast with her sister Chrysothemis, who is woman as Weininger or Kraus described her, wishing for a woman's destiny (*ein Weiberschicksal*), characterized by Hofmannsthal as 'weibliche'.

Hofmannsthal said that his play *Elektra* was to do with 'the dissolution of the concept of individuality', to show 'the ego as a manifestation of forces'.[20] The 'individuality' referred to here would be that of the woman, who must thereby lose her Kundry-like character. Behind this Weininger-like wish lies *The Birth of Tragedy*, promoting the loss of the self as social being, as human: Nietzsche, as so often in modernist discourse, is appropriated for a reactionary position in regard to gender. Nietzscheanism thus appears in Elektra's Dionysiac dances, where the stage direction calls her a Maenad. (Salome's dance, by contrast, is entirely within her control.)

In an opera whose first chords are the 'Vater' motif, the sin against patriarchy is absolute, and even though men appear but seldom on-stage, women are nowhere, neither Klytämnestra nor Elektra, nor Chrysothemis, whose lament is that she will never have children, never be given her 'orthodox' (Weininger-like) position within patriarchal society, and is never given her name on-stage. Even the maidservants at the beginning replicate patriarchal violence by the beating they give to the fifth maidservant. Aegisthus has no status: the triumph of the events rests with Agamemnon and Orestes, the complete hero, who comes as though back from the dead, and whose voice is appropriately baritone, not the heroic tenor, as though to align him with patriarchy. The tenor role is given to Aegisthus: he is truly bisexual, in Weininger's terms, with an emphasis on the female side.

But the text, though more negative about Elektra than Wilde's *Salome* was about that heroine, is also powerfully influenced by Freud and Brauer's *Studies in Hysteria* (1895), which began to challenge those official fantasies of hysteria which made the woman inherently unstable and which affected Weininger.[21] Hysteria, in Freud's work, is a product of repression, as though everything seizes up because the woman has been locked into a process whereby she cannot speak or reminisce freely. The body's symptoms become ways of reading the mind's repression. This would be particularly relevant to the portrayal of Klytämnestra, whose walking-stick proclaims a hysterical paralysis, and who significantly cannot remember the moment of killing Agamemnon. (The lines are cut in the opera.) She has repressed the memory, which means that the body now becomes a symptom of that

[20] Quotations from W. E. Yates, *Schnitzler, Hofmannsthal, and the Austrian Theatre* (New Haven: Yale University Press, 1992), p. 144, and Benjamin Bennett, *Hugo von Hofmannsthal: the Theatres of Consciousness* (Cambridge: Cambridge University Press, 1988), p. 103.

[21] On the Freudian aspects of the text, see Lorna Martens, 'The Theme of the Repressed Memory in Hofmannsthal's *Elektra*,' *German Quarterly*, 60 (1987): 38–51; idem, 'From the Armchair to the Stage: Hofmannsthal's *Elektra* in its Theatrical Context', *Modern Language Review*, 80 (1985): 637–51. Also on Hofmannsthal, see C. E. Williams, *The Broken Eagle: The Politics of Austrian Literature from Empire to Anschluss* (London: Paul Elek, 1974), ch. 1 especially.

repression, and her avoidance of Elektra is the awareness that this daughter is the memory that she has repressed itself.

The opera, like the play, marshalls powerful images of the repressed: in the well on-stage, suggestive of the unconscious and of darkness (there is also a well on-stage in *Salome*); in the buried axe; in the proliferation of references to animals and animal behaviour as the 'other' of human behaviour. There are frequent comparisons to animals and to animal behaviour, howling and scrabbling about on the floor; reduction of people to animal-like characteristics, the train-bearer of Klytämnestra as a serpent, or the maidservants as horse-flies. But beyond Freud's sense of hysteria as a product of repressed memory (perhaps memory of a primal rape, whether in reality or in fantasy) is the other hysteria I have discussed, which makes the text both Freudian and Weininger-like: the ascription of instability to women, especially in relation to the womb. Thus Elektra is characterized by the Third Maid as pregnant with a vulture in her body; she is sex-obsessed, lesbian in relation to her sister, and sees sex and murder in linked terms.

This fusion of Freud and Weininger, where Freud stands for a comparatively enlightened stance on women as having repressed narratives and Weininger for a portrayal of them as having the worst features of Kundry, makes Hofmannsthal ambiguous. Of course, there is Sophocles behind this, and the Greek myths in which all this is one episode; but Hofmannsthal has, very complexly, been prepared to recast this material in the light of Freud, and to recontain it in favour of a masculinity by reference to a discourse marked by Weininger. That requirement of masculinity may also be the reason for his stress on ethical choice (Elektra's constancy) and on action. This contrasts with Hofmannsthal's earlier aesthetic position of the 1890s, in which decade he excelled as a poet, and which he relinquished after the crisis described in the 'Letter of Lord Chandos' (1902). In *Elektra*, written a year after this imaginary letter recording a crisis of a man who can no longer write, there is the effort to ground action in something below the rationalism of the humanist self.[22] The desire is for personal authenticity, established on a basis that goes beyond personal character.

And yet Elektra, pushed to extremity, seems to achieve nothing, certainly not in her own person. Nor is there any political change or legitimation at the end of the

---

[22] The nature of the crisis, as a response to the philosopher Mach's belief that we can know no more than our sensations, is described in Stephen Toulmin and Allan Janik, *Wittgenstein's Vienna* (New York: Simon and Schuster, 1973), pp. 112–17. The authors' account of Weininger is also important; see pp. 71–7. The discussion compares Weininger with Kraus. See also Allan Janik, *Essays on Wittgenstein and Weininger* (Amsterdam: Rodopi, 1985).

opera; certainly no redemption for anyone. In that sense, she is sterile, like her sister, and may point to a sterility which Hofmannsthal felt within himself, expressed in the 'Chandos Letter' and suggestive of his position in Vienna. Traditionally, Hofmannsthal criticism focuses on the issue of his feelings of sterility, and these should be examined in the light of Weininger, for whom the ethical replaced the aesthetic like the male the female. The feeling of being unable to write only marked Hofmannsthal out as Jewish, for Weininger saw the non-belief of the Jew as the emblem of the nihilism of contemporary culture.

The discourse that motivated Weininger towards an ethical position identified with the male and affected so many rightist intellectuals after him has political determinants which should be inspected. Hofmannsthal represented Austrian liberalism, whose Jewish character was assimilated into that Catholic Viennese culture which, at the end of the nineteenth century, was collapsing towards its own version(s) of fascism. Vienna in 1900 witnessed both anti-liberal mass movements and a largely Jewish cultural modernism. The dominant voice was opposed to such modernism. Vienna had had as mayor, from 1897 to his death in 1910, Karl Lueger. The anti-Semitism preached by Weininger was official policy in Vienna; for Lueger, elected on an anti-Semitic ticket, represented the Christian Socialists, who were in power till 1919. They were anti-liberal, anti-capitalist—where capitalism was associated with Jewishness—anti-socialist, and drew on Catholic support.

This party, which had strong resemblances to the later German Nazi party—Hitler admired Lueger—had begun in the early 1890s. Lueger's Austrian nationalism, pro-Habsburg and anti-German, contrasted with the pan-German nationalist party of von Schönerer, who wanted the break-up of the Austro-Hungarian Empire and the unification of 'German Austria' with the German Reich. This party looked back to 1882 and to the nationalistic German 'Linz programme', which by 1885 had incorporated within it anti-Semitic statements.

Both Lueger and Schönerer had been liberals, as had Viktor Adler, who formed the socialist Social Democratic party in 1889. Liberalism had had hegemony in Vienna since 1848, but its collapse came about with Austria's loss to Italy in 1859, to Prussia at Sadowa in 1866 (the moment of the 'Blue Danube' waltz), and the *Ausgleich*, the compromise made with Hungary in 1867, whereby a dual monarchy—*kaiserlich und königlich*—replaced simple rule from Vienna. Lastly, to destroy the liberals, there was the stock-market crash of 1873. *Die Fledermaus*, which dramatizes the bankruptcy of the bourgeoisie, followed a year later, as if to cheer them up. (As though to point up its contemporary relevance, this operetta, unusually for the genre, was set in modern dress.) In common with much of Europe, the dual monarchy went through a depression between 1873 and 1896 (it was the prompting for much anti-Semitism), reaching its nadir around 1880. The breakaway from liberalism had been marked in the Viennese 'Pernerstorfer circle' formed in 1867. This group, pro-German, anti-bourgeois, socialist, and national-istic, took over Wagner's ideas: membership of the German nation was cultural, with art as the unifying force; the *Volk* was stressed as an idea, so was vegetarian-ism, and Bayreuth was a focal point. But this circle disappeared after the stronger infusions of anti-Semitism in the 1880s.[23]

Viennese middle-class music offers an imaginary state to occlude the reality of these events. The waltz begins around 1840; operetta (Offenbach, then von Suppé) became part of Viennese bourgeois existence after 1860. Wickham Steed, *The Times* correspondent in Vienna (1902–13), described the Viennese as 'a people who had been deliberately taught for generations that their one duty was to eat, drink and be merry and to leave the affairs of state to the management of the dynasty and its servants'.[24] Operetta was useful to the state: but distinctions should be made. Kraus, who disliked Johann Strauss and Lehar, admired and played Offenbach. A hint as to how to think of Offenbach comes from Siegfried Kracauer, a member of the Frankfurt Institute alongside Adorno, and associated with Benjamin. His study of Offenbach (1937), effectively draws attention to his operettas as the only form of art sanctioned in the proto-fascist Second Empire of Napoleon III. He sees it as the fullest expression of that Empire, and, by its total lack of criticism, actually a mockery of it. In *Orphée aux Enfers* (1858), the chorus is public opinion; the idea of revolution, including the 'Marseillaise', is declared an illusion; and everything disappears before the cancan (an Algerian dance from 1832 revived by Offenbach), which implies Dionysiac delight going further and further and mocking everything. In *La Belle Hélène* (1864) nothing more of human responsibility is allowed in than an appeal to 'Fate'; there is no public opinion, and certainly no duty or honour. *La Vie Parisienne* (1866) makes new use of contemporary material, and allows room for both Bohemia and the servant class; in fact, it marks the moving away from Offenbachian operetta as the possibility of a left-wing criticism of the Empire emerges. The sense of total opportunism and the acceptance of impermanence which makes it fit for the

---

[23] See William J. McGrath, *Dionysian Art and Populist Politics in Austria* (New Haven: Yale University Press, 1974).

[24] Quoted by Steven Beller, *Vienna and the Jews 1867–1938* (Cambridge: Cambridge University Press, 1989), pp. 176–7. The book has a useful section on Weininger, pp. 221–7.

Empire is also matched by its laughter, 'which shattered the contemporary silence and lured the public towards opposition while seeming only to amuse them'.[25] The laughter, quite unsentimental and effectively nihilistic, could be dangerous, as the Dionysiac always is.

There is nothing like that in Viennese operetta, where the tone is for ever sentimental. Or, to quote Lueger, 'The true Viennese always mixes seriousness and levity, laughter and tears. Every Strauss and Lanner waltz laughs and cries at the same time, as do Schubert's dances.'[26] To refer to the 'true Viennese' is coercive, as sentimentality always proves itself to be. 'Wien Du Stadt meiner Traume' (Vienna, city of my dreams), a lyric of 1913, composed by Rudolf Sieczynski, portrays the place which, years before the Third Reich, at least from 1910, practised boycotts of Jewish shops, thus marking out those it considered not 'true Viennese'. Hofmannsthal and Strauss accept that prescription of sentimentality, and that is the mark of their work being part of the culture of official sentimentality, which is also, not accidentally, a culture of fascism.

The last three decades of the nineteenth century saw a bourgeois liberal hegemony disappear before different nationalisms (fifteen languages were officially recognized in the Empire), before a nationalistic socialism, and before anti-Semitism and the triumph of politicians such as Lueger and Schönerer who understood the age of the crowd. The promotion of what Karl Kraus called 'the rigor mortis of *Gemütlichkeit*' could only act as an ideology to prevent the emergence of anything else less quasi-fascist. That is illustrated by Austria's national face of patriotism in the 1914–18 war, as though something uniquely Austrian was being defended. Kraus showed that the appetite of the Viennese for operettas continued through the war (Timms, *Karl Kraus*, p. 331). The semi-official kitsch continued, as did the appeals to patriotism. Hofmannsthal's enthusiastic reaction to the war meant that he joined up and then did a desk job, while speaking for patriotism, and hence for Weininger-like values which he must have seen were also nihilistic. The nationalistic patriotism continued in Hofmannsthal—for instance, in the essay written after the war, 'Preusse und Oesterreicher' (1919), comparing Prussian values unfavourably with Austrian humanity and charm.

This was a move towards sterility, and the play *Elektra*, though earlier, suggests the relevance of the subject. The three principal women are marked by an equal

---

[25] Siegfried Kracauer, *Offenbach and the Paris of his Time* (London: Constable, 1937), p. 231.
[26] Quoted by Richard S. Geehr, *Karl Lueger: Mayor of Fin de Siècle Vienna* (Detroit: Wayne State University Press, 1990), p. 275.

hysteria which fastens on the subject of fertility. Klytämnestra laughs at the thought that her son Orestes has been killed; Chrysothemis laments her lack of children; Elektra turns images of revenge into images to do with the womb. It is disorder in the absence of patriarchy: no moral or political order is visible in Mycenae, where rule (that of Aegisthus) is in any case illegitimate. Yet the hysteria prevents the possibility of a movement forward. It is as though Hofmannsthal's writer's block were linked to disabling thoughts about the feminine, as though not being able to move forward in his thinking in this regard stopped him from thinking differently within this culture of fascism: 'culture' most literally, since Vienna was exactly the place where fascism was being cultured.

ELEKTRA

To pass from this play to the opera *Elektra* is to feel an anti-modern instinct within Strauss. Unlike *Salome*, it is not a question of camp turning into something more simply critical of the woman while also being romantic; it is more a question of everything in *Elektra* being made affirmative and thus rendered more like kitsch. It appears, for example, in the rewritings that follow Salome's last monologue 'Ob ich nicht höre?' She is crouching, animal-like, on the threshold; but the opera, unlike the play, makes her join in a conventional opera duet with Chrysothemis, thus denying the idea of repression as a factor working in human relationships, especially this relationship between the two sisters; additional words are given to her to be sung 'with enthusiasm':

> Wir sind bei den Göttern, wir Vollbringenden.
> Sie fahren dahin wie die Schärfe des Schwerts
> durch uns, die Götter . . .

(We are with the gods, we who accomplish. They travel on, like the sharpness of a sword, through us, the gods . . .)

and from then on to the exit of Chrysothemis, Hofmannsthal's inserted material shows Elektra becoming more and more upbeat: identifying herself with the moon (in a reference to *Salome*) and concluding with the non-Freudian and complacent

> Ai! Liebe tötet!
> Aber keiner fährt dahin
> und hat die Liebe nicht gekannt!
> (Ah! Love kills, but no one dies without having known love.)

It is a strong movement backwards from the modernity of *Tristan*. Something of the reactionary thought behind the impulse towards that duet may be gauged from Strauss's prescription to Hofmannsthal of what the inserted material should contain: 'nothing new—just the same contents, repeated and working towards a climax'.[27] A kitsch impulse already shows itself in the Viennese waltz strains heard in Elektra's first solo and in the reinsertion of the woman out of the play's disturbing Freudian, 'modern' hysteria into a role where her anger and madness are contained by the male. Another addition to the libretto may be given for illustration: the recognition of Orestes. Hofmansthal was made to add the words beginning:

> Es rührt sich niemand! O lass deine Augen
> mich sehn, Traumbild, mir geschenktes
> Traumbild, schöner als alle Träume!
> Hehres, unbegreifliches, erhabenes Gesicht,
> o bleib' bei mir! Lös' nicht
> in Luft dich auf, vergeh' mir nicht, ...

(No one is stirring. O let my eyes gaze at you, a vision in a dream, a vision granted to me, fairer than any dream! Noble, ineffable, sublime features, oh stay by me! Do not melt into air, do not vanish from my sight.)

The woman's passion is contained, and the male takes over: that is evident in the lyrical, warm music for the 'Recognition scene', and it fits that Strauss simply wished Hofmannsthal to provide him here with 'a few beautiful verses' (Gilliam, *Elektra*, p. 42). And Hofmannsthal obliged, for the kitsch impulse overtook him too, the influence of, pre-eminently, *The Merry Widow* (Vienna, 1905). Orestes is the Siegfried figure, especially as Weininger characterizes him, or he is Siegmund in relation to Sieglinde. In any case, he provides the myth of the complete hero. That he comes on anonymously aligns him to those other Wagnerian heroes who do the same. As Elektra sings to Orestes about the innocent awe with which she used to look at her body and her hair, seeing herself in the light of the moon, she puts herself back into 'normal' behaviour and heterosexuality, as though she passes from the power of the patriarch (the dead Agamemnon) to the patriarch's son; yet this reascription which may be regarded either as healing or as a measure of the text's desire to recontain the woman does not last; Elektra is marked for death, unlike her sister.

[27] Quoted by Bryan Gilliam, *Richard Strauss's* Elektra (Oxford: Clarendon Press, 1991), pp. 221–2.

Of course the music is modern, and was recognized as scandalously, shamelessly, so. Yet it ends on a C major chord (no harm in that, but it is significant), and later on Strauss was to think of it and *Salome* as having music analogous to 'fairy music by Mendelssohn',[28] just as he also wanted (in the period of *Die Ägyptische Helena*) not to 'degenerate into the so-called realism of *Salome* or the eccentricities of today's modernists' (quoted by Del Mar, *Richard Strauss,* ii. 333). This rewriting of his own history permits a final thought about *Elektra.* Its 'Vater' motif means that its aspirations are patriarchal: it looks back for revenge, and all the women are punished through their non-relationship to patriarchy, whether they have destroyed it (like Klytämnestra) or cannot get fully into it (like Chrysothemis) or whether in some ways they have freed themselves from it, like Elektra in her extremity of behaviour and refusal of a norm. In this sense the opera inscribes within it its own reactionariness; it cannot find a politics which makes the dead patriarchy less important than the live women. That seems to me paradigmatic of Strauss's failure. There is a connection between that relationship towards the dead and a reactionary politics, as there is between the newer approaches to sexual relations and gender implied in both Wilde's and Freud's texts, which fit a newer politics, which Strauss never bothered to work through. The result was that the form his modernism took was to use the new in the service of the old. In many ways, that was a typical duality within modernism, and it is one which can easily be mapped on to the dual strategies of fascism.

[28] Quoted by Michael Kennedy, *Richard Strauss* (London: Dent, 1976), p. 78.

7
Conducting from the Right: Strauss, Kitsch, and Nihilism

Strauss operas involve questions of kitsch and camp, and the differences between these two. Adorno, considering Wagner, put kitsch and camp together: if Strauss's operas *are* kitsch, they offer little to offset the culture of fascism (which showed its opinion of Hofmannsthal when his statue in Salzburg was destroyed by the Nazis in 1938 and his books were banned). But in so far as they are camp, they suggest at least the existence of a gender politics to contest the reactionary discourse about women and femininity I have referred to already and which I summarized under the name of Weininger. They may subvert quasi-fascist discourse from the inside. In this chapter, I want to go into these issues again, by considering Hofmannsthal / Strauss operas later than *Elektra*, and then by looking at one detail—the nihilism Strauss was forced into in the 1930s, which is traceable in his encounter with Zweig, his collaborator after Hofmannsthal, and with the Nazis, who made him a collaborator.

Camp, unlike kitsch, contains a resistance to bourgeois taste. In *Der Rosenkavalier*, the silver rose Octavian offers to Sophie, which is one of Hofmannsthal's 'allegories', as he called them, might be a kitsch symbol in one context; but perhaps its very artificiality contains a critique of the whole simulacral nature of the age of the Baroque (as Hofmannsthal, among others, wished to reinvent this for Austria). This might even bring the rose close to camp. But both Hofmannsthal and Strauss also endorsed elements of kitsch themselves. Strauss admired Johann Strauss and his waltzes, calling him 'the most endearing of all God-gifted dispensers of joy'.[1] Anyone pondering the idea of the kitsch creation of a Never Never Land of Vienna in *Der Rosenkavalier* (1911), home of Mozart but possessing the very different comic solidity of *Die Meistersinger*, might ponder the irony of this music being written by a Bavarian and first heard in Dresden. *Die Frau ohne Schatten* (Vienna, 1919), which backs the idea of woman as Frau, not Weib, functions by its use of fantasy and Oriental motifs. As has often been noticed, it

---

[1] Michael Kennedy, *Richard Strauss* (London: Dent, 1976), p. 10.

may be associated with *Turandot*—two operas about women who cease to be sexually inviolate—and, as in *Turandot*, these elements push opera towards the limits, so that it becomes questionable whether anything can be said in the operatic medium again without resorting to such remoteness. Certainly Strauss drew back after the event from repeating such 'romantic opera'; but it could be argued that the move was at the price of blandness, of kitsch. If difficulty of expression is the issue, the sense of being unable to say anything, this repeats the problem outlined in Hofmannsthal's 'Chandos Letter'. In 1916, Strauss sent Hofmannsthal plans for a satirical comedy with himself as an Offenbach figure, adding: 'You'll probably say Kitsch. But we musicians are known for our bad taste in aesthetic matters' (quoted by Del Mar, *Richard Strauss*, ii. 236). If the tides were running out, if there was a sense in composer and librettist alike that there was little that could be said, this draws attention to the nature of the political culture the men were in and of, which could be confronted only by another politics, not by the profession of a liberal stance which evaded the political realm.

To continue with the ambiguous, kitsch/camp gender politics in Strauss and Hofmannsthal and the way women are constructed in their later operas, I want to discuss *Die Frau ohne Schatten* (1919), refer to *Der Rosenkavalier, Ariadne auf Naxos* and *Die Ägyptische Helena*, and conclude with some comments on *Arabella*. At the beginning of *Die Frau ohne Schatten*, the spirit-messenger, the voice from the world of pure spirit, which the empress has left behind, asks the nurse, a female Mephistopheles, whether the empress has acquired a shadow. The nurse replies 'Durch ihren Leib' wandelt das Licht / als wäre sie gläsern' (Through her body the light moves, as if she were made of glass). And the falcon sings that if the woman casts no shadow, 'der Kaiser muss versteinen' (the Emperor must turn to stone). Here is intensely interesting material, which like *Elektra*, assumes the work of Freud. The nurse says that the light passes through the woman's body as though she were made of glass. Glass as an emblem of the purity of the woman's body reappears at the end of *Arabella*. The absence of the shadow derives from *Les Contes d'Hoffmann* (1881), where Dapertutto robs Schlemil of his shadow and Hoffmann of his reflection. But the important change from the Schlemil is that the focus is now on the woman and the woman's body. The loss of these things—shadow and reflection—implies the breakdown of self-awareness, the loss of a sense of the *je ideal*, the self that looks from the mirror in Jacques Lacan's psychoanalysis, which confirms an awareness of the self as a discrete whole, by giving a narcissistic image for the self to nurture. Theweleit in *Male Fantasies* saw the inability to establish such a narcissism as a crisis moment in Western culture, which explains the fascist obsession with borders and their lack. But the body made of glass seems even more interesting, especially as it calls on several accounts of madness, including a famous one in Descartes's 'First Meditation' on the subject of the things we may doubt, where the mad person fantasizes that his body is made of glass. Behind Descartes lies a tradition, which includes the mad king of France, Charles VI, who thought just that.

The body made of glass represents a wish to do away with the body altogether, to eliminate any sense of body flow, of the body having contents, which spill out as tears, blood, milk, sweat, urine, faeces, or any product associated with child-birth or sexual intercourse. It seems to link to a precise fear of the body as other. The mad person, on one reading of Descartes, is the one for whom the body is totally other, totally instrumental. The shadow that the woman fails to cast suggests menstrual blood, since it is specifically stated that the emperor has been with the woman every night for the past twelve months: that he has desired her every night. Perhaps that is a tactful way of suggesting that there has been no cessation of intercourse on account of her periods; or perhaps that reads too literally—though I am not sure whether reading can be too literal. If she has no period, of course, there can be no conception of a child. There is a return to the sense of sterility found in *Elektra*. If my reading is accepted, then the opera stands for something relating to male fantasies of the woman as the hysterical object: the opera's achievement is to reinvoke the woman, but not as a feared other, who must be contained by masculinist ideology.

Julia Kristeva, in her study *Powers of Horror*, a text which ends up discussing the anarcho-fascist writer Céline, is suggestive here. I referred to her in relation to Theweleit (Chapter 1), but I would like to come back to her in more detail in the context of a discussion of the maternal. Kristeva argues that the first repression that takes place in the child, which is never wholly 'successfully' carried out, is of the mother. The subject must separate itself off from the feminine, from the mother's body, in a violent revulsion away from the body's liquids, which are identified with the power of the maternal and the feminine. Menstrual blood is most strongly repressed as a marker of the power of the mother and of sexual difference.[2]

But the woman is also liable, in spite of herself, to turn the emperor to stone, a figure which yet again suggests castration fear (Freud), like beheading (again, this

---

[2] Julia Kristeva, *Powers of Horror: An Essay on Abjection*, trans. Leon S. Roudiez (New York: Columbia University Press, 1982), p. 71.

relates *Turandot* to *Die Frau ohne Schatten*).[3] The opera records the desire to save the male, and it links to fears of artistic impotence. The composer in *Ariadne auf Naxos* comments that 'human vulgarity, staring like Medusa, grins at us in the face'. To suffer from the demands of mass or consumer culture is perceived as a form of castration. As with Zerbinetta in that opera, the text makes the woman the antithesis of the castrating females such as Salome which were conjured up in nineteenth-century male fantasies. In *Ariadne* the only person likely to become stone is Ariadne herself; as Zerbinetta says to her, she wishes in her grief to be 'Als wären Sie die Statue auf Ihrer eignen Gruft' (like a statue on your own tomb). Women in these Strauss / Hofmannsthal operas *post Elektra* become the antithesis of Kundry, obsessed with sexuality and destroying the male in the process: it is mass culture, not the woman, who will prove the Medusa (though mass culture may also be characterized by the modernist as feminine). There is no need to argue whether Freud's readings of male horror at female 'lack' are 'right' or not; it is important only to see that he belongs to the same moment as Hofmannsthal, within a dominant culture which is neurotically anxious about otherness and its own lack.

But the opera tests the woman, not the man, and the attitude to the woman's body is complex. For Catherine Clément, opera is the art-form which thrives on the 'undoing of women', and her insights gain from the point that the only corporeal thing that matters about the diva is the incorporeal voice: the voice for which any soprano's physical appearance will be forgiven (I do not think the same is true of the tenor). The woman's voice, which indeed undoes her, is that fetishized 'object' that no reproduction can make too pure, as though it came from a glass body. While nineteenth-century opera allows the woman to sing, while punishing the character's every innocent deed or guilty passion, it does so by exclusion of all else except the voice—everything of the body, which also evokes, returning to Kristeva, everything of the mother.

In these operas, it seems that the body is brought back. Hofmannsthal's texts are often self-reflexive, fastening on the subject of the theatre. This may reflect on the theatricality of Austrian and Viennese baroque, which is designed to allow for Austria to present an image of itself, as in the Salzburg festival. But *Der Rosenkavalier* or *Ariadne auf Naxos* (second version, Vienna, 1916) emphasize emotions as transient performances. Zerbinetta in *Ariadne* has no workaday name or character

---

[3] Freud, 'On Sexuality', in *The Penguin Freud*, vol. 7 (Harmondsworth: Penguin, 1977), p. 281, for beheading, p. 311 (the idea of Medusa) for turning to stone.

in the *Vorspiel* she *is* her performance as a character out of the Harlequinade, Zerbinetta on-stage and off. There is nothing below her appearance: this makes her Dionysiac, and makes the *buffo* world Dionysiac, following *The Birth of Tragedy*: no wonder the opera concludes with the triumph of Bacchus over Ariadne's attempts at deep subjectivity. *Elektra* may evoke the patriarch, but at its centre are three women who sing with greater and greater intensity throughout the opera, foregrounding the concept of performance. Three women also sing in the opera that follows, *Der Rosenkavalier*, in the last trio and duet, where the voices soar, and it is not clear which voice is being heard, whether that of the stage women or the putative male—that is, Octavian, the 'trousers-role' (a conscious piece of 'theatre'). This is music whose lyricism baffles criticism, but which means that heterosexual relationships are being theatrically presented through a medium where the woman playing Octavian is taken out of that invisible role which nineteenth-century opera had imposed on her (the same goes for the composer in *Ariadne*). Susan Sontag, in her 'Notes on Camp', in finding Strauss camp, says that in comparison to Shakespeare's comedies with their cross-dressing, *Der Rosenkavalier* is 'epicene' (*Against Interpretation*, p. 280). There seems a triple argument here. 'Epicene', as a characterization of *Der Rosenkavalier*, suggests, negatively, the occlusion of sexuality, and the reduction of everything to pure voice, which is what seems to be reversed in *Die Frau ohne Schatten*. But equally, an effect of *Der Rosenkavalier* is to change the presentation of the woman, to take away the investment in the sexual woman, the 'Weib'. This would contrast with *Salome*. The woman, made male, is no longer the object. And thirdly, within the gender politics of the opera, Octavian moves from the Marschallin (Act 1) to Sophie (Act 2) to Baron Ochs (Act 3) in a mixture of sexual and quasi-sexual unions which confuse gender identity as much as Octavian's near-opening words refuse the distinction between 'du' and 'ich'. In other words, there is a complex process in this opera whereby the woman loses her single status as an object and becomes something else, more elusive, less definable, but paradoxically without losing her body on the way.

The woman without a shadow is effectively a woman without a body, pure voice only, the fetishized object of pure glass, or like the 'Alles-wissende Muschel' of *Die Ägyptische Helena*. The change occurs when the empress seeks visibility, a shadow, a recognition of herself as a woman. That is repeated as an idea in what happens to Zdenka (*Arabella*), whose cross-dressing, as a reversal of Octavian, means that her femininity is denied by her being treated as though she were male. Visibility characterizes the humans, Barak and his wife, in *Die Frau Ohne Schatten*. There are several sexisms in the text as regards those two, an obvious one being the denial of a name to the wife. But pursuing a positive reading, rather than one stressing the text's political and cultural conservatism, it may be noted that the wife has effectively been deprived of a narcissistic stage: when the nurse and the empress try to give her a hair-band, she says that she lacks a mirror, and has to do her hair over the trough. A magic transformation then occurs: the dyer's wife finds herself surrounded by slave girls who now feed her narcissism by their solicitations, and a large mirror is given to her, while the voice of the empress is heard singing 'Willst du um dies Spiegelbild / nicht den hohlen Schatten geben?' (For this image in the mirror, will you not give the hollow shadow?). This suggests a difference between the meaning of the reflection and that of the shadow. The reflection enables narcissism, which, Freud argues, is the basis of love relationships, while the shadow continues to feed that sense of self by suggesting its plurality, its otherness.

It seems important that the text should come back to images of narcissism. Hofmannsthal could have read Freud on the subject, where he discusses not only the importance of narcissism in women (it produces the strongly positive woman who feels no lack), but also parental love, which he sees as 'nothing more than the parents' narcissism born again, which, transformed into object-love, unmistakably reveals its former nature'.[4] The lack of children in the marriage of the dyer and his wife causes mutual blame. It may be worth thinking about this in terms of a deficiency in narcissism, a deficiency compounded by the choice of the text to make the marriage conditions as miserable as possible, with the surrounding brothers of the dyer living there.

The opera is marked by a *Gemütlichkeit* as regards marriage, traceable back to *Die Zauberflöte* perhaps, and showing itself in the watchman at the end of the first act, praising sex within marriage, the character coming from the no less bourgeois *Meistersinger* watchman. But taking away its self-conscious appeal to goodness and to the values of earlier operas, which it relies upon to establish its points, it may be considered as a liberal allegory. Keikobad would be the spirit-ruler as a figure of total control, annihilating the world of humans and the world of the body in the name of purity, his motif heard at the beginning, like another 'Vater' motif. The human world is seen as degraded and miserable. Its oppressed,

---

[4] Freud, 'On Narcissism: An Introduction', in *On Metapsychology*, pp. 82–3 for narcissistic women, p. 85 for the relationship to the baby. Thomas A. Kovach, *Hofmannsthal and Symbolism* (New York: Peter Lang, 1985), ch. 3, discusses *Die Frau ohne Schatten* in terms of opposition to the aesthetic sense which is seen in the emperor, and which is the source of artistic sterility and petrification, and is redeemed by the self-sacrificial aspect of women—the empress here, but see also the Marschallin.

poverty-stricken figures, whom the nurse despises as the emblems of otherness, represent that which the fascist mentality wants to control. Perhaps they are even to be thought of as Jewish, or at any rate as 'degenerates'; hence the brothers' deformity, in an instance of Jewish self-hatred in Hofmannsthal. The woman lacks children because she lacks narcissism, and lacks narcissism because she lacks children. The empress at first tries to buy the shadow she needs, but has to learn that she can only have it through service, so that 'humanity' is seen to be something to be learned. This allegory would fit the attempt to find a national unity for Austria, a theme current for Hofmannsthal throughout the years of the composition of the text (1911–19).[5] Whereas in *Elektra* there is complete submission to the dead patriarch and to his values, that is not the case at the end of *Die Frau ohne Schatten*. The empress will not drink from the fountain of golden water that is offered to her, which would give her the shadow she needs. 'Blut ist in dem Wasser, ich trinke nicht!' (Blood is in the water; I will not drink). The motif of pure water characterizes *Arabella* too, and reading it in the light of *Die Frau ohne Schatten* as an allegory might rob it of its coyness in that opera and make it less like kitsch. Blood in the water would be an apt reminder of the violence inherent in the culture of fascism. Water without blood would be the desire for a culture not premised on injustice and the defeat of the 'other'.

If the opera shows the women having to learn, Barak is not so portrayed. He is given a dignity throughout, especially in the orchestral interlude (Strauss's idea, not derived from Hofmannsthal's writing), in which, as Del Mar says, Strauss 'attempted to portray Goodness pure and simple' (*Richard Strauss*, ii. 176). Such a warmly diatonic moment in a score otherwise full of violent dissonance raises a question, however, about the function of the disharmonies. Adorno argued that they were there 'merely to titillate' (*In Search of Wagner*, p. 64). If the music can move so easily between modernist expressionist chromaticism and atonality and more conventional harmony, then it implies that neither is being held on to as giving any representation of the way things are. The chromatic music does not, as it does in Adorno's Schoenberg, reinforce any alienation felt between writer and society. What is involved in writing major inspirational music such as that

---

[5] Hofmannsthal is treated as an allegorist by Michael P. Steinberg, *The Meaning of the Salzburg Festival* (Ithaca, NY: Cornell University Press, 1990), ch. 5. This interesting study compares Hofmannsthal on allegory with Benjamin (see above, Ch. 1). A difference between the two is that allegory in Hofmannsthal builds up a complete system, whereas in Benjamin it shows the breakdown of systems of thought, but the completeness in Hofmannsthal may parody, by its over-perfection, the claim to be complete: may thus re-fragment systems of thought.

composed for Barak, music which reappears at the end of the act with the voices of the nightwatchmen (and the result is very beautiful), is illuminated by the story told by Otto Klemperer of the year 1911, when Strauss expressed his respect for Mahler, but added that he was always 'a little frightened of him'.

Strauss then observed that Mahler had always sought redemption. He had simply no idea what kind of redemption Mahler was thinking of. Strauss' precise words were: 'I do not understand what I am supposed to be redeemed from. If I can sit down at my desk in the morning and get some kind of inspiration, then I certainly do not need redemption as well. What did Mahler mean by it?'[6]

If this anecdote is put alongside *Die Frau ohne Schatten*, which, like *Die Zauberflöte*, obviously has redemption for its subject, something very suggestive appears in Strauss. Mozart's text has revolutionary implications: Strauss has no sense of the conflictual ideologies of post-war Europe, and the allegorical meaning I have suggested would be meaningless to him. In which case, the opera would be closer to kitsch than camp. (The libretto in any case would not permit the thought of camp.) Yet the opera does not seem kitsch—read allegorically, for instance—and in that way suggests that Strauss's musical text belongs to powerful, urgent discourses of which he was not consciously aware.

The same fantasies of total control, this time exercised by Aithra, run through *Die Ägyptische Helena*, where Menelas is to live his life in a state of false consciousness as regards his wife, and is himself murderous and fantasizes killing. This too can be read as an allegory of the 1920s, where the need that Hofmannsthal feels is for a national art that will protect Austria from both its inner violence (the forces of anti-Semitism and of potential Austro-fascism) and what he takes to be its violence from outside. Here the clue is given in a letter to Strauss:

If this present day is anything it is mythical—I know of no other expression for an existence which takes place in front of such frightful horizons—for this encirclement with millennia, for this flooding into our identity from the East [?Russia] and the West [America], for this fearful inner distance, this raging inner tension, this here and elsewhere which is the hallmark of our life. Let us write mythological operas, it is the truest of all forms, believe me. (Quoted by Del Mar, *Richard Strauss*, ii. 312).

The myth that takes place in *Die Ägyptische Helena* is of reconciliation and of a working-through of Menelas's anger by a series of repetitions and workings-through, analogous to psychoanalysis, which enable him to face reality and his

---

[6] Quoted by Peter Franklin, *The Idea of Music* (London: Macmillan, 1985), p. 19.

wife. *Arabella* is also a myth of Vienna, and of a union between Vienna and the rest of the old empire. By the time of this opera, the bankruptcy of liberal Vienna can be put on-stage. In *Arabella*, the bourgeoisie have to be rescued from financial embarrassment. They are shown to be as lacking in credit as they are in *Die Fledermaus*, with which the text shows some similarities—for example, in the structure of the second act. But as with the operetta, 'credit' means little more than having money; the sense of a class having, or needing to have, anything else to its credit is cheerfully avoided. The hero is himself patriarchal, 35 and widowed. He is the Croatian Mandryka, who sells off his lands to 'the Jew in Sissek' who wants to buy them (again, Hofmannsthal's implicit self-hatred is revealing). That he is older makes Arabella's classic statement the more necessary in the context of the opera's ideology—'und selig werd ich' sein und gehorsan wie ein Kind' (And I shall be so happy and obedient as a child). She sings it to a Slavonic folk-tune, before Mandryka has been seen on-stage, and it reappears as a motif elsewhere, later, when he has arrived. The effect of its use before and after he has been seen is to minimize any sense of choice (there seems an echo here of Senta's feelings before the entry of the Dutchman). The impression is given that events must move on as they do: Austria, in the perfect mythology of a united nation, is saved from a purer world outside the capital by those of its subjects who owe it a debt of gratitude.

Fitting this lack of choice, there is in the heroine no independent woman, or spirit of a possible threat to patriarchy. But the relationship between sisters, Arabella and Zdenka, has more interest, and recalls the strange eroticism felt between Elektra and Chrysothemis and between Zerbinetta and the composer or Ariadne. Chrysothemis's desire for children echoes in Zdenka's frustration, and Zdenka's passion, her breaking out of disguise and her commitment to her own sexuality in her affair, is a fascinating aspect of this text's transgressiveness. But the opera is not named for her, and Arabella is no Elektra; the woman has been recontained in the official feelings of bourgeois ideology, so Arabella meditates on wandering with Mandryka through fields and high and silent forests.

Der Rosenkavalier allowed an epoch to go, while celebrating it. 'Alles zerläft zwischen den Fingern' (All slips through our fingers) is its renunciatory message, which tries to turn Schopenhauerian resentment about the past into something positive. The Marschallin may rise in the night and neurotically stop the clocks, like Miss Havisham (Hofmannsthal adding Freudian hysteria to Schopenhaue-rian/Nietzschean revenge against time's 'it was'), though she says that people must not be afraid of time; but it is a question whether the opera itself tries to stop the clocks. Perhaps that is an effect of highly conservative productions: the use of waltz material in eighteenth-century Vienna is anachronistic, but it may be proleptic. The eighteenth century sings to nineteenth-century music about time passing. In *Arabella*, the clocks have not been stopped, for the setting is now bourgeois, and 'quite close to our time as it is, more ordinary, less glamorous, more vulgar' (Hofmannsthal, quoted by Del Mar, *Richard Strauss*, ii. 392). *Arabella* is also concerned with disappearance, like *Der Rosenkavalier*. This is the last ball before Lent, so Arabella must be betrothed this night; she must dance a last waltz to say goodbye to her childhood before she grows up—but the operetta motif and the use of the genre of operetta means that she never needs to grow up, never even has to acquire the equivalent of the 'shadow' of *Die Frau ohne Schatten*. The sense of urgency meets an equal sense of things working out right, and there is little sense of inner or outer conflict, except when this is allowed in with Zdenka. It seems that in this opera both librettist and composer surrender to acquiescence. There is no need for people to take destiny into their own hands, or to find that their destiny might be tragic. Criticism of *Arabella* has become complicit with this acquiescence—for example, 'to music which might have fallen from heaven itself, the celebrated "staircase" music, slowly and with solemnity she descends towards him, the consciousness of her symbolic act growing with every step'.[7] I would rather ponder the connections between sentimentality and acquiescence, where sentiment is not spontaneous feeling but ideology itself, which slowly paralysed Hofmannsthal, and in Strauss's case meant that he had to do nothing to find himself named by Goebbels as president of the new Reichsmusikkammer, the body which was to control music in the Nazi regime.

CONFRONTING NAZISM: FROM STRAUSS TO HEIDEGGER

In Klemperer's view, Strauss's creative and original production was finished by the time of the outbreak of the First World War. The justice of this assessment need not be argued over here; its severity must be seen in the light of Klemperer's disgust that Strauss, unlike himself, did not leave Germany in 1933. Klemperer saw Strauss giving way to money, since in Germany there were fifty-six opera-houses, but in America only two (in New York and San Francisco). 'That would have

---

[7] Kenneth Birkin, *Arabella* (Cambridge: Cambridge University Press, 1989), p. 36.

reduced my income', he records Strauss telling him.[8] In so saying, Strauss placed himself in a culture where he could do nothing new but could only tell himself that he was able to preserve the past. Composers and writers of the 1920s and 1930s, in a not entirely dissimilar discourse from the Nazis, who found popular music decadent, felt a sense of crisis about the status of opera and high art as a concept. The result is that opera and theatre became part of a museum culture.

At the end of the First World War, the energies of Hofmannsthal and Strauss were devoted to a consolidation of the order they felt was going or was lost. Hofmannsthal's energies, along with those of the Austrian-born Max Reinhardt (1873–1943), went into the creation of the Salzburg Festival, a silver rose indeed. Like the European-wide movement to establish national theatres, the festival concept itself derives from nineteenth-century bourgeois culture, as a self-conscious reinvention of popular, pre-bourgeois culture, now reinterpreted along bourgeois lines. Bayreuth was the outstanding example, as with Wagner in 1851, 'the coming Revolution must necessarily put an end to this whole *theatrical business of ours* . . . I shall run up a theatre on the Rhine and send out invitations to a great dramatic festival: after a year's preparations I shall then perform my entire work within the space of four days' (*Selected Letters*, p. 234). The theatre to be constructed for the occasion would be of wood. Wagner wanted to destroy the building after the performance, as if to prevent the work becoming part of a museum culture. Bayreuth was completed in 1876 to house the 'poem of the stage festival *The Ring of the Nibelungs*' as Wagner called it in 1862, when the libretto was published.[9] As for Salzburg, the movement for a festival there had its beginnings in 1870, with the setting-up of a Mozart museum, followed by a music

[8] Peter Heyworth (ed.), *Conversations with Klemperer* (London: Victor Gollancz, 1973), pp. 41–2.

[9] Bayreuth had been a huge public gesture from the beginning. In 1864, Ludwig had commissioned Gottfried Semper (1803–73) to design a monumental festival theatre in Munich, to stage Wagner. Semper's ideas, as expressed in his *Bemerkungen über vielfarbige Architectur und Skulptur bei den Alten* (1834), had envisaged architecture as the total artwork, determining the nature of public life in Greece (as drama festivals also determined it). Wagner agreed that painter and sculptor belonged to the overarching *Gesamtkunstwerk* of architecture, and the Leipzig architect Otto Bruckwald built Bayreuth to Semper's plans. On Semper and Wagner, see Dieter Borchmeyer, *Richard Wagner: Theory and Theatre*, trans. Stewart Spencer (Oxford: Clarendon Press, 1991), pp. 68–72. See ibid., pp. 18–23 for a discussion of Gottfried Keller's ideas for festival competition there as inspired by Swiss choral festivals and a Swiss festival of the procession of local guilds. Borchmeyer sees Bayreuth as a reminder to Wagner of Switzerland and of its republicanism and national awareness. See 'Wagner's Bayreuth disciples', in David C. Large and William Weber, *Wagnerism in European Culture and Politics* (Ithaca, NY: Cornell University Press, 1984); Geoffrey Skelton, *Wagner at Bayreuth* (London: Barrie and Rockcliff, 1965), and his *Bayreuth: The Early Years*, ed. Robert Hartford (London: Victor Gollancz, 1980). See also Beat Wyss, '*Ragnarök* of Illusion: Richard Wagner's "Mystical Abyss" at Bayreuth,' *October*, 54 (1990): 57–78, which suggests that in the design of Bayreuth, 'the eye of justice' looks out from the stage controlling the spectators.

festival (1877), and the opening of the Internationale Mozart Stiftung (1880). This pairing of nationalism and culture may be compared, for instance, with the opening of the Shakespeare Memorial Theatre in Stratford in 1879. That had been linked to movements for a national theatre in Britain, set in motion in 1848, effectively as a counterbalance to the year of revolutions. In 1847, Shakespeare's 'birthplace' had been bought: the national theatre in Britain was to provide 'a house for Shakespeare' (the title of Effingham Wilson's 1848 pamphlet on a national theatre). Similarly, D'Annunzio records in *Il fuoco* his wish for a 'Latin Bayreuth', an Italian national theatre, near Rome, to stage his own plays and those of the Greeks and Racine.

The Salzburg Festival in both nineteenth and twentieth centuries was intended to rival Bayreuth in terms of its shrine value, but became its polar opposite when Bayreuth reopened after the war in 1924 on a strongly nationalist note, identified with Hitler both personally and politically. Toscanini, a presence at Salzburg after 1934, declined to conduct at Bayreuth in 1933. As if in response, Pfitzner declined an invitation to Salzburg, in protest at the Austrian banning of the Nazi party in May 1933. Salzburg for Hofmannsthal represented the ideal of the preservation of Austria of the Baroque period, of Mozart, of older church music, of the Enlightenment, and of the popular culture which inspired *Die Zauberflöte*. The war ended this Habsburg Austria, reducing it to a state of only eight million people. As a conservative institution, the Festival in the years up to the Second World War never produced a new opera, though it gave hearings to *Ariadne auf Naxos* in 1926 and the revised *Die Ägyptische Helena* in 1933; its operatic repertoire comprised Mozart, Strauss, Gluck, Johann Strauss, and, when Toscanini conducted, Verdi. But the past could be supported only by the modernizations of technology. The Festival meant tourism, and 'culture equals business', according to Franz Rehrl, the provincial governor who assumed authority over Salzburg. The festival became more like a theme park when Reinhardt struck a deal with the Archbishop of Salzburg in 1922 for the use of a church which would allow high ticket prices. This last display of the spirit of Salzburg pushed Karl Kraus into a denunciation of the Salzburg spirit that made him leave the Catholic Church.[10]

---

[10] See Stephen Gallup, *A History of the Salzburg Festival* (London: Weidenfeld and Nicholson, 1987), pp. 28, 34 for Rehrl; see Frank Field, *The Last Days of Mankind* (London: Macmillan, 1967), pp. 145–6 for Kraus and Salzburg. On the political (anti-Semitic) reception of the Salzburg Festival, see Michael P. Steinberg, 'Jewish Identity and Intellectuality in Fin de Siècle Austria: Suggestions for a Historical Discourse', *New German Critique*, 43 (1988): 3–33. See also Yates, *Schnitzler, Hofmannsthal and the Austrian Theatre*, pp. 201–17.

Strauss was involved with the Salzburg Festival, as well as being artistic director of the Vienna State Opera (1920–4),[11] conservative in this and in what he wrote, defending himself in 1924, according to Romain Rolland, with the words: 'Haven't I the right, after all, to write what music I please? I cannot bear the tragedy of the present time. I want to create joy. I need it.'[12] The 'tragedy of the present' refers to conditions in the Weimar Republic, which had been inaugurated amidst powerful class struggles (the 'November Revolution' of 1918, the founding of the German Communist party on 30 December, and the deaths of Rosa Luxemburg and Karl Liebnecht, killed by the *Freikorps* in January 1919 in the 'Spartacist Uprising'). It is worth recalling the conventional periodizing of 1918 to 1933 which sees events in three stages. The years 1918–24 were a time of strong republicanism and of workers' movements against the authoritarian legacies of pre-war German industrialization. The Nazi party, first named as such in October 1920, generated Hitler's putsch in Munich (the attempt to take over the state government of Bavaria) in November 1923, the year of Germany's worst inflation. The year 1922 had seen the murder of Walther Rathenau, the Jewish German industrialist and Weimar statesman, who had dreams of synthesizing the development of technology and the realm of culture. This assassination was anti-Weimar, anti-Semitic, and, though modern, anti-modern, representing a fear of technology which the Nazis were to exploit. The second stage, 1924–29, more stable fiscally and industrially, saw industrial control and restraint, exhibited in the importing of Taylorism and Fordism into factories. These were the years of *Neue Sachlichkeit*, a 'new objectivity' in art and music, and a 'realism' operating in both industrial relations and art. After the collapse of Wall Street in 1929, reaction took hold in the form of economic depression, distrust of parliamentary methods, and a swing to the Right, whose consequences in 1930 and 1932 and on 30 January 1933 entailed the triumph of the National Socialists.

An account of what happened to Strauss in the Nazi years must proceed not simply biographically, as though his personal response was everything that was important. In terms of their personal dealings with fascism, very few people seem

---

[11] For Strauss's conservatism with regard to the repertoire at Vienna, see Del Mar, *Richard Strauss*, ii. 220, and Hofmannsthal's critique of Strauss's 'neglect of the higher standards of intellectual existence' (ibid., ii. 222). The conservatism can be paralleled with the Italian opera-houses of 1922, comparing their repertoire with what would have been standard in the mid-nineteenth century, when so much they did would have been less than fifteen years old. In 1922 there would not even have been any Strauss, let alone Busoni. 'The passion for new works had metamorphosed into a passion for new interpretations of nineteenth-century works' (Sachs, *Music in Fascist Italy*, p. 56).

[12] Quoted by Myers (ed.), *Richard Strauss and Romain Rolland—Correspondence*, p. 165.

to have emerged uncompromised; and the culture of fascism being so pervasive, it would be surprising if it were otherwise, for that culture exceeded personal awareness, preventing individuals from seeing into what a subject position they had been put. A question important for this study is how the discourse of art and of a high culture which must be protected maps on to that political fascism, and whether it produces an intellectual fascism of its own. To elevate 'art' into a separate category, as modernism did, including the conservative modernism of Strauss, means that it necessarily excludes those who cannot appreciate it or are said not to be able to. In the 1920s and 1930s, such exclusivity was threatened by the power of popular culture, much of it American, and all of it reliant on 'techno-logical reproducibility'. Suddenly the pure products of high art looked dated, their exclusivity challenged, and even made kitsch-like. The fears this generated appear in the correspondence between Strauss and Stefan Zweig in the years after Hofmannsthal's death (1929), when Strauss was searching for a new librettist.

Two aspects of their correspondence with each other can be identified; first, the question of art. On 21 January 1934, Strauss wrote to Zweig: 'Must one become seventy years old to recognize that one's greatest strength lies in creating kitsch?' In the same letter, with reference to *Der Rosenkavalier* and *Arabella*, he wrote: 'What suits me best are South German bourgeois sentimental jobs.'[13] This is shameless. But such scepticism can be heard from the beginning of his association with Zweig, who reports that 'He knew well indeed, he said, that as an art-form, opera was dead. Wagner was so gigantic a peak that nobody could rise higher. "But," he added, with a broad Bavarian grin, "I solved the problem by making a detour round it." '[14]

Later, in 1934, Strauss and Zweig debated plot details for the opera that became *Der Freidenstag* (with a libretto by Josef Gregor). Zweig found 'the tie-in between the heroic element and the love episode a bit too operatic in the unfortunate sense of the word'—he originally wrote 'kitschig' (3 Oct. 1934, in Zweig, *World of Yesterday*, p. 59; see also p. xix.). Strauss replied, agreeing, but asking 'Where does the kitsch end and the opera begin?' (10 Oct. 1934, ibid., p. 61). To work with kitsch was no problem for Strauss: he freely admitted his search for 'joy' to be

[13] *A Confidential Matter: The Letters of Richard Strauss and Stefan Zweig*, trans. Max Knight, with a foreword by Edward E. Lowinsky (Berkeley and Los Angeles: University of California Press, 1977), p. 39. On the collaboration between Zweig and Strauss, see Michael P. Steinberg, 'Politics and Psychology of *Die Schweigsame Frau*', in Marion Sonnenfeld (ed.), *The World of Yesterday's Humanist Today* (Albany, NY: State University of New York Press, 1983).

[14] Stefan Zweig, *The World of Yesterday* (London: Cassell, 1943), p. 279.

escapism, his own talent being that of the bourgeois sentimentalist who knew opera was dead. We shall need to keep to this confession of kitschiness permeating his art in what follows. We shall also find it interesting to note how differently he and Zweig use the words 'opera' and 'operatic': Zweig critically, as though opera is now seen to be just operatic; Strauss conventionally, as though he is kept back—or keeps himself back—from that awareness.[15]

Meanwhile, to take another subject of the correspondence and to fill in the context, in 1933 Jewish collaborations in artistic productions were forbidden. In 1934, the music of the non-Jewish Hindemith was banned for its modernism, its 'decadent' spirit (the nudity of *Neues vom Tage* (1929) and the art-versus-politics theme of *Mathis der Maler*). Furtwängler's attempt to defend Hindemith in an open letter to the newspaper *Deutsche Allgemeine Zeitung* on 25 November 1934 proved provocative to the regime and popular to those outside it, as was evidenced by the applause Furtwängler received when he conducted *Tristan* in Berlin in the presence of Goering and Goebbels. Nor was Berg acceptable: hence Kleiber conducted the première of the 'Symphonic Pieces' from *Lulu* on 30 November, and resigned from the Staatsoper on 4 December. In a speech on 7 December at the Berlin Sportspalast, Goebbels attacked Hindemith:

Purely German his blood may be, but this only provides drastic confirmation of how deeply the Jewish intellectual infection has eaten into the body of our own people. To reach that conclusion has nothing in the least to do with political denunciation. Nobody can accuse us of trying to inhibit true and genuine art through petty or spiteful regulations. What we wish to see upheld is a National Socialistic outlook and behaviour, and no one, however important he may be in his own sphere, has the right to demand that this be confined to politics and banished from art. Certainly we cannot afford, in view of the deplorable lack of truly productive artists throughout the world, to turn our backs on a truly German artist. But he must be a real artist, not just a producer of atonal noises.[16]

With the current so running against Hindemith, Furtwängler capitulated the following February, after a meeting with Goebbels. It was evident to the Jewish

---

[15] For a discussion of opera as essentially 'operatic'—requiring excess—see Herbert Lindenberger, *Opera: The Extravagant Art* (Ithaca, NY: Cornell University Press, 1984). The same writer's article, 'From Opera to Postmodernity: On Genre, Style, Institutions' in Marjorie Perloff (ed.), *Postmodern Genres* (Norman, Okla.: University of Oklahoma Press, 1988), pp. 28–53, discusses the resistances of opera to modernization, contrasting it with the museum.

[16] Quoted by Geoffrey Skelton, *Paul Hindemith: The Man Behind the Music* (London: Victor Gollancz, 1975), pp. 122–3. On the relation of this to Berg's atonalism, see Douglas Jarman, *Lulu* (Cambridge: Cambridge University Press, 1991), p. 79.

Zweig that this doomed his own collaboration with Strauss on *Die schweigsame Frau*. The première in Dresden on 24 June 1935 took place with Nazi permission but clearly with official dislike: perhaps the Nazis found it necessary to tolerate Strauss's trespassing at that moment, but the composer was soon put in his place. On 15 June 1935 Zweig wrote to Strauss a now lost letter commenting on the two occasions when Strauss had compromised with the Nazi party: by substituting for Bruno Walter, excluded from conducting in Berlin in 1933, and again at Bayreuth in 1933. Strauss's offended and indignant reply of 17 June, in which he says that Zweig nearly makes an anti-Semite out of him, was intercepted by the Nazis, and made the occasion for his forced resignation from the presidency of the Reichsmusikkammer.

It is worth quoting part of that letter, where Strauss says that he only knows 'two types of people, those with and those without talent. The people exist for me only at the moment they become audience . . . what matters is that they pay full price for admission.' Even at such a moment of being confronted with a possible reading of his past actions, Strauss shuffles the matter off by claiming that what he did was for the continuance of art and the orchestras concerned, and by playing the card that the only division that mattered for him is that of artistic talent. He cannot see the contradiction between acknowledging elsewhere his work to be kitsch, and defending himself by saying that it is important. The appeal to art is that whereby he avoids assuming responsibility, though he has already virtually conceded that art to be value-free. It is disingenuous, in that it forces the questioner to submit to art as an absolute value, even though art can also, separately, be acknowledged to be only kitsch.

Such doubleness in Strauss, such an inconsistency into which he allows himself to be driven, is almost the definition of what Nietzsche describes as 'incomplete nihilism' (*Will to Power*, sect. 28). Incomplete nihilism is the form which is not 'genuine', not nihilistic in the sense that Nietzsche sees himself as nihilistic, not marked by an awareness of the changing character of modernity which is producing nihilism. In incomplete nihilism, the hollowness of what is practised— the sense that its values have devalued themselves—is accepted, at least unconsciously, and yet not acted on, in the belief that to follow out the consequences of nihilistic thought would be too dangerous. The empty and illusionistic is therefore still embraced. Strauss knows that what he composes is kitsch; he knows that modernity has passed him by, and that he is outside it (there seems to be some evidence to suggest that he telegrammed Goebbels congratulating him on his criticism of Hindemith, for instance). Yet, at crucial moments, he is ready to defend what he has done as art. (It is noticeable how he reveals his hollowness of attitude, at least unconsciously, in his wholly instrumental attitude to people as recorded in the letter to Zweig: they matter as long as they have paid for their seats.)

Strauss, as the modern he had been and remained in part, was affected by a discourse of nihilism, which meant that there could be no principle which would allow him to distinguish between art and kitsch. Perhaps the very condition of modernity is that in its unhooking of the category of autonomous art from truth, art is devalued from its earlier position as a highest value because it was concerned with truth, just as truth itself is devalued. These devaluations are the work of nihilism, which shows up the illusory nature of the grounds on which judgement is made. The attempt to stop such nihilism led Hofmannsthal to the Salzburg Festival, with its fetishizing of the Catholic Baroque (art linked to religion), and prompted him further to urge a 'conservative revolution' in Munich in 1927. Here he was not alone: there was the analogous 'reactionary modernism' of Jünger and the 'stählerne Romantik'—the 'steel-like romanticism' proposed by Goebbels, in contrast to *völkisch* pastoralism. Such differing forms of incomplete nihilism were all taken up by the culture of Nazism, which may be defined, almost, as an artificial attempt to preserve values manipulatively, while knowing the lack of grounds for them, knowing their readiness to succumb to the charge of relativism. It is worth remembering how many of the Nazis were artists or failed artists themselves. Hitler was a painter and amateur architect, Speer a considerable architect, Rosenberg (like Churchill) a landscape-painter, Goebbels a writer, Ziegler, of the 'Entartete Kunst' exhibition, an artist. Mussolini, to change countries, played the violin, and gave himself out as interested in music.

Yet, while agreeing that fascism wished to protect certain values in its incomplete nihilism, the Nazis were able, like Jago in *Otello*, to expose incomplete nihilism in others. In April 1933 Furtwängler tried to resist the Jewish/non-Jewish distinction that was being made with reference to the choice of musicians for the Berlin Arts Festival, and he wrote an open letter to Goebbels, declaring that he was 'first and foremost an artist . . . and therefore apolitical in the sense of party politics', and that he only recognized one distinction, 'between good and bad art'. Discrimination should be against 'those artists who are themselves rootless and destructive, and who seek to succeed through kitsch'. The true artist, by contrast, was 'helping to build up our culture'. Goebbels's public response to Furtwängler reads as an emollient:

You may rest assured that any appeal made in the name of German art will get a sympathetic hearing from us. Artists of real talent, whose extra-artistic activities do not conflict with the basic norms of state, society and politics, will, as was always the case in the past, receive our warmest support and encouragement in the future.[17]

He side-stepped the Jewish question in this response. And clearly the highest value that existed for Goebbels was the state, in the interests of which everything was to be subordinated: this is borne out not only in his speech about Hindemith, but in the terms in which he addressed Furtwängler:

Politics, it too, is an art, perhaps the most elevated art and the greatest that exists, and we—who give form to modern German politics—we feel ourselves like artists to whom have been conferred the high responsibility of forming, beginning with the brute masses, the solid and complete image of the people. The mission of the artist is not only to unify, but goes much further. He is obliged to create, to give form, to eliminate what is sick, to open the way to what is healthy.[18]

If Goebbels worked by aestheticizing politics, that was because he had seen through the idea of art as an autonomous humanist discourse. Adorno knew that, which is why he believed that the autonomous work of art had to be brought back, even at huge cost. Furtwängler was trying an argument that had become devalued, and the contrast between his position and Adorno's is striking. By making art an absolute, and non-political, its arbitrary status became clear. His reference to kitsch, which also implies an aversion to the new and the experimental, means that he must avoid modernity. Nihilism, to quote Nietzsche, 'stands at the door', and finds Furtwängler obliged to respond with older arguments whose applicability has gone. Furtwängler's *völkisch* sympathies and his support for Pfitzner, which demonstrated his musical conservatism, his nationalism, and his retreat into high culture, belong with many other aspects of German retreat in the 1920s and 1930s, such as in Strauss. Despite elements of heroism with regard to the Third Reich, they make Furtwängler too similar to that culture to be able to contest it adequately.

Here I would like to add for discussion an intellectual more intellectual than Strauss or Furtwängler and more compromised by the Nazis than either—Heidegger. One recognition that Nazism enforced and that Heidegger makes plain is

[17] Quoted by Fred K. Prieberg, *Trial of Strength: Wilhelm Furtwängler and the Third Reich*, trans. Christopher Dolan (1986; London: Quartet Books, 1991), pp. 340, 53.

[18] Quoted by Michael E. Zimmerman, *Heidegger's Confrontation with Modernity* (Bloomington, Ind.: Indiana University Press, 1990), p. 99.

that autonomous art, outside politics, the subject of aesthetic contemplation, is disappearing through the power of technology, which enframes it and allows it to survive while showing up its inability to exist outside politics and technology. If art can exist only within the conditions laid down by technology, technology becomes a kind of nihilism which questions older forms of culture and ways of living. If art is not autonomous, it becomes political. As Philippe Lacoue-Labarthe put it, discussing Germany's 'national aestheticism' and referring to Syberberg's critique of Hitler's Germany in his films:

the political model of National Socialism is the *Gesamtkunstwerk* because, as Dr Goebbels very well knew, the *Gesamtkunstwerk* is a political project, since it was the intention of the *Festspiel* for Bayreuth to be for Germany what the Greater Dionysia was for Athens and for Greece as a whole: the place where a people, gathered together in their State, provide themselves with a representation of what they are and what grounds them as such. Which does not merely mean that the work of art . . . offers the truth of the *polis* or the State, but that the political itself is instituted and constituted . . . in and as a work of art.[19]

Something of postmodernism is implied in this model. The *Gesamtkunstwerk* is the situationists' 'society of the spectacle', in which all reality has become codified in terms of a flattering image; it is even Baudrillard's simulacrum, where, in a stage beyond Guy Debord, reality has disappeared, and the image only reflects back on another image. Wagner's dream of a unification of all the arts ends with the fascist achievement of everything being turned into public display and the displacement of the real by the power of technology. Heidegger joined the Nazi party out of a crisis sense that technology represented a nihilistic challenge, demonstrating the ability to enframe everything within its scope, including autonomous human subjectivity, which it showed up as an illusion. The 'inner truth and greatness of the Nazi movement' was that here the challenge was not ducked: here was 'the encounter between global technology and modern man'. He hoped that Nazism would force into the open the illusory sense of humanism and the human subject—hence Heidegger's wish to promote crisis and bring to an end the concept of autonomous art as the product of the imaginative genius.

But this thought was dysfunctional for Nazism. Lacoue-Labarthe points out that Heidegger's work in the 1930s was concerned with overcoming aesthetics (*Heidegger*, pp. 77, 86). Heidegger's essay 'The Origin of the Work of Art'

---

[19] Philippe Lacoue-Labarthe, *Heidegger, Art and Politics*, trans. Chris Turner (Oxford: Blackwell, 1990), p. 64. See also Rainer Stollmann, 'Fascist Politics as a Total Work of Art: Tendencies of the Aestheticization of Political Life in National Socialism', *New German Critique*, 14 (1978): 41–60.

(1935–6) defines art in non-specific terms, as an event which brings about a new truth, a new way of seeing, which happens, for instance, 'in the act that founds a political state'.[20] This refers to the Nazi state, and fits the rhetoric of Goebbels, who also saw the state as a work of art, just as the idea of Hitler as the 'architect of the state' was meant to be not just metaphor, but also to give a sense of Hitler as an artist. Yet the argument that sees the work of art as political also contains a reverse position. The critique of aesthetics in Heidegger's essay is apparent early on, and it challenges the sense that an artwork can be known and judged according to any rules, or a view that the new artwork can be expected to fit any prior way of conceptualizing reality to which it is supposed to be adequate.

In contrast to Heidegger, the Nazis stood against modernism as the art of incompleteness and non-representation. The classicism of Arno Breker in sculpture or Speer in architecture dehistoricized classical models by making them the emblem of perfection, complete wholes to which nothing else could be added. The cult of the classical body emphasized not only the ego as armour, but discipline, militarism, and expansionism; the order of classical buildings became the image for the military spirit of the parade-ground, and the smoothness of form of the body imaged the unified and impregnable authoritarian personality. Benjamin's idea of the aestheticizing of politics suggests the triumph of a system in which art takes a prior place before people, and that politics is a matter of total control, analogous to the coolness of classical art, which is the image of total power. But for Heidegger, art is outside the conditions of modern life, which yields instead only its packaged image, or its reality added to by the joint powers of technology and the art market:

To gain access to the work, it would be necessary to remove it from all relations to something other than itself, in order to let it stand on its own for itself alone. But the artist's most peculiar intention already aims in this direction. The work is to be released by him to its pure self-subsistence. It is precisely in great art . . . that the artist remains inconsequential as compared with the work . . .

. . . the works themselves stand and hang in collections and exhibitions. But are they here in themselves as the works they themselves are, or are they not rather here as objects of the art industry? . . .

. . . The Aegina sculptures in the Munich collection, Sophocles' *Antigone* in the best critical edition, are, as the works they are, torn out of their own native sphere. However high their quality and power of impression, however good their state of preservation,

[20] Martin Heidegger, *Poetry, Language, Thought*, trans. Albert Hofstadter (New York: Harper and Row, 1971), p. 62.

however certain their interpretation, placing them in a collection has withdrawn them from their own world. But even when we make an effort to cancel or avoid such displacement of works—when, for instance, we visit the temple in Paestum at its own site or the Bamberg cathedral on its own square—the world of the work that stands there has perished . . .

World-withdrawal and world-decay can never be undone. . . . (pp. 40–1)

Heidegger dismisses museum culture, the idea of the artist as the privileged being in relation to the work of art, aesthetic appreciation, the culture industry which turns the work into kitsch and the absolute autonomy of the work of art. He allows that all may be over for art, and that it cannot be fetched back again, even by an aestheticizing of politics. It may be imagined what he would have thought of the Salzburg Festival, where the technologies of tourism and business frame a museum culture. The two icons of Nazi art and rhetoric—the classical and the Gothic—are especially declared by him to be finished. If Heidegger rounds on aesthetics, that is an example of him continuing the work of technology—that is, exposing the pretensions of human subjectivity to be in control of its artefacts, and showing that there can be no such thing as eternal art. Technology has focused the crisis nature of art already: its skills of preservation of art in museums, for instance, is conducive only to producing the image of art, or even the simulacrum.

OPERA AS MUSEUM CULTURE

To return from Heidegger to Strauss is to realize that the two men's experiences of Fascism are comparable answers to questions that both felt in differing measures needed answering. Heidegger's pessimism concerning art and technology made him think that the Nazis were the only people capable of government because of how they related to technology; this contrasts with those who thought that Nazism was only a 'political fashion' and would pass, and that things would be the same as they were before. Heidegger was right in his sense of there being a crisis, but hopelessly wrong in his response to it. At the end of June 1935 Strauss was humiliated by the Nazis, by losing control of the Reichsmusikkammer. In an introspective moment on 3 July 1935, with Zweig also lost to him as a future collaborator, he wrote confessional thoughts to himself, providing the evidence of splits in the self, caused by contradictory discourses each of which played a part in constructing him:

I almost envy my friend Stefan Zweig, persecuted for his race, who now defiantly refuses to work with me in public or in secret because, he says, he does not want to have any 'special privileges' in the Third Reich. To be honest, I don't understand this Jewish solidarity and regret that the 'artist' Zweig cannot rise above political fashions. If we do not preserve artistic freedom ourselves, how can we expect it from soap-box orators in taverns? (Knight (ed.), *Letters*, pp. 109–10)

The contradiction constructed between artist and friend is revelatory. If he tries to defend his own position as artist and his idea of art as a privileged area of human conduct, which in his case means defending nihilism, he is forced to a recognition of Zweig as the 'friend' he does not have. Zweig is the 'other', whose position is not understood, but is none the less sought after. The whole of the correspondence between the two shows Strauss seeking unconsciously but strenuously a validation from the Jewish other. This could be read in Lacanian terms, in terms of 'desire of the other', which I referred to in discussing *Otello*. He needed Zweig more than Zweig needed him, since his own bad faith required validation by the (persecuted) other. He desired Zweig's position as the other, but he tried to play this down through his declaration of the assumption of the superiority of 'art' above all else—art which he considered united all people of talent, and thus made thought of 'otherness' unnecessary. (There are no others: art is there for all.)

Several points emerge from this. If Strauss may be thought of as a good subject of fascism, as he was after he was worked over once, his problems show themselves in his attitude to the other. Zweig Zweig's approval was, unconsciously desired, consciously dismissed in the name of art which reconciles all, same and other, because it appeals to all. Talk about the universality of art continues its hegemony today, and, as before, serves as a form of exclusion. Zweig's stated oppositions are seen as subordination to 'political fashions'—an interesting understatement. The 'other's' discourse has been safely removed: when the fashions change, life will return to normal. The incomplete nihilism of Strauss means that the voice of the other, which would necessitate a new set of interpretations, is not heard.

Between the opening of *Die schweigsame Frau* and these musings on paper, there was a further exchange between Zweig and Strauss, when the former recommended that an orchestral arrangement of the opera be made for smaller, less prestigious musical forces in smaller theatres (with less than Strauss's normal hundred-plus players: the orchestra in Strauss must always speak at top level[21]). Strauss's response to Zweig was sharp:

[21] Romain Rolland commented that Strauss needed too much 'music'; this demand made him unsympathetic to *Pelléas et Mélisande* (Myers (ed.), *Richard Strauss*, p. 156). Compare Strauss's reaction to *Pelléas*

My, what odd ideas you have! Why should I become popular at any price, that is, tied to the rabble and performed in every low-class theatre . . . this I leave to Léhar and Puccini . . . I'm thinking of true places of culture, medium-sized and large opera-houses that are to be enabled to present the masterpieces of our German opera literature in the manner the composer deserves.

The letter even anticipates Goebbels's help in doing this (28 June 1935; Knight (ed.), *Letters*, p. 101).

Even allowing for Strauss's state of mind at the end of that June, this response seems symptomatic of the incomplete nihilism which makes him think that the illusion of great art can be defended. He is neither Léhar nor Puccini—kitsch composers, as far as he is concerned—and therefore he belongs with great art, which excludes the common people—excludes the other, so excludes Zweig. Is there the admission here that the powerful musical forces he requires are designed to keep him apart from the low-class, from the popular? And why should Strauss think that a museum culture of great operatic works, of necessity all of the past, was worth keeping—let alone creating? Such an enterprise, if it had been carried out, would have belonged to the aestheticization of politics carried out by the Nazis, as part of their society of the spectacle. But he must have been aware that at that moment Nazism was exacting barbarisms such as the exclusion of composers (Schreker, Zemlinsky, Hindemith, Schoenberg, Berg, Weill) who made up so much of modern German musical composition, to say nothing of his own librettist. The appeal to the past is a means of collaborating with the Nazis in their negative sense of modernists in music as cultural Bolsheviks, Jews in music, people with non-Aryan sympathies, and degenerates. He could not so exclude the present and exalt the past masterpiece if his belief in art were not actually that it was only an illusion, at best kitsch. In the belief that Nazi Germany might create such opera-houses as he wanted, Strauss went beyond both the élitism and nationalism of the Salzburg Festival and the populism celebrated at the end of *Die Meistersinger*, of the festival as the place to revive the traditions of the *Volk*.

with that of Mascagni, who also wanted music to serve an extreme state: 'The music makes one think of those cinema musicians who play, modestly and timidly, their little airs, while the most extraordinary episodes unfold on the screen' (quoted by Mosco Carner, *Major and Minor* (London: Duckworth, 1980), p. 141).

8

'Entartete Musik': Reading the Nazis and the Schreker Case

There is only one kind of immoral art—and that is art that is boring.

Paul Bekker on *Elektra*

SCHREKER AND WILDE

This chapter explores decadence and nihilism in the senses in which these terms are constitutive of fascist rhetoric and also a critique of fascism. Two odd couples run through my consideration of this: Wagner and Nietzsche, Wilde and Schreker, with Franz Schreker (1878–1934) opening and closing the chapter. His reputation was made by his 'decadent' opera *Der ferne Klang* (1912). In the 1920s he taught in Berlin, a city reckoned since the 1890s to be at the heart of decadence. Romain Rolland thought that *Salome*'s decadence, along with Strauss's modernism and rejection of past musical traditions, originated in his association with *fin de siècle* Berlin. After the war, Berlin represented Weimar culture. When Hindemith was invited by Schreker to teach at the Berlin Musikhochschule in 1927, it had three opera-houses, the Staatsoper with Erich Kleiber, who had conducted the première of *Wozzeck*; the Kroll, with Klemperer; and the Städische Oper with Bruno Walter. Furtwängler directed the Berlin Philharmonic; Schreker directed the Hochschule; Schoenberg taught at the Prussian Academy of the Arts; Zemlinsky, his brother-in-law, was Kappellmeister at the Kroll. Kurt Weill, Bertolt Brecht, and Paul Dessau were also in Berlin. Virtually all these left in 1933 or 1934. Alexander Zemlinsky (1871–1942) did not survive musically after 1933 and the Nazis, and Schreker, broken by the experience of rejection, on account of being Jewish, and accused of writing internationalist and degenerate music, died of a heart attack.

Schreker was branded because he wrote about branded souls (*Gezeichnete*): people haunted by their sexuality or deformity or perversity. What was called his over-refined orchestration and the lack of 'masculinity' in his music were also standard criticisms. The Nazis included his work as 'degenerate'—*Entartete*

Musik—in an exhibition in Düsseldorf in 1938. Max Nordau's *Entartung* (Degeneration) of 1892 had provided the word from biology, 'defining a plant or animal which has so changed that it no longer belongs to its species'; the project attacked works that did not fit a 'German' culture. Hans Severus Ziegler, the theatrical manager of the German National Theatre (Weimar), who initiated this exhibition, called Schreker's work that of a 'Jewish scribbler', saying that 'there was no sexual-pathological aberration that he did not set to music'. He was 'the Magnus Hirschfeld of opera composers'.[1] (Hirschfeld (1868–1935) was the sexologist best known for his pioneering work on homosexuality.)

Schreker's operas, like Zemlinsky's, use Wilde as one inspiration, and so involve themselves with self-reflexive questions about art and pleasure and bourgeois experience. In 1908, while composing words and music for *Der ferne Klang* (written 1903–10), he wrote music for a pantomime of Wilde's short story 'The Birthday of the Infanta' (1889, published in book form in *The House of Pomegranates*, 1891). In 1922, Zemlinsky set the story as a one-act opera, *Der Zwerg*, to a libretto by the Viennese Georg Klaren (1900–62), who had written a study of Weininger. (The opera's revival in 1981 by Hamburg State Opera used a revised libretto which changed the title back to Wilde's.) Zemlinsky's title not only focuses on the dwarf, but 'orientalizes' the topic, by making him a gift from a Sultan, kept prisoner for the past ten years, aware of his loss of freedom, and not, as in Wilde, a child of nature. Thus the subject of imperialism is a subtext of this opera. The Infanta in Zemlinsky is 18, which increases the sexual tension; the

---

[1] Quoted by Peter Franklin, 'Distant Sounds—Fallen Music: *Der ferne Klang* as "Woman's Opera?"' *Cambridge Opera Journal*, 3 (1991): 162. For Schreker, see Christopher Hailey, *Franz Schreker 1878–1934: A Cultural Biography* (Cambridge: Cambridge University Press, 1993), an excellent study. Peter Franklin's work is important for a reading of Schreker: see also his chapter on Schreker in *The Idea of Music* (London: Macmillan, 1985) and his article in *Opera* 43 (Jan. 1992): 26–30. See also Carl Dahlhaus, *Schoenberg and the New Music* trans. Derrick Puffett and Alfred Clayton (Cambridge: Cambridge University Press, 1987). Opera North's programme for *Der ferne Klang* (1992) is useful. On Zemlinsky, see the article in *Opera* 34 (1983): 841–6 by Horst Weber, who also writes on him in the *New Grove Dictionary of Music*, and Alfred Clayton, 'Zemlinsky's One-Act Operas', *Musical Times*, 124 (1983): 474–8, who also writes on him in the *New Grove Dictionary of Opera*.

On 'Entartete Kunst', see Stephanie Barron (ed.), *'Degenerate Art': The Fate of the Avant-Garde in Nazi Germany* (New York: Harry N. Abrams and Los Angeles County Museum, 1991), p. 11. The volume is on the Nazi exhibition of 1938, and the section by Michael Meyer, 'A Musical Façade for the Third Reich', makes clear the comprehensive nature of the attack on modernist music. What was attacked included jazz, swing, Jewish musicians (Klemperer's 1933 *Tannhäuser* was referred to as 'Jews against Wagner'); 'degenerate music', which included Berg, Bloch, Hindemith, Krenek, Schoenberg, Schreker, Stravinsky, Toch, Webern, and Weill; 'alien' entertainment music, and 'Jewish operetta' (pp. 180–2). See also Erik Levi, 'Music and National Socialism', in Brandon Taylor and Wilfried van der Will (eds.), *The Nazification of Art* (Winchester: Winchester Press, 1990), pp. 158–82.

dwarf is a dandy with a dagger. Zemlinsky's version is more violent (verismo-like in the ending), and more intense, if anything, than Wilde's: at the end the dwarf dies in a state of hysteria, marked by fate in every sense, deformed and feminized. But, in addition to this interest in setting 'The Birthday', both composers planned to work on an opera, for which Schreker provided the libretto for Zemlinsky, who told him to 'write about the tragedy of the ugly man' (Hailey, *Franz Schreker*, p. 65), but which Schreker eventually set himself, calling it *Die Gezeichneten*—those branded or marked by fate—which took the Wilde plot much further.

Wilde's short story tells of the Spanish princess's twelfth birthday, at a court where Spain's imperialism and the aggrandizement of Spain are subtly suggested, and are tied into the corruption of the Catholic Church, an institution which was a source of fascination to all modernists unhappy with modernism, affecting *Parsifal*, *Otello*, and *Tosca* and the religiosity of *Hänsel und Gretel* (which requires fourteen 'angels' in production), touching also nineteenth-century 'decadents' such as Huysmans and Wilde, and producing the whole theatricality of the Salzburg Festival. The court is also highly artificial; the Infanta's mother's body has been embalmed, not buried, treated as a fetish and a relic. Among other entertainments, the Infanta is danced to by the dwarf picked up from the forest, the child of nature, who makes her laugh, so that she throws him a white rose, which he receives with all the elevated dignity of an opera-singer with pretensions to a discerning public. The opera-singer is specifically a castrato, and the reference suggests the way the luxuriant court or church embalms and fetishizes the voice at the expense of the person. 'Pressing the flower to his rough coarse lips he put his hand upon his heart, and sank on one knee before her, grinning from ear to ear and with his little bright eyes sparkling with pleasure.' So overjoyed is he by the request that he should dance again for her that he thinks of himself as a courtly lover, and steals into the palace, where for the first time he sees himself in a mirror. The shock of seeing his own ugliness and realizing that this is what caused the laughter of the Infanta kills him, and she has the last word on recognizing he died of a broken heart—'For the future, let those who come to play with me have no hearts.' She is a Salome or a Lulu in her ability to step over the feelings of others, without what justifies Salome, the provocation offered by men. In the first paragraph, where she wanders in her gardens, 'the pomegranates split and cracked with the heat, and showed their bleeding red hearts,' which is suggestive both for the book-title and for the spoiling of hearts that takes place at the end; it also suggests the heartlessness that will pervade the text, the ability to refuse all questions of sympathy or feeling in favour of a pure aestheticism, a stress on matters of external beauty.

As always in narrative, the question of who speaks in the text is important; this narration is indirect free discourse, which means that it does not come from a single viewpoint; it presents matters from neither the dwarf's perception nor the court's, but shifts between these so that its sympathies are ambiguous, mocking the reader's emotions towards the figures and incidents displayed. Does it mock the dwarf's romantic naïveté as much as court artifice? The last line suggests that it is the princess who has no heart, which means the end of the Romantic tradition of the innocent child and the beginning of the tradition of the sexually aware one. The line also implies the folly of allowing any assessment from the outside or setting any emotional store by the opinion of others. The mirror the dwarf looks in evokes the assessment he imagines he gets from society—namely, its mocking laughter. Acceptance of this valuation kills him. Indirect free discourse indeed, with its refusal of a single narrative standpoint, prevents even a clear objective perception by the reader of what the dwarf actually looks like: the text refuses to act as a mirror.

None the less, the text remains nihilistic in scope. It builds up to the degradation of the dwarf, and refuses the possibility of a traditional humanist reading which would allow for the introduction of feeling. In fact it mocks this. Such sadism— not coincidentally, the word comes from Krafft-Ebing's regulatory textbook about sex, *Psychopathia Sexualis*—is part of a pleasure which takes an aesthetic delight in beauty as opposed to taking up a moral position. It is, I believe, a large part of what both Zemlinsky and Schreker derived from Wilde. It fits the nihilism, which is both Wildean and Nietzschean in scope, the desire to press on and prove humanistic illusions to be only illusions. As a way of testing behaviour, the sadism is different from that in *Das Rheingold*, to which both Wilde's story and Zemlinsky's opera are indebted. Alberich the dwarf is mocked by the Rhine maidens, and the portrayal of inner and outer ugliness in him has a sadism which connects with contemporary discourses of degeneracy, anti-Semitism, and class hatred of the industrial bourgeoisie; but certainly the text is weighted against Alberich and in favour of the Rhine maidens and love, which Alberich denies (though the Rhine maidens on one reading can be seen as vacuous, predatory females, anticipative of Strauss's Salome). The humanistic reference to love centres Wagner's text: we know how we are to respond to Alberich, when he negates love in favour of the will to power. Nothing like that happens in Wilde's text. In Thomas Mann's short story 'Little Herr Friedemann' (1897), where a dwarf is rejected by a married woman and drowns himself, the text's nihilism is incomplete, since the text implies that the dwarf has been systematically turning his back on experience and emotions: he is knocked off his balance, which comes about from his ability to repress feeling, by attending a performance of *Lohengrin*. In contrast to Wagner and Mann, there is nothing in Wilde's text to centre the reading: no residual humanism to invite the reader to take up any single position. Rather, all valuations become illusory, ideological. Nihilism fits in part with the modernism of the text, which backs the individual solely against a societal assessment, and where individual self-perception can shift as the societal one cannot. This holds also for Wilde's *A Florentine Tragedy*, which Zemlinsky set (Stuttgart, 1917), where the wife's assessment of her husband changes, and where identity itself seems to shift within the emotional relationship set up between the three people on-stage: husband, wife, lover.

A source for Wilde's nihilism may be *Tannhäuser*, a key text for Wilde; Dorian Gray sits in his box at the Opera, 'listening in rapt attention to *Tannhäuser* and seeing in the prelude to that great work a presentation of the tragedy of his own soul' (*Picture of Dorian Gray*, ch. 11). Tannhäuser breaks up the order of the singing contest in the Wartburg by praising sensuality and the Venusberg. If the Venusberg is the dream which he wants to waken from in the first scene, so is the Wartburg later. When he sings in the contest, 'As if awakening from a dream, Tannhäuser now speaks, his whole demeanour betokening him to be in the grip of uncanny [*unheimlich*] forces,' these forces, heard in the orchestra, are those of the Venusberg, whose music momentarily reappears. The uncanny in Freud comes from the coming to light—the emergence from repression—of something that has been hidden, and which is discovered to be familiar. Both worlds are dreams; both involve a woman who is a figure of the other one; both worlds are allegories of each other. The ascetic world is an ideological representation which keeps a symbiotic relationship with the Venusberg. Tannhäuser is revolted by both worlds in turn. Whatever situation he is in, he identifies with the other side, which means that there can be no closure to the text—only the attempt to make it Christian by a miraculous flowering of the papal staff.

This makes the text disturbingly nihilistic in its questioning of bourgeois culture. When Tannhäuser sings about the Venusberg, however illusory that world too is, he effectively lifts the lid off the values of the dominant order at the court—which also happens to be highly militaristic, demonstrated most clearly by the willingness of the men to kill him—and shows up their emptiness. The opera does not allow for that reading to be sustained, since it projects Elisabeth as the heroine, and pushes towards both redemption and the abandonment of sexuality; none the less, everything here is equivocal. The 'poisonous book' which Dorian Gray is given to read in chapter 10, which, importantly, corrupts his moral sense (it is probably *A Rebours*), suggests two ways of taking *Tannhäuser*. The book comes across to Dorian Gray as the description of 'the life of the senses', which is rendered in terms of 'mystical philosophy', so that 'one hardly knew at times whether one was reading the spiritual ecstasies of some medieval saint or the morbid confessions of a modern sinner'. *Tannhäuser* on this basis might be a secret text of sexual ecstasy, inscribed in the language of renunciation. As has been neatly said, '*Tannhäuser* almost becomes a code word for experimentation with forbidden pleasures.'² The Venusberg, which anticipates Klingsor's magic garden, the brothel in *Der ferne Klang*, and the grotto in *Die Gezeichneten*, may be seen as a reminder of what bourgeois taste really wants, examples of its debased, repressed reality.

In a nihilistic text, cruelty becomes a form of testing bourgeois societal values, as in Wilde's *Salome*. Impelling the need for such sadism is a recognition of the casual cruelties permitted in incomplete nihilism, or, better, what Nietzsche calls 'nihilistic religion' (*Will to Power*, sect. 152). Religious nihilism denies that it is nihilistic: it simply declares the real world, as opposed to the spiritual one, to have no value at all. Wilde chooses Spain not only for colour and for the inspiration of Velázquez, but because it allows him to focus on religious cruelty—the *auto-da-fé*. In a line cut after the first edition of the text, he makes the Grand Inquisitor, a virtuoso of violence, think that 'while it was only right that heretics and Jews and people of their kind should suffer', it was intolerable to watch puppets going through the motions of suffering.³ Wilde must have known about anti-Semitism as a feature of the end of the nineteenth century, as he was to know of the persecutions imposed (by a society characterized by both incomplete and religious nihilism) on the stigmatized, the *Gezeichneten*. The Grand Inquisitor's line is suggestive for fascist discourse and implies that the suffering of the dwarf takes place because the dwarf stands for a whole range of marginal figures, who must look at themselves in a mirror not of their own making.

---

² Anne Dzamba Sessa, *Richard Wagner and the English* (London: Associated Universities Press, 1979), p. 103. See also the chapter on Wilde in Stoddard Martin, *Wagner to The Waste Land* (London: Macmillan, 1982).

³ See Wilde, *The Complete Shorter Fiction of Oscar Wilde*, ed. Isobel Murray (Oxford: Oxford University Press, 1979), p. 15.

Die Gezeichneten (Frankfurt, 1918), Schreker's most fully articulated revision of Wilde, has as its subject the love of the deformed Genoese nobleman Alviano Selvago for Carlotta, who as a painter wants to do his portrait, and seems, so he thinks, attracted to him. She is pursued by another nobleman, Count Tamare. Alviano Selvago tries to compensate for his ugliness by using the grotto on his private island of Elysium as a brothel-cum-playground for the patrician class; but the murders of women on it have shocked him into wishing to give it to the people, and keep it no longer for private use. In the last act, Carlotta is raped by Tamare in the grotto, and Selvago kills him; but Carlotta, with her last breath, repudiates him, and calls out for her lover Tamare. Selvago staggers out, in a state of distraction.

The Wilde short story is only source material here: Schreker has transformed it by intensifying its themes. The dwarf is transmuted into a deformed nobleman, who is a mixture of idealist and pimp for a society even more opportunistic than he is; Carlotta is a version of the ideal woman, as the dwarf thought the princess was, but the effect of her completing the painting of him (as a portrait of the soul) is to make her lose interest in him, which makes for a critique of art and aestheticism; and then she succumbs to the intoxicating pleasures of the island, and enjoys them, which theme, derived from Weininger, indicates that the woman is beyond traditional feeling as this is considered in bourgeois society. She is a nineteenth-century Salome figure or a Lulu. Curiously, what interests her are the hands of various subjects; the cult of the hand suggests the cult of the leader, the impulsion towards the fascist, perhaps the desire to be possessed.[4] Significantly, she is portrayed as ill, with a weak heart: that is how she has been marked by fate. But this makes her nothing like the consumptive heroines Mimi or Violetta; rather, it seems to increase her sexual interest (just as in *The Magic Mountain* sexuality is promoted by the attractiveness possessed by those suffering from tuberculosis). In being an artist and in her sexuality, she affronts bourgeois society, and shows the drive towards experience and speed which is characteristic of modernity: when she has finished the painting, she has finished with the subject of the painting. But that modernity is trumped by something else: the opera shows the triumph of male sadism, a heartlessness more terrible than the Infanta's; it also engages, despite its Renaissance setting, with decadence, seen as the truth behind an established society.

---

[4] The Fascist interest in hands is discussed by Derrida, '*Geschlecht* II: Heidegger's Hand', in Tom Sallis (ed.), *Derrida and Philosophy* (Chicago: University of Chicago Press, 1987), ch. 12.

MANKIND'S DESTRUCTION AS AESTHETIC PLEASURE

At this stage, it is necessary to clarify the term 'decadence'. As a term of abuse or as part of a positive statement, like Nietzsche declaring himself to be decadent (preface to *The Case of Wagner*), decadence means nothing objectively, the question to be asked about it being who is describing what as decadent and why. It is a term of conservative reaction, part of a discourse insisting on order. In Wilde and Nietzsche, naming the self as decadent is an attempt at dissociation from bourgeois culture. But I want to turn to a third sense.

Nietzsche associates decadence with nihilism. The preface to *The Case of Wagner* calls Wagner a decadent, saying that decadence has been Nietzsche's greatest preoccupation. But decadence belongs within the whole sphere of nihilism, which also has plural senses for Nietzsche. It is a key word to describe the inner condition of European Christian bourgeois society and a coming state of crisis, one he intuits as on the point of arriving: 'Nihilism stands at the door: whence comes this uncanniest of guests?' (*Will to Power*, §1).

For Nietzsche, Schopenhauer and Wagner are important because they know the illusory nature of the highest ideals (e.g. those of the Wartburg and of Christianity). Schopenhauer pushed at the weaknesses of Christianity; Wagner ultimately propped them up. But both see that 'the highest values devalue themselves' ibid., §2). Christianity proposes moral and ethical systems to be more important than life: Socratic Christian morality prefers an abstract system of values to life, life being nothing outside moral judgements. This devaluation of life Nietzsche sees as nihilistic. But these values show in the course of time that they lack a *raison d'être*. Although they have been proposed as an absolute, as more important than life, their devaluation becomes manifest. As the aphorism continues, 'the aim is lacking, "why" [i.e. "why should I follow this value?"] finds no answer.'

The historical decline of Christianity means that 'one interpretation has collapsed; but because it was considered *the* interpretation it now seems as if there were no meaning at all in existence, as if everything were in vain' (ibid., §55). A nihilistic text would abandon any idea of the world interpreted in such a way as to yield values, and a text offering values does not escape nihilism, for values belong to the baggage of Christianity and the philosophy which has made values part of the will to truth. The upheavals implied in 'modernity', 'the problem of the nineteenth century' (ibid., §111), creates 'a nihilistic movement', which might be fruitful, since there might appear 'the most extreme form of pessimism, genuine *nihilism*. Such a nihilism could be 'the sign of a crucial and most essential growth, of the transition to new conditions of existence', and in that sense Nietzsche declares himself a nihilist (ibid., §112; cf. §585). So nihilism indeed stands at the door, but its 'uncanny' nature recalls Freud again, that the uncanny is simultaneously strange and unfamiliar and known and recognized. The late nineteenth century has been nihilistic without knowing it in its commitment to the 'will to truth'. A text may look affirmatory (like *Tannhäuser*), but underneath is nihilism, even, says Nietzsche, in 'present-day music' (ibid., §51). Wagner could not have been so systematic in his mythologizing in *The Ring*—the leitmotifs helping to close the narrative gaps, which are also filled in repeatedly by the characters' summarizing of events—if he were not anxious about consistency, about maintaining a will to truth. But the moral, affirmatory intentions of Verdian and Wagnerian opera are there out front—appeals to patriotism, sacrifice, militarism, honour, love, and the importance of patriarchy, for example.

Though nihilism is concealed within the illusionistic structure of European culture and aesthetics, Schopenhauer in *The World as Will and Representation* makes aesthetic contemplation the highest form of knowledge. In contrast to this, Benjamin, as I suggested in the Introduction, sees aesthetics as part of the arsenal of fascism, which depoliticizes the political by turning it into a work of art. Benjamin's comment is amplified in his discussion of Ernst Jünger, the militarist, technocrat, and writer.[5] The critique of Jünger picks up two aspects of fascist discourse, its aestheticizing and its acceptance of an ideology of sacrifice and failure. Benjamin accused Jünger of a glibness about the 'First World War', talking as though wars could be continued endlessly, metaphysically, and vitalistically, if not in actuality, without realizing the power of technology to bring about not further heroism, but 'total disorganization'.[6] Jünger's 'cultic' attitude to war Benjamin calls a 'decadent' *l'art pour l'art* attitude (p. 122). Technology and aesthetics occlude politics and the nature of modern war itself. War can be thought of as something 'cultic', productive of heroism, with technology as an aid to that, not as the obliteration of any heroism or of the human. The machine is beautiful; the human body must become the machine. This is futurist talk, which denies the body: for Jünger, modernization was a necessary aspect of German

---

[5] For Jünger as a 'reactionary modernist', see Jeffrey Herf, *Reactionary Modernism: Technology, Culture and Politics in Weimar and the Third Reich* (Cambridge: Cambridge University Press, 1984). Ch. 4 is on Jünger.

[6] Walter Benjamin, 'Theories of German Fascism: On the Collection of Essays *War and Warrior* edited by Ernst Jünger', *New German Critique*, 17 (1979): 121. The essay on Benjamin by Ansgar Hillach, 'The Aesthetics of Politics', same issue, pp. 99–119, is relevant.

nationalism. In *Der Arbeiter* (The Technocrat, 1932,) technology is 'the mobilization of the world through the *Gestalt* of the worker' (quoted by Herf, *Reactionary
Modernism*, p. 101), by which he meant that the abstract will (like Schopenhauer's)
that shaped history and destiny as a will to power was aesthetic, a will to form, to
create the model of the worker, who is formed on the model of the soldier.

Benjamin further accused Jünger of being in the grip of an ideology which
taught that the Germans lost the war 'out of their innermost existence'; that defeat
was something 'characteristically German'. To lose the war was to fulfil German
destiny; it belonged to the desire to will the abyss, to live with an open wound.
Jünger took 'the loss of the war more seriously than the war itself', in a state of
mind fertile for the growth of Spenglerian theories of 'the decline of the west'.
Jünger had to spiritualize, to think in an idealist way that effaced present reality,
so that the 1914 war was praised for giving back ideals and cutting out decadent
living.[7] Benjamin quotes from an associate of Jünger who declared that dead
soldiers were going 'from an imperfect reality to a perfect reality, from Germany
in its temporal manifestation to the eternal Germany' ('Theories', p. 125). When
everything, including nature, is idealized, technology reduces the reality of nature
to death, to a landscape of death.[8] 'The new nationalists' metaphysical abstraction
of war signifies nothing other than a mystical and unmediated application of
technology to solve the mystery of an idealistically perceived nature' (ibid., pp.
126–7). The hero presented and romanticized by these German nationalists,
impossible in actual warfare, is no more than 'the dependable fascist warrior'
(ibid., p. 127). In the same way, Brünnhilde, armed and in her first appearance in
Die Walküre, is the male fantasy myth of the warrior maiden, representing an
aestheticizing of warfare as well as the fantasy of the hardened, armoured self,
which, denying the body, makes her virtually male.

If the aestheticizing of war is the end-product of a Schopenhauerian approach
to aesthetic contemplation, how does it compare with Nietzsche and his 'We have
art lest we perish of the truth' (*Will to Power*, §822)? Nietzsche reverses the
situation: art for him is not fixed; rather, it is the means of bringing about different
interpretations, ways of seeing life as a sequence of improvisatory interpretations

---

[7] On the sense of liberation felt in August 1914 with the approach of war, see Eric J. Leed, *No Man's Land:
Combat and Identity in World War I* (Cambridge: Cambridge University Press, 1979).

[8] On Jünger's attitude to the body, see Russell A. Berman, 'Written Right Across Their Faces: Ernst
Jünger's Reactionary Modernism', in *Modern Culture and Critical Theory: Art, Politics and the Legacy of the
Frankfurt School* (Madison: University of Wisconsin Press, 1989), pp. 99–117. It becomes clear that Jünger's
fascism starts with a dislike of people's faces.

in contrast to the dominant powerful interpretations which masquerade as 'truth'. The 'transvaluation of all values' he asks for entails thinking in a new way altogether from the older vocabulary of values and value-judgements.

In the light of Benjamin on a decadent art for art's sake attitude, it can be seen that the people Nietzsche views as decadent are the 'moral priests' of society; they are not those whom bourgeois/fascist culture would call degenerate, like Schreker, on racial, social, or sexual grounds. They have the power of naming and constructing social degenerates and decadents, and are activated by a fear or dislike of the body, which itself promotes an aesthetic attitude in self-protection. Nietzsche thus sees decadence as a revulsion from the body which has been constructed as sick. Returning to the extract from *The Gay Science*, section 368, which I discussed in Chapter 1, it will be remembered that the 'cynic' had physiological objections to Wagner's music. Wagner is experienced as a challenge to the body, and the response made by the cynic on the body's behalf is that it expects from music that which will give it ease. But such a wish can come only from someone who describes his body in terms of 'iron, leaden life'. What is really wished for is that the music will put the body to sleep, as at the end of *Die Walküre*. The cynic finds that the music foregrounds his body; the comment 'You really are merely not healthy enough for our music' makes the cynic decadent, wishing for a music which will obliterate the body. It is implied that thinking comes from the body, and is a corporeal process, so the important initial question is how the body is conceptualized. The enlightened Wagnerian points away from a listening which comes out of the body's 'melancholy' (*Schwermut*), which would be nostalgic, death-driven, and implies another way of listening, which would not be confirmatory of the body as weary and death-driven. Decadence is identified with those who despise life in the body, who put it down in favour of the ascetic ideal, who feel that life is a sickness: Schopenhauerians, and those who show by their politics that they are ready to wish universal destruction on others, like Jünger, and on themselves. Linking decadence with nihilism entails seeing that both have to do with a perception that the body resists being made a servant of the will. The self's attempts to impose order on it by setting up a scale of values are nihilistic, while its preaching of melancholy and pessimism on that basis is decadent.

This may be illustrated, in conclusion to this part, through Wotan in Act 2 of *Die Walküre*. After deciding that Siegmund must die, he gives an account to Brünnhilde, full of his own self-idealization and riddled with motifs of the frustration of his will, of his failure to produce a free son. The failure to achieve autonomy induces self-loathing—'Zum Ekel find ich / ewig nur mich / in allem, was ich erwirke' (With loathing I find eternally myself in all my hand has created). Valhalla, built for his own protection against the defeat of the gods, proves a virtual prison to him, since the power of the ring is outside it, and is liable to revert to Alberich and prove fatal to Wotan. He can do nothing to avert this. His highest values—desire for total control—devalue themselves. All he has worked for seems empty, so he is not prepared to save anything. When he sings 'Was frommte nir eigner Wille? Einen Freien kann ich nicht wollen' (What good is my will to me? I cannot will a being that is free), he shows his will to be the source of his being. Positively, not being able to will a being that is free could lead to a new orientation which realized that failure was not simply a matter of historical contingency, but that being free was not a product of will-power: what is free stands outside rules and the investments of the individual subject.[9] But Wotan does not move that way. He continues to see himself everywhere he looks, and self-hatred, a negative form of his earlier self-idealization, follows in a desire for the end: 'Nur eines will ich noch: das Ende, das Ende' (Only one thing I want, the end, the end).

This has gender-implications. Brünnhilde, who has already called herself Wotan's will, asks what she must do, and is told that she can only be the blind slave of his will. She has no other status than as an automaton, whereas Wotan is so full of resentment that he declares he could destroy the world he once took delight in, as though referring to his negative attitude to her. In the same way, he wishes that Alberich and his son may let their envy gnaw greedily on Valhalla, ('zernage ihn gierig dein Neid'). Brünnhilde's listening to Wotan and response to him is dialogic: it implies the possibility of another reaction to his monologistic utterances.

Wotan indicates his decadence in the sacrifice of his eye, which proclaims his attitude to his body. In *Rheingold*, scene 2, he tells Fricka that he lost it to win her; in *Götterdämmerung* the First Norn says that he lost it to receive wisdom, which is connected with domination—breaking off the branch from the world ash-tree in order to make his spear. In his scene with Brünnhilde his self-representation indicates that these things are the same. Demands for possession, whether sexual or in terms of knowledge—the will to truth which is also the will to power—are not to be separated or romanticized. Nihilism and decadence are part of the same thing: the will to the end.

---

[9] Cf. Nietzsche: 'All perfect acts are unconscious and no longer subject to will; consciousness is the expression of an imperfect and often morbid state in a person' (*Will to Power*, § 289) p. 163.

'*Fin de siècle*,' murmured Lord Henry.

'*Fin du globe*,' answered his hostess.

'I wish it were *fin du globe*', said Dorian, with a sigh. 'Life is a great disappointment.'

(*Picture of Dorian Gray*, ch. 15)

Thus for Nietzsche, decadence is not to be identified with the degenerate other; it is inscribed in what is bourgeois about bourgeois culture. To read Wagner is to read both modernity and bourgeois culture, which is why 'we must first be Wagnerians'. This is very different from Weininger's comparison of Wagner to Christ or from H. S. Chamberlain's hagiography. But it explains why Schreker and Berg, for instance, had to be Wagnerians to grasp the inner core of the culture they described. Strauss moving away from Wagnerian decadence, anti-Semitism, and anti-feminism, as in *Salome*, towards the kitsch world of bourgeois culture in *Arabella* shows how much was lost. Perhaps kitsch is the non-recognition of decadence. For Nietzsche, decadence, even that of Wagner, is not to be discarded:

Waste, decay, elimination need not be condemned: they are necessary consequences of life, of the growth of life. The phenomenon of decadence is as necessary as any increase and advance of life: one is in no position to abolish it. Reason demands, on the contrary, that we do justice to it. (*Will to Power*, §40)

In the same aphorism he refers to 'socialist systematisers'—which would include Stalinists, but also National Socialists—who suppose that there could be circumstances 'in which vice, disease, prostitution, distress, would no longer grow.—But that means condemning life.' A society advancing confidently will still form 'refuse and waste materials. The more energetically and boldly it advances, the richer it will be in failures and deformities.'

And with that quotation, I return to Wilde's 'The Birthday of the Infanta', which shows how much artificiality, how much kitsch, is necessary for the denial of 'deformity'. If Nietzsche diagnoses decadence as part of a refusal of life, a way of regarding life as sickness and the body as degenerate, then decadence cannot be dismissed simply as a kind of individualistic utterance that has no necessary place within discourse. Being Wagnerian as a Nietzschean is a necessary part of a discourse which is facing up to the nihilism that stands at the door. And on my account of *Die Walküre* Act 2, I think that Wagner is Nietzschean in his reading of Wotan's decadence and nihilism. In some ways, Nietzsche's discourse recognizes this: despite all its criticisms, it is not distanced from Wagner.

In the Nietzschean part of Franz Schreker's operas, there is again no flinching from showing what he takes to be the inner condition of bourgeois society. In

1918, in a letter to Paul Bekker which shows the influence of Weininger, he said: 'I do not see human beings as either good or evil. At the mercy of their passions, the most sublime of which I think is the sexual urge, they are of necessity full of conflict, like the will of nature itself' (quoted by Hailey, *Franz Schreker*, p. 351). It is now time to look at Schreker's opera *Der ferne Klang* in the light of this interest in the shamelessness of the sexual urge and the importance of decadence.

DER FERNE KLANG: MUSIC AND DECADENCE

Der ferne Klang (The Distant Sound) asks what decadence is and where it is to be found, and answers by pointing to bourgeois culture, not to the person on its margins such as the woman Grete. The plot turns on the decision of the musician Fritz to leave his fiancée Grete, to search for the source of his inspiration, which comes to him as a distant sound, like a harp, the instrument Adorno associates with *art nouveau*.[10] Grete is *petit bourgeois*, and is forbidden by her mother to help herself financially by going into service, while her father wants to sell her off in marriage after he has lost money at skittles. In desperation she runs away and nearly kills herself, but is led by a mysterious old woman, identified in the last act as a procuress, to a brothel, the Casa de Maschere, in the Venetian lagoon, where in Act 2 she is the star. The playground atmosphere, like Monte Carlo and like the island in *Die Gezeichneten*, proclaims the triumph of repro and kitsch culture, though the brothel scene fits generally with the intensity of verismo opera. The attitude to women which this opera diagnoses is that they are to be sold, whether by bourgeois marriage or as sexual objects or by being sacrificed on the altar of aesthetics, while the male pursues art. None the less, the brothel is not presented for shock value; on the contrary, it is the place which gives room to Grete, and it has a positive sense of thrill about it as well. It is the condemnation of Fritz's puritanism that he wanders into the brothel, is repelled by seeing his love as a prostitute, and rejects her.

Deserted twice, Grete in the third act is reduced to the status of a street-walker, and wanders past the performance of Fritz's opera *The Harp*, which we take to be *Der ferne Klang*, and is immediately won over by it. Critics of *The Harp* agree that the last act is wrong because, it seems, the piece ends with helpless longing, without any resolution in terms of the musician finding the woman he needs. The

---

[10] Theodor Adorno, *Quasi una fantasia*, trans. Rodney Livingstone (London: Verso, 1992), p. 135. The essay on Schreker dates from 1959.

last scene of the opera proper concludes with a reconciliation between composer and Grete when he seems to hear the music and dies, knowing now that the last act was indeed wrong ('der letzte Akt ist verfehlt'). No *Liebestod* follows. In this scene, Grete appears to him 'in a simple dress, very pale, unlike her appearance before with flashy clothes and make-up', and the stage direction indicates a basic bourgeois attitude underlying the thrilled, fascinated attitude to decadence and the sexual woman: a contradiction within Schreker's own text.

But in rejecting mere longing and helplessness, the opera seems to reject its own resolution, and also the enervations of Wagnerian opera. Fritz is decadent, his death being an indication of a persistent denial of life he has carried through, which is symbolized by his ability to reject Grete. As in the match of different sounds in the second act, the music aims at a sensuousness which is a critique of that decadence, just as there is another 'distant sound' heard in the first act—that of the train. This points to a music which is not outside technology, which is therefore outside the mystificatory sense of art having nothing to do with modern life, but something to be pursued for its own sake. The celebrations of technology—the train, broadcasting, and amplification—are a feature of Schreker's pupil, Krenek, in *Jonny spielt auf* (1927), another piece which was part of 'Entartete musik', a modern text which thus proclaims both its good and its evil, its good in trying to advance music, to find opera a future with jazz and in its self-reflexivity about opera as a form and a practice, and its evil (its decadence) in that probably automatically—that is, unconsciously—it makes the musician who plays kitsch on the violin Jewish.

Klemperer called Schreker's work 'inflation music', as a reminder of Weimar culture and its hyper-inflation, and named him 'the German Puccini' (Heyworth, *Conversations with Klemperer*, pp. 47–8). Yet Klemperer's imagery of inflation is more apt than he realizes, for it fits the age of technological reproducibility in which Schreker moves. A repro culture must devalue the appeal to humanistic values that Klemperer makes. In Schreker, despite elements of bourgeois seriousness, the commitment is not to humanistic seriousness. What the conservative critic Walter Niemann said of Strauss, that 'healthy sensuousness often gives way to sick corrosive perversity', also refers to him—'it is the total absence of any *ethos*, of any inner moral, ennobling power and grandeur which imposes so much upon modern music the stamp of death' (Hailey, *Franz Schreker*, p. 44). This refusal of the ethical in the situation where art is reproducible through and through, down to its finest effects, is evident too in Paul Bekker's contrasting of Schreker with Wagner, whose characters, he says, embody the humanistic 'will', while Schreker's stand only for emotion, and his orchestra 'longs for dissolution in the colourful shimmering of the incorporeal vision' (ibid., p. 91). This is different from the atmosphere of *Tristan*: it is nearer to being a parody of that. Schreker is inspired by 'the *deliquescence* of sound' (my emphasis), by its disappearance in its purity as the technological takes over.[11]

Inflation and repro culture and the highest values devaluing themselves go together, and produce the music's mixture of modernism and the popular. *Der ferne Klang* has elements of Wagner, and is also reminiscent of the Viennese waltz. The music is both modernist-Mahlerian (it was dedicated to Bruno Walter), and works on the Strauss–Puccini axis. In Act 2, Grete appears in a way reminiscent of Léhar's merry widow. The Viennese influences, as well as the extravagant plots, caused Berg, initially receptive to Schreker, to call *Die Gezeichneten* 'a bit kit-schy'.[12] Berg, a modernist composer who was himself called decadent, tries to save the values of European art in this term. Similarly, the anti-modernist Berlin music critic Alfred Heuss calls Schreker's works 'sexual kitsch operas' (Hailey, *Franz Schreker*, p. 146).

Alongside this series of depreciations of Schreker, many of which anticipate the Nazi critique, Adorno's critique in *Quasi una fantasia* stands out. He says that Schreker's music 'fails to construct an ego' (p. 143), which suggests that it is outside the fascist wish for the ego as armour, but is vulnerable to fascist attacks on just that count. He continues:

It stands outside the demands of culture. But because it springs from a compulsion which is *more potent than shame* and testifies to the truth of things that culture proscribes, it gives expression to doubts about the value of culture as such. Schreker consciously deserts to the realm which culture has distanced itself from and consigned to *the vulgar*. The fact that culture has to reject this reminds us of the limitations of its power and ultimately of its own failure: unable to effect a reconciliation between the drives and itself, it holds them down

---

[11] Despite the use of technology in *Der ferne Klang*, the new technologies disturbed Schreker (Hailey, *Franz Schreker*, pp. 226–40). His response to radio and film was to think that it had brought the distant sound too near. The use of technology in *Lulu* should be compared. *Lulu* has many points of contact with Schreker's dramatic themes, but perhaps under the influence of Louise Brook's performance of Wedekind's Lulu in *Pandora's Box* (1929), it casts Lulu as dangerous to men and as a fatal animal: a masculinist interpretation also visible in the dependence on Wedekind's presentation of the lesbian Countess Gesch-witz, where, influenced by *Psychopathia Sexualis*, lesbianism, as something unnatural, is associated with masochism—just as Lulu herself seems masochistic in relation to Jack. The countess is not allowed a free spontaneous gesture of love towards Lulu.

[12] Letter to Schoenberg, quoted by Christopher Hailey, in Douglas Jarman (ed.), *The Berg Companion* (London: Macmillan, 1989), p. 228. See the essays by Derrick Puffett and by Hailey for the context of German and Austrian opera and the influence of Schreker on Berg.

by force. This has led to those increasingly powerful feelings of discontent which Freud described . . . Schreker refuses to join in the repression of the drives. (my emphasis)

Adorno does not distinguish between culture and middle-class culture, but his insight is vital. Schreker's shamelessness, that mark of modernity, aligns him with the vulgar, with popular culture; and the popular is seen to be the realm of the excluded from high culture. Arguments about commodity fetishism and the culture industry seem to have disappeared here. In the light of Freud's *Civilization and its Discontents*, the realm of high culture, which Adorno actually aligns with repression and force, is seen now to operate at too high a price.

It is strange and interesting to see Adorno allowing his stress on autonomous art to be challenged by Schreker. But Schreker may point towards the eclecticism of popular culture and to a modernity which uses technology and resorts plainly to the categories of pleasure. Alluding to Schreker's birthplace, and hence to his internationalism, Adorno finishes his essay by saying that 'the profession of Schreker's father would have been the true title of the opera he was never able to write: the photographer of Monte Carlo' (*Quasi una fantasia*, p. 144). It may also suggest a new gender politics by which the popular may be thought. It has been argued that the romantic musical inspiration which Fritz follows in the first act of *Der ferne Klang* is gendered in masculine terms (which would not make it a Kundry, but would rather associate it with Weininger). But that is the same as the *Liebestod*: when Isolde asks if it is she only who hears the music, she identifies its compelling force—which her music only signifies—with Tristan himself. In Schreker's opera, Grete has to sing Fritz's music. In unison with him in the first act she sings about the nature of his inspiration: 'Wie wenn der Wind / mit Geisterhand über Harfen streicht' (As when the wind touches with ghostly hand the strings of a harp). As the deserted *traviata* of Act 2, she has to wait, like Violetta, for him to come back into her life, so the opera dramatizes the undoing of both women and a criticism of opera forms both Italianate and Wagnerian and the whole romantic-realist patriarchal nineteenth-century tradition, which allows for that undoing.

Such an account suggests that opera in its fully developed late nineteenth-century and modernist forms is being challenged in its nature as 'sound', with the power of emotional disturbance this has, engendering distant longings that can lead only to death. The anti-Schopenhauerian resonances of this argument are plain. Schreker may fetishize music, but he also critiques it as decadent, since its being and non-being, as a denial of life, destroys the woman. The search for the distant sound robs Grete of Fritz. She is a Gretel without a Hänsel, a Marguerite deserted by Faust. Music shows itself to be on the side of the loutish (e.g. the skittle-players, or Dr Vigellius's narration of the competition, which has a full orchestral and choral backing) and the coarse (perhaps the gypsy band heard in the brothel), an agency of a society that the woman must everywhere fight against. She sings in the third act, in dialogue that in character belongs with the characteristic music of *Wozzeck*—'die schöne Musik—ich bin durch Unglück so tief—so tief—gesunken' (The beautiful music—made me sink so deep—so deep—in misfortune). This, it seems, is not simply because of Fritz's desertion of her, but entails the whole complex of musical features the opera gives—most atmospherically felt in the varied sounds, choral and orchestral, on- and off-stage, heard at the beginning of Act 2.

Wagnerian music and modernist music—that which Fritz pursues, like the etiolated composer Max in *Jonny spielt auf*—is thus to be gendered in male terms. The postmodernist critic Andreas Huyssen argues, in *After the Great Divide*, that modernism, for all its revolutionary potential, couches itself in a rhetoric which makes it masculine and popular culture feminine, like Le Bon's crowd. The whole realm of the popular is thus downplayed, marginalized. It might be another example of what Fredric Jameson refers to as 'the modernist as fascist'. Adorno's wholesale rejection in the 1930s of the popular and his uncompromising stand in favour of Schoenberg's music are heroic, but they also involve sidelining the popular, which the device of referring to it as part of 'the culture industry' does not quite compensate for. Huyssen refers to a contradiction in modernist and realist discourse, which is able to have things both ways about 'mass' culture. Drawing on T. S. Eliot's conservative modernism as expressed in 'Notes Towards the Definition of Culture' (1948), Huyssen speaks of the

traditional dichotomy in which mass culture appears as monolithic, engulfing, totalitarian, and on the side of regression and the feminine ('totalitarianism appeals to the desire to return to the womb' said T. S. Eliot) and modernism appears as progressive, dynamic and indicative of male superiority in culture.[13]

The fear of mass culture overwhelming the self, or society, is reminiscent of the terms in which Theweleit's fascists think.

---

[13] Andreas Huyssen, 'Mass Culture as Woman: Modernism's Other', in *After the Great Divide* (London: Macmillan, 1986), p. 58.

Perhaps such an argument, which locates a conservatism in modernism in gender terms, might explain the modernists' insistence on art as a privileged area. Art, which Fritz pursues, becomes part of the will to truth, which he also exhibits, as when he rejects Grete at the end of Act 2. We are back to Nietzsche's sense of nihilism. But nihilism would include a dismissal of the popular and of mass entertainment. Peter Franklin suggests that the plot of *Der ferne Klang* involves Hollywood elements, and that Grete herself is constructed as a popular heroine out of the materials that would become basic to popular cinema, just as the high violins and glissandi on the harps in the opera are suggestive of Hollywood music. Then Fritz's abandonment of Grete might be read as an allegory of the marginalizing of the popular and of mass entertainment.

The same point about the woman as the expression of popular culture could be made about Puccini, with whom Klemperer compared Schreker. Those critics who say that, given time, Puccini would have become a good writer of Hollywood music are right in so far as Puccini's area of interest is melodrama (Sardou and Belasco), and melodrama, as distinct from 'straight' theatre, had, from its very origins in the eighteenth century, a marginal function, one which contrasted with the dignity of straight plays, which in Britain could exist only in those 'proper' theatres which had a royal patent. Melodrama, whose typical theme is the woman isolated and tested and suffering, thus becomes a vehicle for the expression of non-noble, non-establishment thoughts and actions.[14] The persecutions of Tosca and Madame Butterfly, like those of Grete, belong to a culture that, by its identification with the popular, is also associated with women. To fault melodramatic plots for being excessive, for instance, may be to enter into a masculine discourse which judges from the standpoint of the accepted and the proper. Certainly it is hard to think of Schreker's operas fitting into the pieties of the Salzburg Festival, and indeed *Die ferne Klang* was not performed in Vienna until 1991.

Aside from attacking his Jewishness, for the Nazis to take Schreker as degenerate was to do, only with more intensity, what the prevalent canon of bourgeois taste would do ultimately anyway in its protection of its own decadence. It comes across as a desire to protect value even as a simulacrum when the music and the age together have brought about the disappearance of value. In that sense, it is interesting that the postmodernist Baudrillard reads fascism as a nostalgia for power when the society it grows up in is powerless, where the basis for power is

---

[14] See Christine Gledhill's introduction to the volume she edits, *Home is Where the Heart Is: Studies in Melodrama and the Woman's Film* (London: BFI, 1987).

thought to have gone.[15] That weakens the impact of fascism perhaps, as it underestimates the power that is at work for control in societies, but it describes the melancholy that impels it, none the less.

[15] Baudrillard, 'Simulacra and Simulations', in Mark Poster (ed.), *Jean Baudrillard, Selected Writings* (Cambridge: Polity, 1988), pp. 180–1.

9
Post-Opera? After Brecht

Only opera persists in its 'splendid isolation'. The opera-going public still represents a closed group seemingly removed from the large theatre-going public. 'Opera' and 'theatre' are still treated as two completely separate concepts. In recent operas the dramaturgical style employed, the language spoken and the subjects treated would all be completely unthinkable in contemporary theatre. And one still hears, 'That might work in the theatre, but not in opera!' Opera was established as an artistic genre of the aristocracy, and everything one calls 'operatic tradition' only underlines the class basis of this genre. Today, however, there is no other artistic form in the entire world whose bearing is so unabashedly engendered by established society. The theatre in particular has moved quite decisively in a direction that can rather be described as socially regenerative. If the bounds of opera cannot accommodate such a rapprochement with the theatre of the times, then its bounds must be broken.

Weill, quoted by Hinton, *Kurt Weill*

Kurt Weill's opinions about opera in 1929 do not quite coincide with Strauss's comment to Zweig that, as an art-form, opera was dead. They are obviously less reactionary, though they are demonstrably of the same moment. A familiar question about opera in the 1920s was whether it could have a future. The issue was inseparable from the anxieties felt about the privileged nature of high art in contrast to American popular culture and kitsch; it was central to debates about modernism. Busoni, as a non-Wagnerian, expected that with Wagnerism superseded, 'in the future the opera will be the chief, that is to say the universal and one form of musical expression and content'.[1] His *Outline for a New Musical Aesthetics* (1907, rewritten in 1916) urged a modernist, Nietzsche-inspired looking towards the future.

Pfitzner responded to Busoni in *The Dangers of Futurism*, 'a book written from beginning to end in the spirit of the Third Reich', as the Nazi journal *Die Musik* said in 1933.[2] Pfitzner accused Busoni of ignorance of German music. For him,

[1] Susan C. Cook, *New Opera for a New Republic* (Ann Arbor: UMI Research Press, 1988), p. 11.

[2] Quoted by Beaumont, *Busoni*, p. 98. For a comparison of Busoni and Pfitzner, see Antony Beaumont in *Opera* (1990): 1184–8.

music was part of the profundity of the German soul, and he attacked the modernism of Schreker, Schoenberg, Mahler, and Zemlinsky in a pamphlet directed at the music critic Paul Bekker, *Die neue Ästhetik der musikalischen Impotenz*. Bekker was attacked by Pfitzner on many counts, including his view that music should be judged according to its capacity to generate an audience, and that the symphony from Beethoven onwards had the ability to create a community out of disparate listeners, an argument which attempted to relate music to people and to use, to find reasons for admiring music that were not simply formalistic. Berg responded to Pfitzner in 'Die musikalische Impotenz der neuen Ästhetik Hans Pfitzners' (1920), a paper arguing that music was not simply profound and the expression of an inspiration beyond analysis but, instead, totally susceptible to analysis. Much could be added about the masculinism of 'impotence', making Pfitzner a Klingsor.[3]

In the 1920s Berg represented one way forward for opera. *Wozzeck* engages with social issues through and through, including proto-fascist militarism among army personnel. The opera's atonality suggests that the working class it deals with can be thought of only in terms of dissonance. Indeed, atonalism was associated by *Die Musik* with 'musical communism' and twelve-tone method, as in *Lulu* (heard in Zurich in 1937), with a rejection of 'natural hierarchy' and the assumption of 'an absolute equality of rights' which made it not only socialist but decadent as the Nazis understood that term—'This music is the mirror of that world that staggered into a [First] world war.'[4]

But this modernism was not endorsed wholly by Berg's contemporaries. Schoenberg's scepticism about *Wozzeck* came about from his dislike of audiences and of theatricality and his hesitancy about the idea that opera could communicate immediate experience. These doubts reflected his sense of alienation being the condition of social existence, only falsely and superficially negated by the claim to be able to offer a direct theatrical/operatic experience, and they compare interestingly with Brecht's suspicion of theatricality, as much as they contrast with Brecht's interest in popular theatre. And Weill saw *Wozzeck* as a 'grandiose conclusion' to the Wagnerian tradition.[5] It was all up for opera, unless Wagner could be recovered from.

---

[3] On this debate, see Carner, *Major and Minor*, pp. 253–7; it is perhaps inevitable that the musicologist should ultimately want to side with Pfitzner.

[4] Quoted by Douglas Jarman, *Lulu* (Cambridge: Cambridge University Press, 1991), pp. 42–3. Compare Alfred Rosenberg saying that 'atonality contradicts the rhythm of the blood' (quoted by Meyer, *Politics of Music*, p. 21).

[5] See on this Douglas Jarman's essay on Weill and Berg in Kim H. Kowalke (ed.), *A New Orpheus: Essays on Kurt Weill* (New Haven: Yale University Press, 1986), pp. 147–8.

In this last chapter I will look at Brecht's work with Kurt Weill and the critique of opera offered there. Since it licensed so much of the respectability of the musical (musicals are now likely to turn up in the repertoire of opera-houses), I will close with some comments on contemporary mainstream music-theatre. I comment a little on *Die Dreigroschenoper* (1928) and *Happy End* (1929), but my focus is on *Aufstieg und Fall der Stadt Mahagonny*, which proved its questionable status as opera when it opened to a riot at the Leipzig Opera on 9 March 1930, accused of degeneracy by the Nazis, six months before the election which gave them their breakthrough: 18 per cent of the vote (14 September 1930). German nationalism did not like to see Germany presented in *Mahagonny* as though it were America, and this was another source of the riots, apart from Weill's Jewishness and Brecht's Marxism. *Die Dreigroschenoper*, which, like *Happy End*, opened in Berlin, at the Theater am Schiffbauerdamm, and not in an opera-house, had come before the crash of 1929, and had proved popular. The tone of *Mahagonny* was darker and less assimilable by the bourgeoisie who had enjoyed seeing themselves represented as gangsters in *Die Dreigroschenoper* and even felt flattered thereby. *Mahagonny* did not tap into anything sympathetic in the bourgeois, and the production was accused by the *Allgemeine Musikzeitung* of 'making an opera stage of the rank of the Leipzig one, where today *Fidelio*, tomorrow *Tristan* and Good Friday probably *Parsifal* appears, into a playground for criminals, whores, pimps, a gathering place for Communist demonstrations.'[6]

These Brecht/Weill operas may be contextualized by seeing how the practice of music shifts in the 1920s, with competing ideological values being ascribed to it in this, almost the last, decade of European opera; the moment after which, it may be argued, the form ceased to matter politically. In the 1920s, when expressionism as subjective autonomous art was replaced by *Neue Sachlichkeit*—new objectivity, new realism—Hindemith introduced *Gebrauchsmusik*—music for use—at the innovatory Donauschingen (Baden-Baden) Chamber Music festivals. Brecht, Weill, and Hindemith collaborated in 1929 at this festival on two *Lehrstück* plays, involving radio, music, drama, and poetry.[7] *Gebrauchsmusik* fits with both film music and jazz, imported into Europe in part through American intervention in

---

[6] Quoted by Patty Lee Parmalee, *Brecht's America* (Columbus, Oh.: Ohio State University Press, 1980), p. 177. In the Berlin production of 1931, with Zemlinsky conducting, not at the Kroll, the home of avant-garde opera (which in any case was to close in 1931), it was not mounted so much in opera style: Lotte Lenya, not an opera-singer, now sang Jenny, for instance.

[7] On this, see Roswitha Mueller, *Bertolt Brecht and the Theory of Media* (Lincoln, Nebr.: University of Nebraska Press, 1989), ch. 2.

the First World War and with 'Zeitopern', topical operas, which Susan Cook defines in terms of their comic genre, reliance on parody, satire, and burlesque (*New Opera*, p. 4). Krenek, Hindemith, and Weill are Cook's examples of *Zeitopern*, which we may see, in Bakhtinian fashion, as a mixed genre—dialogic, lacking a single, dominating voice. Weill's term for *Die Dreigroschenoper* was *Zwischengattung*—an 'in-between genre';[8] musically, it derived from cabaret, farce, variety, Viennese and Offenbachian operetta, as well as nineteenth-century operatic forms. And *Gebrauchsmusik* comes near to breaking up the category of high art. Hindemith in 1920 wrote to his publisher telling him that he could produce to order either 'good kitsch' or 'decent music'.[9]

This contrasts strongly with Strauss and Hofmannsthal and with Reinhardt's Salzburg Festival. Reinhardt accepted the importance of the *Gesamtkunstwerk*, and his career—which moved towards Hollywood in the 1920s and which Kraus even compared to Hitler's in its populism—shows a determination to make the theatre more and more inclusive of the people. There is a consistency between the building of the Grosses Schauspielhaus in Berlin in 1919, a theatre to seat 3,000, and his encouragement of open-air theatre at Salzburg in 1921. Everything is to be theatricalized; all gives way to spectacle, so much so that in Salzburg, the whole layout and architecture of the city becomes the theatre. This was true of the staging of *Jedermann* (Everyman) and *Das grosse Welttheater*, two allegories going back to the Middle Ages and the Baroque respectively, presented in versions written by Hofmannsthal, who relied on the past to offer such lessons in morality. When the divisions between actor and audience, fiction and reality, play and the world, are eroded, a space is opened up for fascist uses of reality as theatre. The open-air theatre proves coercive, just as the category 'entertainment', which Reinhardt used to describe what he was producing (in contrast to what he saw as the drabber theatre of naturalism and realism), serves religious ritual and moral teaching designed to persuade. The doubleness of the enterprise is its effectiveness. Is this entertainment, or is it for real effect? The undecidability is the point. Reinhardt's scope was popular culture—he brought Cecil B. de Mille's *King of Kings* to Salzburg for its première—and kitsch, whereby the city is tranformed

---

[8] Stephen Hinton, *Kurt Weill: The Threepenny Opera* (Cambridge: Cambridge University Press, 1990), p. 186.

[9] Quoted by Stephen Hinton, *The Idea of Gebrauchsmusik* (New York: Garland Publishing Co., 1989), p. 162. Bekker spoke of 'madcap, jaunty Paul Hindemith' (ibid., p. 165), referring to what was non-bourgeois in his music (its use of dance rhythms). Kitsch, it seems (which as a choice of word indicates an anxiety in Hindemith about what he was writing), cannot be given a single meaning as inoffensive art: this kitsch seems capable of challenging the bourgeois.

into stage scenery—and it was also like Wagnerian opera in its claims to attention.[10]

In Reinhardt's powerful and brilliant open-air productions, claiming a whole city for effect, the dream of Gurnemanz escorting Parsifal to the Grail ritual is fulfilled: here time becomes space. Bloch saw that line as epitomizing the spirit of the *Buhnenweihfestspiel* (Bloch, *Essays*, p. 167), so a line of thought might go as follows. A whole collapse of movement and history takes place in the capacity of music and ritual to spatialize, simplify, and synthesize, and this happens when *Parsifal* is added to the festival plays of *The Ring* cycle. The assumption has gone that these works belong to temporary festivals to be performed in some wooden building: we are now in the presence of the absolute. Such fetishizing of art and its equation with a total reality, with dimensions of time and space being lost, is at the heart of Salzburg, where typical dramatic texts celebrate time itself as only a play, hence unreal; where the only reality is the mystic space from which God views the world. With such a powerful unconscious set of co-ordinates activating the festival, everything of otherness has been annihilated: relativity has gone; nothing matters but the absolute. As has been noticed so often in this study, the art that fascism kills is unconsciously quasi-fascist itself.

Brecht and Weill's collaboration is antithetical to all this. Opera is turned against opera, so that the audience should be not passive figures, separated by the proscenium arch and the darkened auditorium and the mystic abyss of the Wagnerian orchestra pit, but active producers of the text. But it is not just an opposition to opera or theatre as spectacle. Brecht wrote a programmatic piece entitled 'Notes on the Opera' (1930) relating to *Aufstieg und Fall der Stadt Mahagonny*, expressing his scepticism about opera, calling it 'culinary art' produced to feed official good taste and to go down well, consumer art that, even when it is 'renovated', still appeals to a public definable as 'the opera-going public', the public for whom these changes must ultimately be tailored. *Mahagonny*, which he conceded had traditional operatic features, 'pays conscious tribute to the senselessness of the operatic form'.[11] Or, as he put it in 1935, 'the theme of the opera . . . is the cooking process itself' (ibid., p. 87); that is, its topic is the culinary attitude of the public. It is in this essay that he emphasizes 'the impossibility of any renewal of the operatic medium in the capitalist coun-

---

[10] On Reinhardt, see Styan, *Max Reinhardt*; Margaret Jacobs and John Warren (eds.), *Max Reinhardt: The Oxford Symposium* (Oxford: Polytechnic, 1986). For an overview of the theatre, see John Willett, *The Theatre of the Weimar Republic* (New York: Holmes and Meier, 1988).

[11] John Willett (trans. and ed.), *Brecht on Theatre* (2nd edn., London: Methuen, 1974), p. 35.

tries . . . any innovations introduced merely lead to opera's destruction. Composers aiming to renew the opera are bound, like Hindemith and Stravinsky, to come up against the opera apparatus' (ibid., p. 88).

At stake in this theory of culture with culinary art at its apogee is a theory of fascism, which carries over into *Aufstieg und Fall der Stadt Mahagonny*. Brecht's viewpoint is different from Thomas Mann's Wagner-inspired nihilism about German culture as productive of fascism. For Brecht there was nothing inherent in German culture which should necessarily incline it to fascism; Nazism was the product of capitalism, which in a moment of intense pressure, feeling itself to be in crisis, will always legitimate a particular form of repressive power. Big business was behind the rise of Hitler, and financed his way to the Reichstag. The criticism of German culture would be not of its Schopenhauer-driven longings for its own destruction, its nihilistic will-to-power, its non-rationality, but of its inevitable relationship to capitalist formations, which financed it and which it served. The politicizing of art, recommended by Benjamin, who was influenced by Brecht on this, is in response to fascism's aestheticizing of politics, and is also the alternative to the culinary art that capitalism hands down.

Mann and Adorno rejected such a politicizing in the name of autonomous art. Brecht's politically engaged form of art, which makes no pretence to autonomy, was criticized by both Adorno and Mann—who none the less found Brecht 'very gifted, unfortunately'.[12] One difference separating Brecht's work from Mann's is that it functions in the realm of the comic, the carnivalesque, which also separates it from the astringencies of Schoenbergian composition. It is not surprising to find Adorno complaining that Brecht had reduced the menace of the Nazis in *The Resistible Rise of Arturo Ui* to a 'trivial gangster organisation'.[13] In this case, humour for Adorno would be not only a way of playing down the virtually unrepresentable horrors of Fascism, but also a falsely reassuring mechanism, reinforcing a feeling of common identity in the audience and failing to convey a sense that this society already lives in a state of alienation.

Adorno has perhaps been proved right here in his pessimism, as against Benjamin and Lukács: present-day productions of Brecht, despite his decisive impact

---

[12] Quoted by Eric Bentley, *The Brecht Commentaries* (New York: Grove Press Inc., 1981), p. 32. For relationships between the two writers, see the essay by Hans Mayer, 'Thomas Mann and Bertolt Brecht: Anatomy of an Antagonism', *New German Critique*, 6 (1975): 101–15.

[13] New Left Review (ed.), *Aesthetics and Politics* (London: Verso, 1976), p. 183. On *Arturo Ui*, see Ernst Schürer, 'Revolution from the Right: Bertolt Brecht's American Gangster Play *The Resistible Rise of Arturo Ui*', *Perspectives on Contemporary Literature*, 2 (1978): 24–46.

on twentieth-century European and American theatre, are likely to be culinary art themselves—part of an artistic establishment. The subversive can be contained by successive performances and exposures of the work by the culture industry. In a related way, Benjamin's hope in 'The Work of Art in the Age of Mechanical Reproduction' that the infinite reproducibility of the work of art would take away from its unique 'aura' has not quite worked. The aura is the cultic, exalted status of the work of art, defined as such by its possession of such uniqueness. But the aura has reappeared through the star system and through the manipulations of those who control the processes of reproduction, so 'art' still exists as a privileged category, in spite of the fact that its auratic appeal is hyper-real and simulacral through the power of technology. But popular culture, too, exists through the power of technology. There is no room for the return of femininity or a different gender politics in Andrew Lloyd Webber, for instance. Kundry would find it hard to laugh in the empty spaces of *The Phantom of the Opera*.

'OH MOON OF ALABAMA'

Composers who aim to put new blood in the opera are inevitably (like Hindemith and Stravinsky) brought up against the whole operatic apparatus. Great apparati like the opera, the stage, the Press etc. impose their views as it were incognito.

Brecht, quoted by Willett, *The Theatre of Bertolt Brecht*

Mahagonny breaks with the opera formulae associated with Verdi and Puccini, Wagner, Strauss, and Schreker, in that it is not half in love with what it is bound to criticize, as they are. This holds even though Brecht, in annoyance with the music of *Mahagonny* (particularly its rich orchestration, including violins, which Brecht disliked for their inevitable warmth of tone), called Weill a 'phoney Richard Strauss'.[14] The presentation of the city of Mahagonny breaks with that older European culture, in that it represents the global culture of capitalism, in which money buys everything and which has the power of violence to sustain it. The culinary process involved in producing opera is its topic, in that Mahagonny is the place where money buys entertainment and sex—'Geld macht sinnlich' Fatty and Trinity Moses sing in the first act (Money makes sensuality/sexiness). 'Mahagonny' Widow Begbick translates as a 'city of nets', nets to catch people, every kind of trap and net, including, of course, fish-net stockings. Perhaps the

---

[14] John Willett, *The Theatre of Bertolt Brecht* (London: Eyre Methuen, 1964), p. 132.

title, *City of Nets*, of Otto Friedrich's book about Hollywood in the 1940s is appropriate for depicting the character of Mahagonny, especially if, like Adorno, we think of the destiny of Wagnerian opera being cinema. But to relate Mahagonny simply to the culture industry is to minimize its critique of international capital so that it does not pick up on a uniquely German culture. English/American, as well as German, appears in the songs. In this space, sex has become Americanized; so the 'Alabama Song' (to a tune devised by Brecht himself) celebrates nostalgia for a mythical west, yet the song demands, as everything does in this opera, a double reading. It is full of the sexual desire that builds the city of nets, a self-destroying desire, as Jake the glutton sings, before he falls dead of over-eating:

> Jetzt hab ich gegessen zwei Kälber
> und jezt esse ich noch ein Kalb.
> Alles ist nur halb, alles ist nur halb,
> Ich ässe mich gerne selber.

(Now I have eaten two calves / and now I'll eat another calf. / Everything is only done by halves, / I'd like to devour myself.)

Desire constructs the self and destroys it in turn. That desire is not 'natural', but is set up discursively, is implied by the framing of these words by on-stage bar music, which plays while Jake sings, constructing his words by its own kitsch. None the less, the energy that does things by halves is replaced in *Mahagonny* by a desire that throws everything into the ring, but could thereby revolutionize existing senses of the Western bourgeois subject: devour that in turn. Jake evokes not just the capitalism that eats other people or the calculated violence of fascism, but the self-consuming violence that belongs to a political, economic, and technological crisis moment which was called from the outside 'the decline of the West' and was exploited by the Nazis for reactionary effect.

Mahagonny is Sodom and Gomorrah. As a place built under the rubber tree, it is reminiscent of India as mediated through Kipling, and so a reminder of imperialism, for Mrs Begbick appeared earlier, in Brecht's play about British rule in India, *Mann ist Mann* (just as Jenny comes from Havana, Cuba then being under US protection). But the city is also suggestive of Berlin, and London, which had been the setting for *Die Dreigroschenoper*, which helps inspire the Jack the Ripper scene in *Lulu*. The city is also Chicago, setting for *In the Jungle of Cities*, *Happy End*, *Saint Joan of the Stockyards*, and *Arturo Ui*. It may be Miami, but it comments on America generally, not on the place which will be for ever a frontier, as in *La Fanciulla del West*, which is finally to sentimentalize it, but as the place which mushrooms into its golden age overnight. If we look back to nineteenth-century opera, the building of a city may even evoke the setting-up of the Bayreuth Festival, recalling that Wagner thought of Bayreuth becoming the 'Washington of art' (quoted by Gutman, *Richard Wagner*, p. 433). Or Valhalla might serve as a contrast.[15] Wotan creates Valhalla as a form of safety (a safety net), for protection: this reveals his conservatism, long before his will has been frustrated. Widow Begbick justifies Mahagonny more aggressively, but no less disingenuously

> Aber dieses ganze Mahagonny
> ist nur, weil alles so schlecht ist,
> weil keine Ruhe herrscht
> und keine Eintracht,
> und weil es nichts gibt
> woran man sich halten kann.

(But this entire Mahagonny / exists only because everything is so evil, / because no peace reigns, / and no harmony / and because there is nothing / upon which one can rely.)

Mahagonny looks like a place for security; but, unlike Wotan, Widow Begbick is a dialectician. Because no peace reigns, which is a comment not on the Schopenhauerian will but on the violence of the jungle of cities, she creates a security where no peace will reign either.

Jenny and the six girls, the first sharks (*Haifische*) who swim into the net—so different from the sharks alluded to in the song of Mack the Knife which opens *Die Dreigroschenoper*—sing of having lost the 'good old Mamma', so they too have no security, just as their suitcases suggest that they are for ever on the move. The city is energized by the power of women as much as by the longing for gold; the women come first, followed by Jimmy and his friends, who come not from

---

[15] See Rowland Cotterrill, 'In Defence of Mahagonny', in Keith Bullivant (ed.), *Culture and Society in the Weimar Republic*, (Manchester: Manchester University Press, 1977), p. 197, who compares the work to *The Ring*, and also compares Italian opera, whose subject-matter is the frustrations of the tenor hero, with German opera, which depicts 'the construction and defence of human civilization as a whole', starting with *Die Zauberflöte*. On *Mahagonny*, see also John Milfull, *From Baal to Keuner: The 'Second Optimism' of Bertolt Brecht* (Bern: Herbert Lang, 1974), ch. 1. On Weill generally, apart from Kowalke's compilation, see Ronald Sanders, *The Days Grow Short: The Life and Music of Kurt Weill* (London: Weidenfeld and Nicolson, 1980). See also Peter Branscombe, 'Brecht, Weill and *Mahagonny*', *Musical Times*, 102 (1961): 483–6. David Drew, *Kurt Weill: A Handbook* (London: Faber, 1987) is important; for Weill's work on Broadway, not discussed here, a start may be made with John Mauceri, 'Sugaring the Pill: Weill on Broadway', *Opera*, 40 (1989): 536–43.

southern Alabama, the name with palindromic securities (like 'mamma'), but from northern Alaska. They appear like Jack London heroes with money to show for their labour. They wish to be able to do anything in the city. Having been exploited, they understand the rules of the game: they have a right to exploit. Jimmy's defiance of the more protectionist Mrs Begbick takes place in the highly operatic scene 9, and makes him more representative of Mahagonny (compare his name 'Mahoney') than she is in his forcing desire to its crisis. The scene is set up as kitsch, with the stage direction specifying a white cloud moving across the sky (a Hollywood musical effect—but there is more to it than that, and I will come back to it), while the pianist plays 'The Maiden's Prayer'. Jake says 'Das ist die ewige Kunst' (That is eternal art), art being one of the things you pay for (and recognize as art because it is paid for). Jimmy responds to this valuation of art by appealing to nostalgic memories of labour in Alaska, sung to the waltz strains of 'The Maiden's Prayer'.[16] His self-pity, which has already been expressed in the words of the previous scene, 'O Jungens, ich will doch gar kein Mensch sein' (Boys, I don't want to be a human being), constructs his operatic defiance of Mrs Begbick. His words repeat her earlier ones, which I quoted earlier. 'With your entire Mahagonny / no man will ever be happy / for too much peace reigns / and too much harmony / and because there is too much / upon which you can depend.' His position is a dialectical one in relation to Widow Begbick's; whereas she has set up a fake—a kitsch—peace and harmony, he presses, like a complete nihilist, towards the opposite, for the unsettling of this bourgeois order, and for the undoing of the 'human, all too human'.

At this point, the hurricane threatens. Operatically, this is like Erda telling Wotan that nothing can survive, that destruction is the universal law; but in terms of Jimmy's desire for happiness, which is purchased without peace and harmony, the hurricane symbolizes Jimmy's anarchism, his dialectical disruption of an order already premissed to be fake. The hurricane approaches, and the men of Mahagonny sing a Bach-like chorale, which derives from the music given to the guards during the final testing scenes in *Die Zauberflöte*: a city can survive only if it takes heed of its own precariousness of existence and realizes that this is dependent on something other than itself, to which it must be responsible. But that is ideology for the emergent bourgeoisie, it seems. Jimmy responds to it as a discourse which does not hold now: 'Peace and harmony they do not exist / but hurricanes they

---

[16] 'Jimmy's misfortune is told us in the same way that Sigmund Romberg uses in *Rose Marie*' (Michel Perez, sleeve-notes to CBS recording, 1972).

do . . . And just like that is man / he must destroy whatever exists . . . what horror holds a typhoon / compared to man when he wants his fun?'

Such recklessness recalls the nihilism of which Nietzsche speaks at the end of *The Genealogy of Morals*: man would rather will the abyss, nothingness, than will nothing at all—only in Nietzsche the nihilism does not recognize itself as such; it is more the basic drift of European nihilism attending the development of the West. With Jimmy, it is definite, like his subversion of opera, and it is infectious: Mrs Begbick sings that 'bad is the hurricane, worse is the typhoon, but worst of all is man'. This backs up Jimmy's earlier position, where he had wanted not to be a human being. There is a redefinition implied here of what the 'human' is: Jimmy and the people of Mahagonny have gone beyond humanism into a situation where no traditional sanctions like those evoked by hurricanes could mean anything. Hence Jimmy breaks the narrative flow of the scene by coming down to the footlights and addressing the bourgeois audience, telling them to do the forbidden:

> Wenn es einen Gedanken gibt
> den du nicht kennst,
> denke den Gedanken.
> Kostet er dich Geld, verlangt er dein Haus:
> Denke ihn, denke ihn!
> Du darfst es!
> Im Int'resse der Ordnung.
> Zum besten der Stadt.
> Für die Zukunft der Menschheit.
> Zu deinem eigenen Wohlbefinden
> darfst du!

(If there exists a thought / with which you're not acquainted, / think that thought. / If it costs you money, if it demands your house of you, / think it, think it. / You may do it. / In the interest of order, / For the best of the town. / For the future of mankind. / For your own well-being, / you may!)

Jimmy urges transgressiveness which would be anarchistic in character, getting outside the homogeneity of bourgeois society, acting as impersonally and anarchistically as the typhoon; but the contradiction turns on transgression which is for the sake of order, transgressiveness which is said to be upbuilding the community. In one way, this is the voice of a nihilism which needs to get outside humanism as bourgeois ideology, but it is also reactionary violence that it leads nowhere except to the strong ordered state. The crisis moment is not faced for what it is; there is no emergence of another set of possibilities.

At that point (scene 12), the hurricane makes a detour round Mahagonny, as though in a parody of Hindemith's *Hin und Zurück* (1927), where time is reversed half-way through, thereby avoiding tragedy. But there is no connotation of that here: it is as though the hurricane gives up, leaving the city to the far worse forces inside it. Jimmy's will-to-power is compounded by his *laissez-faire* capitalism as he sings that 'in this life you must make your own bed, / and none will show you the trick; / so lie down and get kicked if you want to, / but as for me, I'd rather stand and kick'. These sentiments are repeated to him, and developed by Jenny in the second act (scene 16), when Jimmy can find no one to help him pay for his whisky. In the narrative order of *Mahagonny*, putting things this way round means that the reprise of the number comes before Jenny's original has been heard. In this way the text reverses expectations and conventional operatic/musical logic. But such reversals are everywhere in the text. When the men line up outside the brothel in the second act, in the new, permissive, rich, post-hurricane Mahagonny, Mrs Begbick tries to smarten up their treatment of women, to make it less determinedly single-minded—'Spit out that gum, / first wash your hands / Give her time / and say a few words to her', and adds in contrast to Act 1, 'Geld allein macht nicht sinnlich!' (Money by itself does not make sensuality/sexiness). This gem of a statement (men are not attractive to women just because they can pay for them) opens up the whole question of how money interests are covered over by ideology, and are not allowed to be recognized for what they are. When money is plentiful, capitalism shows itself expansive and full of fetishistic attention to detail that occludes its real nature; when money is tight, as it was in 1929, and when Jimmy cannot pay, it shows its violence.

The trial for Jimmy which follows his lack of money (and suggests that the whole opera is a trial of Mahagonny) evokes the unstable crowd, who follow uncritically all the pronouncements of the court, and do so to a fast march rhythm, as though Weill summons up the militarism of fascist mass meetings. Jimmy goes to the electric chair at the end, in a situation that recalls the condemnation to execution and then the pardon of Mack in *Die Dreigroschenoper*. That was a parody of grand opera, an operatic conclusion to a text well outside opera conventions, like *The Beggar's Opera* in relation to Handelian opera. But there is nothing to alter the logic of bourgeois capitalism in *Mahagonny*, save for one scene (no. 14) on which I would like to comment briefly. The brothel sequence closes with Jenny and Jimmy singing the 'crane duet', counterposed by their positions on-stage, sitting on chairs at some distance from each other, Jimmy smoking, she putting on make-up. This distance both is and is not reflected in the duet, where the presumed absence of sensuality in their relation to each other is replaced by a different kind of sensuality in the music and words. The vocal line wanders between the two of them, as though drifting, hardly ever letting them sing together, and the words are written in a tight Dantean *terza rima*, which, on account of this verse-form, stands out as different from anything else in the writing. The verse evokes the cranes and the clouds and the force of the winds which carry them, but which could lead them off into the void. The cranes are lovers only for a brief time; they will separate soon, but while the moment lasts, it is as though for ever—'So scheint die Liebe Liebenden ein Halt' (So love to lovers seems a stop in time). Only with this last line, recalling the human world, is a gloss put on the cranes; nor do Jimmy and Jenny sing about themselves. In effect, the poem evokes the huge difference between the direction of the energies of *Mahagonny* and the possible other directions celebrated by the crane duet. The text opens up a space whereby the sense of alternative existences, those which celebrate the cloud and evanescence, rather than the city, may be articulated. The crane duet offers a vision of life as other to the characters, and neither text nor music idealizes the vision of the cranes flying against the clouds. Even the white cloud of scene 9 offers a view of otherness in contrast to the all-consuming will that appears in the inhabitants of Mahagonny.[17]

OPERA AND *NEUE SACHLICHKEIT*

> The great buildings of the city of New York and the great discoveries of electricity are not of themselves enough to swell mankind's sense of triumph. What matters more is that a new human type should now be evolving, at this very moment, and that the entire interest of the world should be concentrated on his development. This new human type will not be as the old type imagines. It is my belief that he will not let himself be adapted by machines but will himself adapt machines.
>
> (Brecht, quoted by Willett, *The Theatre of Bertolt Brecht*, p. 114)

The parable nature of the text encourages a reading of *Mahagonny* which looks for the politics subtending the text and the discourses that have put it together,

---

[17] My colleague Antony Tatlow reads the crane duet in the light of Daoism; see his *Repression and Figuration: From Totem to Utopia* (Hong Kong: University of Hong Kong, Department of Comparative Literature, 1990), pp. 112–17.

sometimes unconsciously. Mahagonny's name suggests mahogany, the brown wood, and Brecht first thought in terms of a 'Mahagonny opera' in 1924 (Parmalee, *Brecht's America*, p. 97) at the time when he was still in Munich, had seen the brownshirts, and thought the men on the march looked like wooden soldiers. Mahagonny embodies something of the fascist state in the total power it wields, and brown may also suggest faecal matter: Jimmy calls Mahagonny a 'manure pile'. Something of a military discipline may survive in the men of Mahagonny singing their chorale, or in the funeral march that concludes the opera. Jimmy's reference to the bar of Mandalay (scene 8) associates him also with Kipling's soldiers out in Burma (and his Irish name would fit here: many recruits to the British army for the colonies were Irish, on account of their poverty and inability to get jobs). The song of Mandalay is referred to (not sung) in no. 14 in an intertextual reference back to *Happy End* (no. 9), where it is sung, turning out to be about a brothel frequented by soldiers who shoot the door down if someone is too long inside with the girl. This and *Happy End*'s songs 'Surabaya Johnny' and 'Bill's Beerhall in Bilbao', as well as *Die Dreigroschenoper*'s 'Der Kanonensong', uncover the Brechtian associations between imperialism, militarism, and fascism. But if fascism is a subject of the text, it does not take the form of Germanic militarism, with its appeal to a nineteenth-century ideology and romanticism. In the types presented in the opera there is the very class that fascism touched most closely.

Yet the building of the city of Mahagonny so fast and to such a pitch of organization and making it offer so much to consumerism are suggestive of the power of technology, which *Neue Sachlichkeit* celebrated. I began this section with Brecht's careful comments in 1928 on the impact of futurism, refusing to aestheticize the machine. The two *Lehrstück* plays he wrote with Hindemith in 1929 deal with technology, specifically the power of aviation, both for its potential and for its abuse. The aviator about whom Brecht originally wrote one of the *Lehrstück*, Lindbergh, became a Nazi, and Brecht changed the name of the play, from *Lindberghflug to Der Ozeanflug*. Even in the 1920s, *Neue Sachlichkeit* could be seen as politically ambiguous, because it appeared to describe the triumph of technology, which made it seem that social problems had disappeared, and all that needed to be done was to submit to them. *Neue Sachlichkeit* was criticized by writers on the left in Germany—by Brecht and Benjamin and Eisler—because to hold to it as the new and hegemonic matter-of-factness meant accepting that reality was as it was described and could not be changed. It belonged with the rationalizations and modernizations of the 1920s, suggesting that class issues had been replaced by a world where all that counted was automation and rationalization.

Ernst Bloch saw *Neue Sachlichkeit* in terms of a movement towards fascism. A philosophy of art and music which stressed objectivity went along with commodification and reification of human relationships typical of capitalism. 'In the place of the expressionist dreams, "explosive concentrations", even storms, an incomparable "realism" set in, namely that of a reestablished world, of a truce with bourgeois existence. . . . Behind the installed rationalities remains the utter anarchy of economic profiteering.'[18] Thus *Neue Sachlichkeit* is the 'falsely immediate', the art of the community which pretends that this society is not in a state of alienation. The argument returns to Adorno on Schoenberg's determination not to produce art which puts itself into immediate relationships with social conditions. Adorno called *Neue Sachlichkeit* a 'false façade' and a 'diversion away from social conditions' (quoted in Kowalke (ed.), *New Orpheus*, p. 67). *Neue Sachlichkeit* describes Hindemith's music; Adorno and Bloch, however, take Kurt Weill as being nearer to surrealism. In a review of *Die Dreigroschenoper* Adorno commented on the work's difference from the audience it played to successfully:

for even when consumed purely for pleasure, *The Threepenny Opera* remains menacing: no community ideology is present, neither in terms of subject-matter nor musically, since nothing noble or transfigured is postulated as a collective art, but rather the dregs of art are salvaged to find the right tone for the dregs of society. (Quoted by Hinton, *Kurt Weill*, p. 133)

There is no pretence in Kurt Weill's music that art is a way of reconciling a society, or that it can be the 'official' ideology of a society, by which that society can (mis)recognize itself.

Neue Sachlichkeit affects Heidegger, who, despite his apparent antipathy to technology, shows that it cannot be stopped, and in this he was influenced by Ernst Jünger, who dreamed of a society energized as soldiers were, and organized as a factory might be, in a state of total mobilization (*totale Mobilmachung*). In *Mahagonny*, the four men—Jim, Jake, Bill, and Joe—operate like nostalgic veterans, pushing the society back home further along the road towards total commitment to action of any sort, so long as it is action. The sense of nihilistic

---

[18] Quoted by Stephen Hinton in Kowalke (ed.), *New Orpheus*, p. 65. See also, generally, John Willett, *The New Sobriety, 1917–1933, Art and Politics in the Weimar Period* (London: Thames and Hudson, 1978). For a view of the regressiveness towards fascism of *Neue Sachlichkeit* in relation to the visual arts, see Benjamin H. D. Buchloh, 'Figures of Authority, Cycles of Regression', *October*, 16 (1981): 39–68.

desperation ('I think I'm going to eat up my hat,' as Jimmy sings in scene 8) speaks for the feeling of having run through the comforts of technology and consumerism, but of still needing more. Jünger stands for the 'will to will', for a promotion of warrior virtues, while Jimmy stands for a will that would pull down any aspect of bourgeois respectability in Mahagonny/Weimar; while at the same time his behaviour and pleasures in the second act are bourgeois, shallow, and parochial—that aspect of the Nazis which would promote kitsch itself. (To cut the brothel scene, as Klemperer wanted to do before he would conduct the opera at the Kroll, or as had to happen before the Leipzig production could take place, misses the critique the opera is making of bourgeois taste—though perhaps the authorities in Leipzig understood the critique all too well.) Jimmy, for a brief moment the culture hero of Mahagonny, is not at the centre at all: he is an exploited figure never able to recognize that he is held by a controlling ideology.

Jünger's influence was one such form of control. He argued that the war had displayed an ideal of technology plus vitalism, of the energies of the blood and of the will-to-power fusing together. His sense of struggle as the law of life fitted his aggressive modernizing, where the body would become identifiable with the machine, the aviator being one example of body and machine, industrial work being another. Jimmy and Jünger are different aspects of the reactionary conservatism and ideology of *Neue Sachlichkeit*, Jimmy being the worker Jünger hoped to bring into his plans for modernization. Mahagonny is the metropolis as a triumph of technology, but relying on a will-to-power which leaves nothing behind, neither Jimmy nor Mahagonny. But the opera sees also the end of technology. 'Is there no telephone?', Jenny sings in the 'Benares Song'. 'Oh sir, God help me, no' is the answer. There is nowhere to go at the end, since Benares has been struck by an earthquake, and the burning of Mahagonny, which may echo *Götterdämmerung* in a way, continues the subject of loss which begins with the loss of the good old mamma.

SPRINGTIME FOR HITLER

Though fascism may no longer operate as a large-scale political movement (though this is very disputatious), not only have its lessons been taken over within the culture industry, but it continues as a subject (e.g. in the cinema) to be a huge audience-puller. Brecht and Weill coincide with and mark the end of opera (and the need, therefore, to reinvent it), and its move to something more overtly popular in the musical. In the gap left by the disappearance of opera as a popular

form which is still being written, Broadway and Hollywood musicals have continued, and as an epilogue I want to refer to their relation to the political. There is
little enough overt reference to politics in most Hollywood musicals, though some
have a racial awareness (*Show Boat* and *Porgy and Bess*), and some are also socially
exclusionary (*Oklahoma!* and *Carousel*). *Springtime for Hitler*, the musical with
very witty Busby Berkeley imitations, which is performed in Mel Brooks's film
The Producers, might be the text to continue with the opera/fascism connection—
or Bob Fosse's musical *Cabaret*, based on *Goodbye to Berlin*. In thinking of their
relationship to mainstream American politics, the distinction between kitsch and
camp can be evoked again; *Springtime for Hitler* makes fascist sympathies camp,
which has implications for gender politics at least. At its strongest, the Hollywood
musical, despite its relentless diatonicism and cheerfulness, is self-reflexive, sur-
veying itself in a way not necessarily narcissistic; and even though it is committed
to the optimism of American ego psychology, it is able to see that in an ironic
light, and to make fun of its own format, as is indicated in the way that so many
musicals turn out to have as subject-matter the idea of putting on a show—as, say,
in *Kiss Me Kate*, or even in *The Producers*.

A tendency in recent musicals has been the reinstatement of the idea of the
Gesamtkunstwerk: partly in Sondheim, but certainly in Andrew Lloyd Webber
musicals and in Claude-Michel Schönberg's *Les Misérables* (1980) and *Miss Saigon*
(1989). In these musicals, the self-awareness and self-reflexiveness of an audience
are cut out by their smoothness and through their aiming at a total experience.
They are helped by amplification of orchestral sound and miking of singing (so
that they can use actors trained in naturalistic acting rather than people who are
primarily singers) and by reliance on spectacle which is enframed by technological
reproduction. These musicals range in subject-matter from Eva Perón to Viet-
nam, so making politics spectacular, and make claims on using 'serious' books and
lyrics (art being fetishized and made a conventional referent of high seriousness
via the use of Georges Seurat (*Sunday in the Park with George*), or T. S. Eliot (*Cats*)
or the history of cinema (*The Phantom of the Opera*, *Sunset Boulevard*)). The title
Aspects of Love, while saying nothing precise in itself, apes a serious intention—this
is Andrew Lloyd Webber on love, like Bryan Magee on Wagner (*Aspects of
Wagner*). They announce that the musical has come of age—is the new opera,
indeed—because of this engagement with 'serious' (non-camp) issues. In Britain,
the Royal Shakespeare Company presented *Les Misérables* (in 1985) as if to confirm
the high-class nature of the musical now: its claim to be considered art. The
revolutions in France which made the barricade a dominant image for the

nineteenth century, through Delacroix and other romantic artists, and which stood for resistance, are now turned into spectacular images in *Les Misérables*, Delacroix's theatricality being re-theatricalized, in a coerciveness which makes resistance almost impossible, because everything now exists at the level of entertainment.

I do not find the Lloyd Webber and Schönberg musicals interesting musically (popular and consensual, aimed at a white, middle-class audience), but they require attention because they are hugely popular and contributory to a state of affairs where, over the past few years, almost half of London's theatres, for instance, have been putting on musicals at any one moment. They have also influenced the production styles of operas and, of course, perceptions of opera. They are mainstream politically and in terms of gender politics, and it is easy to fault them for excluding otherness in their promotion of the idea that the whole community can join in the singing (a little homophobia in *Les Misérables*, for instance). Sondheim's *Pacific Overtures* (1977) is just as much an 'Orientalist' piece in its representation of Japan as *Iris* or *Madama Butterfly*: its values are mainstream American, even if—especially if—it thematizes 'the Japanese enthusiastic endorsement of the American economic and cultural model'.[19] But what of their wish to aspire to the conditions of opera? (After all, opera and these musicals which deal with world-historical events have music right the way through, and opera is 'grand', spectacular, like these musicals.) *Miss Saigon* presents itself as outdoing *Madama Butterfly*, which means that it rests on the culture industry's assessment of Puccini's text as grand opera, as art. *Miss Saigon* assumes an unquestioned value for the earlier text, which it thus supports. Yet Puccini operas are not confident about themselves as 'art' in relation to their tradition. These musicals must first reify and make a fetish out of the status of great art, on which they are parasitic: just as Lloyd Webber depends on fetishizing the history of the cinema. The art that is produced is simulacral.

In not being able to question what 'traditional' opera does, these musicals have an important difference from Brecht, where text and music work differently from each other, and deliberately so. Brecht's theatre is based on the separation of those elements in it that would otherwise prove coercive in their theatrical realism and impose a unidirectional way of thinking on the audience. If the operatic form is broken up into something more analogous to the musical/operetta form, that is not only a resistance to the status of opera as élitist art, but is to take apart opera's

---

[19] Tom Sutcliffe, 'Sondheim and the Musical', *Musical Times*, 128 (Sept. 1987):

seamlessness, to abolish the sense of the music being so commanding that it cannot be touched.[20] The movement in Brecht and Weill towards closed numbers in operas (in *Die Dreigroschenoper* and in *Happy End*, and to a lesser extent in *Mahagonny*) was a way of cutting out the powerful appeal offered by the music in the Wagnerian *Gesamtkunstwerk*. That drive to hold an audience uncritically, Brecht linked to the large and pompous use of 'social gesture' in Nazism—hugely self-important gesturalism and monumentalism, which has its analogues in Wagner—and which Brecht replaced by deliberate use of banality and vulgarity, and by the wholly unpatronizing, non-kitsch use of people in *Mahagonny*—people who make no use of public gesture in their lives. If the large gesture associated with the leitmotif or the strong and obvious Verdian climax has gone in Brecht/Weill, together with the loss of a singing style which neutralizes the utterance in the belief that the music says it all in its musical gesturalism, that is replaced in Brecht by a 'gestic' utterance and musical style and acting which are intended to offer the ability to double-read each situation, to punctuate it, to suggest that each situation contains within it its own alternative.[21] The crane duet is a fine example of the *gestus*, of an alternative presented to the situation on-stage, a commentary here saying, enjoy it while you can.

The musicals I have described reverse Brecht's procedures by going back to operatic forms to increase audience identification with a total event. If something about each of the operas I have written about resists, if only by its musical complexity, the ability to articulate it fully with reactionary positions, if something about each resists the *Gesamtkunstwerk* as much as it tries to approach it, the same cannot be said about the postmodern musical. This uses every aid to create it as entirely homogeneous with the society it plays to and helps to create, and every technological signifier available to promote it as artistic, to give it cultic status. In Lloyd Webber musicals and Schönberg 'operas' the drive is to make everything in them nearer approaches to the commanding and to the absolute.

---

[20] For further, post-Brechtian approaches to opera, see the collection of essays I edited, *A Night In At the Opera: Media Representations of Opera* (London: John Libbey and Arts Council, 1994).

[21] On the *gestus* in Brecht, see Peter Brooker, *Bertolt Brecht: Dialectics, Poetry, Politics* (London: Croom Helm, 1988), pp. 50–9. John Willett gives a good quotation from Brecht on his version of *Antigone* which has relevance for opera: 'The essential was to avoid that revolting convention which demands that the actor should tackle any fairly long verse passage by, as it were, pumping himself full with some emotion which will roughly cover the lot.' Thus Brecht urges the importance of the 'caesura', of syncopating rhythms in speech, on the analogy of jazz, bringing 'contradiction' into the verse (*The Theatre of Bertolt Brecht*, p. 101). The danger in opera is that 'serious music . . . clings to lyricism and cultivates expression for its own sake' (ibid., p. 130).

This, backed with resources of capital no opera ever could lay claim to, gives them their power, and suggests a new way in which the late nineteenth-century dream of opera as ritual and consecration and as aesthetic image for the nation has become translated into a highly profitable form of domination.

Bibliography

I have included here virtually everything referred to in the footnotes, and added in texts which though not referenced, have proved useful in writing this study.

ABBATE, CAROLYN, *Unsung Voices: Opera and Musical Narrative in the Nineteenth Century*, Princeton: Princeton University Press, 1991.

ADAMI, GIUSEPPE, *Puccini: A Critical Biography*, London: Duckworth, 2nd edn., 1974.

—— (ed.) *Letters of Giacomo Puccini*, trans. Eva Makin, rev. edn. Mosco Carner, London: Harrap, 1974.

ADLER, FRANK, Introduction to 'On Fascism', *Telos*, 40 (1979): 95–108.

ADORNO, THEODOR W., *Prisms*, trans. Samuel and Sherry Weber 1967, London: Neville Spearman, 1955.

—— *Minima Moralia*, trans. E. F. J. Jephcott, London: New Left Books, 1974.

—— *In Search of Wagner*, trans. Rodney Livingstone, London: New Left Books, 1981.

—— *Aesthetic Theory*, trans. C. Lenhardt 1970, London: Routledge, 1984.

—— *The Philosophy of Modern Music*, trans. Anne G. Mitchell and Wesley V. Blomster, London: Sheed and Ward, 1973.

—— *Quasi una fantasia*, trans. Rodney Livingstone, London: Verso, 1992.

—— with HORKHEIMER, MAX, *The Dialectics of Enlightenment*, trans. John Cumming, London: Verso, 1979.

ARATO, ANDREW, and GEBHARDT, EIKE (eds.), *The Essential Frankfurt School Reader*, Oxford: Blackwell, 1978.

ARBLASTER, ANTHONY, *Viva La Libertà: Politics in Opera*, London: Verso, 1992.

ASHBROOK, WILLIAM, *The Operas of Puccini*, Oxford: Oxford University Press, 1985.

—— and POWERS, HAROLD, *Puccini's* Turandot: *The End of the Great Tradition*, Princeton: Princeton University Press, 1991.

ATLAS, ALLAN W., 'Crossed Stars and Crossed Tonal Areas in Puccini's *Madame Butterfly*', *Nineteenth-Century Music*, 14/2 (1990): 186–90.

AYCOBERRY, PIERRE, *The Nazi Question: An Essay on the Interpretation of National Socialism 1922–1975* (1979), trans. Richard Hurley, London: Routledge and Kegan Paul, 1981.

BAKHTIN, M. M., *The Dialogic Imagination*, trans. Caryl Emerson and Michael Holquist, Austin, Tex.: University of Texas Press, 1981.

BALDINI, GABRIELE, *The Story of Giuseppe Verdi*, trans. Roger Parker, Cambridge: Cambridge University Press, 1981.

BARRON, STEPHANIE (ed.), *'Degenerate Art': The Fate of the Avant-Garde in Nazi Germany*, New York: Harry N. Abrams and Los Angeles County Museum, 1991.

BARROWS, SUSANNA, *Distorting Mirrors: Visions of the Crowd in Late Nineteenth-Century France*, New Haven: Yale University Press, 1981.

BATAILLE, GEORGES, *Visions of Excess: Selected Writings 1927–1939*, ed. Allan Stoekl, Manchester: Manchester University Press, 1985.

BAXANDALL, MICHAEL, *The Limewood Sculptors of Renaissance Germany*, New Haven: Yale University Press, 1980.

BEAUMONT, ANTONY, *Busoni the Composer*, London: Faber, 1985.

BELLER, STEVEN, *Vienna and the Jews 1867–1938*, Cambridge: Cambridge University Press, 1989.

BENJAMIN, WALTER, *Illuminations*, trans. Harry Zohn, London: Cape, 1970.

—— *The Origin of German Tragic Drama*, trans. John Osborne, London: Verso, 1977.

—— *Charles Baudelaire: A Lyric Poet in the Era of High Capitalism*, trans. Harry Zohn, London: Verso, 1983.

—— 'Theories of German Fascism', *New German Critique*, 17 (1979): 120–8.

BENNETT, BENJAMIN, *Hugo von Hofmannsthal: The Theatres of Consciousness*, Cambridge: Cambridge University Press, 1988.

BENTLEY, ERIC, *The Brecht Commentaries*, New York: Grove Press Inc., 1981.

BERGHAHN, VOLKER R., *Militarism: The History of an International Debate 1861–1979*, Leamington Spa: Berg, 1981.

BERGSTEN, GUNILLA, *Thomas Mann's Doctor Faustus* (1963), trans. Krishna Winston, Chicago: University of Chicago Press, 1969.

BERMAN, MARSHALL, *All that is Solid Melts into Air*, London: Verso, 1983.

BERMAN, RUSSELL A., 'Written Right Across Their Faces: Ernst Jünger's Reactionary Modernism', in *Modern Culture and Critical Theory: Art, Politics and the Legacy of the Frankfurt School*, Madison: University of Wisconsin Press, 1989, pp. 99–117.

BIRKIN, KENNETH, *Arabella*, Cambridge: Cambridge University Press, 1989.

BLOCH, ERNST, *Essays on the Philosophy of Music*, trans. Peter Palmer, ed. David Drew, Cambridge: Cambridge University Press, 1985.

BORCHMEYER, DIETER, 'Richard Wagner and Anti-Semitism', *Wagner*, 6 (1985): 1–18.

—— *Richard Wagner: Theory and Theatre*, trans. Stewart Spencer, Oxford: Clarendon Press, 1991.

BOSWORTH, RICHARD, *Italy and the Approach of the First World War*, London: Macmillan, 1983.

BOULEZ, PIERRE, *Orientations*, ed. Jean-Jacques Nattiez, trans. Martin Cooper, Cambridge, Mass.: Harvard University Press, 1986.

BOURDIEU, PIERRE, *The Political Ontology of Martin Heidegger* (1988), trans. Peter Collier, Stanford, Calif.: Stanford University Press, 1991.

BOWLER, ANNE, 'Politics as Art: Italian Futurism and Fascism', *Theory and Society*, 20 (1991): 763–94.

BRADLEY, A. C., *Shakespearean Tragedy*, London: Macmillan, 1904.

BRANSCOMBE, PETER, 'Brecht, Weill and *Mahagonny*', *Musical Times*, 102 (1961): 483–6.

BRAUN, EMILY (ed.), *Italian Art in the Twentieth Century*, Munich: Prestel-Verlag, 1989.

BRIDGES, GEORGE, 'The Almost Irresistible Appeal of Fascism, or, Is it Okay to Like Richard Wagner?', *Germanic Review*, 64 (1989): 42–8.

BROCH, HERMANN, *Hugo von Hofmannsthal and His Time*, trans. Michael P. Steinberg, Chicago: University of Chicago Press, 1984.

BROOKER, PETER, *Bertolt Brecht: Dialectics, Poetry, Politics*, London: Croom Helm, 1988.

BUCHLOH, BENJAMIN H. D., 'Figures of Authority, Cycles of Regression', *October*, 16 (1981): 39–68.

BUDDEN, JULIAN, *The Operas of Verdi*, 3 vols., London: Cassell, 1973–81.

BULLIVANT, KEITH (ed.), *Culture and Society in the Weimar Republic*, Manchester: Manchester University Press, 1977.

BÜRGER, PETER, *Theory of the Avant-Garde*, trans. Michael Shaw, Minneapolis: University of Minnesota Press, 1984.

BURSTON, DANIEL, *The Legacy of Erich Fromm*, Cambridge, Mass.: Harvard University Press, 1991.

BUSCH, HANS, *Verdi's Aida: The History of an Opera in Letters and Documents*, Minneapolis: University of Minnesota Press, 1978.

—— *Verdi's* Otello *and* Simon Boccanegra *in Letters and Documents*, 2 vols., Oxford: Clarendon Press, 1988.

CANETTI, ELIAS, *Crowds and Power*, trans. Carol Stewart (1960), New York: Seabury Press, 1978.

CARNEGY, PATRICK, *Faust as Musician*, London: Chatto and Windus, 1973.

CARNER, MOSCO, *Puccini: A Critical Biography*, London: Duckworth, 2nd edn., 1974.

—— *Major and Minor*, London: Duckworth, 1980.

—— *Tosca*, Cambridge: Cambridge University Press, 1985.

CARROLL, DAVID, 'Literary Fascism or the Aestheticizing of Politics: The Case of Robert Brasillach', *New Literary History*, 23 (1992): 691–726.

CARSTEN, F. L., *Fascist Movements in Austria: From Schönerer to Hitler*, London: Sage, 1977.

CASELLA, ALFREDO, *Music in My Time* (1941), trans. Spencer Norton, Norman, Okla.: University of Oklahoma Press, 1955.

CHAMBERLAIN, J. EDWARD, and GILMAN, SANDER L. (eds.), *Degeneration: The Dark Side of Progress*, New York: Columbia University Press, 1985.

CHESSICK, RICHARD, '*The Ring*: Richard Wagner's Dream of Pre-Oedipal Destruction', *American Journal of Psychoanalysis*, 43 (1983): 361–74.

CHICKERING, ROGER, *We Men Who Feel Most German: A Cultural Study of the Pan-German League, 1886–1914*, Boston: Allen and Unwin, 1984.

CLARK, MARTIN, *Modern Italy 1871–1982*, London: Longman, 1982.

CLARK, T. J., *The Absolute Bourgeois*, London: Thames and Hudson, 1973.

CLAYTON, ALFRED, 'Zemlinsky's One-Act Operas', *Musical Times*, 124 (1983): 474–8.

CLÉMENT, CATHERINE, *Opera or the Undoing of Women*, trans. Betsy Wing, Minneapolis: University of Minnesota Press, 1988.

—— and CIXOUS, HÉLÈNE, *The Newly Born Woman*, Minneapolis: University of Minnesota Press, 1986.

COHEN, MARGARET, 'Benjamin's Phantasmagoria', *New German Critique*, 48 (1989): 87–108.

COOK, SUSAN, *New Opera for a New Republic*, Ann Arbor: UMI Research Press, 1988.

COOPER, MARTIN (ed.), *The New Oxford History of Music: The Modern Age 1890–1960*, Oxford: Oxford University Press, 1974.

CORAZZOL, ADRIANA GUARNIERI, 'Opera and Verismo: Regressive Points of View and the Artifice of Alienation', *Cambridge Opera Journal*, 5 /1 (1993): 39–53.

CORMACK, DAVID, 'Thomas Mann, Hans Eisler and the New Bayreuth', *Wagner*, 2 (1981): 44–63.

COWLING, ELIZABETH, and MUNDY, JENNIFER, *On Classic Ground: Picasso, Léger, de Chirico and the New Classicism 1910–1930*, London: Tate Gallery, 1990.

DAHLHAUS, CARL, *Schoenberg and the New Music*, trans. Derrick Puffett and Alfred Clayton, Cambridge: Cambridge University Press, 1987.

—— *Richard Wagner's Music Dramas*, trans. Mary Whittall, Cambridge: Cambridge University Press, 1979.

D'ANNUNZIO, GABRIELE, *The Triumph of Death*, trans. Georgina Harding, London: Dedalus, 1990.

DEATHRIDGE, JOHN, *Wagner's Rienzi: A Reappraisal Based on a Study of the Sketches and Drafts*, Oxford: Clarendon Press, 1977.

—— Review of Theodor W. Adorno, *In Search of Wagner*, *Nineteenth-Century Music*, 7 (1983): 81–5.

—— (with DALHAUS, CARL), *The New Grove Wagner*, London: Macmillan, 1984.

DELEUZE, GILLES, *Nietzsche and Philosophy*, trans. Hugh Tomlinson, Minneapolis: University of Minnesota Press, 1983.

—— and GUATTARI, FÉLIX, *Anti-Oedipus*, trans. Robert Hurley, New York: Viking, 1983.

DEL MAR, NORMAN, *Richard Strauss*, 3 vols. (1962) London: Barrie and Jenkins, 2nd edn., 1978.

DERRIDA, JACQUES, *Spurs: Nietzsche's Styles*, trans. Barbara Harlow, Chicago: University of Chicago Press, 1978.

—— *The Ear of the Other: Autobiography, Transference, Translation*, ed. Christie McDonald, Lincoln, Nebr.: University of Nebraska Press, 1985.

—— *Margins of Philosophy*, trans. Alan Bass, Brighton: Harvester Press, 1986.

—— 'Economimesis', *Diacritics*, 11 (1981): 3–25.

DiGAETANI, JOHN L., and SIREFMAN, JOSEF P., *Opera and the Golden West: The Past, Present and Future of Opera in the USA*, Cranbury, NJ: Associated Universities Press, 1994.

DIPROSE, ROSALYN, 'Nietzsche, Ethics and Sexual Difference', *Radical Philosophy*, 5 (Summer 1989): 27–33.

DORFLES, GILLO, *Kitsch: The World of Bad Taste*, New York: Bell Publishing Co., 1969.

DOWDEN, STEPHEN D., *Sympathy for the Abyss*, Tübingen: Marx Niemeyer Verlag, 1986.

DRAKE, RICHARD, *Byzantium for Rome: The Politics of Nostalgia in Umbertian Italy 1878–1900*, Chapel Hill, NC: University of North Carolina Press, 1980.

DREW, DAVID, *Kurt Weill: A Handbook*, London: Faber, 1987.

ELEY, GEORGE, *From Unification to Nazism*, Boston: Allen and Unwin, 1986.

ELLMANN, RICHARD, *Oscar Wilde*, London: Hamish Hamilton, 1987.

ENGEL, ELLIOT, and KING, MARGARET F., *The Victorian Novel Before Victoria*, London: Macmillan, 1984.

ETLIN, RICHARD A., *Modernism in Italian Architecture, 1890–1940*, Cambridge, Mass.: MIT Press, 1991.

EVANS, RICHARD J., *In Hitler's Shadow*, New York: Pantheon Books, 1989.

EWEN, DAVID (ed.), *The Book of Modern Composers*, New York: Alfred A. Knopf, 1942.

FARIAS, VICTOR, *Heidegger and Nazism*, ed. Joseph Margolis and Tom Rockmore, Philadelphia: Temple University Press, 1989.

FEDER, STUART; KARMEL, RICHARD L.; and POLLOCK, GEORGE H., *Psychoanalytic Explorations in Music*, Madison, Conn.: International University Press, 1988.

FELICE, RENZO DE, *Interpretations of Fascism*, trans. Brenda Huff Everett, Cambridge, Mass.: Harvard University Press, 1977.

FERRY, LUC, and ALAIN, RENAUT, *Heidegger and Modernity*, Chicago: University of Chicago Press, 1990.

FIELD, FRANK, *The Last Days of Mankind*, London: Macmillan, 1967.

FIELD, GEOFFREY G., *Evangelist of Race: The Germanic Vision of Houston Stuart Chamberlain*, New York: Columbia University Press, 1981.

FLETCHER, IAN (ed.), *Decadence and the 1890s*, London: Edward Arnold, 1979.

FORSYTH, KAREN, *Ariadne auf Naxos by Hugo von Hofmannsthal and Richard Strauss: Its Genesis and Meaning*, Oxford: Oxford University Press, 1982.

FORTUNE, NIGEL (ed.), *Music and Theatre: Essays in Honour of Winton Dean*, Cambridge: Cambridge University Press, 1987.

FOSTER, HAL, 'Armor Fou', *October*, 56 (Spring 1991): 65–97.

FOUCAULT, MICHEL, *Language, Counter-memory, Practice*, ed. Donald F. Bouchard, Ithaca, NY: Cornell University Press, 1977.

—— *The History of Sexuality*, Harmondsworth: Penguin, 1981.

FRANKLIN, PETER, *The Idea of Music*, London: Macmillan, 1985.

—— 'Distant Sounds—Fallen Music: *Der ferne Klang* as "Woman's Opera?" ', *Cambridge Opera Journal*, 3 (1991): 159–172.

—— Review of John Williamson, *The Music of Hans Pfitzner*, Music and Letters, 74 (1993): 611–13.

FRAYLING, CHRISTOPHER, *Spaghetti Westerns: Cowboys and Europeans from Karl May to Sergio Leone*, London: Routledge and Kegan Paul, 1981.

FREUD, SIGMUND, *Standard Edition of the Works of Sigmund Freud*, ed. James Strachey, 24 vols., London: Hogarth Press, 1953–74.

—— *On Sexuality*, in *The Penguin Freud*, vol. 7, Harmondsworth: Penguin, 1977.

—— *On Metapsychology*, in *The Penguin Freud*, vol. 11, Harmondsworth: Penguin, 1984.

—— *Civilization, Society and Religion*, in *The Penguin Freud*, vol. 12, Harmondsworth: Penguin, 1985.

—— *Art and Literature*, in *The Penguin Freud*, vol. 14, Harmondsworth: Penguin, 1985.

FRIEDHEIM, PHILIP, 'Wagner and the Aesthetics of the Scream', *Nineteenth-Century Music*, 7 (1983): 63–70.

FULCHER, JANE F., *The Nation's Image: French Grand Opera as Politics and Politicised Art*, Cambridge: Cambridge University Press, 1987.

GALLUP, STEPHEN, *A History of the Salzburg Festival*, London: Weidenfeld and Nicholson, 1987.

GASCHÉ, RODOLPHE, 'The Falls of History: Huysmans's *A Rebours*', *Yale French Studies*, 92 (1988): 183–204.

GATTI, GUIDO, 'Gabriele D'Annunzio and the Italian Opera-Composers', *Musical Quarterly*, 10 (1924): 263–288.

—— 'Ildobrando Pizzetti', *Musical Quarterly*, 9 (1925): 96–121, 271–86.

—— 'The Works of Giacomo Puccini', *Musical Quarterly*, 14 (1928): 16–34.

GAY, PETER, *Freud, Jews and Other Germans*, Oxford: Oxford University Press, 1978.

—— *The Bourgeois Experience: Victoria to Freud*, Vol. 1: *The Education of the Senses*, Oxford: Oxford University Press, 1984.

GEEHR, RICHARD S., *Karl Lueger: Mayor of Fin de Siècle Vienna*, Detroit: Wayne State University Press, 1990.

GENSTER, JULIA, 'Lieutenancy, Standing In and *Othello*', *English Literary History*, 57 (1990): 785–809.

GILBERT, ELLIOT L., 'Tumult of Images: Wilde, Beardsley and *Salomé*', *Victorian Studies*, 26 (1983): 133–59.

GILLESPIE, MICHAEL ALLEN, and STRONG, TRACY B., *Nietzsche's New Seas*, Chicago: University of Chicago Press, 1988.

GILLIAM, BRYAN, *Richard Strauss's* Elektra, Oxford: Clarendon Press, 1991.

—— *Richard Strauss and His World*, Princeton: Princeton University Press, 1992.

GILMAN, SANDER L., *Conversations with Nietzsche*, Oxford: Oxford University Press, 1987.

GLEDHILL, CHRISTINE (ed.), *Home is Where the Heart is: Studies in Melodrama and the Woman's Film*, London: BFI, 1987.

GOLSAN, RICHARD J. (ed.), *Fascism, Aesthetics and Culture*, Hanover, NH: University Press of New England, 1992.

GOOCH, JOHN, *Army, State and Society in Italy, 1870–1915*, London: Macmillan, 1989.

GOSSETT, PHILIP, 'Becoming a Citizen: The Chorus in *Risorgimento* Opera', *Cambridge Opera Journal*, 2 /1 (1991): 41–64.

GRAMSCI, ANTONIO, *Selections from Cultural Writings*, ed. David Forgacs and Geoffrey Nowell-Smith, London: Lawrence and Wishart, 1985.

GRAND, ALEXANDER J. LE, *The Italian Nationalist Association and the Rise of Fascism in Italy*, Lincoln, Nebr.: University of Nebraska Press, 1978.

—— *Italian Fascism: Its Origins and Development*, Lincoln, Nebr.: University of Nebraska Press, 1982.

GREEN, MARTIN, and SWAN, JOHN, *The Triumph of Pierrot*, London: Macmillan, 1986

GREENBLATT, STEPHEN, *Renaissance Self-Fashioning: From More to Shakespeare*, Chicago: University of Chicago Press, 1980.

GREGOR, A. JAMES, *Young Mussolini and the Intellectual Origins of Fascism*, Berkeley and Los Angeles: University of California Press, 1979.

GREGOR-DELLIN, MARTIN, *Wagner*, London: Collins, 1983.

GROOCH, JOHN, *Army, State and Society in Italy, 1870–1915*, London: Macmillan, 1989.

GROOS, ARTHUR, 'Lieutenant B. F. Pinkerton: Problems in the Genesis of an Operatic Hero', *Italica*, 64 (1987): 654–75.

—— and PARKER, ROGER (eds.), *Reading Opera*, Princeton: Princeton University Press, 1988.

—— —— (eds.), *La Bohème*, Cambridge: Cambridge University Press, 1986.

GROSZ, ELIZABETH, *Sexual Subversions*, Boston: Allen and Unwin, 1989.

GUTMAN, ROBERT, *Richard Wagner*, Harmondsworth: Penguin, 1977.

HAILEY, CHRISTOPHER, *Franz Schreker 1878–1934: A Cultural Biography*, Cambridge: Cambridge University Press, 1993.

HAMILTON, RICHARD F., *Who Voted for Hitler?*, Princeton: Princeton University Press, 1982.

HANFSTAENGEL, ERNST, *Zwischen Weissen und Braunen Haus. Memoiren eines politschen Aussenseiters*, Munich: Piper, 1970.

HANSLICK, EDUARD, *Music Criticisms 1846–99*, trans. Henry Pleasants, Harmondsworth: Penguin, 1963.

HARGREAVES, ALEC G., *The Colonial Experience in French Fiction*, London: Macmillan, 1981.

HARRISON, THOMAS, (ed.), *Nietzsche in Italy*, Saratoga, Calif.: Anma Libri, 1988.

HASLAM, MALCOLM, *In the Nouveau Style*, London: Thames and Hudson, 1980.

HAY, JAMES, *Popular Film Culture in Fascist Italy*, Bloomington, Ind.: Indiana University Press, 1987.

HEIDEGGER, MARTIN, *An Introduction to Metaphysics* (1935), trans. Ralph Manheim, New Haven: Yale University Press, 1959.

—— *What is Called Thinking?*, trans. J. Glenn Gray, New York: Harper and Row, 1968.

—— *Poetry, Language, Thought*, trans. Albert Hofstadter, New York: Harper and Row, 1971.

—— *The Question Concerning Technology and Other Essays*, trans. William Lovitt, New York: Harper and Row, 1977.

—— *Nietzsche*, trans. David Farrell Krell, 2 vols., New York: Harper and Row, 1979.

HELLER, THOMAS C.; SOSNA, MORTON; and WELBURY, DAVID E. (eds.), *Reconstructing Individualism*, Stanford, Calif.: Stanford University Press, 1986.

HERF, JEFFREY, *Reactionary Modernism: Technology, Culture and Politics in Weimar and the Third Reich*, Cambridge: Cambridge University Press, 1984.

HEPOKOSKI, JAMES, *Otello*, Cambridge: Cambridge University Press, 1987.

—— *Falstaff*, Cambridge: Cambridge University Press, 1983.

HEYWORTH, PETER (ed.), *Conversations with Klemperer*, London: Victor Gollancz, 1973.

HINTON, STEPHEN, *The Idea of Gebrauchsmusik*, New York: Garland Publishing Co., 1989.

—— *Kurt Weill: The Threepenny Opera*, Cambridge: Cambridge University Press, 1990.

HOBSBAWM, ERIC, and RANGER, TERENCE, *The Invention of Tradition*, Cambridge: Cambridge University Press, 1983.

HOROWITZ, JOSEPH, *Understanding Toscanini*, London: Faber, 1987.

HUDSON, GLENDA A., *Sibling Love and Incest in Jane Austen's Fiction*, London: Macmillan, 1992.

HUGHES, H. STUART, *Oswald Spengler: A Critical Estimate*, New York: Charles Scribner, 1962.

HULTEN, PONTUS, and CELANT, GERMANO (eds.), *Italian Art 1900–1945*, New York: Rizzoli, 1989.

HUSSEY, DYNLEY, *Verdi*, London: Dent, 1940.

HUYSMANS, J.-K. *A Rebours*, trans. as *Against Nature* by Robert Baldick, Harmondsworth: Penguin, 1959.

HUYSSEN, ANDREAS, *After the Great Divide*, London: Macmillan, 1986.

IRIGARAY, LUCE, *Marine Lover of Friedrich Nietzsche*, trans. Gillian C. Gill, New York: Columbia University Press, 1991.

IRIYE, AKIRA, *Pacific Estrangements: Japanese and American Expansion 1897–1911*, Cambridge, Mass.: Harvard University Press, 1972.

ISHERWOOD, CHRISTOPHER, *The World in the Evening*, London: Methuen, 1954.

JACOBS, MARGARET, and WARREN, JOHN (eds.), *Max Reinhardt: The Oxford Symposium*, Oxford: Polytechnic, 1986.

JAMES, HAROLD, *A German Identity: 1770–1990*, New York: Routledge, 1989.

JAMESON, FREDRIC, *Fables of Aggression: Wyndham Lewis, the Modernist as Fascist*, Berkeley and Los Angeles: University of California Press, 1979.

—— *The Political Unconscious: Narrative as a Socially Symbolic Act*, London: Methuen, 1981.

—— *Late Marxism: Adorno or, the Persistence of the Dialectic*, London: Verso, 1990.

JANIK, ALLAN, *Essays on Wittgenstein and Weininger*, Amsterdam: Rodopi, 1985.

JARMAN, DOUGLAS, *Lulu*, Cambridge: Cambridge University Press, 1991.

—— (ed.), *The Berg Companion*, London: Macmillan, 1989.

JOHN, NICHOLAS (ed.), *Falstaff*, London: John Boyar, 1982.

—— (ed.), *Turandot*, London: John Calder, 1984.

JOLL, JAMES, *Intellectuals in Power*, London: Weidenfeld and Nicolson, 1960.

JONAS, ILSEDORE B., *Thomas Mann and Italy*, trans. Betty Crouse, Birmingham, Ala.: University of Alabama Press, 1979.

KAPLAN, ALICE YAEGER, *Reproductions of Banality: Fascism, Literature and French Intellectual Life*, Minneapolis: University of Minnesota Press, 1986.

KAPLAN, JULIUS DAVID, *The Art of Gustave Moreau*, Epping: Bowker Publishing Co., 1982.

KASHER, STEVEN, 'The Art of Hitler', *October*, 59 (1992): 49–85.

KATZ, JACOB, *The Darker Side of Genius: Richard Wagner's Anti-Semitism*, Hanover, NH: University Press of New England, 1986.

KENNEDY, MICHAEL, *Richard Strauss*, London: Dent, 1976.

KERMAN, JOSEPH, *Opera as Drama*, London: Faber, 1956: rev. edn. 1988.

KERSHAW, IAN, *The Hitler Myth: Image and Reality in the Third Reich*, Oxford: Clarendon Press, 1987.

KIMBALL, DAVID, *Italian Opera*, Cambridge: Cambridge University Press, 1991.

KOESTENBAUM, WAYNE, *The Queen's Throat: Opera, Homosexuality and the Mystery of Desire*, New York: Poseidon Press, 1993.

KOFMAN, SARAH, *The Enigma of Woman: Woman in Freud's Writings*, trans. Catherine Porter, Ithaca, NY: Cornell University Press, 1985.

KOVACH, THOMAS A., *Hofmannsthal and Symbolism*, New York: Peter Lang, 1985.

KOWALKE, KIM H. (ed.), *A New Orpheus: Essays on Kurt Weill*, New Haven: Yale University Press, 1986.

KRACAUER, SIEGFRIED, *Offenbach and the Paris of his Time*, London: Constable, 1937.

KRAFFT-EBING, RICHARD VON, *Psychopathia Sexualis*, 10th German edn., trans. F. J. Rebman, London: Rebman Ltd., 1901.

KRAMER, LAWRENCE, 'Culture and Musical Hermeneutics: The Salome Complex', *Cambridge Opera Journal*, 2 (1990): 269–94.

—— '*Fin de Siècle* Fantasies: *Elektra*, Degeneration and Sexual Science', *Cambridge Opera Journal*, 5/2 (1993): 141–65.

KRELL, DAVID FARRELL, *Postponements: Woman, Sensuality and Death in Nietzsche*, Bloomington, Ind.: Indiana University Press, 1986.

KRISTEVA, JULIA, *Powers of Horror: An Essay on Abjection*, trans. Léon S. Roudiez, New York: Columbia University Press, 1982.

KRONICK, JOSEPH G., 'Review Essay: Dr Heidegger's Experiment', *boundary* 2, 17/3 (1990): 116–53.

KÜHNEL, REINHARD, 'Problems of a History of German Fascism: A Critique of the Dominant Interpretations', *New German Critique*, 4 (1975): 26–50.

KUNDERA, MILAN, *The Unbearable Lightness of Being*, New York: Harper and Row, 1984.

LACAN, JACQUES, *Écrits: A Selection*, trans. Alan Sheridan, London: Tavistock, 1977.

LACOUE-LABARTHE, PHILIPPE, *Heidegger, Art and Politics*, Oxford: Blackwell, 1990.

LAQUEUR, WALTER, *Young Germany: A History of the German Youth Movement*, London: Chatto and Windus, 1973.

—— *Fascism: A Reader's Guide*, (1967), Harmondsworth: Penguin, 1979.

LARGE, DAVID C., and WEBER, WILLIAM, *Wagnerism in European Culture and Politics*, Ithaca, NY: Cornell University Press, 1984.

LEAVIS, F. R., *The Common Pursuit*, London: Chatto and Windus, 1951.

LEDEEN, MICHAEL A., *The First Duce: D'Annunzio at Fiume*. Baltimore: John Hopkins University Press, 1977.

LEED, ERIC J., *No Man's Land: Combat and Identity in World War I*, Cambridge: Cambridge University Press, 1979.

LEER, DAVID VAN, 'The Beast of the Closet: Homosexuality and the Pathology of Manhood', *Critical Inquiry*, 15 (1989): 587–605.

LEHNERT, HERBERT, and PFEIFFER, PETER C., *Thomas Mann's* Doctor Faustus: *A Novel at the Edge of Modernism*, Columbia, SC: Camden House, 1991.

LESÈR, ESTHER H., *Thomas Mann's Short Fiction*, New York: Associated University Presses, 1989.

LEVI, ERIK, *Music in the Third Reich*, London: Macmillan, 1994.

LINDENBERGER, HERBERT, *Opera: The Extravagant Art*, Ithaca, NY: Cornell University Press, 1984.

LOWENTHAL, DAVID, *The Past is a Foreign Country*, Cambridge: Cambridge University Press, 1985.

LOWINSKY, EDWARD E., *A Confidential Matter: The Letters of Richard Strauss and Stefan Zweig*, trans. Max Knight, Berkeley and Los Angeles: University of California Press, 1977.

LUNN, EUGENE, 'Tales of Liberal Disquiet: Thomas Mann's *Mario and the Magician*: Interpretations of Fascism', *Literature and History*, 11 (1985): 77–100.

LYTTELTON, ADRIAN, *The Seizure of Power: Fascism in Italy 1919–1929*, Princeton: Princeton University Press, 1987.

MAGEE, BRYAN, *The Philosophy of Schopenhauer*, Oxford: Oxford University Press, 1983.

MANN, THOMAS, *Stories of Three Decades*, trans. H. T. Lowe-Porter, New York: Alfred A. Knopf, 1936.

—— *Death in Venice*, trans. H. T. Lowe-Porter, Harmondsworth: Penguin, 1955.

—— *Buddenbrooks*, trans. H. T. Lowe-Porter, Harmondsworth: Penguin, 1957.

—— *The Magic Mountain*, trans. H. T. Lowe-Porter, Harmondsworth: Penguin, 1960.

—— *The Genesis of a Novel*, trans. Richard and Clara Winston, London: Secker and Warburg, 1961.

—— *Doctor Faustus* (1947), trans. H. T. Lowe-Porter, Harmondsworth: Penguin, 1968.

—— *Reflections of a Nonpolitical Man*, trans. Walter D. Morris, New York: Fredrick Ungar Pub. Co., 1983.

—— *Thomas Mann Pro and Contra Wagner*, trans. Allan Blunden, London: Faber, 1985.

MAREK, GEORGE, *Richard Strauss: The Life of a Non-hero*, London: Victor Gollancz, 1967.

MARKS, ELAINE, and COURTIVRON, ISABELLE DE (eds.), *New French Feminisms*, Brighton: Harvester, 1981.

MARTENS, LORNA, 'From the Armchair to the Stage: Hofmannsthal's *Elektra* in its Theatrical Context', *Modern Language Review*, 80 (1985): 637–51.

—— 'The Theme of the Repressed Memory in Hofmannsthal's *Elektra*', *German Quarterly*, 60 (1987): 38–51.

MARTIN, GEORGE, *Aspects of Verdi*, London: Robson Books, 1988.

MARTIN, STODDARD, *Wagner to the Waste Land*, London: Macmillan, 1982.

MARX, KARL, *Surveys from Exile*, trans. Ben Fowkes, Harmondsworth: Penguin, 1973.

MATTHIEU, PIERRE-LOUIS, *Gustave Moreau*, London: Phaidon, 1977.

MAYER, HANS, 'Thomas Mann and Bertolt Brecht: Anatomy of an Antagonism', *New German Critique*, 6 (1975): 101–15.

McCLARY, SUSAN, *Carmen*, Cambridge: Cambridge University Press, 1992.

McFARLANE, JAMES, and BRADBURY, MALCOLM (eds), *Modernism*, Harmondsworth: Penguin, 1976.

McGRATH, WILLIAM J., *Dionysian Art and Populist Politics in Austria*, New Haven: Yale University Press, 1974.

MELLERS, WILFRID, *Music in a New Found Land*, New York: Hillstone, 1975.

MELTZER, FRANÇOISE, *Salome and the Dance of Writing*, Chicago: University of Chicago Press, 1987.

MEYER, MICHAEL, *The Politics of Music in the Third Reich*, New York: Peter Lang, 1991.

MEYERS, ROLLO (ed.), *Richard Strauss and Romain Rolland: Correspondence*, London: Calder and Boyars, 1968.

MILFULL, JOHN (ed.), *From Baal to Keuner: The 'Second Optimism' of Bertolt Brecht*, Bern: Herbert Lang, 1974.

—— (ed.), *The Attractions of Fascism*, New York: Berg, 1990.

MILLINGTON, BARRY, *Richard Wagner*, London: Dent, 1984.

—— 'Parsifal: A Wound Re-opened', *Wagner*, 8 (1987): 114–20.

—— 'Humperdinck's Other Masterpiece', *Opera*, 43 (Feb. 1992): 153–8.

—— 'Nuremberg Trial: Is there Anti-Semitism in *Die Meistersinger*?,' *Cambridge Opera Journal*, 3 (1992): 247–60.

—— (ed.), *The Wagner Compendium: A Guide to Wagner's Life and Music*, London: Thames and Hudson, 1992.

—— and SPENCER, STEWART, (eds), *Selected Letters of Richard Wagner*, New York: W. W. Norton, 1987.

—— (with SPENCER, STEWART) (eds), *Wagner in Performance*, New Haven: Yale University Press, 1992.

MORRIS, PAM, 'Rerouting Kristeva: From Pessimism to Parody', *Textual Practice*, 6 (1992): 31–46.

MOSCOVICI, SERGE, *The Age of the Crowd*, Cambridge: Cambridge University Press, 1985.

MOSSE, GEORGE L., *The Crisis of German Ideology: Intellectual Origins of the Third Reich*, London: Weidenfeld and Nicolson, 1964.

—— *Nazi Culture*, London: W. H. Allen, 1966.

—— *The Nationalization of the Masses*, Ithaca, NY: Cornell University Press, 1975.

—— *International Fascism: New Thoughts and New Approaches*, London: Sage, 1979.

—— *Nationalism and Sexuality: Respectability and Abnormal Sexuality in Modern Europe*, New York: Howard Fertig, 1985.

MUELLER, ROSWITHA, *Bertolt Brecht and the Theory of Media*, Lincoln, Nebr.: University of Nebraska Press, 1989.

MÜLLER, ULRICH, and WAPNEWSKI, PETER, *Wagner Handbook*, trans. and ed. John Deathridge, Cambridge, Mass.: Harvard University Press, 1992.

MYERS, ROLLO (ed.), *Richard Strauss and Romain Rolland: Correspondence*, London: Calder and Boyars, 1968.

NATTIEZ, JEAN-JACQUES, *Wagner in Performance*, New Haven: Yale University Press, 1992.

—— *Wagner Androgyne: A Study in Interpretation*, trans. Stewart Spencer, Princeton: Princeton University Press, 1993.

New Left Review (ed.), *Aesthetics and Politics*, London: Verso, 1976.

NEWMAN, ERNEST, *The Life of Richard Wagner* (1937), Cambridge: Cambridge University Press, 1976.

NEWSON, JOHN, 'Hans Pfitzner, Thomas Mann and *The Magic Mountain*', *Music and Letters*, 54 (1974): 136–50.

NICOLAISEN, JAY, *Italian Opera in Transition: 1871–1893*, Ann Arbor: UMI Research Press, 1980.

NIETZSCHE, FRIEDRICH, *The Case of Wagner: A Musician's Problem*, trans. Anthony M. Lucdovici, Edinburgh: T. N. Foulis, 1911.

—— *The Birth of Tragedy and The Genealogy of Morals*, trans. Francis Golffing, New York: Doubleday, 1956.

—— *Philosophy in the Tragic Age of the Greeks*, Chicago: University of Chicago Press, 1962.

—— *The Will to Power*, trans. Walter Kaufmann and R. J. Hollingdale, New York: Vintage Books, 1967.

—— *Basic Writings of Nietzsche*, ed. Walter Kaufmann, New York: Modern Library, 1968.

—— *The Gay Science*, trans. Walter Kaufmann, New York: Random House, 1974.

—— *Ecce Homo*, trans. R. J. Hollingdale, Harmondsworth: Penguin, 1979.

—— *Untimely Meditations*, Cambridge: Cambridge University Press, 1983.

—— *Human, All Too Human*, trans. R. J. Hollingdale, Cambridge: Cambridge University Press, 1986.

NISH, IAN H., *The Anglo-Japanese Alliance*, 2nd edn., London: Athlone Press, 1985.

NOLTE, ERNST, *Three Faces of Fascism*, trans. Leila Vennewitz (1963), London: Weidenfeld and Nicolson, 1965.

NOSKE, FRITS, *The Signifier and the Signified: Studies in the Opera of Mozart and Verdi*, 2nd edn. Oxford: Clarendon Press, 1990.

NOWELL-SMITH, GEOFFREY, *Modernity and Mass Culture*, Bloomington, Ind.: Indiana University Press, 1991.

NYE, ROBERT, *The Origins of Crowd Psychology*, London, Sage, 1975.

OLIVER, KELLY, *Reading Kristeva*, Bloomington, Ind.: Indiana University Press, 1993.

OXAAL, IVAR (ed.), *Jews, Antisemitism and Culture in Vienna*, London: Routledge, 1987.

PALADILHE, JEAN, *Gustave Moreau: His Life and Works*, London: Thames and Hudson, 1972.

PARKER, ROGER, and BROWN, MATTHEW, 'Rehearings: Late Verdi: "Ancora un bacio": Three Scenes from Verdi's *Otello*', *Nineteenth Century Music*, 9 (1985): 50–62.

PARKES-PERRET, FORD, 'Thomas Mann's Silvery Voice of Self-Parody in *Doctor Faustus*', *Germanic Review*, 64 (1989): 20–30.

PARMALEE, PATTY LEE, *Brecht's America*, Columbus, Oh.: Ohio State University Press, 1980.

PELS, DIK, 'Treason of the Intellectuals: Paul de Man and Hendrik de Man', *Theory, Culture and Society*, 8 (1991): 21–56.

PERLOFF, MARJORIE (ed.), *Postmodern Genres*, Norman, Okla.: University of Oklahoma Press, 1988.

PETERS, H. F., *Zarathustra's Sister*, New York: Crown Publishers, 1977.

PICK, DANIEL, *Faces of Degeneration: A European Disorder, c.1848–1918*, Cambridge: Cambridge University Press, 1989.

PIERROT, JEAN, *The Decadent Imagination 1880–1900*, trans. Derek Coltman, Chicago: University of Chicago Press, 1981.

PLANT, SADIE, *The Most Radical Gesture: The Situationist International in a Postmodern Age*, London: Routledge, 1992.

POIZAT, MICHEL, *The Angel's Cry: Beyond the Pleasure Principle in Opera*, trans. Arthur Denner, Ithaca, NY: Cornell University Press, 1992.

PORTER, ANDREW, *A Music Season*, London: Victor Gollancz, 1974.

POSTER, MARK (ed.), *Jean Baudrillard: Selected Writings*, Cambridge: Polity, 1988.

POWELL, KERRY, *Oscar Wilde and the Theatre of the 1890s*, Cambridge: Cambridge University Press, 1990.

PRIEBERG, FRED K., *Trial of Strength: Wilhelm Furtwängler and the Third Reich*, trans. Christopher Dolan (1986), London: Quartet Books, 1991.

PUFFETT, DERRICK, *Salome*, Cambridge: Cambridge University Press, 1989.

—— (ed.), *Elektra*, Cambridge: Cambridge University Press, 1989.

RABINBACH, ANSON G., 'Towards a Marxist Theory of Fascism and National Socialism', *New German Critique*, 3 (1974): 127–53.

REICH, WILHELM, *The Mass Psychology of Fascism*, trans. Vincent R. Carfagno (1946), 3rd edn., New York: Simon and Schuster, 1970.

REID, DONNA K., *The Novel and the Nazi Past*, New York: Peter Lang, 1985.

REMPEL, JOHN W., and REMPEL, URSULA M., *Music and Literature*, Winnipeg: University of Manitoba, 1985.

RICH, MARIA F., 'Opera USA Perspective: Puccini in America', *Opera Quarterly*, 2 (1984): 27–45.

RICHARDSON, ALAN, 'The Dangers of Sympathy: Sibling Incest in English Romantic Poetry', *Studies in English Literature*, 23 (1985): 737–54.

ROBERTS, DAVID D., *The Syndicalist Tradition and Italian Fascism*, Manchester: Manchester University Press, 1979.

ROBERTS, JEANNE ADDISON, *Shakespeare's English Comedy*, Lincoln, Nebr.: University of Nebraska Press, 1979.

ROBINSON, PAUL, 'Is *Aida* an Orientalist Opera?' *Cambridge Music Journal*, 5/2 (1993): 133–40.

—— *Opera and Ideas: From Mozart to Strauss*, Ithaca, NY: Cornell University Press, 1985.

ROGGER, HANS, and WEBER, EUGEN, *The European Right: An Historical Profile*, London: Weidenfeld and Nicolson, 1965.

RÖHL, JOHN C. G., and SOMBART, NICOLAUS, *Kaiser Wilhelm II: New Interpretations*, Cambridge: Cambridge University Press, 1982.

ROSAN, ELLEN, 'Criticism and the Undoing of Opera', *Nineteenth-Century Music*, 14 (1990): 75–83.

ROSE, PAUL LAWRENCE, *Wagner: Revolution and Race*, London: Faber, 1992.

ROSENBERG, JOHN D., *Carlyle and the Burden of History*, Oxford: Clarendon Press, 1985.

ROSSELLI, JOHN, *Music and Musicians in Nineteenth-Century Italy*, London: B. T. Batsford, 1991.

ROTH, JACK J., *The Cult of Violence: Sorel and the Sorelians*, Berkeley, and Los Angeles: University of California Press, 1980.

SACHS, HARVEY, *Music in Fascist Italy*, London: Weidenfeld and Nicolson, 1987.

—— *Toscanini*, London: Weidenfeld and Nicolson, 1978.

SADIE, STANLEY (ed.), *New Grove Dictionary of Music*, 20 vols., London: Macmillan, 1980.

—— (ed.), *New Grove Dictionary of Opera*, 4 vols., London: Macmillan, 1990.

SAFRANSKI, RÜDIGER, *Schopenhauer and the Wild Years of Philosophy*, trans. Ewald Osers, London: Weidenfeld and Nicolson, 1989.

SAID, EDWARD, *Orientalism* (1978), Harmondsworth: Penguin, 1985.

—— *Culture and Imperialism*, London: Chatto and Windus, 1993.

SALLIS, TOM (ed.), *Derrida and Philosophy*, Chicago: University of Chicago Press, 1987.

SANDERS, RONALD, *The Days Grow Short: The Life and Music of Kurt Weill*, London: Weidenfeld and Nicolson, 1980.

SANTNER, ERIC L., *Stranded Objects: Mourning, Memory and Film in Postwar Germany*, Ithaca, NY: Cornell University Press, 1990.

SCHOPENHAUER, ARTHUR, *Parerga and Paralipomena*, trans. E. F. J. Payne, Oxford: Clarendon Press, 1974.

—— *The World as Will and Representation*, trans. E. J. Payne, 2 vols., New York: Dover, 1966.

SCHORSKE, CARL E., *Fin de Siècle Vienna: Politics and Culture*, New York: Alfred A. Knopf, 1980.

SCHULZE, HAGEN, *The Cause of German Nationalism* (1985), trans. Sarah Hanbury-Tenison, Cambridge: Cambridge University Press, 1991.

SCHÜRER, ERNST, 'Revolution from the Right: Bertolt Brecht's American Gangster Play *The Resistible Rise of Arturo Ui* ', *Perspectives on Contemporary Literature*, 2 (1978): 24–46.

SEDGWICK, EVE KOSOFSKY, *Between Men: English Literature and Male Homosocial Desire*, New York: Columbia University Press, 1985.

SEGAL, LYNNE, *Slow Motion: Changing Masculinities, Changing Men*, London: Virago, 1990.

SESSA, ANNE DZAMBA, *Richard Wagner and the English*, London: Associated Universities Press, 1979.

SETON-WATSON, CHRISTOPHER, *Italy from Liberalism to Fascism, 1870–1925,* London: Methuen, 1967.

SHAKESPEARE, WILLIAM, *The Merry Wives of Windsor,* ed. H. J. Oliver, London: Methuen, 1971.

—— *Othello,* ed. M. R. Ridley, London: Methuen, 1958.

SHAW, LEROY R.; CIRILLO, NANCY R.; and MILLER, MARION S. (eds.), *Wagner in Retrospect,* Amsterdam: Rodopi, 1987.

SHEEHAN, JAMES J., *German History 1770–1866,* Oxford: Clarendon Press, 1989.

SINCLAIR, PETER R., 'Fascism and Crisis in Capitalist Society', *New German Critique,* 9 (1976): 87–112.

SKELTON, GEOFFREY, *Wagner at Bayreuth,* London: Barrie and Rockcliff, 1965.

—— *Paul Hindemith: The Man Behind the Music,* London: Victor Gollancz, 1975.

—— *Bayreuth: The Early Years,* ed. Robert Hartford, London: Victor Gollancz, 1980.

—— *Mussolini's Roman Empire,* London: Longman, 1976.

—— *Mussolini,* London: Granada, 1983.

SMITH, DENNIS MACK, *Italy and Its Monarchy,* New Haven: Yale University Press, 1989.

SONNENFELD, MARION (ed.), *The World of Yesterday's Humanist Today,* Albany, NY: State University of New York Press, 1983.

SONTAG, SUSAN, *Against Interpretation and Other Essays,* New York: Octagon, 1986.

SOUCY, ROBERT, 'Drieu la Rochelle and Modernist Anti-Modernism in French Fascism', *Modern Language Notes,* 95 (1980): 922–37.

SPACKMAN, BARBARA, *Decadent Genealogies: The Rhetoric of Sickness from Baudelaire to D'Annunzio,* Ithaca, NY: Cornell University Press, 1989.

STACHURA, PETER D., *The German Youth Movement 1900–45,* London: Macmillan, 1981.

STANLEY, JOHN L., *From Georges Sorel,* Oxford: Oxford University Press, 1976.

STYAN, J. L., *Max Reinhardt,* Cambridge: Cambridge University Press, 1982.

STEADMAN, JOHN M., 'Falstaff as Actaeon: A Dramatic Emblem', *Shakespeare Quarterly,* 14 (1963): 231–44.

STEAKLEY, JAMES D., *The Homosexual Emancipation Movement in Germany,* New York: Arno Press, 1975.

STEIN, JACK, *Richard Wagner and the Synthesis of the Arts,* Detroit: Wayne State University Press, 1960.

STEINBERG, MICHAEL P., 'Jewish Identity and Intellectuality in Fin de Siècle Austria: Suggestions for a Historical Discourse', *New German Critique,* 47 (1988): 3–33.

—— *The Meaning of the Salzburg Festival,* Ithaca, NY: Cornell University Press, 1990.

STERN, FRITZ, *The Politics of Cultural Despair,* Berkeley and Los Angeles: University of California Press, 1961.

STERN, J. P., *Hitler: The Führer and the People,* London: Fontana, 1975.

—— *Nietzsche,* Cambridge: Cambridge University Press, 1979.

STERNHELL, ZEEV, *Neither Right nor Left: Fascist Ideology in France*, trans. David Maisel, Berkeley and Los Angeles: University of California Press, 1986.

STOLLMANN, RAINER, 'Fascist Politics as a Total Work of Art: Tendencies of the Aestheticization of Political Life in National Socialism', *New German Critique*, 14 (1978): 41–60.

STRONG, TRACY B., *Friedrich Nietzsche and the Politics of Transfiguration*, Berkeley and Los Angeles: University of California Press, 1988.

STYAN, J. L., *Max Reinhardt*, Cambridge: Cambridge University Press, 1982.

SULEIMAN, SUSAN ROBIN (ed.), *The Female Body in Western Culture*, Cambridge, Mass.: Harvard University Press, 1985.

SUTCLIFFE, TOM, 'Sondheim and the Musical', *Musical Times*, 28 (Sept. 1987): 487–90.

SZYLIONICZ, IRENE L., *Pierre Loti and the Oriental Woman*, London: Macmillan, 1988.

TAMBLING, JEREMY, 'Passion and the Abyss in Britten and Mann', *New Universities Quarterly*, 35 (1981): 323–40.

—— *Opera, Ideology and Film*, Manchester: Manchester University Press, 1987.

—— *Confession: Sexuality, Sin, the Subject*, Manchester: Manchester University Press, 1990.

—— *Narrative and Ideology*, Milton Keynes: Open University Press, 1991.

—— (ed.), *A Night In At the Opera: Media Representations of Opera*, London: John Libbey and Arts Council, 1994.

TATLOW, ANTHONY, *Repression and Figuration: From Totem to Utopia*, Hong Kong: University of Hong Kong, Department of Comparative Literature, 1990.

TAYLOR, BRANDON, and WILL, WILFRIED VAN DER (eds.), *The Nazification of Art*, Winchester: Winchester Press, 1990.

TAYLOR, GARY, 'The Fortunes of Oldcastle', *Shakespeare Survey*, 38 (1985): 85–100.

THALHEIMER, AUGUST, 'On Fascism', *Telos*, 40 (1979): 109–22.

THAYER, JOHN, *Italy and the Great War*, Madison: University of Wisconsin Press, 1964.

THEWELEIT, KLAUS, *Male Fantasies*, 2 vols., Cambridge: Polity, 1987, 1989.

THOMAS, R. HINTON, *Nietzsche in German Politics and Society*, Manchester: Manchester University Press, 1983.

TIMMS, EDWARD, *Karl Kraus, Apocalyptic Satirist*, New Haven: Yale University Press, 1986.

TOULMIN, STEPHEN, and JANIK, ALLAN, *Wittgenstein's Vienna*, New York: Simon and Shuster, 1973.

TRAVERS, ANDREW, 'An Essay on Self and Camp', *Theory, Culture, and Society*, 11 (1993): 127–43.

TYRELL, JOHN, *Czech Opera*, Cambridge: Cambridge University Press, 1988.

VANDEN BOSSCHE, CHRIS R., *Carlyle and the Search for Authority*, Columbus, Oh.: Ohio State University, 1991.

WAGNER, RICHARD, *Prose Works*, trans. William Ashton Ellis, 8 vols., London: Kegan Paul, 1894.

—— *My Life*, trans. Andrew Gray, Cambridge: Cambridge University Press, 1983.

WAITE, GEOFF, 'The Politics of Reading Formations: The Case of Nietzsche in Imperial Germany (1870–1919)', *New German Critique*, 29 (1983): 185–209.

WAKE, CLIVE, *The Novels of Pierre Loti*, The Hague: Mouton, 1974.

WALKER, FRANK, *The Man Verdi*, London: Dent, 1962.

WARTOFSKY, MARS W., *Feuerbach*, Cambridge: Cambridge University Press, 1977.

WEAVER, WILLIAM, *The Golden Century of Italian Opera*, London: Thames and Hudson, 1980.

—— and CHUSID, MARTIN (eds.), *The Verdi Companion*, New York: W. W. Norton and Co., 1979.

WEBER, EUGENE, *Action Française: Royalism and Reaction in Twentieth-century France*, Stanford, Calif. Stanford University Press, 1962.

—— *Varieties of Fascism*, New York: Van Nostrand Reinhold, 1964.

WEINER, MARC A., *Undertones of Insurrection: Music, Politics and the Social Sphere in the Modern German Narrative*, Lincoln, University of Nebraska Press, 1993.

WEININGER, OTTO, *Sex and Character*, 6th edn. Heinemann, 1906; New York: AMS reprint, 1975.

WHITE, ALAN, *Within Nietzsche's Labyrinth*, London: Routledge, 1990.

WHITTALL, ARNOLD, 'Carl Dahlhaus, the Nineteenth-Century and Opera', *Cambridge Opera Journal*, 3 (1991): 79–88.

WICHMANN, SIEGFRIED, *Japonisme*, London: Thames and Hudson, 1981.

WILDE, OSCAR, *The Works of Oscar Wilde*, ed. G. F. Maine, London: Collins, 1948.

—— *The Complete Shorter Fiction of Oscar Wilde*, ed. Isobel Murray, Oxford: Oxford University Press, 1979.

WILLETT, JOHN, *The Theatre of the Weimar Republic*, New York: Holmes and Meier, 1988.

—— *The Theatre of Bertolt Brecht*, London: Eyre Methuen, 1964.

—— (trans. and ed.), *Brecht on Theatre*, 2nd edn., London: Methuen, 1974.

—— *The New Sobriety, 1917–1933, Art and Politics in the Weimar Period*, London: Thames and Hudson, 1978.

WILLIAMS, C. E., *The Broken Eagle: The Politics of Austrian Literature from Empire to Anschluss*, London: Paul Elek, 1974.

WILLIAMSON, JOHN, *The Music of Hans Pfitzner*, Oxford: Clarendon Press, 1992.

WOHL, ROBERT, *The Generation of 1914*, Cambridge, Mass.: Harvard University Press, 1979.

WOLIN, RICHARD, *The Politics of Being: The Political Thought of Martin Heidegger*, New York: Columbia University Press, 1990.

WOOLF, S. J. (ed.), *European Fascism*, London: Weidenfeld and Nicolson, 1968.

WYSS, BEAT, '*Ragnarök* of Illusion: Richard Wagner's "Mystical Abyss" at Bayreuth', *October*, 54 (1990): 57–78.

YATES, W. E., *Schnitzler, Hofmannsthal, and the Austrian Theatre*, New Haven: Yale University Press, 1992.

ZAGONA, HELEN GRACE, *The Legend of Salome and the Principle of Art for Art's Sake*, Geneva: Oroz, 1960.

ZIMMERMAN, MICHAEL E., *Heidegger's Confrontation with Modernity*, Bloomington, Ind.: Indiana University Press, 1990.

ZONDERGELD, REIN A., 'Riccardo Zandonai: The Master of the Fake Emotion', *Opera*, 35 (1984): 1191–6.

ZUCKERMANN, ELLIOTT, *The First Hundred Years of Wagner's Tristan*, New York: Columbia University Press, 1964.

ZWEIG, STEFAN, *The World of Yesterday*, London: Cassell, 1943.

ŽIŽEK, SLAVOJ, *The Metastases of Enjoyment: Six Essays on Women and Causality*, London: Verso, 1994.

Index

This Index mainly comprises names, but topics as well when their place for discussion in the text cannot be easily deduced from the mention of names. I have had to be very selective here: there are no entries for 'fascism' or 'gender' for instance, for these would simply be too many to be useful. Operas merely mentioned in the text are not cited here separately from a general reference to the composer.